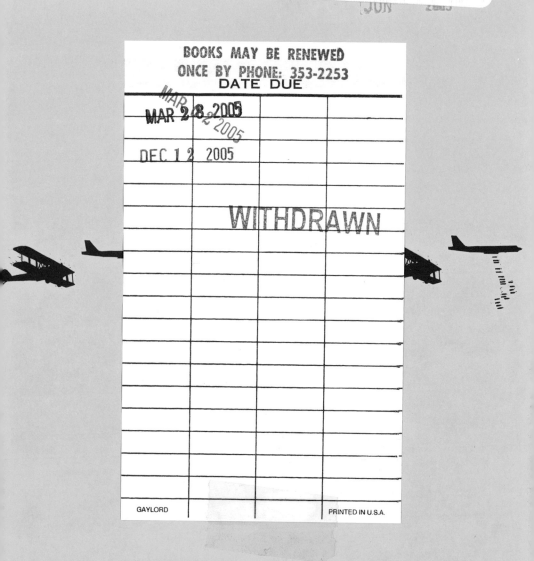

THE FINAL FRONTIER

THE FINAL FRONTIER

AMERICA, SCIENCE, AND TERROR

◆

DOMINICK JENKINS

VERSO

London • New York

First published by Verso 2002
© Dominick Jenkins 2002
All rights reserved

1 3 5 7 9 10 8 6 4 2

Verso
UK: 6 Meard Street, London W1F 0EG
USA: 180 Varick Street, New York, NY 10014–4606

www.versobooks.com

Verso is the imprint of New Left Books

ISBN 1–85984–682–3

British Library Cataloguing in Publication Data
A catalogue record for this book is available from the British Library

Library of Congress Cataloging-in-Publication Data
A catalog record for this book is available from the Library of Congress

Typeset in Dante by M Rules
Printed and bound in the UK by
Biddles Ltd, Guildford and King's Lynn
www.biddles.co.uk

Contents

In despotic statecraft, the supreme and essential mystery is to hoodwink the subjects, and to mask the fear, which keeps them down, with the specious garb of religion, so that men may fight as bravely for slavery as for safety, and count it not shame but highest honor to risk their blood and lives for the vainglory of a tyrant.

Baruch Spinoza, *Theological-Political Treatise*

Acknowledgements

This book has been many years in the making in the course of which I have received extraordinary help and assistance. During the research and writing I have particularly valued the unwavering support, practical help, and intellectual provocation from my parents, Rosemary and Hilary Jenkins, to whom this book is dedicated, my great aunt Senator Florence Bird, and my brothers and sister, Harriet Hunnable, Denzil Jenkins, and Raphael Jenkins. I also treasure the encouragement, assistance, and ideas of my friends in Canada: Kevin Graham, Marlene Goldman, Jim Gilbert-Walshe, Alison Keith, Anita George, David Kraft and Debbie Field, Liz de Fretas, Oliver Schoenborn, Brian Pronger, Jim Bartley, and Amina Mire; in Italy: Marco Montorie and Moira Woods, and in England and Ireland: Ruth Young, Susan Howarth, Patricia Lewis, Marjorie Thompson, Stephen Montgomery, Sandy Balfour, Ingrid Falk, Rorry Macmillan, Malyn Newitt, Kevin O'Rourke, Jo Murphy-Lawless, Oisin Murphy-Lawless, Anne Bottomley, Rooha Variava, Robin Robertson, Ian Willmore, and Alison Holmes. I have very much valued the solidarity and aid of activists, organizers, and thinkers in the peace, disarmament, and environmental movements. In many ways this book is for them. Among those who spring to mind are Yunus Yasin, Janet Bloomfield, Mauplia Kelley, Greg Mello, Rebecca Johnson, David Lowry, Kathleen Sullivan, Jill Perry, Rachel Western, Stephen Young, Arjun Makhijani, Tam Dalyell MP, David Chaytor MP, Jenny Holland, Colin Hines, Steve Wright, Eric Fawcett, Alex Wellington, and my friends at Campeace and Scientists for Global Responsibility in Cambridge and Science for Peace in Toronto. As a mathematician who had to learn to write I am especially appreciative of the help of Dido Davies, Ruth Van Velsen, Elsbeth Heaman, Anne and Peter Walshe, and James Ingram who have helped me to transform my thoughts into prose. In negotiating the world of publishing, John Henderson has been a good guide and I have much appreciated the strong commitment of Tim Clark and Tariq Ali at Verso to seeing this book into print. The Republic of Letters lives. I have repeatedly found that experts in different disciplines have taken time to listen to my ideas and to give me irreplaceable guidance and encouragement. I thank David Dyzenhause, Robert Cuff, Julian Perry-Robertson, Paul Rogers, David Edgerton, Linda Etchart, Scilla Elsworthy, Toni Erskine, Sue Golding, Priya Gopal, Nicholas Labanca, Brendan Simms, Gwyn Prins, Donald Worster, Bill Readings, Dimitri D'Andrea, Sonia Lucarelli, Daniela Belliti, Richard Overy, David Nobel, Ernesto Laclau, Robert Cuff, Michael Byers, Paul Hirst, Roy Porter, Brian Balmer, Paul Schulte, Alison Keith, Robert Accinelli, and Donald MacKenzie. I have especially valued the encouragement and guidance of my doctoral supervisor André Gombay, assistant supervisor Rebecca Comay at the Department of Philosophy, and Ian Hacking at the Institute for the History and Philosophy of Science and Technology at the University of Toronto. While at Cambridge I have been lucky to have the expertise of John Thompson to sharpen my understanding of American history, and of Simon Schaffer and Martin Kusch to deepen my understanding of the history and philosophy of science.

Introduction

New York in Ruins

On 29 July 1921 General "Billy" Mitchell of the US Army Air Service led a force of heavy bombers from Virginia to New York. After flying down Broadway to Battery the bombers picked landmark buildings as their targets – the Woolworth Building, the Treasury, and the Customs House. They then proceeded to pulverize the city in a simulated bombing raid. Afterwards Mitchell landed on Long Island to brief the press corps. He estimated that the twenty-one tons of bombs his bombers had pretended to drop would have completely paralysed the city. Next day the New York *Herald* ran a banner headline:

CITY IN THEORETICAL RUINS FROM AIR RAID

SURVIVORS FLEE STRICKEN ISLAND SEEKING SHELTER IN
COUNTRY. GENERAL MITCHELL SAYS SO.

The sun rose today on a city whose tallest tower lay scattered in crumbled bits of stone . . . Bridges did not exist . . .

The sun saw, when its light penetrated the ruins, hordes of people on foot, working their way very slowly and painfully up the island. A few started with automobiles but the masses of stone buildings barricading the avenues soon halted their vehicles. Rich and poor alike, welded together in a real democracy of misery, headed northward. They carried babies, jewel cases, bits of furniture, bags, joints of meat and canned goods made into rough packs.

Always they looked fearfully upwards at the sky . . . bodies lay like revellers overcome in grotesque attitudes . . . The majority had died swiftly of poison gas.[1]

The attack was intended to capitalize on Mitchell's rise to stardom following his earlier demonstration of the power of the bomber by sinking ex-German warships. Mitchell's transformation into a national hero had been carefully planned as part of his campaign to show that America should now rely on bomber aircraft, not battleships for its defence. To outflank navy admirals' attempts to claim that these sinkings proved nothing because the targets were stationary, undefended, and obsolete, Mitchell, with the help of the Eastman Kodak company, had developed a system to film the attack from the air, rush the film to New York for development, and then distribute the film so that it would be seen in big-city cinemas across America the next day. The formula of pictures plus the story of a little man taking on the massed forces of the navy "trust" was unbeatable. When the trials culminated in the spectacular sinking of the battleship *Ostfriesland*, Mitchell was instantly acclaimed across America. Now, by bombing Manhattan, Mitchell enabled New Yorkers to witness with their own eyes the devastating power of the bomber. This was part of a larger campaign by the Army Air Service and aircraft manufacturers to persuade Americans that they had to support the rapid development of aviation or face disaster (see photographic essay, Part 3). When Mitchell then went on to lead mock bombing attacks on Philadelphia, Wilmington, Baltimore, and, to add insult to injury, the Naval Academy at Annapolis, the result was a storm of publicity in which the nation's newspapers sought to outdo each other with accounts of the projected utter destruction of these cities.

In his 1925 book *Winged Defence*, complete with romantic photograph of himself as youthful air ace behind the cover, Mitchell spelled out the implications. The fact that "aircraft can fly anywhere that is air" meant that "frontiers in the old sense – the coast lines or borders – are no longer applicable".[2] Whereas in the past the inhabitants of America's interior cities had been safe from the dangers experienced by the inhabitants of the frontier, now all Americans were living on the frontier where they might at any moment face a sudden annihilating attack. The frontier no longer referred to a line at the border of the nation. The frontier was now everywhere. The only way the old situation could be restored was through technology. To defend cities against bombers there was no alternative except the development of an air force with sufficient fighter planes to stop an attack or bomber planes to deter it. Mitchell went on to imagine a future in which aircraft and radio held out the potential for world domination:

> If a nation ambitious for universal conquest gets off to a "flying start" in a war of the future, it may be able to control the whole world more easily than a nation has controlled a continent in the past. The advent of air power has made every country and the world smaller. We do not measure distances by the unit of miles, but by the unit of hours. Communications all over the world today are instantaneous . . . Airplanes

can be talked to while in flight anywhere. The airship or Zeppelin can cross any ocean. Should a nation, therefore, attain complete control of the air, it could more nearly master the earth than has ever been the case in the past.[3]

Through aerial supremacy a nation would be able to instantly launch the kind of attack on the cities of any country that did not accept its overlordship which Mitchell had asked New Yorkers to imagine could devastate their city, without that nation being able to deter such an attack through the capacity to reply in kind. It might not even be necessary to actually carry out such attacks, as the very ability to do so would enable such a nation to bend the actions of others to its will through implicit threats of such an attack.

In his later book *Skyways* published in 1930 after he had been court-martialled and dismissed from the army for insubordination, Mitchell reinforced the idea that airpower could offer world mastery through maps of the globe showing the flight distances between New York, San Francisco, Peking, Tokyo, and other world cities. He conveyed the idea that the rapid development of the aeroplane was making all parts of the world contiguous through a map showing the speed with which air transportation was shrinking the time taken to go from one part of the United States to another. By 1930, he claimed, air transportation had already reduced the globe to one sixth of its former dimensions.[4] Mitchell balanced his vision that aircraft made possible world domination by claims that aerial war was actually more humane because it would deter war entirely or quickly result in victory by the side with superior air power.[5] Moreover, the rapid development of civilian air transportation would soon lead to the universal triumph of civilization. "There is no place on the earth's surface that air power cannot reach and carry with it the elements of civilization and good that comes from rapid communication."[6]

Mitchell's simulated attack supported a fiction. There was no possibility that any European power could cross the Atlantic with a bomber force sufficiently large to carry out anything more than a superficial gas attack on New York. As such the media blitz that followed his mock attacks on America's cities stands in stark contrast to the brief mention received by an *actual* air attack against the inhabitants of an American city some months earlier. In May 1921 a mob of 10,000 whites invaded the black part of Tulsa, Oklahoma. As they advanced, they looted small businesses and shops and set homes on fire. Armed blacks defended their homes. To overcome the unexpectedly fierce resistance the white mob enlisted the help of eight planes, some manned by police, and rapidly improvised dynamite bombs, which were dropped on black neighbourhoods which the mob had already set alight using oil and gasoline. Most of the black ghetto was burnt to the ground and between 150 and 200 black people, the majority of whom were women and children, along with 50 of the white invaders, lost their lives.[7]

Mitchell's simulated attack on New York was a sign of things to come. In articles published in 1932, Mitchell described in detail how air power could be used against Japan: "What Japan is in deadly fear of is our air force . . . These towns, built largely of wood and paper, form the greatest aerial targets the world has ever seen . . . Incendiary projectiles would burn the cities to the ground in short order."[8] Mitchell's vision rapidly became reality. The following year the Boeing corporation won the Army Air Corp's competition to design a long-range multi-engine bomber. The XB-17 was tested in 1935, and by 1938 mass production of the Boeing B-17 Flying Fortresses was under way. America now began to formulate plans for the fire-bombing of Japanese cities. In late 1940 the US advisor to the Chinese air force, retired Air Corps General Claire Chennault, proposed a plan for basing hundreds of US bombers in China. From there these forces would be able to "burn out the industrial heart of the Empire with fire-bomb attacks on the teeming bamboo ant heaps of Japanese cities".[9] Franklin Roosevelt was "simply delighted" by Chennault's scheme. When it proved unworkable he turned to other ways of using bombers against Japan. In February 1941 Admiral Husband Kimmel in Hawaii was asked by Chief of Naval Operations Admiral Harold Stark, apparently acting under White House orders, to develop plans for "making aircraft raids on the inflammable Japanese cities (ostensibly on military objectives)". In mid-1941 B-17 bombers and incendiary bombs were moved to Hawaiian and Philippines bases from which they could bomb Japan. The goal was to have 340 of these bombers ready by February or March of 1942. Claimed to be a closely guarded secret, the plan was widely reported in the press. In October 1941 *The United States News* published a two page map showing routes and flying times for US bomber raids on the cities that formed "the head and the heart of industrial Japan". The strategy was to use the force to persuade Japan to abandon her imperial ambitions, and if that did not work to rapidly defeat Japan without the need for ground troops. At a secret briefing for press bureau chiefs and senior correspondents, Army Chief of Staff Marshall declared: "We are preparing an offensive war against Japan . . ." The first aim would be to deter war by officially informing the Japanese about the bomber build-up and the intention to bomb their cities. Should this fail, Marshall continued, America would wage war "mercilessly" and "Flying fortresses will be dispatched immediately to set the paper cities of Japan on fire."[10]

Notoriously, Japan did not wait until America had built up its bomber forces and sought instead to ensure that Japan started what Japanese militarists increasingly regarded as an inevitable war in the best position, striking first at Pearl Harbour in December 1941. Official Japanese observers had been present at Mitchell's demonstration that bombers could sink battleships. It seems that the lesson he had taught had been well learned, but by the wrong people. Whereas Japan and Germany had developed tactical air forces to aid their armies, in the inter-war period Britain and America had developed strategic air forces made up of heavy bombers. The result was that in the total war that followed Pearl Harbour, it was Britain and America that took the devastation of cities to its greatest heights. But whereas Mitchell had imagined that air power would be more humane, the unexpected ability of civilian populations to endure and the steadily mounting bombing raids to break that endurance meant that bombing led to ever higher civilian deaths without bringing quick victory. The airmen's desire to prove the bomber could bring victory on its own meant that the attack Mitchell had asked New Yorkers to imagine on their city was, in reality, carried out by the Royal Air Force and US Air Force in their deliberate creation of firestorms which consumed Hamburg, Dresden, and Tokyo and the atomic bomb blasts which destroyed Hiroshima and Nagasaki and left the survivors dying of radiation poisoning.[11] Truman's belief that the bomb would give America clear superiority over Russia only led Stalin to accelerate Russia's own bomb, so that within a few years New Yorkers indeed faced the danger that their city could be annihilated.[12]

These histories complicate any simple response to 11 September. They show that in seeking to secure themselves against imagined terror in the past, Americans have ended up exercising terror over others and contributing to the creation of a world in which such terrors are real. This book is a detective story in which I investigate how Americans first became trapped in such a world. I turn to the period after the First World War when Billy Mitchell and others first sought to convince urban Americans that changes in technology meant they now lived on a frontier where they might be attacked at any moment. I focus on how the presidency on the one hand, and scientists, engineers, big business, and the military on the other, worked together to produce a frontier in which we are threatened by "outlaws" armed with high-technology weapons, and presented the extension of their power as the *only* way in which Americans can defend themselves against this threat.

To present a complex argument in an easily accessible way Chapter 1 gives an overview of the whole book. The later chapters then look at the material presented in greater depth and from new points of view. To continue the detective analogy, in the later chapters the reader discovers that the initial "crime" and "trail of evidence" was a diversion to lure them in the wrong direction. They come to see that the initial "suspects" were small fry, and going to the root of the matter discern the "master criminals" lurking in the background. The book has three parts. In the first part I am interested in how the imperative to stop terror is transformed into the perfection of new means to exercise terror. I look at the way the creators of America's first weapons laboratories sought to transform the relationship between science and law by arguing that urban Americans were now living on a high-technology frontier in which they could be annihilated at any moment by German aircraft carrying poison gas bombs. I uncover the untold story of how America came to see itself as the guardian of international law with the right to use high-technology terror to deal with outlaw states.

In the second part I look at the way the struggle to gain the vote within America so as to combat the white community's use of lynch terror to control African Americans was subordinated to Woodrow Wilson's crusade to make the world safe for democracy. I focus on a diabolical deal. In return for accepting elite rule and giving up Americans' struggle to extend democracy within the United States, the elite would praise them as heroes fighting to extend democracy throughout the world.

In the third part I argue against the idea that science and technology must inevitably lead to new means for exercising terror. I argue that democracy can now only be meaningful if it involves new rights which enable citizens to intervene in decisions about the direction of scientific research and technological development. The old science politics focused on the abuse of scientific discoveries after they had been made. The new science politics must focus on how citizens can decide in which direction new scientific research and technological development should proceed.

The intense emotions engendered by 11 September make a retreat to prepared positions easy, and reflective thought about how we should respond to this new situation difficult. Yet such thought is vital if Americans are not to end up compounding the dangers facing the world. As we no longer have strong emotional investments in the partisan disputes of this era, these investigations give us vitally needed distance. Through the juxtaposition of past and present, we can understand the political and emotional structures we are caught up in, and trace excluded alternatives which suggest how we can now remake these structures to at least lessen the degree to which we are constrained by terror or complicit in it.

PART 1

1

The Infant Stage

How were urban Americans first persuaded that they lived in a frontier situation where, at any moment, they might be attacked by outlaws armed with weapons capable of annihilating whole cities? A passage discussing the 22 April 1915 Germany gas attack in General Amos Fries and Major Clarence West's 1921 book *Chemical Warfare* is a good place to begin. Fries was Director of the US Army Chemical Warfare Service, while West was a leading member of the National Research Council and a reserve major in the Service. It begins by quoting an eye-witness account of the attack by the Rev. O.S. Watkins in the *Methodist Recorder*:

> Then we saw that which almost caused our hearts to stop beating – figures running wildly and in confusion over the fields.
>
> "The French have broken," we exclaimed. We hardly believed our words . . . The story they told we cannot believe; we put it down to their terror-stricken imaginings – a greenish-grey cloud had swept down on them, turning yellow as it travelled over the country, blasting everything it touched, shrivelling up the vegetation. No human courage could face such a peril.
>
> Then there staggered into our midst French soldiers, blinded, coughing, chests heaving, faces an ugly purple color – lips speechless with agony, and behind them, in gas-choked trenches, we learned that they had left hundreds of dead and dying comrades. The impossible was only too true.
>
> It was the most fiendish, wicked thing I have ever seen.

Fries and West then seek to control the effect of Watkin's description. To do so they continue with a statistical analysis which, they claim, proves the humanity of gas:

Medical records show that out of every 100 Americans gassed less than two died, and as far as records of four years show, very few are permanently injured. Out of every 100 American casualties from all forms of warfare other than gas more than 25 per cent died, while 2 to 5 per cent more are maimed, blinded or disfigured for life . . . it is the most humane where both sides are prepared for it, while against savage or unprepared peoples it can be made so humane that but very few casualties will result.[1]

The eyewitness account and the passage that follows it are central to Fries and West's attempt to enrol the reader in a fantasy in which the greatness of absolute power is confirmed by the display of humanity.

Their key tactic in doing so is their presentation of poison gas as a *new* technology, whose possibilities are not yet fully established. All we have are indications of what its potential may be. This turns chemical weapons into a blank space onto which Americans can project their fantasies and imagine them becoming real.[2] We can see such projection at work every day in the psychic investments we make in children. As human beings who cannot yet completely define themselves they become a site onto which we can project our hopes; as really existing persons they give us the licence to dream about a better life. To combat the idea that poison gas use during the World War had already turned it into an old technology whose possibilities were well known, Fries and West take up the idea of the infant and use it as a metaphor to describe the current state of chemical weapons. They are at "the infant stage".[3] Like a mother whose close attention to her child enables her to spot the signs of things to come, scientists on the "inside" of chemical warfare research can now see future developments of chemical weapons that were "undreamed" of at the end of the war. Elsewhere, Fries uses the idea of a technological revolution to underscore the newness of chemical weapons. "No other invention since that of gunpowder has made so profound a change in warfare," he claims, "as gas is making and will make in the future."[4]

By presenting chemical weapons as a new technology, Fries and West seek to institute a *break in time*. They claim that the actual use of chemical weapons in the First World War does not provide a good guide to their future potential. Equally, they claim that the role of the development of armaments, in particular naval armaments, in bringing about the First World War is not a good guide to the likely effect of pursuing chemical weapons research. Through doing this they seek to exclude the views of their opponents from consideration: on the one side, the military establishment's view that four years of war had turned chemical weapons into an old weapon which had not proven to be militarily decisive; on the other side, the post-war disarmament movement's view that just as the development of naval armaments had led to the First World War the development of chemical weapons would lead to a new world war. The result of these moves is to turn chemical weapons into a *site of investment*. Fries and West are taken up and carried along with enthusiasm for the possibilities. Scientific research will lead to new poison gases of far greater effectiveness. Poisonous particulates are being developed which can pass straight through gas masks. Aircraft are being adapted so they can fly over armies or cities and cover them with a fine poisonous mist. Through these fantasies of total power the chemical soldiers intoxicate themselves with the greatness of their task in winning the chemical arms race for America. In doing so they silence any doubts they might have through the strong emotion of enthusiasm:

> The Chemical Warfare Service today is essentially a pioneer. We are all engaged in blazing a trail. Our work is new, and the details of it are highly technical. The possibilities of Chemical Warfare . . . are practically unlimited . . . The eyes of the army and the nation are fixed on the Chemical Warfare Service.[5]

Watkins' eyewitness description of how the German use of gas led to the total collapse of all opposing forces plays a key part in giving credibility to these fantasies of total power. It is reinforced in the photograph entitled "French gas attack seen from an Aeroplane" which accompanies it. From the aerial vantage point, we see a series of plumes of gas being blown towards enemy lines from the French trenches. As our eye catches the tiny and indistinct roads and other features that mark the landscape below us, we are stunned by the vast size of the gas plumes. Then, as we see the plumes extending away to the horizon we begin to comprehend the enormous scale of the attack. The photograph's view-point allows us to imagine ourselves in the position of a military commander directing the attack. This encourages us to share the fantasy of controlling unlimited power. What *Chemical Warfare* does not show us are pictures of the actual effects of gas on people we can identify with. (Indeed, the British Medical Council's *An Atlas of Gas Poisoning*, which contains vivid colour medical drawings showing such effects, was deliberately withheld from the public.)[6] The photograph is a precursor to the photographs of atomic bomb detonations with which we have all become familiar.

The newness of chemical weapons gives Fries and West the freedom to conceive of almost anything being possible. They imagine that chemical weapons will enable a war to be fought in which there are many casualties but few permanent injuries or deaths. Or, against unprepared peoples, a war almost without casualties at all. The selective use of statistics enables them to avoid confronting the fact that new poison gases make maximum casualties with minimum deaths and permanent injuries unlikely.[7] The fantasy element present here can be seen even more clearly in Harvard chemist Norris Hall's 1921 book, *The Next War*. After speculating about the possibility of enlisting "lethal bacteria and protozoa" as weapons, he moves on to proclaim that "The possibility is always present that a gas may be found of such properties that it can secure complete victory without killing or maiming, which is totally impossible with other weapons of war."[8]

This, however, is only the start. Fries imagines that by making war more terrible, chemical warfare research will lead to an end to war itself. This idea is condensed in the slogan he coins for the Chemical Warfare Service. *"Every development of science that makes warfare more universal and more scientific makes for permanent peace by making warfare more intolerable"* (italics in the original).[9] The idea that poison gas would, paradoxically, make war more humane by making it more terrible was shared by General William Mitchell, the leader of the campaign for an independent air force based on a fleet of heavy bombers. Mitchell imagined that the bombing of cities with poison gas would cause mass panic and quickly lead the nation which endured it to sue for peace. This "quick way of deciding a war," he wrote after he had left the army in 1930, would be "really much more humane than the present methods of blowing people to bits by cannon projectiles or butchering them with bayonets".[10]

At the centre of Fries and West's fantasy is a scene in which the exercise of total power over life is reinforced by the display of humanity. In their vision the world is transformed into struggle between rival chemical laboratories in which international law is powerless to set any limit to the development of ever more deadly chemical weapons. In their eyes the earth is essentially a battlefield in which the force of international law is suspended. In this scene the United States represents the forces of humanity and exercises a direct power over life. In the absence of any legal limit, power shows its greatness through its humanity. The exercise of pity and mercy towards human life does not limit power but confirms its greatness.

The presentation of the gas cloud, and the fantasy in which the logical contradictory elements of total control and the exercise of humanity not only co-exist but reinforce each other, is the main tactic employed by Fries and West in *Chemical Warfare* to enrol support for chemical warfare research. Fries and West sought to cloak themselves with the authority of the state through a double movement. First, faced with the power of chemical weapons their reader would have felt his or her own weakness and isolation. *Chemical Warfare* worked to intensify the anxiety. It also took the actual use of chemical weapons, as we have seen, to legitimate a fantasy of the absolute power of poison gas. Second, the educated reader for whom *Chemical Warfare* was intended, was offered a way of escaping from this powerlessness and isolation. He or she was invited to view the world *as if* they were part of a powerful and knowledgeable community of scientists, engineers, corporate businessmen, journalists, statesmen, and soldiers who were in the process of discovering how to protect humanity from them.

Within *Chemical Warfare* the message that the reader is in a world where chemical weapons and the threat they pose are an inescapable reality is reinforced throughout by endless descriptions, technical drawings, and photographs of chemical weapons laboratories, testing grounds, industrial plants, munitions dumps, and wartime chemical warfare operations. The world of chemical warfare is all-encompassing. There is no escape. At the same time these descriptions, technical drawings, and photographs put the reader into the position of a scientist, engineer, businessman, or soldier in control of this new technology. In *Chemical Warfare* this community is represented by the photograph of the wartime Director of the Chemical Warfare Service, Major-General Silbert, at the front of the book. Silbert appears as a calm, benevolent, authoritative patriarchal figure with whom the reader can identify.

Chemical Warfare enables us to see current arguments for continued nuclear weapons research in a new light. We see that the leaders of American nuclear weapons laboratories are repeating the tactics used by the supporters of chemical weapons laboratories. In both cases a technology is presented as new so that the future can be imagined as absolutely different from the past. By instituting an absolute break, arguments that the laboratories are repeating actions that led to disaster can be swept aside. The supporters of chemical weapons can ignore the warning sounded by the consequences of American, German, and British pursuit of the ultimate battleship fleet in the decades before the First World War – a naval arms race which was a major factor in the division of Europe into two armed camps, a division which transformed a local crisis in the Balkans into a world war. The supporters of new nuclear weapons can ignore the warning sounded by the consequences of America's initiation of a nuclear arms race through the bombing of Hiroshima and Nagasaki – an unstable nuclear arms race in which each side's pursuit of superiority and fear of surprise attack may or may not have brought the world to the brink of nuclear war, which saw the waste of human resources on a massive scale, and which led to the proliferation of chemical, biological, and nuclear weapons throughout the globe.[11]

(i) Placing the weapons laboratory at the heart of the extension of the power of the presidency and its "advisors"

To see what was at stake in Fries and West's evocation of the power of future chemical weapons we need to see *Chemical Warfare* as a repetition of earlier statements supporting the expansion of a "grey zone" – an area in which it was ambiguous whether the presidency on the one side, and business, professional, and civil service advisors on the other, were exercising increased powers so as to ensure the survival of the republic or on behalf of their own interests.

The growth of the grey zone was already well under way in the decades before the First World War. Take tariff policy. Following severe recession in the early 1890s, big business and trade associations began to argue that America's very survival depended on assured access to other countries' markets. They began to see tariffs in a new light. In addition to being a means of raising revenue or of protecting industries, tariffs would now be a weapon of economic warfare, a means of breaking a way in for American goods whether foreign countries wanted them or not. To forge the new weapon, business successfully lobbied Congress to hand a large measure of control over tariffs to the executive, which could then use it to punish nations for refusing access to American goods on favourable terms. As smaller economies usually depended more on access to America's giant economy than vice versa, America's existing economic advantage could be used as a basis for generating yet further economic advantage. Then, in a second stage, business lobbied Congress to set up a tariff commission to investigate world trade conditions and determine "scientifically" how the president could use the tariff to improve access for American goods. The same transfer of power to the presidency and to advisory bodies was repeated in other areas of policy such as health, sanitation, naval armaments, social policy, and conservation.

The war saw the further expansion of the grey zone.[12] To mobilize the economy for total war President Woodrow Wilson gained Congressional acceptance for a Committee of National Defence (CND) composed of members of his cabinet, and advised by representatives of the key sections of society on which mobilization depended serving in the National Defence Advisory Council (NDAC). In practice, mobilization was carried out by businessmen seconded from their industries to the subcommittees of the NDAC and the more powerful War Industries Board (WIB), working with officials in the government departments they were supplying. The wartime demands on the time of the secretaries of state for war, navy, state, and other departments meant that close supervision was impossible, while the reliance of the government on these businessmen's expertise, experience, information, and personal contacts within their industries meant that only they, and the government officials they worked with, could determine which policies should be followed. The official status of such businessmen – called dollar-a-year men because they received no salary from the government – as only "advisors" meant that their activities were not restricted by Congress, and they were able to wield great power over any area of policy they could claim was central to mobilization. As these businessmen oversaw their own industries, and in some cases awarded government contracts to themselves, they were in conflict with army regulations and anti-trust laws. Charges of conflict of interest, corruption, favouritism, and profiteering proliferated.

Though the most powerful, the CND-NDAC and WIB were but two of many organizations set up during the war which worked on the basis of close cooperation between business, professionals with key expertise, and government officials. For our investigation two others are of central significance: the Committee of Public Information (CPI) and the National Research Council (NRC). Both were established by President Wilson using executive orders. In the CPI officials from the war, navy, and state departments cooperated with leading journalists to provide Americans with a flood of information. This was carefully selected to support the government's story – that a united America was placing all its energy behind a war to defeat a Germany bent on world domination – supplemented by highly charged images and stories. Depictions likening German officers to wild beasts and atrocity stories about rapes and other horrors were grist to its mill. All this was backed up by discreet censorship of alternative points of view. In the NRC, leading scientists, engineers, businessmen, and officials worked together to apply scientific research to the rapid solution of war problems. These ranged from the use of research to develop new chemical weapons and the means of protecting against them, to the development of a device for detecting submarines, to finding alternatives to difficult-to-obtain raw materials needed by the war economy.

As the end of the war approached, government officials, businessmen, professional experts, and trade unionists sought ways to extend the power they had gained during the war into the peace. The strategy they devised can be seen in an August 1918 address given by the chairman of the Board of Trustees of the Carnegie Institution, Senator Elihu Root. The senator spoke as one of America's senior statesmen and as one of the principal architects of the new assertive presidency supported by expert advice. As William McKinley and Theodore Roosevelt's secretary of war (1899–1904), Root reorganized the army and oversaw its use in the Philippines-American War. Succeeding Hays as Roosevelt's secretary of state (1905–1909), he went on to serve as senator for New York (1909–15). His work negotiating international arbitration treaties brought him the 1913 Nobel Peace Prize. During the years of American neutrality he had played a leading role in the preparedness movement. Working behind the scenes Root had drafted the legislation establishing the CND-NDAC. Root started his address by reiterating the case for the organization of scientific research being carried out by the NRC. "The effective power of a great number of scientific men," he argued, "may be increased by organization just as the effective power of a great number of laborers may be increased by military discipline." The German success in organizing science for "military world dominion" has shown that such organization has now become central to national military power. The challenge facing America, he concludes, is whether individualistic Americans can achieve the level of scientific organization for practical ends as successfully as autocratic government has done by giving direction to a docile and submissive people.

The key part of the address, however, comes near the end where Root argues that the organization of science undertaken during the war needs to be continued after the war's end:

> It would be the height of folly for the law-abiding nations of the earth ever to permit themselves to be left again at a disadvantage in that kind of preparation.

> Competency for defence against military aggression requires highly developed
> organized scientific preparation. Without it the most civilized nation will be as
> helpless as the Aztecs were against Cortez.[13]

The argument is based on the idea that the First World War has shown that the
organization of science is now militarily decisive. Root mixes rational argument
with fantasy. Of course science was important to all sides in the First World War,
but Root goes beyond that to evoke a situation in which the organization of science for war is so potent that even after Germany has been defeated, America
must keep up the organization of science for war. Just as we have seen *Chemical
Warfare* present chemical weapons as a new thing whose future potential cannot
be fixed, so here Root presents scientific organization for war in exactly the same
light. This allows it to become a licence for fantasies about the achievement of
unlimited power through scientific research. Such fantasies are given further legitimacy by recounting the history of the Aztecs' sudden collapse when faced by
Cortez's forces armed with superior technology. (In fact, Cortez's defeat of the
Aztecs was mainly due not to technology but to the support of peoples tired of
Aztec rule.) On this basis, Root argues that the cooperation between government
officials, scientists, and engineers, and business initiated during the war by the
NRC must be continued indefinitely because the civilized world is faced with a
constant threat to its existence. Here the idea that America's very survival hangs
in the balance is used to legitimate the indefinite extension of a wartime measure
established by presidential decree without Congressional legislation.

Root goes on to argue that the same organization of science for war will be
essential to American industry in the post-war competition for international
markets:

> We are not limited, however, to a military objective, for when the war is over the
> international competitions of peace will be resumed. No treaties or leagues can pre-
> vent that, and it is not desirable that they should, for no nation can afford to be
> without the stimulus of competition.
>
>   In that race the same power of science which has so amazingly increased the pro-
> ductive capacity of mankind during the past century will be applied again and the
> prizes of industrial and commercial leadership will fall to the nation which organizes
> its scientific forces most effectively.[14]

This is a reiteration of the argument used to justify cooperation between business
and government officials before the war so that America can continue to have the
access to world markets it was claimed she needs to survive. At the centre of
Root's vision is a concord in which all conflict is resolved. He imagines a harmony
between the advance of pure science and the use of science both for war and for
industrial and commercial advance. Equally, he imagines a harmony between

American success in international markets through scientific research and the advance of mankind as a whole. He excludes the alternative possibility that the struggle to ensure markets for America's surplus product may itself have been a cause of the world war and may be so again. Like Fries and West, then, Root imagines a beautiful harmony between America's achievement of control through new weapons and its exercise of humanity.

The unexpectedly sudden collapse of German forces in late 1918 caused a crisis for President Wilson and for the businessmen, professionals, trade unionists, and government officials who were exercising wartime power in his name. When the Armistice was signed on 11 November 1918, neither had had sufficient time to entrench their new power. Abroad, Wilson was confronted by the fact that Britain and France were no longer dependent on American military power. He therefore had to trade acceptance of Britain and France's dictation of a punitive peace – which one side of him agreed with anyway – for their agreement to his plan for a League of Nations. At home he suddenly found his plans for the League of Nations imperilled by a Senate which refused to accept his dictate as it had during the war. The crisis facing the groups that had exercised power on his behalf was no less severe. Big business faced the threat of being attacked for drawing America into the First World War through a one-sided trade with Britain and France in war materials during American neutrality, and for abusing its wartime position as advisor to the government to extract enormous profits. The army faced the threat of being attacked for using the war to carry out the militarization of America that the nation had gone to war to defeat in Germany. In these circumstances, co-operation began to break down as different groups sought to maintain their wartime gains at the expense of other groups.

The falling out that concerns us emerged within the army. The army general staff sought to use the memory of the German threat while it was still fresh in American minds to secure legislation introducing universal military service. This would reinforce its links with members of the business and foreign policy elite who believed that universal military service would teach young Americans to put the development of America as a great civilizing nation before their class, ethnic group, or region. The general staff needed to deflect the arguments of critics that it was militarizing America. Equally, it needed to deflect critics who argued that the war showed that far from being a place where young men could learn heroically to sacrifice themselves for the nation, the army transformed into mindless automata blindly following the orders of their superiors. The result was that at the same meeting that Chief of Staff General Peyton March and Secretary of State for War Newton Baker finalized plans to introduce legislation calling for universal military service, redescribed as universal military training, they agreed to dissolve the Chemical Warfare Service.[15] In doing so they reiterated the wartime branding of chemical weapons as a diabolical German weapon, and by rejecting them sought to reinforce the wartime claim that the American army was a democratic army of citizen soldiers different in kind from the autocratic German army.

The authors of *Chemical Warfare*, therefore, faced a difficult rhetorical challenge. The book is addressed to an elite audience that, for the most part, already accepts the claim that the defeat of Germany required the temporary extension of the power of the president and his wartime "advisors". Fries and West seek to transfer the authority of this claim to their own.[16] First of all Fries and West open up a gap between the past and the present. Through their presentation of chemical weapons as a new technology, they seek to place their audience in a new situation in which they are threatened by German chemical weapons. They then close the gap by getting the audience to accept that they should be accorded the same authority that the president's business, professional, and official advisors were given during the war. They do this by presenting the situation created by chemical weapon research as *the same* as the wartime situation. The potential power of chemical weapons, especially when joined to that of aircraft, is so enormous that America continues to face a threat to its existence as it did during the war. At the same time they seek to present their claims as the same as those being made by more authoritative figures, such as Elihu Root, about how the threat presented by organized scientific research means that wartime cooperation to push forward research into new weapons must continue in peacetime. These authorities are enlisted to discredit the general staff's claim that it is the staff, and not Fries and West, who should be accepted as authorities about the post-war situation.

They do this by likening themselves to earlier military innovators, and the general staff to conservative generals who mistakenly tried to stop innovation:

> Hannibal, Hasdrubal, Caesar, Napoleon, Frederick the Great, Scott, Grant, and Jackson were all independent thinkers. Each and every one dared to do something that every other general and statesman of his time told him could not be done or that would bring about disaster. They had the courage of their convictions. They had the courage to think out new ideas and develop them, and they had the courage to carry through those convictions, not lone against the opposition of the enemy, but against the opposition of their own people, both in the field and at home.[17]

Here the break in time created by insisting on the radical newness of chemical weapons is repaired. Research into chemical weapons is presented as the next step in a tradition of daring military innovators who made world history. While Fries and West seek to transfer authority from past figures to themselves, they also transfer authority from themselves back to the past. The arrow goes both ways. They implicitly present the wartime extension of the authority of the president and his advisors as a proper one. What is at stake is one way in which the wartime expansion of the grey zone can be continued into the peace. Fries and West offer the presidency and its business, professional, civil service, and military advisors an exchange: in return for supporting the claim that the extra-ordinary wartime powers enjoyed by the presidency and its advisors, in particular the NRC, during the war should be continued into the peace because of the threat of chemical and air weapons, the president and the NRC should support research into new chemical and air weapons.

To the extent that it is accepted by their audience, Fries and West's repetition of the wartime claims made by the president and his scientific advisors entrenches the authority of these earlier claims. The audience's acceptance of their claim in the present has an effect on its relation to the past, the authority of all the earlier claims Fries and West have invoked is strengthened, and the past is consolidated as a foundation for action in the present. But there is an alternative possibility. If the audience does not accept Fries and West's claim, the result will be an earthquake which shakes the whole past chain of authorities they have invoked. If Fries and West's claims on behalf of chemical weapons are a confidence trick, then their audience may wonder about earlier claims made by the president and his "advisors" about the need to go to war with Germany. The tremors may extend even further back to the foundations of the republic itself. Were the Anti-Federalists right to argue that the Constitutional Convention's claims that the states had to endorse the new Constitution as the only way the new republic could maintain its security against the threat of foreign invasion were a confidence trick to reinforce elite power? Was the Declaration of Independence right to claim that the subjects of George III faced an "absolute tyranny" so great that they had no alternative except to found a republic? The tremors may go in other directions as well, leading the audience to ask questions about the authority of earlier military scientific and engineering figures implicitly and explicitly evoked.

(ii) Turning the argument for chemical weapons research back against itself

If Fries and West's *Chemical Warfare* was the book that put the case for poison gas research in 1921, the book against it was "Will" Irwin's *The "Next War": An Appeal to Common Sense*. Going through no less than twelve printings in 1921, Irwin's book was a seminal part of a rapidly expanding disarmament movement.[18]

This movement arose in response to the resumption of America's 1916 naval building programme when the war ended. Wilson resumed building as a way of saying to the British that if they did not support his League of Nations project, America would deprive them of their naval supremacy. When the US Senate voted against ratifying the League Covenant, Wilson continued the building

programme as a way of saying to Americans that if they did not support membership of the League, they would have to pay for a navy second to none. The
vast cost of completing the shipbuilding meant that Americans faced no prospect
of tax relief as they reeled under the double burden of economic recession and
having to pay for the war. No less worrying, the programme threatened to spark
a naval armaments race with Britain and Japan. The result was that when, on 14
December 1920, Senator Borah tabled a Senate resolution calling for newly-
elected President Harding to host a conference to limit naval armaments, he
found he had captured the popular mood. Led by *The New York World*, newspapers across America weighed in with support, as did business groups like the
Los Angeles Chamber of Commerce.

A small number of women's suffrage activists acted as the catalyst which, in
these favourable conditions, precipitated the 1921 disarmament movement.
Writing in the 16 February 1921 *Nation*, Harriet Connor Brown's "Women to the
Rescue" set out their argument.[19] Huge military appropriations showed that
Congress had been captured by the vision of America becoming the world's leading military power. Unless women acted, America would repeat Germany's
mistake and the lessons of the world war would be lost. Owing to their "sex
instinct to cherish and conserve what is valuable for human life", women were in
a unique position to lead, and their recent success in gaining the vote gave them
the power to do so. "We can hold the balance of power. If we keep outside of
political parties, holding ourselves a mobile mass poised to crush the enemies of
the race as they show their heads in the different parties, we may decide elections."
Through a deliberate echo of Genesis, militarists were presented as poisonous
snakes, the crushing of which is up to women. Brown concluded with a call to
arms. "Is it not high time that the women of the world, lifted now by their
enfranchizement into a position of power, should become sex conscious and
work together in every land and all lands for the reduction and final abolition of
armaments?"

When they failed to carry a vote for a disarmament campaign at the February
National Women's Party annual meeting, these activists set up their own organization, the Women's Committee on World Disarmament. Their demand that the
government call an international disarmament conference quickly captured
Americans' imagination. Working through existing organizations, they were rapidly able to mobilize a broad coalition of groups representing America's religious
denominations – women, farmers, workers, educators, and students.

The "Next War" helped to give the campaign a second focus. In it Irwin takes up
the chemical soldiers' fantasy about the absolute power of poison gas, but claims
the gas cloud had escaped its creators' control. The Chemical Warfare Service is
not responding to a German threat, he argues, but is *leading* a chemical weapons
arms race:

American ingenuity solved the problem [of finding the ideal war gas]. At the time of the Armistice, we were manufacturing for the campaign of 1919 our Lewisite gas. It was invisible; it was a sinking gas, which would search out the refugees of dugouts and cellars; if breathed it killed at once – and it killed not only through the lungs. Whenever it settled on the skin, it produced a poison which penetrates the system and brought almost certain death. It was inimical to all cell-life, animal or vegetable. Masks alone were of no use against it. Further, it had fifty five times the "spread" of any poison gas hitherto used in the war. An expert has said that a dozen Lewisite air bombs of the greatest size in use during 1918 might with a favourable wind have eliminated the population of Berlin. . . . Now we have more than a hint of a gas beyond Lewisite. . . . a mere capsule of this gas in a small grenade can generate square rods and even acres of death in the absolute. . . ."[20] (ellipses in the original).

Irwin presents the use of research to discover poison gases as opening up a new era in human history in which mankind is acquiring the ability to destroy civilization itself. For Irwin, 22 April 1915, the day the Germans first used poison gas, is as significant a day as 12 October 1492 or 4 July 1776. It marks a critical reversal. Hitherto, scientists and inventors have worked for the benefit of mankind. "No first class scientific mind was interested in research having for its end to destroy human life."[21] Now that the German attack has been followed by a chemical arms race this has all changed:

From that moment, to use the language of the streets, the lid was off. Nations, instead of mere armies were now mobilized for war. Those great and little scientific minds, engaged hitherto in searching for abstract truth or in multiplying the richness of life and the wealth of nations could be turned towards the invention of the means of destruction whether they wished or no. A new area of human consciousness was brought to fruition.[22]

The war has also seen a second turning point. Previously, war had been waged by professional soldiers. Now, the fact that victory depends upon the organized effort of entire nations has made civilians the target. The result was that "military necessity" led Germany to start the bombing of cities, while the Royal Navy blockade sought to bring about German surrender by starving German civilians.

Irwin places these events within a wider context. Like Root, he sees the war as a battle between the forces of aristocracy and democracy. These forces cut across the warring nations: aristocracy had been in control in Germany; in France and Britain it had been balanced by democracy; and in America democracy had dominated. In Germany aristocracy had learned how to turn the modern forces of science and industrial organization to its own ends. The critical date was the Franco-Prussian war. The result of Germany's stunning military defeat of France in that war had been the total organization of German science and industry for war. The German nation had been completely indoctrinated to play its part.

Within Germany, the aristocracy had transformed war and the state into a national religion. "War was the highest manifestation of the state, the supreme act which gave it glory, the opportunity for the subject to prove his devotion. War was good in itself."[23]

Irwin confronts Americans with a choice. The defeat of Germany has been a victory for democracy. The horror of the war means that support for peace crosses all national boundaries. The danger is reactionary European elites, "men with old ideas, men whose concept of statesmanship is force unlimited", are seeking to maintain their power by playing on nationalist sentiments. The result is tragic: "those returning soldiers, with all their pacifist sentiment, find themselves caught in a wheel".[24] This situation places the United States in the decisive position: "Now is the appointed time to begin action, and we are the appointed people. The lesson of the last war is still fresh in our mind; and unto us, by luck rather than foresight, has been given the dominant position in the world of the next quarter century. The course the United States chooses will largely be the course of other nations."[25] Americans must now decided whether to build on the defeat of autocracy to move the world towards permanent peace through disarmament; or, to lead a new arms race by continuing their naval shipbuilding programme and the development of new chemical and air weapons. "We have as much economic and industrial power to manufacture navies and munitions as any three European nations, more population to furnish soldiers than any two Western European nations. If we arm to the teeth the rest must follow through fear."[26]

Irwin ends with a dramatic passage in which America is placed in the position of Christ being tempted by the Devil. America now has the option of using its scientific, military, and economic power to achieve domination over the entire American continent. It can establish the greatest empire the world has ever seen. But the story of Germany's bid to dominate its neighbours shows the vision is a false one: "Germany listened to the tempter and chose the kingdoms of the world. And Germany in 1921 . . . Behind these gorgeous visions floating in rosy mist lurk death . . . poverty . . . starvation . . . a civilization become offal and ashes. He does not show you these; he knows that he is at war with the purposes of eternity." (Ellipses in the original.)[27]

Irwin interrupts the double movement through which Fries and West seek to present themselves as the authorities Americans should look to for guidance on chemical weapons. He does so by taking the chemical warfare officers' first movement, their presentation of chemical weapons as so powerful they call into question the competence of the general staff's claim to authority over military policy, and giving it a twist. Through their programme of research into new poison gases, Irwin claims, the chemical warfare officers are accelerating a chemical arms race that was begun in the world war. Far from knowing how to control this new danger, the chemical warfare officers are rapidly increasing it to the point where it is beyond anyone's capacity to control. The world is on the verge of an unstoppable chemical and air arms race, which will lead to a war in which civilization itself will be destroyed. Metropolises will be turned into "necropolises". *Here the officers' own tactics for gaining support for research create the opportunity for multiplying resistance to chemical warfare research.* Irwin takes up the officers' presentation of chemical weapons as a new technology and makes it the occasion for negative rather than positive fantasies, nightmares rather than dreams. In these circumstances, Irwin presents the leaders of the rapidly emerging campaign for disarmament as the best guides to follow. He seeks to reverse the chemical officers' attempt to drive their critics in the general staff and military establishment to the margins. Instead, it is the chemical officers who should not be listened to. They are like the Prussian militarists who led Germany to disaster. It is up to the rest of the army to show they are not Prussians by supporting those generals who reject chemical warfare research.

So successful was Irwin's, and more generally the disarmament movement's, turning of the chemical warfare officers' own tactic back against itself that in a few years Fries was desperately trying to squash the idea that chemical weapons promised unlimited power. Erasing his own role in propagating this idea, he now claimed it was a trick used by opponents to discredit chemical warfare research. In his 1924 Annual Report to the secretary for war, Fries complained: "Much has been said of new gases being discovered. Agitators and careless speakers refer to some of these gases as if they had supernatural powers. That is ridiculously erroneous. It is also seriously misleading. Chemicals have very definite limits to their power."[28]

Irwin's book is carefully crafted to gain a hearing for the disarmament movement within the new elite. Irwin was well placed to do so. A journalist who had worked in the Committee for Public Information, he was himself a member of the new elite. To gain a hearing *The "Next War"* does not call into question the basic story the new elite told about itself – that the danger of German autocracy to American democracy meant that it had indeed had the responsibility to mobilize America for total war and then to go to war in 1917. This is both the strength and the weakness of Irwin's intervention. On the one side, it enables him to widen the split between the general staff and the Chemical Warfare Service. On the other side, it reinforces the new elite's belief that those members of the 1921 disarmament campaign who question that story need not be listened to. Irwin's book thus helps to silence American socialists, black radicals, German-Americans, women's suffrage advocates, Christian pacifists, and other groups who argue that the new elite was complicit in the war. The full force of Irwin's call for disarmament lays itself open to being deflected by the new elite: the latter has only to present itself as seeking to ward off an armaments race among the wartime allies and lower the cost of maintaining military dominance over their wartime enemies. It can do this by advocating arms control measures among the wartime allies rather than disarmament. These will stop an arms race among the allies, but, by maintaining their collective military predominance over their wartime enemies, will entrench the division of the world into opposing camps. The result will be to split the disarmament movement in two: a part which accepts the new elite's claim to represent civilization and is content with arms control measures that maintain the power of the elite; and a part which believes that the new elite's complicity in the war's violence calls into question its claim to represent civilization and demands general disarmament.

(iii) Is there something wrong with the very framework used to discuss research into new poison gases?

The juxtaposition of an eyewitness account of the first poison gas attack with the use of statistics to prove gas is a humane weapon sounds a false note. There is a jarring as the two rub up against each other. It is like having one's teeth set on edge when chalk is slowly scraped across a blackboard. The sense of discord is increased when you realize that the horror of the first gas attack is already attenuated by Watkin's description; first-person accounts of being gassed would have made the collision between the two ways of speaking unbearable.

It is not difficult to begin to note reasons for our discomfort. There is a feeling that the languages of strategy, efficiency, investment, nationalism, and humanism do an injustice to the categorical imperative the dead address to us – very roughly "that we must stop the violence done to them from being repeated". There is an intuition that Fries and West may be burying something by moving too quickly over the burning question – why were the dead killed so horribly? To address these issues we need to find terms that sharpen our appreciation of what is at stake. A test of such language will be whether it brings to the fore the problem that the very terms used to talk about violence can, themselves, work to continue that violence.[29] To begin it is helpful to think about the dispute over chemical weapons as analogous to a dispute in a law court. The analogy suggests that there are two very different ways in which the feeling that there is something forced in Fries and West's argument can be taken up.

1. As calling into question whether the arguments the defendants, Fries and West, make to convince the judge in the court case are well made
In their argument the judge appealed to is humanity, and the kind of arguments that this judge will accept are assumed to include such things as how can humanity most effectively defend itself against its enemies while causing the least suffering. Within this court, the relevant questions are such things as whether the

chemical warfare officers make proper use of statistics to prove that chemical weapons are more humane than other weapons.

2. As calling into question the legitimacy of the court to try this case

Is there a complicity between the judges and the defendants? Can the judges decide the case on the bases of whether or not chemical weapons research is a good way of investing capital if what is at stake is whether the gas attack calls into question the extension of capitalist relations to all areas of life? The same problem may arise with respect to the goals of nation building, the exercise of humanity, technological efficiency, and scientific research. Are the court's rules of proof right? Should the prosecution have to prove that chemical weapons research will start a new arms race, or should the defendants have to prove it will not? Should the prosecution have to prove that the current illnesses and deaths of soldiers who have been injured by gas attacks are due to poison gas and not to other factors, or should it be up to the defence to prove that they are not?

Using a distinction introduced by Jean-François Lyotard in his investigation of the injustice done to the victims of the Holocaust, I call the first kind of challenge a *litigation* and the second a *differend*.[30] In this book I explore the idea that the discord in Fries and West's argument signals the existence of a differend. It is a feeling that something ought to be said here but that the very rules of argument used in the elite debate make it difficult to say. The problem can be seen if we look at how the American elite responded to the 1921 disarmament movement. This shows that in making an argument that could be heard within the elite, Irwin helped prepare the way for the elite to neutralize the call for disarmament and peace.

The strength of Irwin's argument was that it widened the split between the War Department and general staff on the one side, and the Chemical Warfare Service on the other. Through its presentation of American chemical warfare research as leading a new chemical and air arms race, it confronted the newly-elected Republican President Harding and the army with a choice: either they could support new chemical and air weapons, in which case they would be branded as no better than the German autocrats America had fought the war against, and as repeating the mistakes of the Anglo-German naval arms race that had divided Europe into two armed camps, so that a local crisis in Serbia was quickly transformed into a cause for a full-scale European war.[31] Or, by pursuing chemical and air disarmament, they could claim that they were leading the civilized world in its search for peace. They could claim to be continuing Woodrow Wilson's work for peace, but to be doing so more effectively.

Confronted by these choices, and the success of the disarmament movement in uniting a broad section of opinion behind it, Harding called Britain, France, Italy, and Japan to a Conference on the Limitation of Armaments (the Washington

Conference). When the expert subcommittee on chemical weapons reported that it was impossible to restrict the use of chemical weapons in war, Secretary of State Hughes stunned the conference by tabling an alternative report headed by General Pershing, who had led America's Expeditionary Forces in the First World War. The general's report repeated and added military authority to Irwin's argument that a chemical/air arms race would lead to a war more devastating than the First World War. The Conference then accepted a treaty drafted by Senator Elihu Root, who with Henry Cabot Lodge led America's delegates to the Conference, reiterating the pre-war ban on the use of chemical weapons in war.[32] As a result, the chemical/air arms race was deferred for a decade until the Nazis seized power in the 1930s and supported the development of new nerve gases.

The weakness of Irwin's argument was also revealed by the Washington Conference. To gain a hearing within the American elite, Irwin had to endorse the elite's claim that they had brought America into the First World War to defeat a German bid for world domination. In endorsing the elite's own story of its past, he prepared the way for Harding to neutralize the disarmament movement. Harding did this by using his power to establish the terms of the Washington Conference. Instead of the *disarmament conference* called for by the 1921 disarmament movement he called an *arms limitation conference*. Equally significantly, he only invited the victorious powers to the conference. This meant that the agenda of the conference was to establish how, under American leadership, the victorious powers could maintain their wartime unity, and reduce the cost of their armaments, while retaining their military superiority over Germany and Russia. This split the disarmament movement in two. On one side were those who accepted the elite's story of why America had fought the war. On this basis it accepted that the actions of the Harding administration were a continuation of the same story. By ending the naval and emerging high-technology arms races among the victorious powers, while retaining America and the Allies' military superiority over Germany and Russia, the administration was taking a key step to ensure long-term peace. On the other side were those who did not accept the elite's story, now consigned to the political wilderness.

The result contributed to a disaster we have not yet escaped. The Conference confirmed the division of the world into hostile camps established by the Treaty of Versailles: the victorious powers on the one side, Germany and Russia on the other. It entrenched exactly the kind of division of the world into friend and enemy groups, the Entente and the Central Powers, that in 1914 had turned a local crisis in the Balkans into a world war. It was a lost opportunity to overturn Woodrow Wilson's failure to deliver on his promise of a "peace without victory" at Versailles. And, by delivering arms limitation rather than disarmament it entrenched the military superiority of the victors. Chemical weapons are a case in point. Root's Treaty did not call for chemical disarmament. It only reiterated the ban on using chemical weapons. By contrast, the Treaty of Versailles demanded German chemical disarmament, while the Washington Conference entrenched the chemical superiority of the victorious powers over the vanquished. The Nazi Party would use both the one-sidedness of the Versailles Treaty and the vulnerability of a disarmed Germany, to help it capture state power and once in power to mobilize Germany for total war.[33] In short, the Conference delivered neither a just peace nor disarmament. Instead, it smoothed the path for a return of world war – against Germany and Japan in the Second World War, against Soviet Russia in the Cold War, and against the formerly colonized world in Vietnam.

This history shows the difficulty the worldwide peace and disarmament movements now face. Works like Jonathan Schell's *The Fate of the Earth*, William Arkin's *Nuclear Battlefields*, and Paul Roger's *Losing Control: Global Security in the Twenty-First Century*, which repeat Irwin's form of argument to gain a hearing for peace and disarmament within the elite, are crucial. Yet, if they are not to open the way up for the ultimate absorption of the call we sense in the account of the first poison gas attack and in many other witnesses to such violence, then they must be complemented by other works that show how the elite translation of such calls betrays them. We must therefore take a critical distance from the main representatives of the peace and disarmament movement to see how their articulations of such calls can themselves be problematic.

My starting points are points at which I experience a feeling of discord between accounts of violence, such as the description of the first gas attack, and the authoritative languages that are used to say what we must do in response to them. Such feelings of discord say that the framework that currently governs debate is inadequate, that within it one "cannot find the words" to say what needs to be said.[34] This feeling does not tell us exactly what is wrong with the elite framework. Our failure to find the words we need may be because we are not the people authorized to say them, or because the people who are listening to us are not the right people to hear them, or because the meaning of what we should say cannot be said in the words available to us, or because the things we need to refer to do not exist. The feeling of pain at not being able to find the necessary words does not immediately tell us what is lacking. We have to search to find new positions from which we can speak, new kinds of listeners, new meanings, and new referents. It is a question of finding a different framework, indeed several different frameworks. The classic term for this is "invention", the discovery of the rules which allow one to judge a particular case. This does not mean creation out of nothing. It is a question of experimenting by placing what has hitherto been marginal at the centre, and by making what has been subordinate primary. The analogy of the law court is useful in showing the double injustice that exists where there is a differend – the double bind that even if you win you lose. Yet if the violence of chemical weapons is not simply opposed to law but reveals the violence of law itself and the need to resist that violence, it will ultimately have to be itself called into question. This work is necessary so that the challenge poised by the critical feeling is not immediately smothered by being converted into a limited claim against chemical weapons. There is a political side to this. The work of invention is also the work of assembling a constituency powerful enough to mount an effective challenge to the domination of the debate by particular groups and their principles.

2

The Marked Leaders of the World

The manipulation of fantasies about technology was only one of the ways that the chemical and air campaigns sought to gain support for weapons research. In this chapter I look at how they sought to manage the political field by presenting themselves as sharing the virtue of American soldiers who had died on the battlefield. The investigation is critical to understanding the tactics that have been used to prevent opponents from using their double status as citizens of a republic and a democracy to oppose the development of strategies for using terror and the weapons needed to execute them. My interest is in how the rights citizens enjoy in theory can be neutralized in practice. In a republic the goals that the state should give priority to in any particular case are up for public debate. This means that, *in theory*, opponents should be able to challenge the chemical and air campaigns' prioritizing the goals of nation building, superior military power, return on capital invested, and technological efficiency, and its insistence that the pursuit of these goals was the best way to achieve peace and justice. In a democracy the people have the right to determine what the government policy should be. This means that, *in theory*, the opponents of chemical weapons research should be able to stop that research if they can convince a majority of Americans of their argument. *In practice*, everything depends on the political middle ground within the power elite, those who command large resources and have not yet decided which side of the argument to support. If the opponents of chemical weapons can win the support of this group, then they will be in a position to win the argument. They will be able to force the leaders of the chemical and campaigns to answer probing questions about the inconsistencies in their argument which suggest that their claimed motivations are different from their real ones. They will be able to challenge the claim that goals, such as military superiority, are being pursued because they are the best way of achieving peace. They will then be able to publicize analogies between cases where it is generally accepted that these goals should not have priority and the case of chemical weapons research. They will be able to offer alternative definitions of what it means to achieve goals such as security and democracy.

What I will be looking at, then, is the tactics used by the chemical campaign to seek to prevent the middle ground within the elite from listening to their critics. To do so, I supplement Fries and West's *Chemical Warfare* with editorials and articles from *The Chemical Warfare Bulletin*. The *Bulletin* was established in the summer of 1919 by the Chemical Warfare Service after the initial general staff attempt to dissolve the Service had been fought off. It was intended to shore up morale among its officers. Through its circulation to recently demobilized chemical warfare officers as well as supportive chemists, chemical engineers, and chemical manufactures, it sought to enable them to take an active part in its campaign to survive. As such, it gives us an invaluable insight into the tactics developed by the leaders of the chemical warfare laboratory.

(i) The story that humanity is progressing

The leaders of the Chemical Warfare Service presented its officers as part of the avant garde of humanity. This avant garde is presented as a benevolent servant, exercising power by clearing away the obstacles which prevent humanity from realizing its potential. They stage a scene in which research into new poison gases is only a small step in the far greater project of overcoming human suffering, this diminishes opposition to new chemical weapons research to an insignificant temporary obstacle that can be brushed aside. This can be seen in the 20 October 1921 *Bulletin of Chemical Warfare* editorial entitled "VISION". The editors provide a revealing tutorial on how the officers of the Chemical Warfare Service should behave as members of the avant garde:

> Of all the qualities that tend to leadership no one is more vital than that of vision, the power to penetrate the beyond, to picture coming events; to anticipate what is coming and to shape a course of action to meet it.
>
> We speak of vision as a quality, in reality it is an art . . . The power of consummate expression in art, music and literature means to the artist precisely what the power of vision means to the man of action, the soldier, statesman, business man who is working out the practical problems of life. The men who possess this power and couple with it courage to force their plans into execution are the marked leaders of the world. It could not be otherwise for the man who sees into the future and

is prepared to meet any emergency inspires confidence. He leads and others follow. They look up to him because they trust and need him.

Especially in pioneer work is this power of vision needed. Where the way is still untrodden and the paths uncut, where new contingencies, new emergencies crop up at every forward step, vision must develop or the mission fails . . .

It is not hard to understand what is meant by range of vision. We must consider what tomorrow will bring forth, what a year, a decade, a century. The Germans on several occasions came dangerously near winning the war because they looked ahead and were one step in advance of the Allies in the use of gas. They failed because they did not look far enough ahead.

The immediate problem of the Chemical Warfare Service is to look ahead and keep always a step in advance in offensive and defensive methods of Chemical Warfare, but the Service cannot stop here, it must look still further into the future, and appreciate the advantages of the benefits arising from a close cooperation with the chemical industry of the country. The leaders in the chemical industry are men of vision also, they not only realize that Chemical Warfare is perhaps the most economical form of National Defense, but they see the value of this cooperation in building up a great national chemical industry, and what this means in the way of national comfort and prosperity.

Even deeper into the future can we penetrate and visualize the day when Chemical Warfare will function more prominently in preventing than in waging war, and it will be employed at full strength in a glorious war against famine and disease, by increasing the yield of the field, and by sweeping before it the germs that prey upon mankind.[1]

This passage is simultaneously a justification of chemical preparedness; an aesthetic spectacle in which the intoxicating spectacle of exercising a godlike power enables the chemical warfare officers to silence any doubts they might have about their work, and a move to reinforce and extend the wartime alliance between the leaders of the Service and the leaders of the chemical industry.

The passage reweaves the progressive story of Americans as pioneers who are developing humanity's potential that was a staple of contemporary America. Lyotard terms such stories "meta-narratives" (literally, stories that are above other stories) because it claims to determine the *final* meaning of all earlier stories.[2] Put in terms of space rather than time, they claim to determine the *universal* meaning of all local stories. By placing the story about the first gas attack within the progressive meta-narrative of American leadership of humanity, Fries and West seek to determine its final meaning. The meta-narrative tells that while human beings share a common human nature, the unity of the human community is currently split into a "we" and a "they". The "we" is an avant garde: a select group who have a vision of mankind as united and are striving to realize it. The avant garde "we" is made up both of the community of those who know (scientists, engineers) and of the community of men of action (engineers, soldiers, businessmen, and statesmen).

By contrast, the "they" is made up of local communities who do not yet have a vision of themselves as part of one human community. The majority of them are men and women of good will whose ignorance and division means they can be intimidated and duped by a minority of ill-willed leaders. The ignorance and division of the "they" also means that it is in thrall to the forces of nature. The "they" is trapped in a cyclical time, caught in a circle in which their ignorance and division mean they are repeatedly subjected to natural disasters such as disease and famine and to the manmade horrors of war and repression.

In terms of international relations, the "we" is the community of civilized nations (America, Britain, France, etc). The "they" are the barbaric or semi-civilized nations (the Philippines, China), and nations which have reverted to barbarism (Germany, Bolshevik Russia). The task of the avant garde is to end the split in the human community. To do this it has the interlinked tasks of research and education, which will end ignorance about the forces of nature and society, and of organizing the good-willed majority to defeat both the forces of nature and the ill-willed minority. This will replace the cyclical time of repeated disaster by the time of progress, ending the split between the "we" and the "they".

How chemical preparedness literature seeks to enrol the support of its readers can be restated using this terminology. The reader is presented with an image of a Germany caught up a cycle of violence and armed with deadly chemical weapons of terrifying power. They are confronted with the spectacle of an unending cycle of violence which they cannot escape. This places them in a world in which they no longer know what to do to protect themselves or others. The leaders of America's chemical soldiers, chemists and chemical engineers, then present themselves as authorities capable of guiding the reader through the dangers of this horrifying new world. They present themselves as part of the avant garde of humanity which has the power to overcome the threat. Recall, here, how the editorial "VISION" instructs on how to present oneself as an authority whom people will trust and follow. The editorial thereby complements the photograph of General Silbert at the beginning of *Chemical Warfare* in showing the officers of the service how they ought to style themselves as leaders. Chemical preparedness is then justified by arguments it claims must convince the whole avant garde. The readers' anxiety at not knowing how to fulfil their obligations to the victims of chemical warfare is relieved. Readers find themselves part of an imaginary community which, if it does not yet have the full answer to the threat posed by chemical weapons, is on the way to doing so. Even if they do not convince the reader of the need for chemical preparedness, these passages work to convince the reader that the leaders of American chemical warfare, science and engineering, and manufacturing are part of an avant garde with the responsibility and the right to lead humanity.

There is no scientific basis for the progressive meta-narratives. The rules of science are that we can only have knowledge about things we can observe. We can observe particular historical events, but we cannot observe whether the actions of a group embody a first cause, humanity, which is realizing itself in history. Yet the leaders of the chemical warfare officers used their presentation of themselves as the avant garde of a mankind in the process of realizing its sovereignty to seek to impose a double silencing on their opponents. In doing so their action was like that of their claimed opposites, the Bolsheviks, whose belief that they were the avant garde of mankind led them to declare that opponents should not be listened to and if such opponents began to gain a hearing they should be eliminated. The process of silencing can be seen by looking carefully at the way the leaders of the chemical campaign redraw the line between those inside and those outside the avant garde. Fries and West's *Chemical Warfare* is addressed to other members of what they regard as America's avant garde. The argument itself indicates who such people are. They are those who accept that the basic question is: How can America's military and diplomatic power be developed so that it can carry out its task as the leader of the civilized world? They are those for whom the key secondary questions are: Which weapons are most effective, least costly, and most humane? Can arms control reduce the cost of military expenditure while maintaining America's military advantage? In the course of the argument, they seek to redraw the line the new elite has established between the "we" and the "they" to their own advantage. This can be seen by looking at how they attempted to dismiss Chief of Staff General March, who had ordered the dissolution of the Chemical Warfare Service after the Armistice, from the group of persons whose views should be listened to. This was done by presenting him as a man whose failure to see that poison gas is more humane than high explosives indicated he was a romantic military conservative,[3] an isolated proponent of irrational views. To do this they contrasted March with the wartime head of the American Expeditionary Forces, General Pershing. March, they claimed, was impervious to reason while Pershing could be convinced by rational argument. Their attempt to open up a division between America's two leading generals failed. At the Washington Conference, as we have seen, Pershing placed the weight of this authority behind the call to outlaw chemical warfare.

The chemical warfare officers use their claim to be the avant garde of humanity to subject the views of groups they place outside the "we" to a double silencing. In the first place, such groups are silenced by being labelled as not worth listening to. But if they gather sufficient support inside and outside the "we" to prevent their being ignored then they are labelled as a danger to society. This then justifies the use of force to isolate or destroy such groups. Such groups are labelled as a danger to society by assimilating their views to the positions of those who are already widely regarded as dangerous enemies of society. During the First World War, pacifists were presented as being the knowing or unknowing dupes of the German militarists; after the war, association with the Bolsheviks became the favourite way of dismissing opponents. The leaders of the Chemical Warfare

Service present it as extremely dangerous to listen to the views of those actively challenging the chemists' attempt to manage the debate. Ironically, this is done by presenting the views of these critics as having the power to spread like that of a contagious disease or a poison in the blood stream. Take the 5 February 1920 editorial of the *Bulletin of Chemical Warfare*. Following the arrest and deportation of suspected anarchists and Bolsheviks across America in late 1919 and early 1920,[4] the editors took the opportunity to recommend that the officers of the Service conduct a campaign to root out any such ideas in their own minds:

> Perhaps only a few weeks ago you had a box of beautiful apples in which you allowed one rotten one to remain. Look at them today and you will find numbers of them rotten to utter worthlessness . . . We may in the first place each of us be likened to the box of apples. In the ideas in your mind somewhere you have some undesirable brain inhabitants – some specked apples – petty jealousies, envy, revenge, or some other . . . Search your mind for petty thoughts, vice, avarice, passion. Root out these undesirables from your mind, not by an effort to suddenly obliterate them, but by a careful well-planned campaign, replacing them with better and nobler thoughts . . . In the second place, avoid contact with bad ideas . . . It was contact of the pure and loyal minds with the ideas of anarchy which now make necessary the vigorous campaign against the Red flag.[5]

The editorial then concluded with a barely veiled threat of ostracism for anyone who did not toe the party line. An officer who did not is presented as having become a socially despicable person who deserves to be excluded from society. In short, our most terrifying fear, isolation, is evoked to enforce collective ideological discipline. The presentation of opposed views as like poison or disease makes it possible to maintain the idea of a "we" that is developing its ideas rationally without having to give serious consideration to the arguments of those outside the "we". The "we" is presented as an organic whole like an apple. The metaphors of poison and disease then convey the idea that opposed views are exterior to that whole. As such they are an attack on the integrity of that whole from completely outside it, even if they are our very own ideas or feelings. As such they do not need to be listened to. Instead, they should be rooted out and their capacity to be an effective political force neutralized by whatever means necessary.

(ii)   The Chemical Warfare Service and the Knights of the Round Table

The post-war dominance of the meta-narrative of progress meant the chemical warfare officers had to make their case by re-articulating that narrative.[6] There was, however, another more important strand to chemical preparedness literature. This understood the American elite and its European counterparts as a "we", but no longer believed that this "we" could be universalized to include the "they".[7] Just as in the progressive meta-narrative, this "we" was idealized. It represented the high point of civilization. Since it could not be universalized by absorbing the "they", this community saw itself as having a right to do *whatever* it believed necessary to defend itself. It had such a right because it represented the best of human achievement. By contrast, the "they" was, at best, irredeemable, and at worst, a threat.

The cynical meta-narrative arises out of a collapse of the progressive meta-narrative. This collapse has an emotional logic. In the progressive meta-narrative, the "we" was able to represent itself as a hero engaged in a struggle to spread civilization to the "they". If we look closely at some of these self-presentations – as we shall see in Addison's memorial address to the First Gas Regiment, or in the writings of Roosevelt and Wilson on the Philippines – what is striking is that there is little interest in the "they". The "they" are only of concern in so far as the struggle to extend civilization to them provides an opportunity for the "we" to display its heroic virtue. One has the feeling that there is something theatrical about the heroic action, that it is being staged before an audience. This audience can only be other elements of the avant garde "we" itself. Faced with the refusal of the "they" to play the part allotted to them in the script, the cynical meta-narrative becomes a way in which the "we" can continue to maintain its heroic role. Only now, the heroic role will no longer be the battle to extend civilization. Instead, it will be the defence of the "we" against the "they", and the denunciation of those elements of the "they" hidden within the "we" who would betray America to the "they" outside. Or, put in more graphic terms, civilization will be imagined as a fortress that must be defended against an attacking enemy outside and against an enemy within who would betray it to the enemy outside.

This second strand can be seen in passages where the story of the need to defend the nation at all costs replaces the story of the achievement of peace through the extension of civilisation. The 5 April 1921 editorial of the *Bulletin of Chemical Warfare* entitled "DO NOT LOSE THE PERSPECTIVE" is a case in point. In presenting America as the ideal "we", the passage emphasizes the impossibility of ever trusting the "they". Equally, it underscores the lethal threat the "they" will pose to America should these nations combine against her and use poison gas to attack her:

> In our quarrel with Germany we must not lose sight of the fact that a good deal of the "peace and good will" of nations to one another is "camouflage." There are many nations who hate us violently, but who realise they are not in a position to combine to attack us. But there is no certainty that this condition will obtain forever . . . Do not lose sight of the fact that we are the biggest thing on earth today. There is only one way to conquer us – lull us to sleep and then smother us with Gas. Most assuredly, because that is the one way that no nation can disarm.[8]

The word "the" in the title shows that here this story is intended to replace the story of mankind progressing towards cooperation and peace. In other passages an appeal is made to history to support the replacement of the progressive meta-narrative by the cynical meta-narrative. Take the *Bulletin of Chemical Warfare* editorial of 20 October 1920. Entitled "SNAP OUT OF IT", it first falsifies the actual historical situation. This is the post-war world in which the United States enjoyed excellent relations with its wartime allies France and England, and good relations with its wartime ally Japan, and in which large sections of all countries were aghast by the world war. This actual state of affairs is ignored. Instead, America is presented as threatened by all the countries of Europe and the East:

> I know of no single instance in Europe which has come under my observation, where an American in any situation has not dominated the situation. Those people don't like it. Europe and the East fear us commercially and militarily. They say nothing, but nurse a growing grudge, and their mental attitude is "Wait!"[9]

This abstraction from the actual state of affairs is then justified by making an appeal to the whole course of history. On this basis the editorial calls for the branches of the army, such as the cavalry, the artillery, and the Chemical Warfare Service, to stop competing against each other and cooperate:

> Look back in the history of the world and you will see that, whenever a parallel situation has existed, that nation which stood in the position we now occupy has always been attacked and in the end conquered. We shall not be conquered – Get together! – Get some team work! – Eyes on the boat and PULL – All together![10]

The conclusion of *Chemical Warfare* legitimates the existence of such a permanent state of war by idealizing it. War is idealized and presented as the natural human condition by evoking the myth of the Knights of the Round Table. This is the myth of a society of heroes who fight, die, and are eternally reborn. Here this myth of a pre-modern society is used to give legitimacy to a thoroughly modern project, the expansion of America's chemical industries and the preparation of America's armies to fight a chemical war. To do this an attempt is made to beautify chemical warfare by presenting it as no different in essence from an idealized picture of medieval knightly combat:

> It is just as sportsman-like to fight with chemical warfare materials as it is to fight with machine guns. The enemy will know more or less accurately our chemical warfare materials and our methods and we will have the same information about the enemy. It is thus a matching of wits just as much as in the days when the Knights of the Round Table fought with spears on horseback. The American is pure sportsman and asks odds of no man. He does ask, though, that he be given a square deal. He

is unwilling to agree not to use a powerful weapon of war when he knows that an outlaw nation would use it against him if that outlaw nation could achieve success by so doing.[11]

Here the modern world is depicted as a continuation of the medieval world of constant battles, and not as the overcoming of the cyclical time of that world by the linear time of modern progress. The cynical meta-narrative justifies the development of a military capable of global power projection just as much as the meta-narrative of America as leading the extension of civilization does. The ideal America depends upon global commerce and investments to acquire the wealth necessary to protect itself. It must have the means to project its power globally so as to protect its commerce and investments. Further, the fact that it cannot convert part of the "they" to its ideals means that it must rely completely on military power to deal with the threat posed by the "they". America must either have sufficiently large military forces to deal with any combination of hostile nations, or adopt an aggressive policy of pre-emptive attack whenever there is a danger that other nations will combine against her. The cynical meta-narrative, then, calls for the domination of the globe through overwhelming military force and pre-emptive attack.

(iii) What was at stake in the struggle over chemical weapons research?

At stake in the editors' bid to strengthen the campaign for chemical warfare research was the fate of the world's largest chemical warfare complex, built as part of secret US army plans to wage chemical warfare on a vast scale. Poison gas was to make the 1919 offensive "a walk to Berlin".

Germany had started chemical warfare. On 22 April 1915 at Ypres on the Western Front its soldiers released 150 tons of chlorine gas from 6000 cylinders along a seven kilometre front.[12] The gas advanced slowly at one kilometre per hour. Initially white, it turned yellow green and rose to a height of between ten to thirty metres. The front collapsed. The Germans, however, had not assembled sufficient troops to turn the collapse into a strategic breakthrough. The attack started a chemical arms race. At first the main gases used were chlorine and phosgene. Initially, attacks were made by releasing a cloud of gas from cylinders. This depended on the wind being favourable. It had the disadvantage that if the wind changed the attacking troops were themselves gassed. To avoid these problems alternative tactics were developed: using artillery to rapidly fire large amounts of shell to build up a lethal concentration of gas at a particular target, and firing gas in special trench mortars.

On the night of 12–13 July 1917 the Germans first used dichlorodiethyl sulphide (mustard gas). This by-passed gas masks by attacking the skin directly. Gas warfare now entered a second, more intense, phase. In March and April of 1918 the British suffered 33,000 casualties from mustard gas alone.[13] Injuries ranged from conjunctivitis of the eye, to injuries corresponding to first and second degree burns, to inflammation of the throat, bronchitis, pneumonia, and death. Again led by the widespread German use of arsenical fillings in "blue cross" shells, the armies also started to use substances which were not true gases but were made up of deadly microscopic particles. As these move much more slowly than gas molecules, instead of bumping into the walls of the charcoal capillaries in the filters of gas masks they could pass right through. Contemporary accounts report the results: excruciating pains in the nose, sinuses, mouth, and throat, and nausea along with "intense mental distress . . . utter dejection and hopeless misery [without] counterpart in any other type of gas poisoning".[14]

During the war the armies used gas on a very large scale. A single cloud gas attack might use hundreds of tons of gas, while by 1918 gas accounted for one in every four artillery shells. Chemical warfare became a contest between national chemical industries. Initially this gave the advantage to Germany. America sought to reverse this by building the plants needed to produce even larger quantities of poison gas and by planning to use gas on a vast scale in 1919.[15] In the United States research into defence (gas masks) and offence (poison gas) soon involved about thirty universities. To speed up research, the campus of the American University in Washington DC was taken over in mid-1917 and most of the research moved there. An American gas mask was developed, new poison gases such as "Adamsite" and "Lewisite" were discovered, and the key problem of how to produce large amounts of mustard gas solved. At its height, this research and development employed over 1200 scientists and engineers.

In 1919 the army planned a dramatic escalation in the use of gas. The commander of American chemical warfare in France, Colonel Fries, called for an American chemical warfare effort over three and a half times the size of the British one. The commander of the American Expeditionary Forces, General Pershing, supported a threefold increase in the number of American gas troops.[16] And in June 1918 the American high command signalled the seriousness of its forthcoming chemical warfare offensive by setting up the Chemical Warfare Service as an autonomous unit. The key role planned for chemical war was emphasized by Assistant Secretary for War Benedict Crowell at the Army Reorganization Hearings in 1920: "Our offensive in 1919, in my opinion, would have been a walk to Berlin, due to chemical warfare. Of course, that was kept as a secret."[17]

These preparations can be traced in the massive expansion of American plants for producing poison gas. The army constructed its own plant, rapidly and on a huge scale. Within nine months it turned a green-field site into the giant Edgewood Arsenal plant. This produced gas in unprecedented quantities.[18] Private contracts for gas were extremely large by European standards. Zinsser and Co. and the National Aniline and Chemical Co. were each commissioned to produce mustard gas plants which would produce a total of 16,000 tons per year – four times the entire British planned total use of gas for 1919.[19]

The earlier than expected end of the war brought about a sudden reversal. In Europe Wilson sought to re-enforce the principles established at the Hague Conferences of 1899 and 1907 forbidding the employment of "poisons or poisonous weapons". The result was Article 171 of the Treaty of Versailles, which ordered Germany to disarm all her chemical weapons and forbade her to manufacture or import them.[20] In the United States, Army Chief of Staff General Peyton March and Secretary for War Newton Baker ordered the dissolution of the Chemical Warfare Service. All responsibility for chemical warfare was to be handed over to the engineers. As staff advice to the Chief of Engineers emphasized, no "funds or special personnel" would be authorized for chemical warfare: the intention was to bring an end to America's chemical warfare establishment.[21]

Facing complete negation of their wartime work and the apparent insult to their heroic efforts in the war, American chemists, chemical engineers, chemical manufacturers, and chemical warfare soldiers (hereafter, the chemists) fought back. The American Chemical Society, the *Journal of Industrial and Chemical Engineering*, the Du Pont Corporation, the Chemical Foundation,[22] and the Chemical Warfare Service launched a campaign for American chemical preparedness. It had two aims: to maintain the Chemical Warfare Service as an independent organization devoted to both defensive and offensive chemical warfare; and to get the government to pass high chemical tariffs and selected chemical embargoes so as to build up America's new artificial dye industries in the interests of national security. All parties would benefit. Chemical warfare officers would maintain their independence; the importance of chemists and chemical engineers for the nation's security would be recognized and they would be able to get employment in the research-intensive new dye industry; and chemical manufactures would gain an increased share of the nation's wealth through tariff protection from competition by foreign chemical manufactures.

The campaign for chemical preparedness was initially successful. Through the support of Congressman Julius Kahn, Chairman of the House Military Affairs Committee, and Senator George Chamberlain, Chairman of the Senate Military Affairs Committee, the Chemical Warfare Service was established on 30 June 1920 by a rider to the Fiscal Year 1920 Appropriations Bill. The years after the war saw a convergence of interests and tactics between the supporters of an offensive chemical warfare capability, led by General Fries, and the supporters of an independent air force with a strategic bombing mission, led by General Mitchell. Both groups sought to assert their independence from the general staff: their leaders sought to break down opposition within the army by getting the public behind them and to convince the public that the population of American cities would soon be vulnerable to annihilation by aircraft carrying new, deadlier, poison gases. Chemical preparedness supporters argued that only the capacity to retaliate could ward off this threat. The air men stressed the necessity for an independent air force. Should they choose to harmonize their demands, they could form an alliance. By telling the same story about the threat these new weapons posed to American cities, they might be able to rally the public behind them and break the grip of the military establishment over the direction of military policy.

As the Washington Conference approached, the future of America's chemical warfare capability was still precarious. The Chemical Warfare Service had just escaped the axe but there was no certainty that it would continue to survive as more than a rump. The general staff had reacted to the failure to close it down by seeking to limit its activities to defence against gas attack. At the same time, as we have seen, 1921 saw the rapid growth of a disarmament movement which made chemical disarmament one of its principal objectives. The danger facing the supporters of an offensive chemical warfare capability was that at such a conference its two opponents would work together to split the coalition for chemical preparedness. On the one hand, the Service's supporters in Congress might become lukewarm. The replacement of Wilson's Democratic administration by a Republican administration meant that arms control was now an issue on which the Republicans had to prove themselves. Equally, with the passage of the 1920 Army Reorganization Bill, the Senate and House military committees had won their battle with March over the future direction of American military policy. They no longer needed the assistance of disaffected groups within the army. On the other hand, America's chemical manufactures had won the high tariffs and selected embargoes they wanted. The growing strength of public opinion against chemical weapons, and the fact that they had already successfully used the threat of foreign chemical weapons to gain the tariff and embargo they wanted, might now lead chemical manufactures to decide it was no longer in their interests to support publicly reviled chemical weapon research.

Recall that Fries and West's *Chemical Warfare* attempted to enrol support through a double movement. They *displaced* Americans by asserting that chemical weapons were an inescapable reality that would soon threaten them; then, they *exploited* that displacement by presenting themselves as the authorities who could guide Americans through this dangerous new world. This history shows that at the time of their book's publication in 1921, Fries and West's claim that chemical weapons were an inescapable reality was *not* a statement of fact. True, chemical warfare had been a massive fact of the world war. But by 1921 the future of American chemical weapons hung in the balance. Indeed, with laboratories shut down, chemical plants mothballed, few officers, poor funding, active hostility within the army high command, growing public antipathy, the prospect of an international treaty reinforcing or going beyond the Hague Conferences, the wartime enemy itself disarmed and under a democratic government, and the threat that the coalition in support of chemical preparedness might come apart – America's offensive chemical warfare programme was in an advanced stage of decomposition. And if the development of new chemical weapons were abandoned in the United States, they might be abandoned in other countries as well. Placed in the context of the post-war battle with the military establishment and with the disarmament movement, the claim that chemical weapons were an inescapable reality is revealed as a political intervention intended to bring about what it asserts to be the case. If the book succeeded in enrolling a sufficient number of Americans in support of an offensive chemical weapon capability then this would become American policy. And if their counterparts in other countries succeeded in doing the same, the threat that the American supporters of chemical preparedness point to would indeed exist. *Chemical Warfare*'s assertion of the inescapable reality of chemical weapons must be understood as an intervention that promoted one possible line of development as opposed to others.

(iv) The glorious dead and the untimely murdered

In the weeks following the publication of "Vision", the pressure on the campaign for chemical weapon research grew. As the 11 November Armistice Day start date of the Washington Conference approached it was caught in a tightening vice-grip between the military establishment's hostility on the one hand and the growing campaign for disarmament on the other. Under these extreme circumstances guarded expressions of dissent began to emerge within the Chemical Warfare Service itself. This can be seen in the Armistice Day address to the First Gas Regiment by its Chaplain J.T. Addison, reprinted in the 21 November *Chemical Warfare Bulletin*. Addison takes up the Bulletin's presentation of the chemical warfare officers as heroes and re-articulates it, to suggest that being a good chemical warfare officer means supporting chemical disarmament at the Conference:

> We meet here today to commemorate with honor those of our own comrades who died in the Great War, and to unite with all Americans in grateful tribute to the Unknown Soldier – the symbol of all our sacred dead. These men gave everything . . . In the hearts of those who were dearest to them and in the hearts of their comrades and of all their fellow citizens their golden stars will shine forever . . . But if we would still continue to think of these men as our comrades, there are laid upon us two serious obligations – to learn from their example and to carry on their work.

What can we learn from them and from the great Army to which we all belonged? The American Expeditionary Forces were an organization united, full of the spirit of enthusiasm and comradeship – and eventually victorious. And why? Because we had a cause that was noble and world-wide and because we encountered tasks that involved great difficulty and grave risk. And if we want any other organization – our city, our church, our state, our nation – to be united, full of the spirit of enthusiasm and comradeship and eventually victorious, then we must see to it that that organization or that institution shall have a cause that is noble and world-wide and that it shall take up tasks that involve great difficulty and grave risks. That is what we learn from our honored dead and from the Army that we all served in common – that you can win the heroic virtues only by tackling big things in a big way.

You must go deeper than what they said they were trying to do. Probably they would have said they were trying to "can the Kaiser" . . . But if that is all they fought for, it wasn't worth the cost. We know, in spite of those who delight to dishonour America, that what they fought for at bottom was liberty and justice and future world peace . . . We must make their motive our motive and their spirit our spirit and never let our nation rest content until the great purpose for which they died is achieved . . .

At this present hour we can do no greater service to our honored dead than to show their spirit of fearless service in aiding the cause of world peace. Unless the nations can learn to live together in harmony, the price of the whole hideous five years of war has been paid in vain. All honor to our President and to both parties of our country for celebrating Armistice Day in the finest possible way – by trying to make real on earth what our soldiers really fought for. Does some one say to us that world peace is impossible? You tell him to wake up. These are the days of the impossible. The war was impossible. Two million men in France was impossible. Every great achievement that the glowing spirit of man has attempted some cowards have always called impossible. If a thing ought to be done it can be. If a great task is to be done to complete the purposes of the war, let us be grateful that America is leading and let us support our country in this great conference with full loyalty – so that America may serve the world by helping to bring the nations together.[23]

The centre of the address is its presentation of America's war dead as models for the soldiers of the First Gas Regiment to follow. The presentation of the war dead as such models was vital to classical republican discourse. Unlike monarchies, republics actively promoted the participation of its citizens in politics.[24] Every citizen was charged with the responsibility of ensuring that the republic was governed in the interests of the whole. It was the duty of citizens to question the advocates of policies – to probe them to see whether they were really acting in the interests of everyone, or whether their polices were really masks behind which they were pursuing their own self-interests. It was the particular nightmare of republicans that one part of society would surreptitiously come to govern in its own interests. This created the danger that the republic might appear no more than an aggregate of self-interested groups. In a crisis the republic would disintegrate into its constituent parts as soon as it became apparent that it was no longer in the self-interest of the parties to work together.

To solve this problem republics have invested those who have died fighting for the republic with great significance. Here were men who, it is claimed, have proven that they put the good of the republic above their own self-interests. They have done this in the only completely convincing way possible – by voluntarily risking their lives for the republic. Their deaths prove the republic is a living ideal. This idea is condensed in Michelangelo's statue of the young David. He stands ready to risk everything for Israel in his battle with Goliath: quietly confident, slingshot ready, stone in hand – the perfect image of the virile Florentine republic. The war dead are models of republican virtue. Hence the importance of the militia in classical republican thought as the place where young men become citizens. In the militia they learn to model themselves on past heroes who have risked all for the republic and they prepare themselves to follow them to the death if necessary.

Addison takes up this idea and reworks it to provide an opening for the idea that the chemical warfare officers should support chemical disarmament at the Washington Conference. It is a high-risk strategy. The soldiers are already angry at the general staff and War Department calling their status as heroes into question by ordering the dissolution of the Chemical Warfare Service. They may unite against anything Addison has to say and brand him as the enemy within. Alternatively, faced with hostility to chemical warfare from respected military figures, leading statesmen, and the disarmament movement, they may follow Addison – if he can provide them with a way of retaining their conception of themselves as heroes.

Addison's appropriation of the voice of the dead is strongly marked in the address. The soldiers are to disregard what the dead *actually* said they were trying to do. And they are not to listen to critics who state the dead were forced conscripts tricked into dying in a war fought for big business, imperialists, and other special interests. Addison does not refute these arguments. Instead, he uses them to reinforce the idea that he is at one with his audience's conception of themselves as heroes by attacking such critics as "those who delight to dishonour America". He then presents America's war dead as having made possible the realization of the American ideal on a world scale. Led by America humanity is becoming one vast republic. By giving their lives to defeat the Kaiser's threat, America's war dead have shown that the idea of republican brotherhood is a living ideal. Like the Americans who died in the War of Independence to establish the republic, they have shown that America provides a model for how humanity can achieve liberty, justice, and peace. Addison challenges his listeners to show that they can match the sacrifice of the dead by setting their own interests and devoting themselves to world peace.

Addison rearticulates a logic of sacrifice that is also at the centre of Fries and West's *Chemical Warfare* and "Vision", based on the exchange of mortal for immortal life. By voluntarily choosing to risk their lives on the battlefield, the dead have shown that America and humanity are living ideals. This means they escape the normal fate of the dead – to become no more than an object talked about by the living. Instead, they remain active as a model for the living to follow. As "golden stars" which will "shine forever", they become like the night stars which are always there to give us orientation. It is only through the sacrifice of the dead that a human community, as opposed to a mere aggregate of self-seeking individuals, is possible at all. This means that the living are in debt to the dead. By evoking a sense of the horrendous size of the world war and the vast scale on which it was fought, Addison invites us to take this idea to an extreme, evoking a sense of an enormous debt to the dead. At the same time, he introduces a rivalry between the dead and the living. If the living are to become heroes like the dead, their achievements have to be on an even greater scale. Only by doing this will the living be able to pay back the dead and achieve immortality in their turn. Equally, the failure to achieve world peace will mean that the dead have "paid in vain".

Addison calls for a *total* identification with the "motives" and "spirit" of the dead. The call is backed up by two threats which are perhaps more powerful for not being directly stated. The first threat is isolation through ostracism by the living community. To avoid this, living Americans must show they are made of the same stuff as the dead heroes. The second is that the living will be forgotten by those who come after them. Addison seeks to exercise control through the way he describes what the living have to do to achieve immortality. In Hobbes' *Leviathan*, the temporal sovereign is a "weak" sovereign in comparison with God. His power is limited since the most he can do is to threaten his subjects with death. By contrast, God can threaten eternal damnation and promise immortal bliss.[25] Here, as in Kliest's play *Prince Frederick of Homberg*, we see the state seeking to exercise strong sovereignty over the army through its ability to determine who is given military glory. And we see Fries and West on the one side, and Addison on the other, seeking to twist this mechanism in different directions. In *Chemical Warfare* what the living have to do to achieve glory is to push ahead with the development of chemical weapons. After describing a line of military heroes who achieved victory by pushing ahead with the introduction of new weapons, they state that if these men had not done so "we may be perfectly sure . . . they would have gone down to oblivion just as has been the case with millions of others who tried the usual things in the usual way".[26] Addison, for his part, seeks to turn this mechanism against chemical warfare research. To do so he redescribes what is new in the present. Instead of chemical warfare being constituted as the new thing, the address makes the international triumph of republican ideas following America's defeat of Germany the new thing. The claim that international politics now proceeds according to American republican ideals makes possible a fantasy no less intoxicating than that presented by "Vision". Americans are now living in the days when the "impossible" is being realized. Through American leadership, the Washington Conference will be able to complete the task of bringing about world peace.

The editors of the *Chemical Warfare Bulletin* saw Addison's address as too powerful to simply ignore, yet felt it was dangerous to draw attention to it. The address was all the more threatening as it was but one of many such 11 November addresses given in churches and synagogues throughout America as part of the Catholic, Protestant, and Jewish joint campaign to support the Washington Conference. To deal with the threat, they took advantage of the fact that Addison had not directly called for chemical disarmament. To do so would have been to lay himself open to the charge of exceeding his religious role as chaplain of the First Gas Regiment. This silence in Addison's address left open the possibility of rearticulating the significance of his address by establishing the context in which it was viewed. To do this, the editors preceded it by an editorial arguing that the best way to achieve peace was to push ahead with chemical weapon research, and followed it by a statement arguing that chemical disarmament was impossible. Sandwiched in this way, Addison's address could be easily digested.

The preceding editorial makes the American nation rather than the republic the model for humanity. The difference is that, whereas the citizens of a republic are expected to prove their virtue, the citizens of the American nation are presumed to be virtuous by the simple fact of being born Americans. Virtuous action is expected of them, it does not have to be proven. In the editorial this idea is extended from the nation to humanity, allowing a transfer of the virtue of those who have died risking their lives for humanity to the living. As the soldiers of the Chemical Warfare Service are human, they must be presumed to share the virtue of the war dead. The Service is presumed to share America's war dead's commitment to peace because "the desire for peace is natural to every normal human being".[27] Chemical warfare soldiers are no different from "firemen" or "police officers" in seeking to deal with threats to humanity. "Their mission is to prevent trouble rather than to foment it." This shifted the balance of proof. Whereas in republican discourse the officers are under suspicion of putting forward measures in their own interests, they are now presumed to be for peace. It is now up to opponents to prove that the campaign against American chemical disarmament shows that they are not committed to peace. To trump the extreme rhetoric of Addison's memorial address, the editorial ends with an even more extreme statement of the argument that chemical warfare research makes for peace than that found in "Vision": *"Every development of science that makes warfare more universal and more scientific makes for permanent peace by making war intolerable."* (Italics in the original.)[28]

The memorialization of the war dead as immortal heroes suppresses a more disturbing possibility – that the dead are unquiet ghosts crying for revenge. When the living are violently killed, those who loved them are left with a burning question: Why did they die? The situation is worst when the circumstances in which those who have died were killed is incompletely known. Even partial evidence that they may have been sacrificed in the interest of the elite becomes politically explosive. The dead become dangerous ghosts.

Shakespeare's King of Denmark in *Hamlet* is such a ghost. His death is *untimely* rather than natural or heroic. As the king's ghost tells Hamlet, his trusted brother murdered him by pouring poison into his ear while he took an afternoon sleep in his orchard. Taken completely by surprise, there was no chance to prove his heroic virtue by risking his life for an ideal in battle. Instead, he is instantly killed by a poison he cannot defend himself against. He has died before his natural time, without being able to complete the tasks he had set himself or to ask forgiveness for his sins. The very fact of his murder has been hidden so that no one seeks to bring his murderer to justice. As his murderer is the now king, the supreme judge in the kingdom, the normal course of justice cannot operate. The ghost must appeal to his son Hamlet to avenge his death, calling on his love and sense of filial duty. As a ghost, the king lacks the evidence to prove that what he says is true. He may be a demon, Hamlet suspects later, sent from hell to ensnare him. Hamlet must invent new ways of finding proof that what the ghost claims to have happened did in fact happen. It is a world in which all certainties are set adrift. The images of the snake and poison call into question the entire political establishment.

The ghost of the conscripted soldier who died from poison gas brings Hamlet up to date. He tells a story that may only be substantiated by details never committed to paper or kept in the files of government departments (American, British, French, German), banks (the House of Morgan), and corporations (Du Pont). He claims he died not for peace or democracy, but to keep up the profits of munitions makers, realize the ambitions of imperialists, gratify the hatred of nationalists, indulge the curiosity of scientists, satisfy the lust for glory of militarists, and alleviate the boredom of the working masses. He argues that President Wilson and his dollar-a-year business and scientific advisors are usurpers. They have seized advantage of the war to impose a new political system on America without the people's consent. Overtaken by a gas cloud there was nothing heroic about his death. He died horribly, gassed like a rat. And he warns that unless the crime is brought to light, and the institutions that carried it out transformed, his murder will be repeated.

3

The German Outlaw

It is now taken for granted that weapons laboratories are essential to national security. This was not true for Americans in the first quarter of the twentieth century. To convince them it was true demanded a great deal of work. I now turn to the leaders of America's chemical scientists and engineers. To persuade Americans to support chemical weapons research, these men produced a threat that only chemical warfare research could counter. I use the word "produce" to indicate they were not telling a lie, but were helping to bring one possible reality a step closer to existing. They made two claims. First, despite her defeat, Germany remained a long-term threat to civilization. Americans should continue to regarded Germany as an "outlaw" nation until she had proved that she no longer wanted to dominate the world scientifically, militarily, and commercially. Second, research must inevitably lead to the discovery of new, deadlier, poison gases. Disarmament treaties were no solution. A nation that had signed a treaty could develop chemical weapons without being caught. Research into new poison gases could easily be disguised as legitimate research into drugs or dyes. The production of poison gases could be disguised as legitimate commercial production. Taken together, these two claims meant that the war had not really ended. America, the chemists argued, faced an outlaw nation whose chemical industry and research would increasingly give it the means to threaten American cities with annihilation. To maintain her independence, and defend civilization, America must make research into chemical weapons and the development of her chemical industries a national priority.

Here I focus on what the chemist's portrayal of Germany excluded: the opportunity for America to cooperate with German liberals and social democrats to permanently marginalize Germans who supported a renewal of war when the time was right; and, that chemical disarmament was possible if a significant number of scientists, engineers, soldiers, and businessmen on both sides supported it.

I also investigate the scientists' and engineers' interest in arguing for chemical weapons research and government support for the chemical industry. These interests included the development of an artificial dye industry that would provide a large number of jobs for chemists and chemical engineers,[1] a new role for themselves in the government of America based on the acknowledgement that America's survival and future greatness depended on chemistry,[2] and the rationalization for their role in the development and production of the high explosives and chemical weapons used by America and the Allies. This history has a message for us today. After the end of the First World War, in their bid to make chemistry central to the modernization of America, the chemists helped squander America's opportunity to mediate a "peace without victory". In doing so, they took the world a step down the road to the Second World War. Today, after the end of the Cold War, this history is being repeated. To secure funding for scientific and engineering projects, leading American scientists and engineers are supporting the production of a new Third World threat – "rogue" or "outlaw" states who are seeking or have acquired chemical, biological, and nuclear "weapons of mass destruction" – which, they claim, only new high-technology weapons can defeat.

(i) "Our industrial salvation"

Before the First World War American chemists and chemical engineers argued that America should emulate the German use of scientific research.[3] In Germany, technical schools, universities, government, manufacturers, and banks, all appreciated research and cooperated to use it to ensure the success of German manufacturing:

> No one at all conversant with the facts can doubt that our industrial salvation must be found in a closer alliance and co-operation between the scientific worker and the actual agencies of production. Such co-operation exists . . . in Germany, and its results are evident throughout the world in the tremendous expansion of German industry.[4]

The chemists pointed to the glory of the German chemical industry, her artificial dye industry, where the extensive use of scientific research had led to the manufacture of a wide variety of new, high-quality dyes. Research had enabled German manufacturers to take over the world market in a few decades.

It is difficult to overstate the chemists' pre-war idealization of Germany. They projected onto Germany their desires for a perfect society. As many of them had studied in German universities or worked in German laboratories, they could claim first-hand knowledge of what was being done there. Germany provided them with the concrete proof that their ideas were not utopian, that research really could transform America into an ever-improving society. They presented American and German political ideals as compatible: "Broadly speaking, democracy has established itself in . . . Imperial Germany, as truly as in the republican United States of America."[5] American chemists deployed the German example in a bid to re-articulate power relations within America. In the university, they argued, scientists should be given the research time and equipment German scientists enjoyed. This was essential if American scientists were to make the discoveries America needed to keep up with Germany industrially. In industry, the nation must establish industrial research laboratories; fund university laboratories and technical schools; speed up the diffusion of new ideas by allowing scientists working in industry to publish most of their research; give scientists the finance they needed to turn discoveries into patentable inventions; and reform patent law to support rapid technological advance. What are now regarded as negative features of Wilhelmine Germany were often praised. In arguing for the development of a national system of technical education, for example, Victor Alderson, dean of the Armour Institute of Technology, evaluated German organization positively in contrast to British *laissez faire*.[6] Equally, they believed America should emulate Germany's quasi-military effort to conquer world markets.

The chemist's strategy for enlisting the support of business and finance had one fatal flaw: there was no compelling reason for business to invest in research, since America's vast natural resources and huge domestic market meant it could secure higher profits through large-scale production. American businessmen and financiers, the chemists lamented, viewed chemical research as an unfamiliar, high-risk, long-term, low-yield investment. This forced the chemists to buttress the commercial case for research with other arguments: only research could conserve America's natural resources, ensure the efficiency of a complex society, stamp out disease in her huge cities, and develop the social reforms essential to avoid the disintegration of America through class war. America was an increasingly complex and interdependent society, they claimed, which was now *dependent* on chemical research if she was to keep up with other nations and avoid collapse. The nation as a whole, whether through private philanthropy or through government grants, should support chemical research so that it became a better investment.

During the First World War the chemists replaced their ideal image of Germany with a harsh, threatening, negative one. The change began during the years of American neutrality. The chemists seized advantage of the interruption of German dye shipments to American textile manufactures to launch a campaign for an American artificial dye industry. To persuade businessmen that investments in the new industry would not be wiped out if a sudden end to the war enabled the Germans to resume shipments to America, they campaigned for a high tariff or temporary embargo on foreign dyes. The chemists faced a potentially fatal obstacle to their campaign: textile manufactures might object to paying higher prices for dyes. To break down this barrier, the chemists portrayed the German dye industry as an enemy. Reversing their earlier idealization of the German chemical industry, they now claimed that in the decades before the start of the war German dye manufactures had cooperated in a relentless campaign to crush all American attempts to manufacture artificial dyes, and had resorted to methods that went beyond acceptable business practice. This enabled them to present textile manufactures who argued against a high tariff as either selfish and unpatriotic, or as the dupes of the German dye manufactures. Stories were told of how German manufacturers were preventing Americans from uniting behind the campaign by threatening the Americans they employed as dye agents with dismissal, and blackmailing textile manufactures into silence by threatening to withhold all dye supplies. "It is useless for anyone to cry 'American dyes for American textiles'," Arthur Prill of the *Daily Trade Record* argued, "while the majority of persons directly connected with the dyestuff industry get their bread and butter from non-American dyestuff makers and while these persons retain control of the so-called campaign."[7] American chemists united behind the campaign. October 1915 saw the American Chemical Society at its annual meeting in Seattle supporting a call for Wilson to enact laws to protect investment in the dye industry.[8]

The chemists had a second, more hidden, reason for portraying German manufacturers as the enemy. This did not appear directly in their statements – indeed, their silence on this issue is deafening – but can be inferred from the changing context in which they found themselves as the war continued. The British blockade of Germany not only interrupted German dye shipments to America, it also ensured that chemical manufacturers in the United States only produced high explosives for the Allies. By late 1915, the tidal wave of Allied orders for munitions had led to an unprecedented boom in the American chemical industry. The leaders of America's chemists and chemical engineers saw a chance to advance their profession by persuading high explosives manufacturers like Du Pont to reinvest war profits in dyes research. They argued that this would give manufacturers a second line to fall back on when the market for high explosives collapsed at the end of the war. By portraying German manufacturers and the German government as combined together in a sinister plot to attack American manufacturers, American chemists were able to avoid seeing themselves as opportunists advancing their position within America by the sale of American high explosives to blow young Germans conscripts to pieces.[9]

When America entered the war in April 1917, Woodrow Wilson depicted Germany as an outlaw nation America had to defeat to restore the rule of international law. Equally, Wilson argued that Germany's autocratic government had to be defeated to "make the world safe for democracy". After the signing of the Armistice on 11 November 1918, the leaders of American chemists and chemical engineers adapted this story. They argued that – despite the Armistice, the Paris peace negotiations, the abdication of the Kaiser, the replacement of the monarchy by a republic, and a new German government led by the anti-military Social Democratic Party – Germany continued to be an outlaw nation. At the same time, they warned that as the years went by German chemical research and her giant artificial dye industry would give her new, deadlier, poison gases. She would be able to threaten American cities with annihilation by bombers or airships carrying poison gas bombs.[10] Claiming that this threat could not be contained by disarmament treaties, they concluded that the American government should support the development of an American artificial dye industry with a tariff and selective embargo.

(ii) The Teutonic heart

To show that Germany would continue to be an outlaw nation, the chemists told a story of the causes behind contemporary events, Germany's (claimed) bid to control the world continued to operate despite the end of the war.

The chemists reinterpreted events to present *all* German actions as caused by the same driving passion. Before, during, and after the Armistice, German actions all showed a relentless and all-powerful drive to exercise global hegemony. This story was tirelessly repeated in the editorials of *The Journal of Industrial and Engineering Chemistry*. At a psychologically critical point shortly after the Armistice was signed, the editorial "A VICTORY OF ARMS, NOT YET OF IDEALS" sought to ward off the danger that American chemists and chemical engineers might agree with Woodrow Wilson that it was the German government alone, and not the German people, who were to blame for the war and that normal relations might soon be re-established with Germany commercially and culturally. There could be no normal relations, the editorial warned, because all German actions flowed from a deep cause, the Teutonic heart's desire to dominate.[11]

The telegraphic style of these editorials presents the argument in extreme condensation. Its details can be seen in the addresses and testimony of Francis Garvan reprinted in the journal. Garvan was at the centre of the campaign for a dye industry. During the war he had been in charge of the Alien Property Custodians' investigation into German manufacturers' attempts to hide their American assets to prevent their seizure. This gave him an in-depth knowledge of German manufacturers' activities in America. Shortly after the war ended, he became the alien property custodian. He was also the president of the Chemical Foundation, the body set up to hold German dye patents seized during the war and to distribute them to American companies. As such he represented the interests of all American chemical manufactures who had invested in artificial dye production.

A lawyer by training, Garvan built up a detailed case against the German chemical industry in reports and in testimony to Congress. Garvan presented all Germany's actions as revealing a single aim:

> Her ambitions are the same in peace and war. Destroy your business competitor by state aid, cartel combination, dumping, full-line forcing, bribery, theft of patents or inventions, espionage, and propaganda! Destroy your military adversary by tearing up sacred treaties, by unlicensed and unbridled submarine and poisonous gas warfare, by the destruction of factories, mines, and vineyards, by terrorism and vandalism.[12]

All these effects are presented as the result of a *single* cause. In the case of the editorial cited above it is the nature of the Teutonic race. For Garvan, this is the Germans falling to the temptation created by discovering the enormous power of research. He dated Germany's desire for domination to the 1860s, when she first began to use research to develop her chemical industry. "It was Germany's chemical supremacy that gave her confidence in her avaricious dream of world empire."[13] This means that Germany's desire for world power had been growing for over half a century. As the war had done nothing to remove this cause, Germany would continue to seek to dominate the world. Indeed, chemical research would make her more powerful and the temptation greater.

Garvan saw scientific research as naturally contributing to the betterment of mankind. Tempted by the enormous power offered by research Germany had turned science towards its own selfish ends. It was the destiny of American chemistry to correct that deviation. This can be seen in Garvan's plea to the Senate dye subcommittee for a dye tariff:

> We felt that we would like to be a part of the taking of the forces of science, developed by them – but which they have only turned to the desolation and destruction of mankind – and placing it in the hands of what we believe is a higher and purer civilization; and see if we cannot, out of the terrible mess of this war, do something constructive with the same scientific forces which heretofore have been devoted to nothing but evil . . . It is only to give American principles, character and energy a chance that we ask you to hold these people off until we get our education. Then we will meet them without any tariff.[14]

The cause of all German actions in Garvan's opinion is not the result of a nature trying to realize itself, but rather an absence or lack. Garvan understood the cause of Germany's desire for world empire in terms of the meta-narrative of humanity described earlier. Mankind is discovering it is *one* as men acquire increased understanding of nature and society and throw off their dependence on nature and other men. The process is understood as one of teleological causality: just as the acorn grows into the oak it has the potential to be, so to mankind is coming together to fulfil its natural potential to cooperate. In doing so men are fulfilling their nature. Within this story, Germany's claimed desire to conquer its neighbours can only be understood in negative terms. She deviated from the path of civilization. This deviation is caused by negative factors – lack of knowledge and failure of the will. Hence the chemist's use of terms like "temptation", "dream", "avarice", and "greed" to explain Germany's postulated deviation from the path of civilization.

Since the war had not removed the cause of Germany's desire for world domination, Garvan concluded the war had not really ended. Germany was simply biding its time. "Industrial Germany was the first to see defeat and forced the military peace, in order that with her industrial equipment intact she might continue that same war by intensified and concentrated economic measures." Garvan invoked a Germany bent on a strategy of commercial domination to explain the 1916 unification of the two cartels that dominated the German dye industry into one giant cartel, the Interessen Gemeinschaft (the I.G., later I.G. Farben), and the issuing of stock to raise its capital to over $400 million:

> It cannot be doubted that this enormous engine of commercial warfare has been created expressly for the expected war after the war, and that it is intended to undertake still more efficiently and on a larger scale the various methods by which German attacks upon all competition are carried out.[15]

The chemists argued that the war had left the real basis of German power untouched. Germany's artificial dye industry had been the key to German power during the war and would be in the future. The nature of the artificial dye industry meant that it could be easily and quickly converted to the production of poison gas or high explosives. Equally, research into new dyes was almost certain to lead to the discovery of new poison gases. On the basis of their expertise, they claim that, as a matter of scientific and technological fact, the cheapest way America could assure itself of the large, immediately available supply of high explosive and poison gases she needed for her national security was through the development of a dynamic artificial dye industry. To popularize this claim, the National Security Council helped the Chemical Warfare Service prepare and exhibit a display showing that poison gases, artificial dyes, medicines, and high explosives all had similar chemistry, and that dye plants could be rapidly converted to the production of high explosives or poison gases.[16]

The chemists stressed that Germany's signing of the Treaty of Versailles, which forbade it to have or import chemical weapons, was no protection. The argument was made the subject of a British book, *The Riddle of the Rhine* by Victor Lefebure, republished in America by the Chemical Foundation.[17] The title echoes the widely read pre-war spy story by Erskine Childers, *The Riddle of the Sands*. Childers' novel tells how secret German preparations to invade England are discovered by two Englishmen on holiday in Germany. Where Childers stressed that an invasion threat may be hidden in inlets to the North Sea, Lefebure underscores the danger that preparations for a surprise chemical attack may be hidden in the I.G.'s chemical plants along the Rhine. The war had shown, he argued, that plants developed to manufacture dyes could be instantly converted to the production of poison gases. Nor could it be discerned whether plants were secretly being used to produce chemical weapons, since this could be hidden by dispersing the stages of production among different plants. Equally, it was not possible to stop commercial laboratories secretly being used to discover new chemical weapons.[18]

(iii) Was there no alternative?

The chemists claimed there was no alternative to chemical preparedness. A review of what was then known about Germany shows that this was a highly debatable and self-interested claim.

Had Germany deviated from the path followed by America, Britain, and France since the 1860s?
There were reasons to doubt it. German actions could be just as well explained by the idea that Germany was acting *like* America in seeking to become a Great Power as by the alternative hypothesis that she was seeking to dominate the other powers. (1) Differences between German and American actions can be explained: by Germany's geographical position between France, Austria-Hungary, and Russia; and by the fact that within the international economy she had long been in a tributary position to Great Britain, and was being increasingly forced into a tributary position by the United States.[19] Equally, the dynamic industrial growth of Russia in the decades preceding the war meant that Germans saw the long-term balance of power shifting against them under the current system of alliances. In 1914, as the Reichstag record states, it was the fear of an invasion by Russia following the Tsar's decision to mobilize, and hatred of Tsarist autocracy, cleverly played upon by the Chancellor Bethmanm Hollweg that led the vehemently anti-militarist Social Democratic Party to support German mobilization and war credits.[20] (2) The actions of German dye manufacturers in using their domination of the market to strangle potential American rivals were no different from those of American oil and sulphur companies in Europe, where they dominated the market.[21] The idea that Germany was acting like America is underscored by the earlier views of the chemists themselves. Before the war they had emphasized the similarity between America and Germany. They had regarded Germany as the model for America to follow, not a deviation to be corrected.

Was post-war Germany an outlaw nation biding its time before launching new wars?
Of course, in the aftermath of the war there was confusion. Even so, there were strong reasons to doubt it; and, more importantly, for believing that if America

and her Allies supported liberal and social democratic forces within Germany a long-term peace could be established. (1) The forced abdication of the Kaiser, who had earlier been presented by the chemists as one of the main forces behind German militarism, and the replacement of the monarchy by a republic. (2) The replacement of the wartime German government by a new government dominated by the Social Democrats and headed by the Social Democratic Chancellor Ebert. Here it is important to recall the long-standing opposition of the German Social Democrats to German militarism before the war.[22] A German Social Democrat/Liberal alliance, emphasizing anti-militarism, anti-communism, and free trade, supported by America, could have permanently isolated groups supporting rearmament and renewed aggression. (3) The grassroots support for such a politics was there for all who cared to investigate. Following five years of war there was widespread disenchantment with the military and a strong desire for peace; equally, many Germans were prepared to ally themselves with their former enemy to protect themselves from a Bolshevik revolution.

Would German chemical research soon give her the capacity to mount a serious threat to its neighbours in the medium term?
This claim does not stand up to much probing. It only appeared credible because Americans were unfamiliar with the real capacities of aircraft and chemical weapons. By presenting them as new technologies whose possibilities were only beginning to be realized, the chemists turned them into a site for popular fantasy about the unlimited power of science and technology. (1) The German chemical industry was in a poor state. It lacked essential raw materials, it was plagued by severe industrial unrest, and Germany's transport system was not working.[23] In addition, the Allies had taken over key German chemical factories, and German chemical weapons researchers had dispersed after the end of the war.[24] By contrast, the American chemical industry was now stronger than it had been before the war. The military defeat of the Central Powers, and the post-war division of the Austro-Hungarian Empire, meant that in the medium term Germany's conventional forces were no match for its wartime opponents. Chemical weapons alone could never have made up for this weakness. Finally, under the Treaty of Versailles, Germany was obligated to carry out general disarmament. (2) It was not obvious that the integration of all German dye companies into one giant company, the I.G., gave the German dye industry a competitive advantage. (We now know that the inflexibility of the I.G.'s constitution prevented German dye companies from adapting to post-war conditions.)[25]

Was chemical disarmament impossible?
What a disarmament treaty requires is not the ability to detect any cheating, but only the ability to detect large-scale cheating that would give a decisive military advantage.

A good treaty establishes processes in which verification and trust reciprocally re-inforce each other. As trust is built up, it becomes more difficult for a government to risk cheating lest its activities be betrayed by its own civil servants, soldiers, scientists, engineers, and soldiers. A good treaty works to break down the distrust and hostil-ity that complete secrecy demands. The idea that chemical disarmament might be possible if the nations concerned had a will to pursue it is suggested by the writings of chemists: (1) American chemists themselves argued that those countries which had an open chemical industry would have an industrial advantage over their rivals. Thus *The Journal of Industrial and Engineering Chemistry* editorialized in September 1918: "Too much secrecy as to certain fancied advantages has already proved in some cases the cause of industry 'dry rot.' Community of knowledge as to scientific achievement, safeguarded by critical discussion of results, will prove so valuable a means of industrial advance that it must not be neglected."[26] If chemists and chem-ical manufactures could be persuaded to pursue openness for national prosperity, they could be persuaded to pursue openness for peace. (2) A treaty with a good ver-ification regime deters cheating. It also gives countries more information about the preparations of a country they do not trust than they would have if they had to rely on their own intelligence alone. It is implausible that a government that had signed such a treaty could be certain that the vast quantities of chemical weapons needed to be sure of having the decisive advantage in a surprise attack could be kept secret. The use of chemical weapons to gain a strategic advantage requires very large-scale preparations: one cloud gas attack alone requires hundreds of tons of gas; large quantities of the gas must be produced and stored; large numbers of gas masks and other equipment for using gas must be produced; and large numbers of troops must be trained in both offensive and defensive chemical warfare.

Would poison gases and aircraft ever give Germany the capacity to wipe out the population of American cities?
This claim is only plausible if the large difficulties in carrying out such an attack are ignored. An enthralling fantasy, it collapses on contact with reality. The shapes of buildings, wind conditions, and the necessity for either accurate bombing or the laying of a gas plume by precise level flying close to the ground all make it diffi-cult to build up a lethal concentration of gas over the whole of a large city.[27] These difficulties are multiplied if the city is defended by either aircraft or anti-aircraft guns, and if the civilian population is equipped with gas masks. They become intractable when the bombers needed to carry out such an attack have to cross the Atlantic Ocean. German chemical weapons could never have been a sig-nificant threat to American cities.

Hindsight is misleading. We must guard against reading history backwards. This is what happens when the National Socialist seizure of power in 1933 is seen as predetermined by German resentment at the imposition of a punitive peace treaty.[28] In *The Origins of the Second World War*, A.J.P. Taylor argues that between 1918 and 1929 there were many points at which Germany, America, Britain, and France could have cooperated more vigorously and successfully to achieve a long-term peace. Without continued insistence that Germany pay reparations because of its alleged sole responsibility for the war, German bitterness at the Treaty of Versailles would probably have been politically insignificant. Even as late as 1929, Taylor reports, "the most popular cry in Germany was 'No More War' not 'Down with the Slave Treaty'".[29] Equally, Germany did carry out the disarmament provisions laid down at Versailles, and as late as 1934 the German army did not believe it was capable of attacking Poland, let alone France.

Viewed in retrospect, the repeated failure of national governments to take full advantage of the intense and widespread desire for peace in the 1920s was a series of lost opportunities. Rulers of France, Britain, and America failed to appreciate, once they had decided against the destruction of Germany, that with the end of Tsarist Russia, the collapse of Austria-Hungary, the weakening of the British Empire, and the devastation of France, the long-term balance of power had shifted in Germany's favour. As French bitterness over Alsace-Lorraine following the Franco-Prussian war had shown, securing an enduring peace depended on negotiating a settlement Germans would see as minimally just.[30] Equally, as the French historian Marc Ferro emphasizes in *The Great War*, the return of world war showed the inadequacy of the American, British, and French elites' view that the "uneasy [post-war] atmosphere, the disunity of the victors, the difficulties of applying Versailles and the crisis of emerging from economic and social reconstruction, were all simply crises of transition and that capitalist society would be able to overcome them just as it would discredit socialism".[31]

(iv) "No other industry offers a livelihood to any such numbers of highly trained scientific chemists"

The chemists presented their demand for an artificial dye industry as driven by the German chemical threat. The history of American chemistry and chemical manufacturing reveals the special interests that lay behind this interpretation. The key elements to consider are the history of high explosives and artificial dyes.

The end of the nineteenth century saw an explosives revolution.[32] Chemists developed smokeless explosives such as cordite, which enabled guns to be fired without their position being given away. They also developed "disruptive" explosives such as picric acid, which could withstand the shock of being fired in an artillery shell. This led to artillery shells and which exploded on impact and which were first used in the Boer War. The First World War saw an insatiable and ever-growing demand for the new explosives. None of the armies had prepared for a long war; all soon faced a critical shortage of high explosive. The British sought to gain the advantage by cutting Germany's supply of the Chilean nitrates it needed to manufacture high explosives, using the Royal Navy's command of the sea to buy American high explosives and to deny them to Germany. Germany responded by building plants to manufacture synthetic nitrogen using the new Haber synthetic ammonia process.

The trade in high explosives and the chemicals to make them brought the American chemical industry into the war on the side of the Allies, and led to the massive expansion of the American chemical industry. In October 1914 Du Pont had an annual smokeless powder capacity of 4500 tons. Three years later its factories at Carney's Point, Haskell, and Parlin had a capacity of 130,000 tons, rapidly rising to 200,000 tons – a forty-five-fold increase.[33] The price of high explosives, and the intermediary chemicals needed for their manufacture, soared. The price of the intermediate phenol in New York rose from 7 cents a pound in early 1914, to 50 cents in January 1915, to 100 cents in February, and 150 cents in July.[34] Du Pont's profits rose from $27 million in 1913 to $270 million in 1917 and $329 million in 1918. Du Pont common stock paid out 458 per cent of its original value in dividends during the war, and the price of the stock increased 374 per cent. This enabled Du Pont to acquire a 25 per cent share in General Motors for $47 million.[35] Through the sale of high explosives and other war materials the Dow Chemical Company increased its profits from $1 million in 1913 to $12 million in 1917 and another $12 million in 1918.[36] For both companies the war brought a more than tenfold increase in annual profits.

Germany developed modern artificial dye manufacturing in the 1860s.[37] This was the world's first industry based on organized scientific research. Manufacturers developed close links with leading chemists in universities and opened up the first industrial research laboratories. Germany soon dominated the American and the world markets for artificial dyes. Of the 24,000 tons of dye consumed by the American textile manufactures in 1913, only 3000 tons were made in the United States. There were several causes for the lack of a native artificial dye industry: there was no adequate supply of coal tar intermediates; German patents blocked innovation; American tariff policy reflected the interests of the textile industry in cheap high-quality German dyes; and businessmen preferred the quick high profits available from investing in large-volume production in other industries to the slower rewards of investing in research into new dyes.[38] The Germans used their commanding position to strangle American attempts to enter the market: when the American firm Benzol Products put the coaltar intermediate aniline oil on the market, German firms cut the price of aniline oil to stop the new venture gaining market share.

With the start of the European war, American chemical scientists and engineers argued for an American artificial dye industry. They saw a dye industry based on research as a step towards making research the engine of the American chemical industry. Equally, they saw an artificial dye industry as the best way of providing employment for chemists. Germany had built its artificial dye industry by using teams of chemists to exhaustively explore thousands of possible chemicals to see whether they would make good dyes. The artificial dye industry was different from other parts of the chemical industry – it alone offered the prospect of large numbers of research jobs. This was of intense concern to American chemists as more and more of them graduated from new university departments of chemistry and chemical engineering. After experiencing full employment during the war, many chemists found themselves unemployed or facing unemployment after the war when an excess of productive capacity brought the booming wartime chemical industry crashing down. The leaders of the campaign for a dye industry and chemical preparedness played on this concern to ensure that American chemists and chemical engineers were squarely behind the campaign. "No other industry offers a livelihood," claimed the Alien Property Custodian Mitchell Palmer in 1919, "to any such large numbers of highly trained scientific chemists nor any such incentive to continuous and extended research."[39]

For their part, manufacturers saw investment in dyes as a way to ensure themselves against the collapse of the explosives market when the war ended. Du Pont led the way. Through an agreement with the German firm of Levinstein, it obtained German know-how, in particular for the synthesis of indigo, and exclusive rights to sell Levinstein dyes in the New World. It built a large dye factory at Deepwater Point in New Jersey, and employed approximately 200 chemists as researchers.[40] The other key firm was the National Aniline and Chemical Co. Following America's April 1917 entry into the war, the Alien Property Custodian seized German dye patents, and sold them to an organization set up to licence their use by American manufactures, the Chemical Foundation. Most of the licenses went to Du Pont and to the National Aniline and Chemical Co.

The end of the war saw American, British, and French chemical manufacturers moving swiftly to protect their investments in dye manufacture. They were strongly supported by their nations' chemists and chemical engineers. At the Paris Peace Conference the American chemical industry urged Wilson to support a British proposal to destroy the military power of the German chemical industry by demanding the surrender of all its trade secrets. They claimed that half a billion dollars worth of investments were at stake.[41] Wilson rejected the proposal as motivated by economic not military interests, and as impracticable because it would never be known when Germany had divulged all its secrets.

In America, Britain, and France, chemical manufacturers, scientists, engineers, and soldiers launched campaigns demanding support for their chemical industries in the interests of national security. In the late 1930s a Senate investigation of the munitions industry, led by Senator Nye, revealed that the American campaign was funded on a massive scale by Du Pont. Between 1918 and 1925 Du Pont contributed over $370,000 to the American Dyes Institute, the Synthetic Organic Chemical Manufacturers Association, and the Chemical Foundation for publicity work.[42] The goal of the campaign was to magnify the dangers the United States would face without a large artificial dye industry. To do this, the chemists and chemical manufacturers decided to concentrate on chemical warfare. By contemporary standards the campaign was on an unprecedented scale, with close cooperation between the American, French, and British campaigns. The Chemical Foundation reprinted books from overseas arguing that national chemical industries must be built up to face the German threat. Du Pont sent an agent to Europe to promote scare stories about the threat of future chemical warfare. The agent fed stories on foreign chemical developments back to American newspapers. Senior officers from chemical companies addressed fraternal and commercial organizations. A typical address was delivered by Dr William Hale, a vice-president of Dow Chemical Company, to the Flint, Michigan, Rotary Club on 16 December 1921. Gas was the most effective and most humane weapon of all time. The mass armies of the world war were a thing of the past. Future wars would be between armies officered entirely by trained chemists. He concluded with a call to arms. "We need a protecting tariff . . . In this war after the war our battle cry must be 'To hell with German imports! Down with everything opposed to American industries!'"[43]

(v) A self-amplifying power strategy

The chemists' writings show the piecemeal development of a strategy to reinforce and extend their power. At the centre of their writings, they produce a picture of Germany as an outlaw nation whose chemical research is making it more and more menacing. This production is a mystification of the real order of cause and effect. Or, to be more precise, since we never have unmediated access to that order, by excluding alternatives and hiding interests they present their interpretation as objective by presenting it as unmediated.

We start with the special interests of the chemical scientist, engineer, manufacturer, and warfare soldier. The leaders of the chemical campaign then combined and harmonized these different interest by crafting a story. Here their action is the *cause*, and the world presented by the story the *effect*. This causal sequence has been revealed by our examination of the chemist's case for an American dye industry. This showed there was nothing necessary about the chemist's interpretation. Strong arguments could be given for other interpretations. The events themselves were insufficient to explain why the leaders of the campaign selected this interpretation rather than others. Their interpretation was "under-determined" by events.[44] Their decision must, therefore, be explained by the special interests of the groups that made up the chemical campaign. Thus the elements of their interpretation – the story which presents America as global sovereign, Germany as long-term outlaw nation, the laboratory as a wild space that cannot be policed, and the need for an American dye industry – are all effects of the chemists' self-interested interpretation of events.

The chemists' story presents the chemists as representing the interests of mankind by hiding the way it was produced. This is achieved through a *reversal* of the order cause and effect.

The story captures and arrests American's attention by focusing it on the spectacle of a wounded monster lurking in its lair, like Grendel in *Beowulf*, restoring its strength, brewing new poisons, waiting until the moment is right for it to take revenge. It enthrals Americans with its account of the underlying causes which make it impossible to tame this monster: the Germans' long temptation by the potential for domination created by being the first people to discover the power of research, and the nature of chemical laboratory and plant as places which cannot be monitored by any disarmament inspectorate. Held in the grip of the story, Americans attention is deflected from the interests that have led the chemists to select this interpretation, and the chemists are able to portray themselves as heroes whose motives are only a concern to defend humanity.

Here cause and effect are reversed. What were effects of the chemist's act of interpretation? Humanity realizing itself, the German deviation, the nature of the chemical laboratory, are presented as causes. One of the causes, the chemist's reweaving of the wartime story, is now presented as an effect. Equally, the chemists implicitly present their own action, which was the cause of their selecting one particular interpretation of events, as an effect. They do this by implicitly presenting themselves as forced to tell Americans that chemical preparedness is the only way of defending humanity.

The chemist's writings reveal a self-amplifying power strategy.[45] They show the chemists using the position they had already achieved through the exercise of power for the further exercise of power. During the war, those chemists who supported the Allies gained control of the American Chemical Society and *The Journal of Industrial and Engineering Chemistry* by presenting the German chemical industry as an enemy, and those Americans who questioned this presentation as their knowing or unknowing tools. The American entry into the war gave the leaders of the campaign details of the German chemical industry's actions in America. Later the Allied victory placed them in a position to give detailed reports on the German chemical industry. Equally, the leaders of the campaign were already in control of laboratories and manufacturing plants. This placed them in a position to make authoritative statements about such places which are difficult to challenge by those without day-to-day access to them. In practice the only way it proves possible to mount such a challenge is if some chemists come over to the side of the critics. In recent decades it is precisely such chemists who have made possible chemical disarmament. The chemists' strategy resembles the technique used to amplify the strength of a radio signal. It is a self-amplifying power strategy. The chemists' power over the laboratory, the factory, and Germany enable them to paint a picture which justifies the maintenance and extension of that power. The reinforcement and extension of their power, in its turn, places them in a position to further reinforce and extend their power.

I have used the language of cause and effect. Equally, we can talk about the chemist's *production* of Germany as an outlaw nation and the laboratory as wild-space beyond international control. The stories told by the chemists contribute to the actual production of both these things, making them more likely. It is a self-fulfilling prophecy. If the Americans, French, and British believe the story told by the chemists – a big "if", since chemists' emphasis on the new chemical terror actually had the unintended effect helping to create a mass movement for disarmament – then they will build up their chemical industries, support their chemical warfare laboratories, and refuse to negotiate chemical disarmament. Their German counterparts will then be in a stronger position to argue that these countries are intent on dominating the world through chemical weapons, and that therefore Germany must build up its chemical weapons in self-defence – which of course includes an offensive capacity to launch pre-emptive attacks. Germany will indeed become, from an American point of view, the long-term outlaw nation the American chemists portrayed it as being. Equally, Germany's understandable unwillingness to cooperate with any international inspectorate will then make German laboratories and factories the dark, obscure, wild and dangerous spaces the American chemists have portrayed them as being.

(vi) "One People, One Danger, One Defence"

The 1921 disarmament movement defeated the chemists and airmens' attempt to enrol Americans in their campaign. In the early 1930s by contrast, the same strategy was successfully used by a coalition between veteran air pilots, air strategists, and aviation engineers on the one side, and the Nazi Party on the other, to persuade Germans to support an authoritarian state. This coalition sought to overcome what it identified as the cause of German defeat in the First World War, the collapse of civilian morale in November 1918. The means used have been described by historian Peter Fritzsche.[46] Instead of seeing themselves as civilians whose defence against air attack should be left up to technical experts (fire wardens, police, Red Cross, civil-defence officials), German men and women should see themselves as soldiers on the home front whose task was to keep the nation working so that German armies could win the war. "Civil defence is part of 'total mobilization'," explained Ewald Sellien, "It is not emergency defence, it is not a means to minimize the dangers of war . . . rather it is the expression of the will to fight and the self-assertion of a great people." The goal of civil defence was accomplished when "the individual thinks, feels, and acts as a fighter" and "is as disciplined as a soldier". All citizens must become "bound into one unbreakable national community".[47] Or as one air-defence poster's slogan summed it up, "One People, One Danger, One Defence."[48]

The coalition sought to enrol Germans into their campaign by saturating society with images and writings showing their total vulnerability to bomber aircraft carrying poison gas. When the Nazi Party seized power in 1933 it placed the whole weight of the state behind the campaign. "For the state, it was crucial that ordinary Germans see their country," Fritzsche writes, "through the eyes of the bombardier – as one vast target. Only then could the organic unity of the fascist nation be realised." Exhibitions showing aerial photographs were organized. These sought to show that big cities, and the nation as a whole, formed a giant system which could be disrupted by air attack. Throughout the 1930s German cities were subjected to simulated air attacks to demonstrate their vulnerability. On 24 June 1933, "unknown foreign" air aeroplanes bombed Berlin with leaflets. The journal *Flugsport* warned that the next time it might be "gas or incendiaries". In Kiel a special wooden village was constructed and set on fire. Then voluntary firemen, Red Cross officials, and members of the Technical Emergency Forces entered the ruins to rescue the "victims" and to extinguish the flames. The event ended with the unexpected deluging of the spectators with tear gas to drive the point home. Across Germany the Reich Air Defence League installed eight foot high dummy bombs, marked with a vivid yellow stripe, in city squares, and aerial explosives dangled from street lamps and streetcar wires. The German Airsports League, founded in 1933, and heavily subsidized by the Nazis, provided another vehicle for educating German's about the aerial danger and, more importantly, through its glider clubs, in persuading civilians that they should be actively involved in defending the nation. The Reich Ministry of Education decided that it was in the "national-political" interest of the state to promote aviation in schools. In physics classes students learnt about the mechanics of flight, in chemistry they studied poison gas, in literature they read the memoirs of air aces, and in history they studied the development of aviation and how Allied restrictions during the 1920s on aviation had left Germany vulnerable to air attack. Teachers also discussed the theories of air strategists, showed students how to wear gas masks, and drilled students in how to remain calm during air raids. School rooms became centres of air mindedness: model aeroplanes hung from the ceiling, posters showing bomber attacks hung on the walls and aeroplane books sat on the shelves.

By convincing Germans that they were in immediate danger from bombers dropping poison gas, high explosives, or incendiaries, the Nazi government persuaded them to join the Air Ministry's Reich Air Defence League. Once enrolled in the League, German civilian men and women would be transformed into home front soldiers. Every apartment building was asked to elect a "house warden". They in turn assigned a fire detail, a hose crew, medical aides, and a dispatcher from among the residents. This formed the bottom of a pyramid linking house wardens to block wardens, district leaders, city-wide air raid officials, and so on up to Air Minister Goering. This enabled the Nazis to involve a large part of the German nation in air defence preparations. By January 1936 there were over 7000 branches of the Reich Air Defence League with a total of over 8 million members. This provided a way of drawing civilians into a web of disciplinary power. The goal was to make Germans feel that they were citizens of the nation first and foremost, and that the divisions of class, education, and status emphasized by liberalism and socialism were purely secondary. The idea was that through participation in air defence measures the sense of civic solidarity and acceptance of hierarchy claimed to exist in small-town Germany would be replicated throughout the nation. The gliding club was seen as a place where Germans from all social groups would learn to work together for the common good through the hard work of manually launching gliders and the enjoyment of flying. The need for national unity also overrode traditional gender roles. German women should not see their roles as restricted to their house and home, but encompassing the nation as a whole. Many house wardens were women, and the Nazi Party kept open auxiliary gliding classes for women. In Ernst Ohliger's 1935 novel *Bomben auf Kohlenstadt* it is Frau Hellman who provides the leadership demanded during an air raid on the Ruhr.

The strategy to enrol the entire population in preparations for air defence transformed Germans understanding of themselves and their world. They increasingly came to see air attacks as an almost inevitable part of their future, while they became more confident that they were prepared to meet the danger and overcome it. Many Germans joined the Reich Air Defence League as a way of proving their loyalty to the regime without having to join the Nazi Party. Yet the overall effect was to transform Germans into collaborators with the Nazi state. What this meant is nicely summed up by Fritzsche in an analysis of a picture of a man in the act of putting on a gas mask. It is, he writes, "a portrait of the collaborator, without illusions about the horrors of air war but ready and able to survive and meet its demands . . . Against a background of searchlights exploring the black sky, the figure appears competent and alert. Recognising the futility of escape, he willingly collaborates in the disciplinary regime of the authoritarian state."[49]

4

A New Declaration of Independence

What we have seen is the masked return of the sovereign right which the Declaration of Independence attacks, and which the Constitution's division of powers appears designed to absolutely prevent.[1] To understand what is at stake, a brief discussion of sovereign right is essential. Supporters of absolute monarchy, such as Jean Bodin, justified the claim that the king must have a sovereign right to suspend the law and exercise direct rule by arguing that the laws cannot work in the midst of riots, insurrection, plagues, famine, or war.[2] The basis for their argument is that for the laws to be applied the lives of the population must be peaceful and orderly. There must, therefore, be a single person, the sovereign, who is the guardian of peace and order. The sovereign is, paradoxically, both inside and outside the law. The sovereign is inside because the law depends on him. At the same time, he is outside. This is because the sovereign must decide when there is a danger to peace and order which threatens to prevent the rule of law. He may then declare a state of emergency, during which the sole criteria of the sovereign's actions is whether or not they are efficient means to restore peace and order. Legal restraints which normally restrict the power of the sovereign are suspended. Only a single person can exercise sovereign right. In those situations where society is riven by conflict, it is essential that there is an authority who can decide whether a state of emergency exists. This means that if the authority to declare a state of emergency is divided between two persons, there is a possibility that they may disagree over whether or not a state of emergency exists at the point when it is most critical that a clear decision is made. The opportunity for the state to make a timely intervention to restore order may be lost.

In their battle with absolutism, Enlightenment thinkers saw the royal pre-rogative, or sovereign right, as a way in which monarchs could illegitimately justify the unlimited extension of their power. While John Locke argued that a place had to be retained for the exercise of sovereign right by the Executive because the laws could not provide for "all Accidents and Necessities",[3] hatred for absolutism led Montesquieu in *The Spirit of the Laws* to imagine it could be done away with altogether. His system of government has no place for a discretionary power whatsoever. The idea that a government could be set up without such a power rested on the Enlightenment belief that nature was a regular system gov-erned by eternal laws. This meant that it should be possible to tell what could be expected in the future by examining the past and to provide for it in setting up a system of government. The founders of the American republic inherited the Enlightenment's denunciation of sovereign right, and Montesquieu's idea that a well-made constitution could do without it. The 1787 Constitution does not have a provision for emergency situations. It sought to avoid giving an single actor a sovereign right to decide that a state of emergency existed and to suspend the law until the exercise of direct power had restored peace and order. Instead, the Constitution sought to deal with the unexpected in two ways. The first was by creating an *unlimited power* which would enable the federal government to over-come any contingency. The second was by dividing and balancing power to prevent its abuse. The authors of the 1787 Constitution believed that checks and balances would prevent the return of absolutism's abuse of power.

On the one hand, the Constitution gave the federal government the right to set up its own taxation bureaucracy rather than depend upon the states, and asserted that it had an unlimited power to tax. Without setting up an equivalent of the Bank of England, it gave the federal government an unlimited right to borrow money on international markets. It gave the federal government the right to raise standing armies and to support a navy, as well as ultimate control over the states' militia. In *Federalist* no. 23, Alexander Hamilton, who had been the New York del-egate to the Constitutional Convention, justifies the Constitution's centralization of powers as necessary to meet all possible threats to the republic, both internal and external:

> These powers ought to exist without limitation *because it is impossible to foresee or to define the extent and variety of national exigencies, and the correspondent extent and var-iety of the means which will be necessary to satisfy them."* (Hamilton's italics)[4]

Here Hamilton answered the question of how it is possible to do without a full sovereign right. To secure the right to life, liberty, and the pursuit of happiness against all possible future contingencies, the federal government must have *unlimited* power. Through unlimited power the republic would be able to dominate all possible contingencies.

On the other hand, Hamilton and co-author of *The Federalist*, James Madison, claimed the Constitution, by keeping America united, would prevent the return of absolute power. The Constitution established a machine which made it impossible to use the power of the central government for illegitimate purposes. It allows the government to raise standing armies for use against other nations in war, but prevents a person or group raising troops with the hidden intent of using them to suppress liberty. It does so by dividing power over the military: it makes the president commander-in-chief, while giving Congress the power to declare war and to fund the military. To ensure that the president has to always return to Congress for military funding, Congress is only given authority to provide military funds for two years. Finally, control over the militia is divided between the federal government and the states. The president is the commander-in-chief of the militia when called into actual service of the United States. Congress is in charge of funding, arming, and disciplining the militia, and of its calling forth to execute the laws of the Union, to suppress insurrections, and repel invasions. The states appoint the officers of the militia and are in charge of its training. Hamilton and Madison's claim that this system would enable the federal government to use military forces to preserve liberty but prevents its abuse, rested on two principles which can be seen in their defence of the Constitution.

Military expertise and timely information

Their claim presupposed that the Congress would have the military expertise and information it needs to decide whether America faces a military threat, and would have them in time for large forces to be raised to meet the threat. This is based on the idea that the American elite, who will form the bulk of the representatives, itself had adequate military expertise. Military expertise was not yet seen as the monopoly of the professional soldier, but as something that members of the elite could acquire through temporary military service. Thus the federal government, not the states, would be in the best position to judge what military threats may exist. It would be the "center of information" which will "best understand the extent and urgency of the dangers that will threaten".[5]

America's geographical situation

Their claim also presupposed that the federal government would not have to constantly maintain a large military force because America's favourable geographical position means there would be sufficient time to raise such forces after a military threat has been detected. This presupposition can be seen in their assertion that America's separation from Europe by the Atlantic means that it would be impossible for the government to keep up large enough military forces to threaten liberty on the pretence that a foreign threat exists when it actually does not. To build the military up to sufficient size to threaten liberty without sparking a general revolt would require the executive and the legislature to collude together over a period of years to gradually build up the military under the pretence that America was threatened by foreign powers. This is impossible, Hamilton claimed, in the absence of a real threat:

> What colorable reason could be assigned in a country so situated for such vast augmentations of the military force? It is impossible that the people could be long deceived; and the destruction of the project and the projectors would quickly follow the discovery.[6]

Equally, Madison argued that the Constitution was the best protection Americans can have against the danger of standing armies because it ensures that Americans will be united in the defence of the nation. Britain's separation from continental Europe, and her navy, have made her "impregnable" to the armies of her neighbours. This has meant her rulers have never been able, "by real or artificial dangers, to cheat the public into an extensive peacetime establishment". If this is true for Britain, he concluded, it will be even more true for the American states provided they have a Constitution which keeps them united.[7]

(i) The leaders of the Chemical and Air Campaign and the return of sovereign right

What I have documented is the rise of a new sovereign right to determine whether a state of emergency exists and to suspend the law.[8] The leaders of the chemical campaign claimed that their position at the heart of the industry and research meant they were uniquely qualified to determine the scale and type of threat facing America. On this basis they claimed that America was now threatened by a German outlaw whose research and industrial development would increasingly give it the means to threaten America's great cities with annihilation. Unless America developed its chemical warfare capacity, she would not be able to defend other nations or herself against the German outlaw. In the second place we have seen the rise of a new right to suspend the law and exercise power outside it. Within the United States the leaders of the campaign had to operate within a political context established by the Constitution. This means it would be politically imprudent to assert such a right openly. Their belief that they had such a right is revealed by actions in which they sought to manipulate the Constitution's division of powers to the point where they no longer operate as a set of checks and balances but instead become a myth which allows the proliferation of unaccountable power to proceed unhindered. This can be seen in two cases. First, the Constitution makes the president the commander-in-chief. When Secretary of War Newton Baker and Chief of Staff Peyton March order the dissolution of the Chemical Warfare Service, and the officers of the Service get their friends in Congress to attach a riders to bills to block the order and then to establish the Service as an independent part of the army, we are in a grey area. On one interpretation, the officers of the Service are an outside power, taking advantage of the division of powers *to execute a strategy of divide and rule*. On another interpretation what we see is a legitimate checking of presidential power by the Congress after it has been over-extended by the war. The ambiguity is significant. It reveals that the complexity of the constitutional system makes it difficult to determine who is ultimately responsible for particular political outcomes, and hence provides interests like the chemical campaign with large opportunities to exercise behind the scenes influence.

The second case is more conclusive. Through elections the power of the federal government is checked by the power of the people. If this check is to be effective, the people must know who is behind campaigns to convince them to vote one way or another. This is essential if they are to be able to make informed judgements about whether a special interest is seeking to pass itself off as the national interest. This means that when Du Pont decides to employ some of the vast profits it made from the sale of munitions during the war to finance the chemical campaign, and uses front organizations to keep the extent of its support hidden, this is a clear case of manipulating the Constitution. We only know that Du Pont did this because the Senate Nye Committee much later forced Du Pont to provide internal correspondence which revealed that it financed the chemical campaign to the tune of a third of a million dollars – a vast sum to spend on propaganda in an age when politics had not yet become a branch of the advertising industry. The chemical campaign's manipulation of the Constitution's separation of powers was significant because it works towards bringing about a difficult-to-reverse change in power relations. Through the creation of an independent Chemical Warfare Service and tariffs and embargoes on the import of foreign dyes – in effect a hidden tax – the leaders of the chemical campaign in big business, science and engineering, the Senate and House of Representatives, and the army reinforced their power, and this in turn placed them in a position to increase their power yet further when new opportunities presented themselves.

While the leaders of the chemical campaign were normally careful to present their actions as respecting the Constitution, and were indeed supported by constitutional authorities, there is one place where the right to act against the Constitution is openly proclaimed. This is in Major General Fries' 20 April 1922 address "Chemical Warfare – Past and Future" to the Army and Navy Club.[9] Fries sought to establish the chemical laboratory as a place where the balance of power could be radically shifted, and the director of the laboratory as a person in a uniquely privileged position to decide the direction of military policy. He was also educating his fellow officers in how to manipulate the political system, and perhaps crowing a little over his success in doing so. In the first part of his address Fries sought to show the assembled officers the *"value of clear thought and prompt action even when it leads to laying violent hands on precedents and regulations"* (my italics). To justify breaking the law, he retold a story from Roman history. In 207 BC Rome is under threat of defeat by Carthage. The Carthaginian armies of Hannibal and his brother Hasdrubal are active in Italy. If they combine, Rome will fall. When the commander of one of the Roman armies, Nero, captures one of Hasdrubal's messengers, he realizes the only way to prevent this is to immediately combine his forces with those of his fellow general, Livius. With "a decision that brands him as one of the great leaders of all time", he instantly decides to do so despite the fact that it meant he must break "one of the most rigid Roman laws". To emphasize that when one breaks the rules one should do so in a way that makes one's actions irreversible, Fries notes that Nero only sent a report back to Rome after he had begun the movement so that *"his action could not be undone when his report reached the Roman Senate"* (my italics). Hasdrubal is surprised by the combined armies of Nero and Livius, and Hannibal informed of his defeat when Hasdrubal's head is thrown into Carthaginian lines the next morning. Rome is saved from disaster and the way cleared for Scipio's final defeat of Hannibal and Rome's destruction of Carthage.[10]

While the leaders of the chemical campaign only discussed their manipulation of the Constitution in places like the Army and Navy Club, where they could be sure of a receptive and discrete audience, and only published them in journals which circulated among like-minded people, they openly proclaimed that, as the self-proclaimed guardian of international law, America had the right to suspend international law when it judged that it was threatened and to exercise unlimited violence to restore order. The Hague Conventions of 1899 and 1907, the Treaty of Versailles, and the Washington Conference *all* prohibited the use of poison gas in war. Faced with such a clear statement of international law the leaders of the chemical campaign argue that there must be two *exceptions*. The first is in the use of chemical weapons to extend the rule of law. In *Chemical Warfare*, Fries and West claim that international law banning the use of chemical weapons cannot be applied to wars with savage peoples, because savage peoples do not themselves obey international law.[11] They are, as it were, "pre-laws". The use of chemical weapons by civilized peoples to conquer savage peoples is justified because it is the most effective and humane way to conquer them. Such conquest is always justified because the triumph of civilization over savagery is the triumph of law and peace:

The most scientific nations should be the most highly civilized, and the ones most desirous of abolishing war. If those nations will push every scientific development to the point where by the aid of their scientific achievements they can overcome any lesser scientific peoples, the end of war should be in sight.[12]

British chemical warfare officers justified using poison gas against the Afghans and tribesmen of the North-West Indian Frontier using precisely this logic. The head of the British effort, Foulkes, responded to scruples in high places by declaring: "tribesmen are not bound by the Hague Convention and they do not conform to its rules".[13] The same logic doubtless justified British experimenting with aerial gas attacks against the Red Army of the Bolshevik "outlaw" when it intervened in the Russian Civil War in 1919.

The second exception is the use of gas to defeat "outlaws" who threaten the rule of international law. Fries and West argued that America was justified in using chemical weapons against "outlaw" nations armed with poison gas. The United States, presumed to be the defender of international law, would be at an intolerable disadvantage if it were not prepared to use it against an outlaw nation that was. Indeed, they argued, it is better to prevent any outlaw nation from being tempted to threaten the international legal order by declaring that "we are going to use chemical warfare to the greatest extent possible in any future struggle". In an article in the 5 March 1921 *Bulletin of Chemical Warfare*, "Chemical Warfare Inspires Peace . . . Carrying of Horrors to Doors of Entire Population a War Deterrent", Fries justifies the use of aircraft to bomb the populations of cities with poison gas. Had the civilized nations been able to threaten the German outlaw with the annihilation of Berlin, he argues, the German emperor would have hesitated and "the war probably never would have been begun". He then goes further, stating that the United States must be ready to threaten the maximum use of chemical weapons not just to deter aggression by an outlaw nation but to insist that other nations respect its idea of what is just. He thus takes the step from defending the existing international order to making a new international order according to American ideas:

> Let the country that is most powerful insist on a square deal and justice, and make it known to the world that it is ready to get that justice, by peace if possible, by war if it must, but that if it is finally force to make war it will be with every element that can be found, secure in the knowledge that the more terrible the war the shorter it will be and the smaller the loss of life and property.[14]

This is a prescription for America to impose its idea of international relations by convincing other nations that it will not hesitate to destroy the populations of their cities by bombing them with poison gas, and that its greater power will allow it to do so without fear of retaliation. It is a prescription for the maximum use of terror as the most efficient way of achieving American ideas of a just world order.

The leaders of the chemical campaign thought justice consisted in mankind's achievement of its potential through the advance and worldwide spread of science, technology, capitalism, and democracy. They had, as we have seen, an intoxicating vision of themselves as the avant garde of a war through which mankind was overcoming war, poverty, famine, and disease.[15] On this view of themselves as the "marked leaders of mankind", the barriers of constitutional or international law are of little importance compared with the larger project of enabling mankind to realize its sovereignty. This means that the free interpretation or the breaking of the law is justified. The chemists see the necessity of breaking such law because of their knowledge of the fundamental laws of nature and society, and because they have the "vision" to see what needs to be done. Many of their fellow countrymen, however, lag behind them by maintaining an irrational attachment to laws. In the same article in which he advocates the maximum use of terror to achieve justice, Fries attacks the authority of man-made laws by representing them as powerless when they conflict with the laws of nature and society. To do so he turns to astro-physics. Though the picture he paints sounds a bit like that of eighteenth-century Newtonian mechanics, it draws its strength from contemporary descriptions of the evolution of stars and galaxies:

> Action is the first law of the universe. Nothing remains permanently stable. All is changing. The planets revolve around the sun; the sun and all the rest of the solar system revolve around other centers. The whole universe, so far as man has yet been able to determine, is in motion . . . Man has often revolted against these everlasting changes. Since recorded history began he has attempted by arbitrary rules to arrest the law of change and fix things for all time. And just as we recognize the constant change is the fundamental law of the universe, just so far we advance in knowledge.[16]

Lee Lewis, the inventor of the gas "Lewisite", by contrast, turns to the laws of evolution to make the same point. The whole history of animal and human evolution, since our "first very great grandparents emerged from the Silurian ooze and began to proliferate", has been one long story of the development of more effective poisons to kill off competitors. The Washington Conference's attempt to "lay down rules for governing all future warfare" is therefore irrational. Just as the Hague Convention failed to stop Germany from using chemical weapons in the world war, so too the Washington Conference's reiteration of the ban on chemical weapons will not stop nations from using chemical weapons in the future.[17] The chemists' self-presentation leads to an ambiguity: is their breaking of the law necessary so as to preserve the law against those who would destroy it, or is it part of their campaign to realize mankind's sovereignty through the world-wide development of science, technology, capitalism, and liberal democracy? Breaking laws for the second reason is easier to justify if it is presented as undertaken for the first reason. This ambiguity means that the constant invocation of the figure of the outlaw can provide an essential alibi for repeated law breaking to achieve utopia.

The history of the chemical and air campaigns shows us the use of science and the progressive narrative to improve an age-old strategy of using terror to exercise control over populations. Through doing so they sought to provide America with a refinement of an old way of exercising power. This strategy depended upon threatening both lives and voices.[18] For analytic purposes it is helpful to separate the two threats, though in practice they are thoroughly intertwined because the inability to protest against terror facilitates its repetition. The first dimension of the strategy is the exercise of control by threatening the bodily life of the population. This is done through the *example, labelling, blackmail* and *asymmetric power relations*.

The first element was the creation of examples through the spectacular destruction of bodies. Through use of bomber aircraft dropping high-explosive, incendiaries and poison gas in 1919 on a scale no other nation could match, the chemists and airmen would have created an example through the massive destruction of life. Plans included the bombing of cities. This would have sent a message to the surviving Germans: "Do what we say, or else we will do to you what we did to them." The 1919 campaign never happened. The chemical and air campaigns, as we will see, sought to make up for this by pointing to the Royal Air Force post-war success in using aircraft against tribal peoples in Somalia, Afghanistan, Mesopotamia (Iraq), and Northern India.

The second element was the use of labelling to legitimate the use of violence. To ensure they had Americans' and other nations' support for the future use of such violence, despite the fact that it was against international law, the chemists and airmen sought to reinforce the wartime labelling of Germany and Russia as "outlaw" nations. They also, as we have just seen, began to legitimate the idea that it was acceptable to coerce foreign governments by threatening to attack their civilian populations, by arguing that this would either make war shorter or stop war happening all together.

The third element was the use of blackmail to turn the moral responsibility that governments had, or ought to have had, for the well-being of their fellow nationals into a means for dictating to them. This was done by making the civilian population rather than the army the target and by seeking to convince governments that they had no way they could protect their population except by capitulating.

The fourth element was the creation of an asymmetric power relation. The chemists and airmen sought to do this by playing on the fantasy that new poison gases, new bombers, and the unprecedented scale of American production would soon give her the ability to annihilate any place on earth if she chose to do so. They sought to turn this fantasy into reality through the rapid scientific and technological development of the chemical and air weapons and their associated industries and by strengthening the relations they had developed during the war with their British and French counterparts.

The strategies' second dimension is the exercise of control and coercion over the voices of those who might oppose it. Here there was a repetition of the terror exercised against bodies as this, too, involved the example, labelling, blackmail and asymmetric power. The reader will be thoroughly familiar with how this was achieved. Through the rearticulation of the progressive meta-narrative the leaders of the chemical and air campaigns sought to entrench an asymmetric power relation in which society was divided into a "we" which commands and a "they" which is commanded. They then subjected anyone who challenged their criteria for assessing the development of new poison gases and bombers to a double silencing. First they silenced such critics by claiming the right to interpret what they said. This was done by presenting these opponents as members of the "they" which had not yet acquired the reason or self-discipline to participate in the avant garde debate. Second, if such critics insisted on being heard the leaders of these campaigns sought to turn society against them by identifying them with groups, such as Bolsheviks, commonly believed to be trying to destroy society itself. Through such silencing, the leaders of the chemical campaign sought to transform opponents (General March, the unknown officer with the wrong ideas) into chilling examples. The message of these examples was: "If you don't accept our criteria for discussion, we will silence you as we silenced them." The result was that those who sought to oppose the development of strategies for exercising terror found themselves caught up in a blackmail similar to that involved in the exercise of terror against bodies. To prevent others being subjected to terror in the future they needed to gain a hearing within the elite. Yet if they sought to gain a hearing by challenging the very framework being used to the exercise of terror by the elite, rather than merely arguing against particular forms of terror, they risked losing their capacity to gain a hearing at all. This is why those who have undergone terror can find bearing witness a traumatic ordeal in which the threat against their voice repeats the earlier threat against their lives which they are seeking to bear witness to and to prevent being repeated.

(ii) Eroding the distinction between the exercise of sovereign power to protect the law against violence and the exercise of violence in defiance of law

The Constitution has a remarkable way of providing for unexpected threats.[19] Under normal circumstances the fact that the executive, the legislature, and the courts all have a part in each other's exercise of power acts to prevent each from encroaching on the other's territory. Thus if the legislature encroaches the executive's territory by passing laws which are really a way of exercising executive power, the president can punish by veto. In exceptional circumstances when the very existence of the republic is threatened, however, the president can use his or her power as commander-in-chief to take extraordinary measures in the expectation that the Congress and courts will not interfere with his or her actions because there really does exist a danger to America itself. In this way the Constitution guards against the presidency using its unstated prerogative powers, hinted at in the designation of the president as commander-in-chief, to exercise arbitrary power while at the same time providing a way in which he or she can exercise such powers in exceptional circumstances to save the republic itself. It becomes impossible, however, to distinguish the president's use of such prerogative from the exercise of arbitrary power if:

First, the clear distinction between normal periods of good order and exceptional circumstances is broken down by the repeated depiction of threats to the republic which justify the continued extension of presidential powers.

Second, the presidency uses its prerogative to alter the very structure of society so as to decisively shift the balance of power within the federal government in its favour.

In such circumstances it becomes impossible to make a sharp distinction between the presidency's exercise of prerogative as the guardian of the fundamental law set out in the Constitution and the autocrat's destruction of the rule of law. In the next part of the book I show that Woodrow Wilson made it increasingly difficult to make such a distinction between the president's action as the guardian of the Constitution and that of his claimed opposite, the Kaiser's autocratic rule over Germany, by repeatedly depicting threats to America which demanded the extension of presidential power at the expense of Congress. It became hard for Americans to see whether the president's demands were really necessary to defend America against real German and Bolshevik threats or whether the presidency was creating bogus threats to convince Americans to support the transformation of America into the leader of a worldwide liberal capitalist revolution. Here I look at how the leaders of the chemical campaign's assertion of a sovereign right also began to erode the distinction between action to protect the rule of law and arbitrary violence. This can be seen in an August 1919 editorial in *The Journal of Industrial and Engineering Chemistry* entitled "A New Declaration of Independence". In it the leaders of the chemical campaign's claim to revolutionary authority, normally hidden, breaks through. The editors proclaim that the September 1919 meeting of the American Chemical Society in Independence Hall in Philadelphia will be "no less significant than the 1776 Declaration of Independence". At the meeting the Society would tell Americans that their liberty now depends on the nation's chemical industry. They then went on to declare that President Wilson's 20 May 1919 address to Congress, in which he supported a tariff on foreign dyes so as to build up the chemical industry in the interests of national defence, showed that the president had endorsed this claim. Without directly saying so, the editors were announcing that America now had a new informal constitutional structure in which the expansion of the chemical industry to prepare for a chemical war is accepted as basic to America's survival as an independent nation. The informality of this new structure, far from being a drawback, had the positive advantage of allowing the leaders of the chemical campaign to exercise power on behalf of national security without limits and without democratic accountability. They justified this expansion of the grey zone by arguing that the war was not over. Germany, despite its change of government, was in reality still an outlaw nation bent on world domination whose chemical and aircraft industries would make her a greater and greater threat to civilized nations:

> The present grip of the chemist upon public thought is due not so much to his industrial achievements as to the conviction that upon his genius and ability depends the future safety of the nation. This may well be, for, however regrettable it may be, the fact must be faced that warfare is becoming more and more a matter of chemistry. Few there be who believe that the signing of the treaty of peace by Germany portends an era of peace. Her leading men frankly avow it does not. Under such circumstances we would be indeed a foolish people if we did not encourage to the utmost that branch of science and its applications which is so intimately bound up with the national defence.[20]

Here the First World War is presented as not really having ended despite the Armistice. This means America faces an indefinite postponement of peace – in effect a permanent state of war. The erosion of the distinctions on which the legitimacy of sovereign right depends at both the national and international level undermine the claim that American liberal democracy, as the guardian of law, is distinct from Prussian autocracy. (As we shall see the classification of Prussia as an autocracy was, itself, questionable and interested.)[21]

The erosion of any credible claim to a significant difference between the leaders of the chemical campaign and their supposed opposites, German autocrats, is compounded when the full details of the chemical campaign's argument are taken into account. The ultimate foundation of their argument, as we have seen, was the production of Germany as an outlaw nation whose industries would soon give it the capacity to threaten American populations. They played on the public's willingness to invest new technology with extraordinary powers to overcome the fact that the Atlantic ocean meant such a threat was not credible, and on the wartime demonization of Germany by the Campaign for Public Information. They made their view appear necessary by excluding an alternative line of development from consideration: the idea that chemical disarmament could reinforce, and in turn be reinforced by, strong American support for German liberals and social democrats. And they hid the interests of the chemical corporations, chemical warfare officers, and chemical scientists and engineers that lay behind this portrayal of Germany. When these additional factors are taken into account, it becomes difficult see any sharp distinction between the chemical campaign's exercise of sovereign right to uphold the law and its opposite, Germany's alleged destruction of law. Nationally, the story of the Constitution's division of powers, which assures Americans that they need not be concerned about the takeover of power, is transformed into a myth which, by deflecting attention away from such a danger, makes it easier for the new power bloc represented by chemical industry to reinforce its wartime hold over the state. Internationally, the story that America went to war to defeat the German threat to international law and to democracy – which, as I will show in Part 2, was doubtful to begin with – is transformed into a myth which justifies the continued extension of American global power through the exercise of high-technology terror.

(iii) Parallels between the chemical weapon laboratories after the First World War and nuclear weapons laboratories after the Cold War

There are close parallels between the post First World War chemical and air campaigns and the post-Cold War campaign by America's nuclear weapons laboratories – Los Alamos and Sandia in New Mexico, and Lawrence Livermore in California. General Fries argued that America had the right to set aside international law and use poison gas as an instrument of terror to defeat "outlaw" nations. With the dropping of the atomic bomb President Truman asserted exactly this right (see Chapter 14). The years that followed saw a close symbiosis between the presidency and America's nuclear weapons laboratories. The laboratories legitimated the claim that America faced a Soviet nuclear threat which could only be met if Congress allowed the president wide scope to act in the interests of national security. In return the presidency ensured the laboratories obtained enormous resources to develop new kinds of nuclear weapons. In 1989 the sudden collapse of the Soviet Union left this power structure without the enemy figure it needed to justify itself. What we have seen as a result is an repetition of the presidency's (see Part 2) and the weapons laboratories' post-First World War production of new enemy figures to replace those they had lost. The first part of the story is told by Michael Klare in his *Rogue States and Nuclear Outlaws*.[22] He describes how the presidency on the one side, and the military on the other, made use of Iraq's invasion of Kuwait to convince Americans that they now faced a Third World so huge it required the continuation of America's Cold War military machine.

Here is how the trick was turned. First, all media attention was focused on Iraq. The presidency's and the military's own motivation was placed in the background. Second, Iraqi military power was presented as a growing threat by disconnecting it from its dependence on American and Soviet support. For a decade the US had viewed Iraq as an ally because of its opposition to Iran. It did not oppose Iraq's invasion of Iran, and when the war turned against Iraq gave it support. Credit was given to buy food and civilian technology with military uses, trucks, helicopters, and computers. Assurances were given to Egypt, Kuwait, Jordan, and Saudi Arabia, that if they sold their US weapons to Iraq they could replace them from American stockpiles. Iraq's development and use of chemical weapons and of ballistic missiles was systematically ignored. Third, the Iraqi threat was inflated. Then Secretary for Defence Richard Cheney spoke about Iraq as a "Third World country that presents us with a first rate military threat". In fact Washington knew Iraq had crippling weaknesses in intelligence, troops, pilots, air defence, naval forces, and command. To hide this, US generals talked up Iraqi strength. Fourth, the Pentagon played on technological fantasies about super-weapons. Taking advantage of public fears of the unknown, Iraq's chemical and biological weapons were equated with nuclear weapons. This was reinforced by the use of the term "weapons of mass destruction" which placed all three in the same category, despite the fact that nuclear weapons are both vastly more destructive and militarily more effective. This allowed Iraqi chemical and biological weapons to be falsely equated with America's nuclear weapons. Fifth, by focusing on the Iraqi dictator Saddam Hussein, Iraq was personified as evil incarnate. Playing up his biological, chemical, and nuclear weapon programmes allowed Iraq to be presented as nothing less than the Antichrist. In fact the US military knew Iraqi use of chemical and biological weapons would not redress the massive disparity in military power, and did not even bother planning for Iraqi use of nuclear weapons. When the war did occur it was a one-sided slaughter. Sixth, the decision to go to war was an act of labelling. By doing so the first Bush administration underlined the fact that Iraq was a nation so dangerous it had to be dealt with immediately by the massive use of force. Seventh, since then America and Britain have sought to fix this image in place. They have played up the danger of Iraq's biological, chemical, and nuclear weapons programmes uncovered by United Nations inspectors far beyond their real military value, and have repeated their original labelling of Iraq with continued air and missile attacks to underscore their claim that Iraq is a tremendous danger. Eighth, Iraq has been presented as exemplifying a larger class of Third World rogue states. So that even if Iraq on its own is not sufficient threat, it is seen as part of a far larger threat represented by the Third World as a whole.

These tactics have worked. In the latter decades of the Cold War there was no real Soviet threat to America. Indeed, it is questionable that there ever was such a threat. To maintain their dominance over allies and to deny aspirations for greater liberty and democracy among their own populations, it served both superpowers to pretend they really were locked in global confrontation.[23] Now this racket has been replaced by a new one. For a decade the presidency and the Pentagon have been able to present Americans with a Third World threat large enough to justify a high-technology military two thirds of the size of the one built up by Reagan's 1980s military expansion. There is no comparison between the destructive capacity of the Soviet nuclear arsenal and the arsenals possessed by Third World "rogue" states. The United States spends twenty-two times more on its military than its seven potential enemies – Cuba, Iran, Iraq, Libya, North Korea, Sudan, and Syria – combined. Yet, for a decade the new "pre-eminent threat" has deflected attention from America's own vast nuclear arsenal and enabled the Pentagon to persuade Americans to maintain military funding at close to Cold War levels.

The mainstream disarmament movement has also repeated the strategy adopted by its post-First World War predecessor. The leaders of the world's non-nuclear states internationally, and supporters of disarmament domestically, have demanded that America show that she is indeed the guardian of international law and absolutely different from "outlaw" states. To prove this they asked the United States to make good her commitment to nuclear disarmament as a signatory of the Nuclear Non Proliferation Treaty (NPT) by signing a Comprehensive Nuclear Test Ban Treaty (CTBT) in 1996. Taken together the NPT and the CTBT could, indeed, be significant steps towards nuclear disarmament. Uranium deposits are only located in some parts of the world, uranium mining is a very large-scale activity which cannot be hidden, and transforming uranium into the type of uranium needed to make an atomic bomb requires hard-to-develop technology. This means that if the will exists it is possible to make it very difficult for a non-nuclear state to acquire the kind of uranium or plutonium needed to build an atomic bomb. These technological facts have made a political deal possible, the Nuclear Non Proliferation Treaty, between the declared nuclear weapon states (Britain, France, America, Russia, and China) and the non-nuclear states. The NPT binds the former to take effective measures to negotiate an end to the nuclear arms race and carry out nuclear disarmament, and to allow the non-nuclear weapon states to acquire the technology needed to develop nuclear power. It binds the latter not to seek to acquire atomic weapons, and to allow an international organization, the International Atomic Energy Agency (IAEA), to monitor their nuclear power programmes to make sure they are not diverting uranium for nuclear power to bomb making. This flawed treaty gives the same body which is responsible for promoting the use of nuclear power the responsibility for checking that civilian nuclear facilities are not being used in bomb-making programmes. Nonetheless it provides a starting point for other treaties by articulating a basic deal which it is in everyone's interests to honour.

The technology of the atomic bomb itself means that a Comprehensive Nuclear Test Ban Treaty, which would ban the nuclear explosions needed to test atomic weapons, would be a major step towards nuclear disarmament. For an atomic bomb to work, explosives must compress uranium or plutonium into exactly the right shape in a very short time period. If this is done correctly a super-critical mass and a runaway nuclear chain reaction will be created resulting in an atomic explosion. If this procedure goes even slightly wrong the bomb will not explode. This means it is not enough to have a blueprint and a knowledge of physics to build a bomb. You also need hard-to-acquire craft skills.[24] To make an atomic bomb without this tacit knowledge is like trying to carry out heart surgery without previous experience using just a text book. The tacit knowledge needed to build an atomic bomb can only be acquired by either repeating the long trial and error process carried out by the original bomb builders, or by learning it from current bomb builders in the course of an apprenticeship. These skills decay unless they are kept up through repeated practice. This means that a CTBT would be a major step towards nuclear disarmament and to stopping the spread of nuclear weapons. It would be a step towards disarmament because it would bring to a stop the cycle in which the development of new kinds of nuclear weapons by one state is immediately countered by the development of further kinds by others. It would help stop the spread of nuclear weapons because, without testing, it would be impossible for scientists and engineers to know they had a working atomic bomb. It is possible to check that no nation is secretly testing atomic weapons by exploding them underground. This is because an atomic explosion, like an earthquake, sets up seismic shock waves which have a distinct signature and can be detected on the other side of the earth.

The Clinton administration's response to the threat to America's reliance on nuclear terror as the ultimate basis for coercive diplomacy posed by these treaties has been close to that of the Harding administration. The latter used its power to set the terms of the Washington Conference to tame the 1921 disarmament movement. It only invited the victorious powers. And it made it an arms control conference not a disarmament conference. The result was it became a way of consolidating the power of the victors of the First World War by preventing their being split by an arms race. In the same way the Clinton administration sought to convert the CTBT from being a step towards nuclear disarmament to being a means for maintaining America's nuclear advantage. As Secretary of State Madeleine Albright put it after the Senate refused to ratify the treaty:

> We simply do not need to test nuclear weapons to protect our security. On the other hand, would-be proliferators and modernizers must test if they are to develop the kind of advanced nuclear designs that are most threatening. Thus the CTBT would go far to lock in a technological status quo that is highly favourable to us.[25]

The administration may have done this because it wanted America to preserve its reliance on nuclear terror to get its way in international relations. Here it should be noted that if it had been able to combine new "usable" nuclear weapons with a working ballistic missile defence shield, America would have created precisely the absolute asymmetrical power relationship that lies at the heart of any strategy for exercising control through terror. On the other hand it is possible that it believed that this was the only way it could gain the support of the nuclear weapons laboratories it saw as essential to persuade the Senate to ratify the treaty. What happened, however, is clear enough. In return for the promise to support ratification by stating that they could maintain the "effectiveness" of America's nuclear weapons without testing, the administration provided the directors of the laboratories with a vast increase in funding and the super-computers and other technologies it deemed necessary to keep America's nuclear arsenal intact.

The heads of the nuclear weapons laboratories were not satisfied. Just as the chemical warfare officers did after the First World War, they believed new nuclear weapons would give America a way in which it could combine control with benevolence. This can be seen in statements in internal publications. These were intended to silence doubts among, and boost the enthusiasm of, scientists and engineers working on new weapons at a time when the Cold War enemy, the Soviet Union, no longer existed. Lawrence Livermore National Laboratory is famous for its role in the development of the hydrogen bomb. In the aftermath of the Second Gulf War, its Director, J.H. Nuckholls, boldly extrapolated from the use of patriot missiles to shoot down medium-range Iraqi missiles during the Gulf War to a space-based missile defence system which would provide the world's cities with security against nuclear attack:

> The Laboratory has made important contributions to the understanding of Third World nuclear weapons capabilities, most recently in Iraq . . . Desert Storm clearly emphasized the growing vulnerability of the world's population centers to attacks by Third World weapons of mass destruction. Recently the US Strategic Defense Initiative has been redirected toward the development of a limited defense system. The Laboratory's Brilliant Pebbles technology is the cornerstone of this initiative.

Brilliant Pebbles puts in space the same kind of smart, superaccurate technologies recently demonstrated so successfully in Desert Storm. Once in orbit, a constellation of Brilliant Eyes would encircle the earth creating "open skies". When activated, these orbiting missiles would intercept and destroy mid- and long-range ballistic missiles carrying weapons of mass destruction. A recent Brilliant Pebbles flight test was largely successful.[26]

Los Alamos National Laboratory is where the Hiroshima and Nagasaki atomic bombs were made. Its top nuclear scientist, Dr. Stephen Younger, argued in support of research to modernize America's nuclear arsenal in an address to laboratory scientists which combined the imagination of absolute power with pleasure in the punishment of transgressors:

> The W-76 warhead is the backbone of America's strategic deterrent. There are lots of these things out there. They are out there right now on submarines, submarines moving very quietly. We don't know where they are. The bad guys don't know where they are. Thirty minutes, however, and they can deliver this type of weapon to just about any target on earth. Okay? So the moral of that story is: don't mess with the United States. You think Texas is bad? Try a Trident submarine.[27]

These two passages show technology providing a license for the laboratories' scientists and engineers to dream dreams in which there is no contradiction between total control based on the ability to annihilate any place on earth, and the display of humanity and benevolence. In the dream the logically impossible is possible. Directly contradictory elements co-exist without difficulty: on the one hand, the combination of nuclear missiles, which can hit anywhere in the world, with a nuclear missile defence shield can be imagined to give America control over the globe by giving her the ability to threaten any country in the world without fear of retaliation. On the other, it can be imagined as enabling America to protect not only its own population but also the population of any other country.

The dream of control with benevolence and the depiction of new enemies has justified the laboratories' continued modernization of America's nuclear and non-nuclear arsenals after the end of the Cold War. A new nuclear weapon, the B61-11, has been developed whose low yield makes it more "usable" against Third World states without nuclear weapons, and further such nuclear weapons are in the pipeline.[28] Weapon systems such as the B-1 bomber and Trident submarine originally intended for fighting a nuclear war with the Soviet Union have been adapted for use against Third World targets. Targeting systems have been modernized and refocused to allow any place on earth to be hit by nuclear missiles at short notice. And nuclear war fighting doctrine has been updated. The role of nuclear weapons was first expanded from deterring the use of nuclear weapons to deterring the use of chemical and biological weapons. According to the February 1996 statement by the joint chiefs of staff, "Doctrine for Joint Theatre Nuclear Operations", Third World proliferation dangers are now the "pre-eminent threat", and nuclear weapons have the task of deterring short, medium, and intermediate range missiles capable of carrying nuclear, biological, or chemical warheads.[29] The role of nuclear weapons was yet further expanded in 2000, with Defence Secretary William Cohen describing the role of nuclear weapons as being "to deter any potential adversary from using or threatening to use nuclear, chemical or biological (NBC) weapons against the United States or its allies, and as a hedge against defeat of US conventional forces in defence of vital interests".[30] The modernization of the nuclear arsenal is complemented by the development of a nuclear missile defence shield[31] and of increasingly accurate, stealthy, and long-range conventional armaments.[32] The arms race is being extended into space with a priority being set on research and development of new space weapons such as the Military Space Plane and Space Based Lasers.[33]

Like the leaders of the chemical campaign the directors of America's nuclear weapons laboratories believe they have a sovereign right to manipulate the checks and balances established by the Constitution if they judged this is necessary to protect America. In 1993 after it was disclosed that the nuclear weapons laboratories were developing nuclear weapons specifically designed for use against rogue nations, Congress banned "research and development which could lead to the production by the United States of a new low-yield nuclear weapon, including a precision low-yield nuclear weapon". To evade the Congressional ban the laboratories decided not to submit the B61-11 to the Nuclear Weapons Council for approval. Immediately after the November 1994 Congressional elections had produced a new committee chairman more favourable to nuclear weapons, however, Assistant Secretary of Defence Frank Miller "reenergized" the project so that it could be completed "before Congress changed again".[34] The result was that by the end of 1996 the new nuclear weapon had entered service. The directors of the nuclear weapons laboratories have also turned party politics to their advantage. In October 1999 Republican senators led by Jesse Helms sought to embarrass the Clinton administration by forcing the ratification of the CTBT to a vote and defeating it. Almost certainly in the belief that they would be rewarded for their treachery by an incoming Republican administration, the directors of the nuclear weapons laboratories now reneged on the deal they had struck with the Clinton administration. They did so by giving expert testimony undermining the administration's claim that the Senate should support the treaty because they had given the laboratories the technology they needed to maintain America's nuclear weapons in working order, and by claiming that other countries would be able to erode America's nuclear advantage by testing their nuclear weapons without being detected.[35] The Republican senators were able to cover their refusal to ratify the treaty with the cloak of expert testimony. The result was the Clinton administration was unable to gain the two-thirds majority it needed to ratify the Treaty.

PART 2

5

Democratic Despotism

In Part 1, I took as my starting point the jarring feeling I experienced from the juxtaposition of a description of the horror of the first poison gas attack with the use of statistics to prove gas was a humane weapon. My hypothesis was that this jarring signalled an incommensurability between what is at stake in the development of poison gas and the languages of science, technology, capital, the nation, and humanism being used to discuss the issue. To show that this was the case, I investigated the way scientists, engineers, military officers, and businessmen who supported chemical and air weapons research, sought to exclude opponents from the public debate. They did this by redrawing the line between critics within a modernizing "we", whose arguments they sought to answer, and opponents outside the "we" who ought not to be listened to – either because "they" were good-willed but ignorant, or because "they" were seeking to destroy civilization itself. At the centre of their attempt to manipulate the political field was a terrorist threat: "Accept our rules for debate or we will silence you." The threat was conveyed by making examples. To convey the threat of what might happen to opponents if they do not accept the chemical campaign's rules of debate, its leaders made General March an example of a man who should not be listened to as he was ignorant and prejudiced, and made socialists and anarchists an example of a group that should not be listened to as it was purely destructive. Though less immediately lethal, these threats had the same structure as the army's message to its own troops "Do what we command or risk a court martial and the firing squad", and its message to the enemy "Do what we command or take your chance with high explosives, poison gas, liquid fire, and other horrors". By claiming that there was no other way to defend America against the threat posed by the alleged German "outlaw", the campaign justified the development of chemical weapons and bomber aircraft. The development of terror weapons which could be used to annihilate the populations of cities was legitimized by claiming they will either deter wars entirely, or make them so short that they will be more humane.

My horror in imagining soldiers choking to death from poison gas seemed a natural point from which to begin the investigation of violence and its repetition. The very naturalness of this starting point, however, needs to be called into question. Why does a certain "we" find this kind of violence the most important kind of violence to address? Might that "we" display a blindness to other forms of violence which serve its own interests? What lies behind, for example, William Irwin's final statement in The "Next War," An Appeal to Common Sense, that of the two great problems facing mankind, the democratization of industry and the achievement of international peace, the latter must have priority because the survival of civilization itself is threatened? To whom does this argument appear to be common sense? This question of whether the absolute priority on stopping war between great powers may do an injustice to other issues is posed with special force by a cartoon in the National Association for the Advancement of Colored Peoples (NAACP) journal, The Crisis, of March 1916.[1] Roughly drawn in pen and ink, it shows Uncle Sam standing horrified on a balcony as he lowers a telescope through which he has just been staring across the Atlantic at an image of the war god Mars. What Uncle Sam does not see, what he avoids seeing, is a huge, savage, muscular figure who strides across the right of the page. The giant's left hand is swinging a rope with a hangman's noose, while in his right is a burning torch. On his leg is written, "Lynch Law", and under his feet is "The South". Below the cartoon, the caption reads: "Uncle Sam Speaks: 'Barbarous UnChristian Europe!'" This question is posed no less strongly by a photograph of a black soldier in Belgian army uniform in The Crisis of December 1918, with the caption: "The Paradox: A Black 'Heathen' of the Congo, fighting to protect the wives and daughters of the white Belgians, who have murdered and robbed his people, against the 'Christian' Culture represented by the German trophy in his hand!"

The injustice of making war between great powers the priority finds expression in a short 1915 essay, "The African Roots of War", in the The Atlantic Monthly by the black activist and intellectual W.E.B. Du Bois. As the editor of The Crisis, Du Bois was one of the leaders of a nationwide campaign by the NAACP against all aspects of white oppression. The centre of this campaign was the reporting of weekly lynchings of black Americans, and an analysis of how the southern whites used lynching to maintain their power over the blacks through terrorizing them.[2] Within the pages of The Crisis, lynching is shown to be but one part of a system of oppression in which propaganda, political manipulation, and economic pressure, were

"Uncle Sam Speaks: 'Barbarous Unchristian Europe!'" Cartoon, *The Crisis*, March 1916, p. 236.

The author gratefully acknowledges the publisher of the magazine of the National Association for the Advancement of Colored People, for the use of this cartoon first published in the March 1916 issue of *The Crisis* magazine.

buttressed by the ultimate weapon of terror. As the title of the journal indicates, the coalition of black radicals and white liberals and socialists who had set up the NAACP after a horrifying lynching *demanded the federal government should recognize that the crisis faced by black Americans was a national crisis which demanded immediate action, and made ending it a priority second to none.* They thus immediately run into the problem that white America values white life more than black life. The NAACP is confronted by a dilemma about how to gain a hearing among white Americans: they can call into question white America's claim to be part of a "we" which forms the avant garde of civilization and their positioning of black Americans as part of the "they" which is not yet civilized; or they can argue that the federal government's protection of black Americans from lynching is the best way to advance other goals valued by white Americans. In the former case, white Americans who believe that they are part of the avant garde of humanity are likely to maintain their hegemony through a double silencing – by dismissing black radicals and their white comrades as part of the "they" which should not be listened to because it is not yet civilized, and, if they insist on being listened to by disrupting the normal working of society through protests, as a threat to the social order itself which must be silenced by force. If this silencing is successful the white claim to represent civilization is further entrenched. In the latter case, a hearing is gained for particular reforms at the cost of reinscribing the idea that white life, as part of the avant garde of humanity, is more valuable than black life – the very view that is used to justify white domination over blacks in the first place.

We can see this dilemma in Du Bois's attempt to gain support from America's peace societies. Following the outbreak of the First World War, Du Bois sought to convince the almost wholly white peace societies to act against lynching by persuading them that it was essential to do so if they were to bring an end to world war. Yet, when he sought to get the peace societies, at their meeting in St. Louis, to discuss whether race prejudice was a prime cause of war, he was immediately rebuffed by the secretary of the meeting, who was "unwilling to introduce controversial matters". In "The African Roots of War", Du Bois spelled out his argument. By starting off his essay with a Latin tag, "Semper novi quid ex Africa", he insists on his status as a Harvard scholar who has done postgraduate studies in Germany to write as a part of the avant garde of humanity reflecting on what civilization can learn from the violence of the European war to make itself more truly civilized. At the same time, he takes issue with progressives who would prevent white civilization from being called into question by presenting the war as due to pre-modern aristocratic elements in Europe that American democratic modernity will overcome.[3] Du Bois draws on the authority of an early writer, Alexis De Tocqueville, who saw the potential for American democracy to become a new kind of despotism, a democratic despotism.[4] Re-working liberal and socialist accounts of imperialism, Du Bois sketches out a theory of modern "democratic despotism" in which American,

British, French, and German democracy were part of a global system of race violence which was a primary cause of the world war. Far from spreading peace, the white extension of civilization was an exercise in dominating other peoples through terror. The war revealed the violence at the very core of white civilization. The extension of democracy in America and in Europe to include the working class was based on the exploitation of coloured people both at home and in the colonies. The anti-democratic nature of this exploitation was rationalized as natural through the doctrine of racial inferiority. Du Bois shows the conflict within the "we" of the new democratic nation. The centre of the new democratic nation was an alliance between capital and the aristocracy of labour, with the latter in a subordinate position. The accord between capital and labour was continually threatened as labour sought higher wages, improved working conditions, and a say in the governance of industry. Industrial peace was maintained by a combination of reward and threat. On the one hand, the domination and exploitation of the coloured world enabled capital to buy off the labour aristocracy. On the other hand, capital could damp down its demands by threatening to give its jobs to unskilled white labour or to coloured labour at home or in the colonies. These antagonisms meant that the unity of the democratic nation under the hegemony of capital was maintained by drawing the colour line. The result was a system in which antagonisms within the white "we" are continually displaced onto the "they". "The resultant jealousies and bitter hatreds tend continually to fester along the colour line."[5]

The demand to buy off the working class at home, and the working classes' own demand for a greater share of national wealth, led to the scramble for colonies abroad. At the same time, the Franco-Prussian war showed that direct military conflict between nations in Europe was too dangerous. This led to the displacement of military conflict between European powers to the colonies. Du Bois gives an impressive list of clashes between great powers in the colonial world: France and England at Fashoda, Italy and Turkey in Tripoli, England and Portugal at Delagoa Bay, England, Germany and the Dutch in South Africa, France and Spain in Morocco, Germany and France in Agadir, and the world at Algeciras. The result of all this was an unstable world system in which the violence displaced to the colonies finally returned to the North Atlantic with the world war: "The Balkans are convenient for occasions, but the ownership of materials and men in the darker world is the real prize that is setting the nations of Europe at each others throats to-day."[6] The scramble for colonies was driven by the desire for unlimited material wealth. To the European imagination, Africa represented a dream of abundance . . . gold and diamonds from South Africa, cocoa from Angola and Nigeria, rubber and ivory from the Congo and palm oil from the West Coast. In the twentieth century the prospect of rendering Africans docile and exploiting African labour presented the possibility of returns "exceeding the gold-haunted dreams of the most modern of Imperialists". Africa offered white men the dream that they could all be aristocrats, possessing wealth without working, able to enjoy the jealousy of their neighbours.

At the same time that Du Bois presented the economic and political relationships between the new democratic despotism and the coloured world, he showed how this relationship was the product of, and reinforced, a distorted white understanding of the relationship between itself and coloured people. The white world, he charged, was only able to endure the "Lying treaties, rivers of rum, murder, assassination, mutilation, rape and torture" which marked its progress by "stopping its ears and changing the subject of conversation while the devilry went on".[7] At the same time, the broad synthesizing vision which integrates all events into a story of progress serves to reassure "most philosophers" who see "the ship of state launched on the broad, irresistible tide of democracy", and to blunt the critical awareness of others who, "looking closer", ask: are we reverting to aristocracy and despotism? "They cry out and then rub their eyes, for surely they cannot fail to see strengthening democracy all about them?"[8] It is the failure to understand that capital has been able to extend democracy to workers while maintaining its dominant position within society only by shifting exploitation to coloured people that has led capitalists, socialists, imperialists, and philanthropists to believe they can work together:

> It is this paradox, which has confounded philanthropists, curiously betrayed the Socialists, and reconciled the Imperialists and captains of industry to any amount of "Democracy". It is this paradox which allows in America the most rapid advance of democracy to go hand in hand in its very centres with increased aristocracy and hatred towards darker races, and which excuses and defends an inhumanity that does not shrink from the public burning of human beings.[9]

Du Bois goes on to show how the domination and exploitation of one race by another distorts all aspects of our thinking, language, feelings, and relationships.

Theoretically, it leads to an account of history which excludes the coloured world's role in the creation and transformation of European civilization

The role that African agriculture, technology, and civilization had in the birth of European civilization is passed over; the role of Africa in the transformation of Europe by Christianity, Islam, and the slave trade is marginalized; and the role that European racism and colonial competition had as a prime cause of the world war is not taken into account.

Linguistically, the term 'democracy' is limited to Europeans and made compatible with despotism

The term 'peace' is restricted to mean peace between North Atlantic democracies, while violence against coloured people is excluded from discussion. The result is that the achievement of peace in Europe will merely mean the continuation of violence against coloured people. "The utmost European Concord will mean satisfaction with, or acquiescence in, a given division of the spoils of world-dominion. After all, European disarmament cannot go below the necessity of defending the aggressions of the whites against the blacks and browns and yellows."[10]

Affectively, human feeling is made compatible with inhumanity
"How can love of humanity appeal as a motive to nations whose love of luxury is built on the inhuman exploitation of human beings, and who, especially in recent years, have been taught to regard these human beings as inhuman?" While white people come to relate to coloured people primarily in terms of the perceived need for pre-emptive attack: "all over the world there leaps to articulate speech and ready action that singular assumption that if white men do not throttle coloured men, then China, India, and Africa will do to Europe what Europe has done and seeks to do to them."[11]

Du Bois's essay displaces America from her position as world educator. Instead, America now appears as one member of a system of North Atlantic democracies in which international and class peace is secured by displacing armed conflict to Africa, Asia, and South America and by the displacement of class domination and exploitation onto coloured people within these nations and in their colonies. The world war represents the return of this displaced violence. White America is part of a world system whose dynamics it has a vested interest in not understanding and which it does not control. Equally, the mind of the white American liberal is displaced from its central position. Its claims to be without prejudice and autonomous are shown to be false. Instead, we see that it systematically fails to understand its own motives; its understanding of its own history is distorted, its language is corrupt. Its claim to be the educator of mankind rests on misunderstanding its place in a system of violence, exploitation, and domination. This leads Du Bois, writing on behalf of the redemption of white liberalism, to re-interpret the significance and implications of America's commitment to democracy and peace:

> We, then, who want peace, must remove the real causes of war. We have extended gradually our conception of democracy beyond our social class to all social classes in our nation; we have gone further and extended our democratic ideals not simply to all social classes of our own nation, but to those of other nations of our blood and lineage – to what we call "European" civilization. If we want real peace and lasting culture, however, we must go further. We must extend the democratic ideal to the yellow, brown, and black peoples.[12]

The dynamic aspect of world history means that unless democracy is extended, there will be a return of world war. Any settlement between nations which merely redistributes spheres of influence will eventually lead to new jealousies. Equally,

such a settlement will not avoid the problem of revolt as the expense of armaments necessitates the limitation of industrial democracy. Finally, the injustices
this system perpetuates must eventually lead to war between the white and
coloured worlds.

Whereas in *The Atlantic* Du Bois addressed educated white Americans as a
whole, in *The Crisis* he addressed a small white readership and a large black readership which were both already outraged by race lynching. Addressing this
mixed audience, Du Bois argued that the war showed that black Americans
were right to see themselves as just as civilized, and hence their lives just as valuable, as white Americans. His September 1916 editorial "The Battle of Europe"
is a case in point.[13] He uses the horrors of the war, "attacks by gas, of raids on
non-fortified towns, of Zeppelins dropping bombs on women and children", to
argue that European civilization, in which he includes white America, can no
longer claim to speak for civilization as such. It can no longer be *the* measure by
which white Americans judge black Americans and find them wanting. At the
same time, he places the war within an optimistic story of human progress: "it
takes no prophet to presage the advent of many things – notably the greater
emancipation of European women, the downfall of monarchies, the gradual but
certain dissolution of caste and the advance of a true Socialism". Addressing
African-Americans, he argues that the war is "a gradual and subtle encouragement to strengthen race predilections and revel in them unashamed". This
opened up the need for "the reassembling of old ideals". Europe can no longer
presume to set the standard for beauty, instead we must appreciate "rich, brown
and black men and women with glowing dark eyes and crinkling hair". Equally,
"the plantation song is more in unison with the 'harmony of the spheres' than
Wagner's greatest triumph". It was a moment for the revaluation and the cele-
bration of African culture: "Life, which in this cold Occident stretched in bleak,
conventional lines before us, takes on a warm, golden hue that harks back to the
heritage of Africa and the tropics." Yet Du Bois did not see the issue as an
either/or choice between European and African civilization; what was called for
was the "reassembling of old ideals" in a higher synthesis. Accepting the standard dichotomy between the active, time-conscious West and the passive,
timeless East, he argued: "Brothers, the war has shown us the cruelty of the civilization of the West. History has taught us the futility of the civilization of the
East. Let ours be the civilization of no <u>man</u>, but of <u>all men</u>. This is the truth that
sets us free."[14]

Du Bois's analysis of the origins of the First World War finds confirmation in
William McNeill's classic work *The Pursuit of Power*. Throughout the nineteenth
century, McNeill writes, Europe "launched itself on a self-reinforcing cycle in
which its military organization sustained, and was sustained by, economic and
political expansion at the expense of other peoples and polities of the earth".[15] It

was this tremendous accumulation of the means of violence, and the reinforcement of an aggressive personality habituated to its use, that ultimately came back
to tear Europe apart in the First World War. Du Bois's challenges us to open up a
debate over race, war, terror, and democracy, in which both ends *and* means are at
stake. At the level of ends, he force us to call into question the assumption that the
goal of putting an end to war between states should have priority over ending race
terror. At the level of means, he leads us to ask whether or not there might be systematic connections between war between great powers, the domination of the
white race over all others, and the role of democratic despotism in both. Du Bois
was quite clear about the status of his own argument as a sketch intended to
open up the question: "The theory of this new democratic despotism," he wrote,
"has not been clearly formulated."

My analysis in Part 2 is intended to help us feel the full force of that challenge
today. It does not itself amount to a theory of democratic despotism, but is
preparatory work towards one. My starting point is the potential of the democratic imagination.[16] This is beautifully expressed by Herman Melville in *Moby
Dick*: "But this august dignity I treat of, is not the dignity of kings and robes, but
that abounding dignity which has no robed investiture. Thou shalt see it shining
in the arm that wields a pick or drives a spike; that democratic dignity which, on
all hands, radiates without end from God; Himself! The great God absolute! The
centre and circumference of all democracy! His omnipresence, our divine equality!"[17] Here it is equality which is presented as the ultimate order of the world.
Initially in the French and American revolutions the idea of equal citizenship is
restricted to white, male, propertied men. Yet, it is immediately taken up by other
groups. They ask: why should we not enjoy equality to since no politically significant differences exist between us and them? Thus Mary Wollstonecraft follows
A Vindication of the Rights of Men with her classic work, *A Vindication of the Rights
of Women*, and the French Revolution leads to "Black Jacobins" using the ideas of
Liberty, Equality, and Fraternity to inspire slave revolts in the Caribbean. Within
America the demand that black Americans have the vote is taken up by black
Americans both as a way of insisting that their life is of equal value to that of a
white man, and as a way of defending themselves against race terror:

> With no sacredness of the ballot there can be no sacredness of human life itself. For
> if the strong can take the weak man's ballot, when it suits his purpose to do so, he
> will take his life also . . . The more complete the disenfranchisement, the more fre-
> quent and horrible have been the hangings, shootings, and burnings.[18]

I am interested in how leading members of the Protestant establishment sought
to tame the threat posed by the democratic imaginary to their right to rule. To do
so I show how they sought to use the Spanish-American and Philippines-American
Wars, and then the First World War, to transform America into an "imperial

democracy". In doing so they sought to prevent groups such as women, workers, or African-Americans using democracy to call into question the right of the establishment to rule America. I argue that they offered Americans a diabolical exchange: in return for giving up the struggle to extend democracy within the United States Americans were offered an intoxicating spectacle in which they would be presented as heroes in a struggle to extend civilization to all the world's peoples. Instead of Americans empowering themselves in a struggle for democracy against Jim Crow laws or in the factory, they would have the glory of sweating, fighting, and dying to extend democracy to the Filipinos by conquering them.

6

The Striking and Stupendous Spectacle

During the First World War America was riven by intense debate over the meaning of democracy. At its heart was a strategy by part of the elite, whom I call the "patrician reformers", to remake America as an imperial democracy. This was crafted by Henry Cabot Lodge, Theodore Roosevelt, and their circle in the 1880s and 1890s.[1] Their programme was a reaction against the transformation of America's Protestant establishment – which they had been born into – after the Civil War.[2] Previously, the families that made up the establishment had legitimized their claim to be a meritocracy, or in Jefferson's terms a natural aristocracy, through their political leadership of America and their openness to rising members of other ethnic and religious groups. Thus Jewish Americans of German origin, of the right sort, were allowed to become members of their clubs and assimilated through marriage. Now, faced with millions of new immigrants from Europe, the establishment began to seal itself off. It embraced theories of Anglo-Saxon race superiority, drawing a sharp line between itself and other ethnic and religious groups by establishing numerous genealogical societies, such as the Daughters of the American Revolution, through which it could trace its descent. And it began to close off a set of spaces, the summer resort, the country club, the metropolitan club, the suburb, the boarding school, and the college fraternity, so that upper-class Protestant Anglo-Saxons, and more importantly their sons and daughters, could be sure that they would only meet other upper-class Protestant Anglo-Saxons.

Lodge and Roosevelt believed that the failure of America's Protestant establishment to lead the nation, and to integrate the leaders of rising groups into their ranks, came at the worst possible time. They painted a picture of a nation on the edge of the abyss. America was dividing along ethnic and religious lines. In the past, the difficulties and dangers of extending the frontier in the face of hostile Indians and a savage wilderness had led members of different ethnicities, religions, and classes to see themselves as citizens engaged in the common task of creating an American nation. The shared dangers had taught the virtues of self-reliance, respect for authority, belief in the rule of law, self-discipline, organization, and cooperation. Now the frontier was closed. Industrialization was drawing millions of poor Europeans to America. Whereas previous waves of immigrants had dispersed across the continent and soon been assimilated, these were not. Instead, they lived among their own kind in America's rapidly expanding cities and identified more with their countries of origin than with the new land they had found themselves in. They had no chance to learn the American story. In some cases they did not even speak English. At the same time, the retreat of the Anglo-Saxon Protestant elite from its task as a meritocracy had left the way open for America's wealthy to devote their lives to material pleasures on the one side and to the super-exploitation of workers in the search for profits on the other. The resentment this produced among workers made them easy prey for agitators: socialists and anarchists who, Roosevelt claimed, argued that the workers ought to pursue their own class interests as the new rich were clearly pursuing theirs. Meanwhile, the rise of the Populists marked the emergence of a radical consciousness among American farmers. The Populists argued that the state served the interests of East Coast financiers and businessmen in hard money and that these same groups exploited their control of the market for agricultural products and the farmers' need for credit. And there was always the terrifying possibility that the Civil War divide between North and South might re-emerge.

The salvation of America, Roosevelt and Lodge believed, lay in the creation of a new frontier. Externally, America had to join European nations in the task of extending civilization to the non-white world. Internally, the slums of America's cities and the immigrant and working-class populations had to be tamed. In colonizing these new frontiers a new generation of America's Protestant Anglo-Saxon establishment would rediscover their historic role as leaders of the nation, repudiating the attractions of being a closed caste and opening up their ranks to the leaders of other ethnic and religious groups who demonstrated their commitment to the nation. The task of extending civilization was no less vital to the education of the "masses". It would teach them the value of the elite's leadership and they would learn the value of self-discipline and organization. In seeing the entire nation engaged in such a vast task, Americans would be impressed by their own collective power. They would come to see themselves, as they had done in the Civil War, the Indian Wars, and in the colonization of new land, as a community of heroes engaged in a struggle upon which the future of humanity depended.

Roosevelt and Lodge sought ways to counter the Protestant establishment's tendency to become a caste. They wrote histories for both children and adults which told how America had been created by many races led by an open meritocratic elite. "It is," Roosevelt said, "a good thing for all America and it is an especially good thing for young Americans . . . to keep in mind the feats of daring and personal prowess done in the past . . . [for] no people can be really great unless they possess . . . the heroic virtues."[3] His multi-volume national epic, *The Winning of the West*, described the colonization of America as the latest step in the onward sweep of the North European Teutonic peoples who had defeated the Roman Empire. Note that at this point Roosevelt, as Woodrow Wilson also did in this period, emphasizes Americans' kinship with the Germans. The heroic exploits of the Western pioneers outdid those of all other European colonists. In fighting the Indians, Roosevelt underscored, they faced "the most formidable savage foes ever encountered by colonists of European stock . . . far more to be dreaded than the Zulus or even the Maoris".[4] Roosevelt and Lodge sought to establish new places where the division of the nation could be overcome. Roosevelt depicted his Dakota cattle ranch, the scout movement's wilderness camps, the football field, and the battlefield as utopian places where the sons of the Protestant establishment could rediscover their historic role, and where Americans could learn to accept their authority. The idea of the battlefield as the place of moral redemption gripped Roosevelt's imagination. As the 1893 depression intensified, Roosevelt came to see war with Spain as vital to the redemption of the nation. On the battlefield vice would be blown away "like chaff" and war would give America "something to think about which isn't material gain". Saddened by the flawed image of Civil War hero Ulysses Grant, he sought a new war which would create new *American* heroes comparable with European figures like Napoleon. America needed war with Spain simply because "the memory of every triumph won by Americans . . . helps to make each American nobler and better".[5]

When America did indeed declare war on Spain in April 1893, the chance came to put theory into practice. Roosevelt resigned his post as assistant secretary of the navy and formed his own regiment, the Rough Riders. This was intended from the start to become a national myth. Roosevelt sought to show Western "plainsmen" and Eastern "swells" fighting together for a national victory. To that end, he and the regiment's initial commander, Colonel Leonard Wood, scattered the 10 per cent of East Coast volunteers amongst the 90 per cent of Western volunteers. The regiment was an idealization of what America was and could be. It showed the sons of New York bankers, East Coast industrialists, and agrarian debtors volunteering to live and fight together to defeat America's enemy. Roosevelt, an Eastern blue-blood, emphasized that his "dearest comrade" and "best subordinate" officer was "Bucky" O'Neil, twice Populist candidate for Congress. One New York sergeant was a leading Gold Democrat, while another from Colorado was a well-known Socialist. In taking the regiment into battle, Roosevelt played the part of an American hero voluntarily risking everything to ensure the liberation of Cuba from Spanish oppression. This went so far as to lead him to disregard how objectives could be obtained with minimal losses. In attacking Spanish positions he "spent blood like water", flinging troops "straight against entrenchements" where they remained "hour after hour, dropping under fire". For Roosevelt, the reckless disregard for his own safety helped redeem his own sense of self-worth. After battle, he wrote, he could now die satisfied that he had left "a name" to his children "which will serve as an apology for my having existed".[6]

For the editors of newspapers concerned to head off anarchist, socialist, and populist claims that democracy entailed taking back the government of America from big business and other interests, Roosevelt's Rough Riders provided a counter-image of an ideal democratic community. It was "the most representative body of men on American soil", in which "cowboys and millionaires" lived and fought together as "equals". It was "democracy . . . the highest and the lowest, the rich and the poor, the young and the old, ready to fight side by side" and "mingle their blood on the Cuban trail". After the war Roosevelt the historian promoted the story of the Rough Riders as the ideal democratic community created by Roosevelt the soldier. He articulated the story that in dying while risking their lives for the nation's ideals the soldiers who had lost their lives had redeemed the nation. Their deaths proved that the nation was not simply an aggregate of self-interested groups. It provided living Americans with a model to guide them. They achieved immortality as national heroes:

> There could be no more honorable burial than that of these men in a common grave – Indian and cowboy, miner and packer, and college athlete – the man of unknown ancestry from the lonely Western plains and the man who carried on his watch the crests of the Stuyvesants and the Fishes, one in the way they had met their deaths, just as during life they had been one in their daring and their loyalty.[7]

Lodge and Roosevelt used the Spanish-American War to give Americans the new frontier they believed was essential now the Western frontier had closed. On 24 April 1898 Roosevelt, then still assistant secretary of the navy, sent a telegram to Commodore Dewey to proceed to Manila and "commence operations against the Spanish squadron". Arriving in Manila Bay on 1 May, Dewey won an immediate victory over the Spanish fleet. The move came at a point when Filipino nationalists, led by Emilio Aguinaldo, had already been in rebellion against Spanish rule of the Islands for a number of years. To take advantage of this, Dewey now transported Aguinaldo, in exile in Hong Kong, back to Manila to lead Filipino nationalists against the Spanish. Filipino and American forces quickly encircled the Spanish in Manila, but Dewey secured the surrender of the Spanish to American forces alone. Fearing betrayal by the United States, the Filipino nationalists quickly moved to proclaim Filipino Independence on 12 June and set up a government on

23 June. When McKinley persuaded Spain to hand over the Philippines to America in the Paris Treaty, American forces found themselves fighting to suppress a full-scale national liberation struggle.

This now became Roosevelt's war. His status as a national hero following the success of the Rough Riders led McKinley to choose him as a running mate when he sought re-election in 1900, making Roosevelt president when McKinley was assassinated in September 1901. To fight the war he turned to his friend, New York corporate lawyer Elihu Root, who had been made Secretary of War by McKinley the previous year. McKinley had underestimated the difficulty of taking the Philippines from the "little brown people". At first the Filipinos fought a conventional war, suffering over 3000 casualties in just the first two weeks. Then in November 1899 Aguinaldo ordered the Filipino army to conduct a guerrilla war. Realizing they could not defeat the United States militarily, their aim was to make retaining the Philippines too costly. Surprised by the success of the guerrilla campaign, America increased its army to 70,000 men and pursued a strategy of territorial occupation. As the war escalated American forces sought to isolate the guerrillas from the general population. The property of suspected sympathizers was confiscated; barrios supporting the guerrillas were burnt; and officers used torture to extract intelligence from captured guerrillas. In the final stage of the war civilians were moved into concentration centres; crops were burnt and cattle killed to deprive guerrillas of supplies; and a policy of executing prisoners of war when American troops were killed in guerrilla ambushes was applied. In his classic essay "Expansion and Peace" Roosevelt justified the war as essential for peace: "Every expansion of civilization makes for peace . . . The rule of law and order has succeeded to the rule of barbarous and bloody violence. Until the great civilized nations stepped in there was no chance for anything but such bloody violence."[8] Relations among the civilized nations, he continued, are becoming more peaceful. "A very marked feature in the world-history of the present century has been the growing infrequency of wars between great civilized nations. The Peace Conference at the Hague is but one of the signs of this growth."[9] By the time Roosevelt declared the end of war on 4 July 1902, some 126,500 Americans had seen active service in the Philippines, 4200 were killed, and 2800 were wounded, while 16,000 to 20,000 Filipino insurgents had been killed, and perhaps 200,000 Filipino civilians had died of famine, disease, and other calamities. Roosevelt, Lodge, and Root defended the war as necessary and righteous. The Filipino people were not yet capable of self-government. They were not a nation but a diverse collection of different groups; while the rebels represented only the Tagalog tribe. A long period of American rule was necessary to give them self-discipline, respect for authority, and other qualities necessary for democratic self-government.

(i) The extension of a network of power over life both more extensive and more penetrating than that created by the Roman republic/empire

Modern liberal democracy first legitimates itself by presenting the absolutist state as a monstrosity in which no one's life is safe and all are slaves.[10] It then justifies itself as acting in the name of humanity against the absolute state. The ambiguity of modern liberal democracy, already identified by Alexis De Tocqueville in his *Democracy in America*, is that under the cover of a claimed complete break with absolutism it can lead to the exercise of sovereign power over life extending itself far further than it could under absolutism.[11] This is because liberal democracy leaves the structure of sovereignty essentially untouched. By banishing a person, the sovereign designates them as an "outlaw" who can be killed without the action being legally a homicide.[12] They are stripped of their legal and customary rights. This reduces them to no more than a living human being who has no duties to the community and which it has no obligations towards. Through the act of banishment, or the declaration of a state of emergency, the sovereign creates a "community" of persons who, as far as the state is concerned, have no relationship to each other except the fact that they are all subject to its unlimited power. The citizens of liberal democracy are none other than this "community" of persons who, from the point of view of the state, are without relation apart from the fact of all being living human beings subject to its power. The difference between absolutism and liberal democracy is the declaration that, from now on, state power will be exercised so as to transform these persons into citizens. This leads to an ambiguous situation. On the one hand the assertion that the simple fact of being born gives rights can empower citizens to contest the exercise of state power on behalf of special interests. Rights to freedom of speech, assembly, the press, and so forth, help to enable the formation of a political society capable of identifying and resisting particular interests manipulating the levers of power under the guise of acting in the general interest. Where particular interests have discovered new ways of doing this which render existing political rights ineffective, these rights need to be supplemented by new rights which enable citizens to perform this vital task. Moreover, the idea that all human beings are equal can lead to demands to extend such right to excluded groups (women, workers, colonized peoples) and to excluded places (the factory, the laboratory, and the colonized world). On the other hand, under the cover of enabling life to realize its potential the self-proclaimed avant garde of humanity can extend the state's power over life far further than absolutism did. The vagueness of what it would be to achieve mankind's realization of its sovereignty allows for power to be extended further and further. At the same time, the avant garde gains control of the power of modern bureaucracy, its members are able to create a network of power far more extensive than under absolutism and, with the help of scientific knowledge, can bring all aspects of life under their control.

The creation of such a network lay at the heart of the patrician reformers' strategy. This can be seen in a 1907 talk by Elihu Root to Yale students.[13] Root presents the elite as having a sovereign right to intervene in every human activity by producing a picture in which life is threatened with multiple catastrophes that only they can avert. Root seduces his audience by speaking to them as if they already were part of the global avant garde of humanity. His talk then gives them a series of instructions on how to extend their rule over every aspect of life.

First, the elite have to explain to Americans that government is needed over every aspect of life. Government is an essential part of "every act" because human life itself depends upon it. If it fails "ruin comes to all" while good government means that success comes according to "capacity and courage". The need to enhance life also justifies the great civilizing nations in governing other peoples. "The fairest and most fertile parts of the earth have been for centuries wilderness and desert because of bad government . . . While under good government industry and comfort flourish on the most sterile soil and under the most rigorous climate."[14]

Second, the elite should show Americans the absolute necessity for government in every aspect of life by demonstrating that modern progress has completely transformed the conditions under which they now live. This can be done by pointing to the situation of modern city dwellers. They are now part of a complex, interdependent whole in which their very life is vulnerable to disasters beyond their control. "Under these circumstances of complete interdependence the individual is entirely helpless."[15]

Third, the complete dependence of every aspect of modern life on government should be demonstrated using vivid examples. The typical city family can be used to show Americans have "no control at all over the things that are absolutely necessary for daily life". The coal they depend upon for heating and cooking may be interrupted at any moment by a strike in a distant coal mine, a strike in a lighting plant instantly cuts off their electric light, and a railway dispute may cut off their most necessary supplies. They are equally vulnerable to disease. "The milk may be full of tuberculosis and the water full of typhoid germs unless some one has tested the cattle and some one enforced sanitary ordinances upon distant farms."[16]

Fourth, the elite's interventions can be justified by describing them as measures which will enable Americans to govern themselves. The Yale students are to persuade Americans to accept the measures they advocate as necessary to enhance life and to avoid disaster. Through doing so the elite will get Americans to participate

in the forms of organization they advocate and to monitor their own performance. This way of governing can be justified in terms of America's democratic
tradition. Here Root offers the students a convenient definition of democracy.
"Popular government is organized self-control – organized capacity for the development of the race."[17]

Fifth, they can deal with anyone who poses a serious challenge to their claim to be
doing no more than enabling the people to govern themselves by turning the wrath
of the community against them. This can be done by emphasizing that such groups
represent the tyranny of the mob, and that this is "the most frightful form of oppression mankind has yet known". Their actions should be identified with past cases of
revolutionary violence. Root provides the students with a convenient list: "Jack
Cade and Wat Tyler rebellions, peasant insurrections, the Red Terror of the French
Revolution, the excesses of the Commune of Paris, the reign of assassination in
Russia, the Jacquerie of Roumania, the perpetual revolutions of South America."[18]

Sixth, to capture the popular imagination Americans should be encouraged to
compare their achievements with ancient Rome. For contemporary Americans
Rome provides an ideal model because it was both a republic *and* an empire.
Root emphasizes that it was the Romans' devotion to their country and the state
that enabled them to develop successful republican self-government and to triumph over the Greeks.[19] Comparing America with Rome will spur a spirit of
emulation and rivalry. Americans can see their greatness when they see how far
their achievements have surpassed those of Rome. They can see that America's
experiment in popular government has "produced an effect upon the constitution
of government throughout the civilized world by the side of which the Roman
dominion sinks to an inferior place as a permanent force". America's strength as
a nation depends upon her citizens' willingness to copy military peoples' willingness to sacrifice themselves for the good of the nation.[20] "Intense devotion to the
State is one of the great elements of strength in the Japanese nation now; it was
one of the chief elements of Roman power."[21]

Root told his audience that the fate of civilization now rested in their hands. The
rise and fall of earlier civilizations suggested that mankind might be trapped in a
cycle. If modern civilization was to escape it would be because America, with the
other great civilizing nations, had found a way of enrolling all the people in government. To ensure that civilization triumphed it was now up to them to extend
government into all aspects of American society:

> Former civilizations were but islands surrounded by vast regions where savagery ruled;
> and they were but civilizations at the top, underlaid by the ignorance and prejudice of

the multitude who had no interest in preserving what such civilization had gained . . .
The hope of the permanence of modern civilization is that it is being built up from the
bottom through the participation of the whole people in that universal, combined
action for the common good which we call popular government.[22]

Root's talk underscores that the patrician reformers saw their exercise of power on
behalf of life as a project they *shared* with their British, German, and French counterparts, that they saw themselves as engaged in a friendly rivalry with, and
emulation of, the current leaders of European imperialism and the past leaders of
Roman imperialism, and that they sought to persuade all Americans to see themselves in the same way. It shows that the patrician reformers, with the European
counterparts, saw themselves as extending a network of power that would, and
ought to, far surpass that created by imperial Rome in both its penetration of
every aspect of the life of society and in its worldwide extent.

(ii) Relaying British imperialism – Toad's motor and Badger's cudgel

For a clear picture of the world Roosevelt sought to build and America's place in
it, I turn to a surprising source, the immortal children's story, *The Wind in the
Willows*, written by his friend Kenneth Grahame. The story starts with two animals, Mole and Ratty, who live on a river and enjoy a life of boating and picnics.
They go to visit Ratty's friend Toad, who lives in a large mansion, Toad Hall.
When they arrive, they find that Toad has abandoned his last enthusiasm, rowing
boats, and is gripped by a new one for caravans. Nothing will content him except
that they all leave at once for a caravan holiday. Catastrophe follows. Frightened by
a motor car, the carthorse bolts, the caravan overturns, and Toad is left gazing into
the distance after his new love.

Mole encounters the other main protagonist in the story, Badger, when he
explores the Wild Wood on a winter's day. As he penetrates deeper in the wood,
he realizes he is lost and as it grows dark he notices what he perceives to be hostile faces looking at him. "Then the faces began. It was over his shoulder, and
indistinctly, that he first thought he saw a face: a little evil wedge-shaped face, looking at him from a hole."[23] These are the faces of the weasels and stoats who live
in the Wild Wood. The Mole hears the patter of feet approaching and a terrifying
whistling. Believing that he is being hunted, he runs blindly through the woods
before hiding in an old tree stump. He is rescued by Ratty, armed with pistols and
a cudgel. By now it is night and the two animals find themselves in the middle of
a blizzard which obscures all paths. Fortunately, they discover the entrance to
Badger's house and are given supper and beds for the night. In the morning
Badger shows Mole his home and the two animals talk about the security, peace,

and tranquillity of being in an underground fortress even right in the middle of the Wild Wood.

As Toad acquires and crashes a series of ever more powerful and expensive cars it is clear he is headed for disaster. Badger now persuades Mole and Ratty that the three of them have to take Toad in hand. Until Toad sees sense, Ratty, Mole, and Badger take him prisoner in his own house. Toad, however, escapes through a window, steals a motor car, is caught, gives cheek to the police, is put on trial, and is sentenced to twenty years in prison. Through the kind heart of the warder's daughter he is able to escape, and after various adventures involving trains, a washer woman, gypsies, the stealing of another car, a chase by police, and a near drowning, he makes his way back to the river. He is told that the stoats, weasels, and ferrets have taken over Toad Hall. On trying to enter, he is shot at by the stoat guards. While the weasels are celebrating their takeover with a great banquet, Badger, Ratty, Mole, and Toad arm themselves with cudgels and pistols and set off down a secret passage to the heart of Toad Hall. The four animals now burst into the great hall, cudgels flying and pistols firing. The weasels are caught unprepared and Kenneth Grahame describes their panic in loving detail. It is a sadistic fantasy:

> My! What a squealing and a screeching filled the air! Well might the terrified weasels dive under the tables and spring madly up at the windows! Well might the ferrets rush wildly for the fireplace and get hopelessly jammed in the chimney! Well might tables and chairs be upset, and glass and china be sent crashing on the floor, in the panic of that terrible moment when the four Heroes strode wrathfully into the room! The mighty Badger, his whiskers bristling, his great cudgel whistling through the air ... There were but four in all, but to the panic-stricken weasels the hall seemed full of monstrous animals, grey, black, brown, and yellow, whooping and flourishing enormous cudgels; and they broke and fled with squeals of terror and dismay ... anywhere to get out of reach of those terrible sticks.[24]

The book ends with a dream of how the weasels, stoats, and ferrets come to accept the overlordship of the four animals, and to point to Ratty, Toad, and Mole as heroes for their children to emulate, before going on to tell how the inhabitants of the Wild Wood themselves relay the terror they had experienced to their infants so as to get them to accept adult authority. "But when their infants were fractious and quite beyond control, they would quiet them by telling how, if they didn't hush them and not fret them, the terrible grey Badger would up and get them."[25]

The story contains all the elements of the patrician reformer's programme, and it is not surprising that Roosevelt claimed to have read it no less than twelve times. It also shows us Grahame, whose employment at the Bank of England placed him at the very centre of late nineteenth-century British imperialism, handing over a British imperialist view of the globe to Roosevelt, the architect of the coming American imperialism, who helped him to spread these ideas in America by finding him a publisher. Toad represents that part of the establishment whose virtue has been corrupted by inherited wealth and the lure of consumerism. His reckless pursuit of material pleasure regardless of the consequences of his actions, symbolized by his out-of-control driving, threatens the very existence of the community. By failing to play his proper role as a patrician who shows a benevolent concern for the whole community, the way is opened for the stoats and the weasels to rise up and take control over Toad Hall. Harmonious social relations within the animal community, however, can be restored through war. Emulating the heroic model provided by Mole, Ratty, and Badger, Toad comes to risk his life in the battle to retake Toad Hall. He shows that, deep down, he remains a virtuous animal who is prepared to put the good of the community before material pleasure. His action restores the legitimacy of the hierarchical order and his inherited wealth.

The story shows the connection between the patrician reformer's strategy for remaking democracy, sovereign right, and the frontier. At the centre of the story are three kinds of justice. There is the justice of the courts. When Toad steals a motor car he is tried before a civil court and convicted according to the law. Then there is the higher justice of the heart. Identifying with Toad as a loveable rogue clearly in the grip of an obsession we ourselves know, we give our support to the warder's daughter who helps him to escape. Finally, there is the justice of the frontier. This is represented by Badger who lives in the middle of the Wild Wood, threatened at every moment by the stoats, weasels, and ferrets. In this frontier situation, Badger relies on the superior force of his cudgel to maintain an armed peace. When the stoats, weasels, and ferrets take over Toad Hall, Badger acts as the sovereign who has the right to decide when a state of emergency exists which requires the suspension of the law and the exercise of direct power. He decides that the very existence of the community is threatened and leads Ratty, Mole, and Toad on an armed expedition to retake Toad Hall. The Wild Wooders' attempt to shoot Toad shows that it is they who have first put the rule of law in danger and are to be blamed for the violence that follows. Note that unlike Toad's crimes, the stoats, weasels, and ferrets' takeover of Toad Hall is given little context. And that unlike the heroes, the stoats, weasels, and ferrets are neither given individual names nor qualities we can identify with. Their overwhelming numbers and the fact that as weasels, stoats, and ferrets their nature is such that they are not to be trusted, mean that the four animals clearly have no other recourse but violence. Catching the weasels and ferrets when their guard is down, their attack overwhelms all resistance by spreading panic among the diners. The animals then show their mercy by pardoning the captured stoats, weasels, and ferrets after only a nominal punishment.

The stoats, weasels, and ferrets might interpret the events recounted in *The Wind in the Willows* very differently. They would probably start by pointing out that

the writer, Kenneth Grahame, has rendered the use of terror against them acceptable by the way he has set up the whole scene. They might point to the elements
of Social Darwinism and Malthusian paranoia in his depiction of themselves –
who are ambiguously the working class, the colonized peoples of Africa, Asia, and
the Americas, women and gays – as creatures whose violent nature and rapid proliferation makes them dangerous and in need of control. Looking abroad to the
almost quarter of a million Filipinos who died in America's conquest of the
Philippines, they might see this depiction as the world turned upside down. They
might see breaking through Badger's snarl the ancient figure of the sovereign as
a Wolf-Man who must be watched least he acquires a taste for blood.[26] They
might strip away the prettying up of violence represented by the use of antique
weapons and see in Badger's hands not a cudgel, but the ultra-modern Gatling
machine gun used by British imperialism to terrorize native peoples. They might
tell another story which looked at how the exemplary violence of the re-taking of
Toad Hall is seen as a repetition of the violence used to enclose Toad's land and to
acquire the wealth to build Toad Hall in the first place. They might note the
sadistic fantasy at the centre of Grahame's account of the terrorization of the
stoats and weasels and so clearly present in the illustrator's depiction of the scene.
And, finally, they might wonder what all these confirmed bachelors are doing
along the river bank in a world without women and ask why their love for each
other ultimately has to be expressed through an orgy of violence.

(iii) Woodrow Wilson's re-articulation of the Lodge–Roosevelt–Root strategy to tame democracy

Then Princeton Professor Woodrow Wilson strongly endorsed Roosevelt, Lodge,
and Root's programme to give America a new frontier. He saw it as a way of persuading Americans to accept rule by a reforming elite in the name of democracy.
The strength of Americans' commitment to democracy meant that this was now
the only way they could be brought to accept what Wilson called "The best
gov[ernment] of the few."[27]

Wilson's rearticulation of democracy appeared as articles in *The Atlantic Monthly*
between 1900 and 1901. In "Democracy and Efficiency", Wilson claims that the
future of democracy is now threatened by "reactionary revolution" unless it can
show itself to be an "efficient" mode of government.[28] He draws a tight link
between the viability of democracy internationally and within the United States.
"We dare not stand neutral . . . we shall not realize these ideals at home, if we suffer
them to be hopelessly discredited amongst peoples who have yet to see liberty and
the peaceable days of order and comfortable progress."[29] The threat to democracy
within America comes from the boss and the machine which threaten to impose

tyranny in America's great cities, and the rise of political parties which have reduced politics to "an infinite play of forces at cross purposes". Following Roosevelt, Lodge, and Root, Wilson argues that these threats arise because America no longer has a frontier which can teach its citizens the true meaning of democracy:

> Until 1890 the United States had always a frontier; looked always to a region beyond, unoccupied, unappropriated, an outlet for its energy, a new place of settlement and of achievement for its people. For nearly three hundred years their growth had followed a single law – the law of expansion into new territory . . . England sought colonies at the ends of the earth to set her energy free and give vent to her enterprise; we, a like people in every impulse of mastery and achievement, had our own vast continent and were satisfied. There was always space and adventure enough and to spare, to satisfy the feet of our young men . . . From coast to coast across the great continent our institutions have spread, until the western sea has witnessed the application upon a great scale of what was begun upon a small scale on the shores of the Atlantic, and the drama has been played almost to the last act – the drama of institutional construction on the vast scale of a continent. The whole European world, which gave us our materials, has been moralized and liberalized by the striking and stupendous spectacle.[30]

The passage is a call to emulate past Americans. It seduces the reader, intriguingly, by presenting seduction at work on others. The reader is presented as a member of the American nation. Past Americans are portrayed as heroes whose actions have a powerful emulative force. Europeans have been compelled to acknowledge their greatness and accept the value of American morality and liberty. The glory their deeds have achieved in the eyes of Europeans and Americans has given them immortality. Their actions have made them a guide for the world to follow.

Wilson describes the frontier solely as a locale for white Americans' heroic action and nation building. Through depicting it as "unoccupied" and "unappropriated" he erases the genocidal destruction of the Indian nations who lived there. A page later Wilson momentarily acknowledges the problem this other history poses for the heroic story of building the American nation, the way the "unpitying force" with which we have "thrust the Indians to the wall whenever they have stood in our way" calls into question America's pretensions that it is more peaceful, just, and liberal than other nations. But Wilson immediately subordinates this other history to America's rivalry with European nations. "Our interests must march forward, altruists though we are; other nations must stand off, and do not seek to stay us."[31]

In his December 1901 "The Ideals of America", written as the Philippines-American War dragged on, Wilson stresses the battlefield as the place where America became a nation. Americans are presented as living in the continuous presence of dead heroes and the battlefields they died on:

We do not think or speak of the War for Independence as if we were aged men who, amidst alien scenes of change, comfort themselves with talk of great things done in days long gone by, the likes of which they may never hope to see again. The spirit of the old days is not dead. If it were, who amongst us would care for its memory and distant, ghostly voice? It is the distinguishing mark, nay the very principle of life in a nation alive and quick in every fibre, as ours is, that all its days are great days – are to its thought single and of a piece. Its past it feels to have been but the prelude and earnest of its present. It is from its memories of the days old and new that it gets its sense of identity, takes its spirit of action, assures itself of its power and its capacity, and knows its place in the world. Old colony days, and those sudden days of revolution when debate turned to action and heady winds as if of destiny blew with mighty breath the long continent through, were our own days, the days of our childhood and our headstrong youth. We have not forgotten. Our memories make no effort to recall the time. The battle of Trenton is as real to us as the battle of San Juan hill.[32]

Here Wilson pays homage to Roosevelt and the Rough Riders as the heroes whose exploits in Cuba have renewed the nation. What is striking in this essay is that having evoked America's origins in the War of Independence, Wilson then goes on to argue that the *true* origin of America lies in the war of 1812. The motive is not difficult to discern. The danger of making the War of Independence the true origin of America is that it will stress that America is first of all a republic. Since Wilson's whole project, like that of Roosevelt, Lodge, and Root, is to make Americans see themselves as first of all a nation, that will not do. To suppress it, Wilson evokes the war of 1812 as the real origin of America: "That was the real war of independence . . . It was then we cut our parties and our passions loose from politics over sea, and set ourselves to make a career which should be indeed our own."[33] To get Americans to support the transformation of America into a great civilizing nation, Wilson had to persuade them to reject Anti-Imperialist League statements that European conquest and colonization of other nations like the Philippines was exactly what the republic had been founded against.[34] To do this he sought to overturn an entrenched way of classifying states.[35] This drew a sharp line between monarchies and republics. Monarchies should not be trusted in international relations: kings and aristocrats are aggressive and domineering; they used wars to justify their existence, and as an excuse for repression.[36] The American republic had been founded against just such a monarchy, George III's England. As republican ideas threatened the existence of monarchies, they were hostile to republics. America's natural ally in international relations was her fellow republic, France; England was not to be trusted. The sharp divide between monarchy and republic was established by a revolutionary overthrow of monarchy by the people. The authors of the Constitution saw the republican and democratic principles as being in conflict. Democracy was seen as tending towards a tyranny in which the majority dominated the minority. Yet the majority of Americans soon came to see republicanism and democracy as mutually reinforcing. Only through the direct involvement of the people in government could the wealthy be stopped from taking over the republic.[37]

To reclassify states Wilson redrew the line separating states Americans could trust from those they could not. The states Americans could trust were those, like England and Germany, in which the people had a *constitutional government* suited to their stage of development.[38] Constitutional monarchies and republican democracies were not separated by a sharp revolutionary divide but by a gradual evolution. The American people had only developed the habits necessary for self-government because their long subordination to the English king had slowly taught them the respect for authority, concern for the common good, obedience to the law, patience with slow change, and other qualities necessary for self-government. The best states, those able to play a leading role in the spread of civilization, were those in which a self-conscious nation had a constitution which fitted the character of its people – Germany, England, and America. The French, Spanish, and Latin American nations, by contrast, were not to be trusted in international relations because their people had not acquired the self-discipline and concern for ideals necessary for democracy. This explained why democracy, "a cordial and a tonic to little Switzerland and big America" has only been a "quick intoxicant or a slow poison to France and Spain, a mere maddening draught to South American states".[39]

Like Roosevelt, Lodge, and Root, Wilson believed that the task of spreading democracy to the Philippines would teach Americans the true meaning of democracy. The Protestant elite would rediscover its role as a meritocracy governing in the interests of the nation, and the people would rediscover the "discipline" of accepting their leadership.[40] The Philippines is the new frontier in which Americans learn to work together as a nation: "Although we have forgot our own preparatory discipline in that kind, these new tasks will undoubtedly teach us that some discipline – it may be prolonged and tedious – must precede self-government and prepare the way for it."[41] America's annexation of the Philippines is providential:

They came upon us . . . with a strange opportuneness, as if part of a great preconceived plan for changing the world. Every man now knows that the world is to be changed – changed according to an ordering of Providence hardly so much foreshadowed until it came . . . The whole world had already become a single vicinage; each part had become neighbour to all the rest. No nation could live any longer to itself, the tasks and duties of neighbourhood being what they were . . . We might not have seen our duty had the Philippines not fallen to us by the wilful fortune of war; but it would have been our duty, nevertheless, to play the part we now see ourselves obliged to play. The East is to be opened and transformed, whether we will or no; the standards of the West are to be imposed upon it; nations and peoples that have stood still for centuries are to be quickened, and made part of the universal world of

commerce and of ideas which has so steadily been a-making by the advance of
European power from age to age. It is our peculiar duty as it is also England's, to
moderate the process in the interests of liberty . . . In China, of course, our part will
be indirect, but in the Philippines it will be direct; and there in particular must the
moral of our polity be set up and vindicated.[42]

Wilson used the task of governing the Philippines to argue for his programme to
remake the government of America. He called for a sweeping reform which
included:

The president

The role of the president must be expanded.[43] In the Constitution the Congress
initiates legislation, while the president can check congressional legislation
through the use of the veto. America's new international role, and the task of governing a complex society, now demand that the president actively initiate
legislation. The president must also take an active role in directing the formation
of public opinion, and use it to control Congress. As the only representative of the
whole nation, if he listens to the sentiments of the nation, and the nation trusts
him, he is able to shape public opinion. Above all since America is now a great
power, the president must have a virtually unrestricted role in foreign affairs.

Professional administration

The president must be supported by a professional administration.[44] Seen as part
of European absolutism, it meant paternalistic rule by a class of servile bureau-
crats, separate from society, trained by the monarch and personally loyal to him.
It was the means used by a Frederick the Great or a Napoleon to exercise despotic
control. Wilson now argued that administration was a neutral tool for exercising
efficient government, an instrument that could be used by either monarchy or
democracy. He claimed administration was objective and non-political by arguing
it had a scientific basis, and stressed its practical value by arguing it was grounded
in business methods. Having severed the link between administration and monarchy, Wilson claimed the former's rapid adoption was essential for America's
new world role. A professional administration was a vital tool of the executive at
all levels, national, state, and city. Its task was to work out how legislation could be
applied in particular instances, and how society needed to be reformed if legislation was to be effective.

Political science

The basis for political reforms was the comparative study of different political systems by political scientists. The Philippines now offered American political scientists
a new laboratory which would enable America to perfect her government at

home.[45] To those who rejected expansion because it might corrupt American government at home, Wilson emphasized the value of the knowledge gained for domestic reform.[46]

Meritocracy

Whereas Roosevelt emphasized the army and the navy as the best places to reform the Protestant establishment, Wilson stressed the university. Modelled on the University of Berlin, Princeton was to transform the parochial views of its students into a national vision through studies in the liberal arts and pure science.[47] In contrast to business which emphasized the pursuit of commercial advantage, and the narrow focus of applied science, the university would enable future leaders to decide how men should cooperate together for the common good. In a move in which the recipients of a Princeton education internalize and appropriate the Constitution's system of checks and balances, Wilson claims that a liberal education will enable them to be "the balance wheel of a free industrial nation".[48]

The people

Wilson saw the people as governed by irrational sentiment. In the Civil War "the ultimate foundations of the structure was laid bare: physical force, sustained by the stern loves and rooted predilections of the masses of men, strong ingrained prejudices which are the fibre of every system of government".[49] Acknowledging that since the French Revolution Americans have come to understand democracy as based on popular sovereignty,[50] Wilson told an evolutionary story about democracy which gives the people a restricted role: choosing between representatives at elections. What ought to differentiate democracy from other forms of self-government was not popular participation in government, but that public office was open to everyone on the basis of merit rather than inherited position. This is the test of popular sovereignty, not the ability of citizens to determine what their representatives should do:

> Representative government has had its long life and excellent development, not in order that common opinion, the opinion of the street, might prevail, but in order that the best opinion, the opinion generated by the best possible methods of general counsel, might rule in affairs.[51]

Universal suffrage was not the key to democracy. "[It is] not universal suffrage [which] constitutes democracy. Universal suffrage may confirm a *coup d'état* which destroys liberty."[52]

The full significance of Wilson's endorsement of Lodge, Roosevelt, and Root's programme is now clear. The annexation and government of the Philippines, Wilson believed, was a splendid opportunity for restructuring the government of

America, developing political science and scientific administration, remaking its governing class, and convincing Americans to accept a weakened principle of popular sovereignty. In teaching the Filipinos obedience, discipline, organization, mutual obligation, and patience, Americans would be reminded of the importance of these habits. The government of the Philippines would re-teach Americans that self-government means a preparedness to be governed, and that popular sovereignty must be mediated by elite representatives. "It is thus that we shall ourselves recognize the fact, at last patent to all the world, that the service of democracy has been the development of ideals . . . [rather than] any absolute qualification of the ultimate conceptions of sovereignty."[53]

7

Bolts from the Blue

The patrician reformers sought to persuade Americans to accept their rule in return for being presented as heroes in a struggle to extend democracy to all peoples. Their interest in transforming America into a great civilizing nation converged with the interests of a second group, the military progressives, who sought to give America a military system like that of European great powers. In this chapter I look at how they sought to persuade Americans that they were wrong to think that the Atlantic and the Pacific meant that America did not need such a military system. The investigation transforms our understanding of the post-1918 struggle within the army between the general staff on the one side and the Chemical Warfare Service and air corps on the other. It shows that in seeking to place themselves at the centre of American military policy, these new units were *folding back* against the general staff the very strategy the military progressives had used to persuade Americans to adopt a German-style general staff in the first place. In doing so they found themselves driven to trump earlier claims about America's vulnerability to foreign attack, and to intensify the military progressives' claim to a sovereign right to intervene in America's constitutional system in order to save it. The chemical and air officers' actions, then, were not a deviation from path followed by the military as a whole, but reveal its inner logic.

(i) The strategy developed by the military progressives

To see how the military progressives argued the defence of American's rights demanded the extension of a new network of power, we need to go back to the foundation of the Military Service Institution in 1878.[1] It was formed by regular army officers, whom I call the "military progressives", on the model of the British Royal United Services Institution.[2] Largely unnoticed by their contemporaries, these officers began to form a strategy for remaking American military power. Its elements can be seen in Major-General Schofield's Inaugural Address, reprinted in the first number of the Institution's new publication *The Journal of the Military Service Institution*.

First, Schofield argues that America faces a potential military catastrophe. The development of long-range firearms of unprecedented destructive power and the vast rise in the size of armies have placed an increased responsibility on her officers. The age of amateurs is over. America's army officers must become professionals. To justify the need for military professionalism, Schofield takes the Declaration of Independence's claim that Americans must fight a war with Britain to secure their right to life, liberty, and the pursuit of happiness as his starting point:

> A fault in the chief, or a failure in a single subordinate, may involve, in an hour, the loss of a battle possibly involving all the accumulated wealth of the people, even their liberty and the safety and honor of the nation. The work of a hostile army is like a fiend of fire. A magnificent city which generations have builded may be destroyed in a single night. So the wealth, liberties, and happiness of a people may be lost in a single day of battle.[3]

Schofield's military audience would have immediately picked up his implicit reference to the 1870–71 Franco-Prussian War, in which Prussian mobilization of over a third of a million men and innovative use of her railway system had enabled her to defeat France's armies in less than a month, leading to the siege of Paris. By placing his argument within the horizon of Prussia's rapid, violent, overwhelming military aggression, and by making the Declaration of Independence his starting point, Schofield is able to fold back against itself the argument that military professionals and standing armies are dangerous to liberty; to the contrary, European events show they are now essential to its preservation. There was, however, the slight difficulty that America was not, like France, in Europe, and seemed an unlikely target for any European military expeditionary force after the Civil War had shown America's capacity to mobilize vast military forces.

Second, Schofield argues there is a military science, which American army officers can study and develop, which will give them the expertise they need to defend Americans against the new threat to their safety, wealth, liberty, and happiness. The argument has two levels. First, the study of military history reveals the principles of military success, which are the same everywhere. The study of Caesar's battles reveals them just as much as does the study of Napoleon's battles. The study of what men do in battle is equivalent to natural sciences' direct observation of nature: "As the student of natural science dives deep into the recess of nature, to learn the facts recorded in natural history, so the military student must intently study the history of military contests and endeavour therefrom to learn the facts."[4] Third, Schofield argues that while the study of military history gives us the general laws of military science, these laws have to be applied. In particular, the development of new means of warfare makes it unclear how these laws are to be applied today. The discovery of the factors that have to be taken into account in applying the general laws of military science in turn calls for the further study of military history.

Through its development of military science, Schofield argued, the new Institution offered the American state control over war. It would enable military officers to judge how the "chances" of war could be reduced to "minimum" and "what enterprises may be successfully undertaken with reasonable chance of success".[5] To support this claim, Schofield invoked the authority of Napoleon. The great French general, he claimed, had conquered Europe due to his ability to analyse just what it was in the battles he fought which had led to his victories. He had shown how chance could be removed from war through its analysis in terms of the "simple ideas of pure mathematics and those of mechanics and the relations they teach between time, motion, and force".[6]

The formation of the Military Service Institution shows us the emergence of a strategy through which regular army officers sought to re-articulate their relations with other groups. Take Congress. Before the creation of the Institution, the army officers were in a weak position: they depended on Congress for appropriations, yet after the end of the Indian Wars there was *no* enemy they could point to justify a large army. The dispersal of officers of what was then a tiny army of about 20,000 across the United States made it difficult for them to come together to formulate a common position. The officers sought to change this. The Military Service Institution provided a way in which its founders could enrol the support of all officers, despite their geographical dispersal, in developing the claim that America faced threats which her military system could not cope with, and that through the study of military science they alone were in a position to give Congress the advice it needed to remake the military system. As a forum for debate, and through the pages of its journal, it could exert a seductive pull on officers unable to display their martial valour for want of a war. It offered an arena in which they could vie with each other to demonstrate their mastery of military science, and to show new ways in which the case for a modern army could be made. It also provided a way of informing America's army officers about how their European counterparts were making the case for military modernization. In this way it could draw the whole officer corps into making the case for America to develop a military system like that of European nations.

The first number of the journal published in 1880 pointed out why it was in regular army officers' interests to back the project. After Schofield's inaugural address had flattered army officers as heroes who must save America, Brevet Major-General James Fry laid it on the line:

> It is to be hoped that this Institution may promote such an understanding, at least in those matters which concern alike all branches of the Service, as to bring about a unanimity of sentiment upon them, and thus render possible a concurrent and potent expression of their views upon points affecting our general welfare.[7]

Fry concludes by emphasizing why it is in the vital interests of army officers to cooperate in this effort: "We all know that the army is the creation of Congress, and that its strength, organization, compensation, etc., must from time to time undergo revision at the hands of the power which created it and by which it exists." Subsequent editions of *The Journal of the Military Service Institution* showed regular army officers, and some National Guard officers, strengthening and refining the strategy set out by Schofield to take advantage of changing opportunities.

(ii) Overcoming American's perceptions that the Atlantic and Pacific Oceans mean the United States does not need a European-style military system

American military progressives faced a problem their European and Japanese counterparts did not. The Union's defeat of the South through the mobilization of vast numbers of militia and volunteers, America's giant economy, and her separation from Europe and Asia by the Atlantic and Pacific Oceans led Americans to believe they already had a military system that was more than adequate to meet any threat. Why, then, fix what wasn't broken? The military progressives themselves were forced to acknowledge the strength of the argument. Thus in 1890 Major-General John Gibbon described a war of invasion as a "highly improbable contingency" because America's railway system, huge agricultural surpluses, and giant manufacturing capacity all favoured its defenders.[8] The transition from sail to steamships actually reduced the range of shipping because it made ships dependent on coal depots.[9] There was also the uncomfortable, but little mentioned, fact that strengthening the navy provided an alternative way of defending America against invasion – which did not raise the historic fear that a professional officer corps and a standing army would be dangerous to liberty. To meet the difficulty, the progressives developed a series of arguments to show the existing system was deeply flawed:

New criteria for assessing the military system shows its repeated failure

To overcome the problem that after the Civil War there was no state that either
wanted to or could conquer the United States, and hence America had an opportunity to develop an alternative military/diplomatic policy to that being pursued
by European Great Powers, the military progressives sought to bury the present
opportunity by falsely equating the present with America's past. This tactic can be
seen in the military progressives' bible, General Emory Upton's *The Military Policy
of the United States*. In it Upton argued that while Americans had largely won
their wars, the lack of a proper military policy meant they had been full of disasters, wasteful of life and money, and unnecessarily long. Upton drove home the
unnecessary loss of life caused through the policy of relying on untrained militia
with savage irony by referring to the question laughingly asked by the veterans of
Gettysburgh as they met fresh militia troops: "Where did they bury their dead?"[10]
The military reformers presented themselves as an avant garde "we" which knows
military science, and the American people as an ignorant "they". The "we" has the
task of educating the "they". The need for a programme of education is set out in
Arthur Wagner's 1886 essay "Popular Military Education". The heart of Wagner's
argument is a characterization of the American voters as lacking the foresight necessary for the development of a rational military policy:

> Yet judging from our past history and the nature of our government, the present
> interest in providing for national defence is a mere spasm of patriotic alarm; and it
> is to be feared that when the popular demand shall have been satisfied, and the
> nation shall have been placed in a good condition of defence, apathy will follow
> interest, and our military and naval preparations will again drift far behind the
> necessities of the country.[11]

The characterization of voters as a collective popular mind incapable of showing
foresight and consistent interest or appreciating key distinctions such as that
between military resources and military strength is a recurrent theme. Thus in
1906 Allen Redwood tells a story to drive home the idea that the voters are incapable of learning from past mistakes:

> History seems to have repeated itself, almost without deviation, from the very begin-
> ning of our existence as an organized republic, and even before that, quite up to the
> time in which we live. Like the Bourbons, we have "learnt nothing", but here the anal-
> ogy ends; we seem to have forgotten most of the lessons we have had drilled into us
> by many and costly experiences in the past. The familiar story of the Arkansas squat-
> ter who did not mend his roof when the weather was fine because it "didn't leak *then*"
> illustrates the happy-go-lucky attitude of the American people upon all questions
> touching military policy so long as the emergency is not actually present.[12]

The modernizers' conclusion was that in a democracy a proper military policy
could only be developed by educating the voters.[13]

America is threatened as much by internal as external dangers

Here again Upton provides a robust statement of the argument. With the memory of the Civil War still fresh in American minds, he argued: "the military policy of a republic should look more to the danger of civil commotion than to the possibility of foreign invasion . . . In less than a century our peace [has] been disturbed by Shay's Rebellion, the Whisky Rebellion, the Great Rebellion, and more recently still the Rail Road Riots of 1877."[14] In a rhetorical twist which highlights the central issue of this chapter, Upton claimed that there was no danger that the use of military force to crush dissent might be repressive since in America the government represented the popular will: "Recognizing, too, that under popular institutions the majority of the people create the government and that the majority will never revolt, it should be our policy to suppress every riot and stamp out every insurrection before it swells to rebellion."[15] Here the presumption that democracy *already* exists, which rules out the very idea that protest could be drawing attention to the suppression of democracy, gives a *carte blanche* for the use of force against all protests. Equally, it presumed that rule by the majority is the *sole* value, and hence that protests by oppressed minorities are necessarily illegitimate. Others emphasized the importance of the military in the protection of property. Thus Captain G.F. Price in 1885 evoked the authority of Hamilton to insist on the importance of the army as the *"Ultima ration regnum"*, and argued that the extension of the franchise to the "criminal and ignorant classes" threatened the public safety and demanded "an army of sufficient numbers . . . to protect property from the assaults of the mob".[16] Lastly, there was a danger that "riots and disorders" might fatally weaken the United States in wartime.[17]

Changes in transportation and commerce make the US more vulnerable to attack

The military progressive claimed the development of transportation and commerce meant it was becoming easier for a European or Asian power to launch a rapid attack on the United States:

> The great lesson of the Franco-German war has not been learned by the United States. . . . while the geographic position of this country has afforded in the past some excuse for neglecting the important duty of military preparations, it affords but little, if any, excuse now. It is no longer so many miles from New York to Halifax or Liverpool; but it is three day's journey to the first, and seven day's journey to the second.[18]

Later officers pointed to the Boer War and the Russian-Japanese War as evidence that armies of hundreds of thousands could be transported to America in a matter of weeks. "With the improvements in methods of transportation," Captain William Mitchell underscored in 1910, "Germany is closer to us than Canada was in 1812."[19] The military progressives urged that, while it might be true that no other nation can conquer America, without a modern military it could not resist being intimidated by the threat of an attack on its coastal cities. Such an attack could be launched from British Canada, Mexico, the Caribbean, or from across the Pacific or Atlantic. Equally, Germany might first gain a foothold in Brazil before attacking, while Japan might use Alaska, Hawaii, and the Philippines as stepping stones. At the centre of their argument was the claim that such an attack might materialize without warning – hence America has to have a large regular army to meet it. The National Guard, besides being decidedly inferior to a modern army commanded by professional soldiers, would not be ready in time. The time needed to train and equip a modern military meant it had to be prepared well in advance of any possible war. Only such an army would give sufficient time for America to turn its enormous latent strength into effective military power.[20]

The growth of American trade will increase the likelihood of war, and demands a modern military to support it

In earlier editions of the journal, contributors argued America's expanding commerce would lead to clashes between her commercial interests and those of other nations. If she is to be able to assert her rights as a trading nation, she must have the military power to resist being intimidated by rivals. Some contributors emphasized that while America could not be conquered, to resist being intimidated she must be able to deter an attack on her cities designed to bully her into submission. Others underscored that America must have the military power to expand her trade even if resisted.[21] In later editions, contributors argued America is now a great commercial and military power. Having the power to take a leading role in the governance of the world implies the obligation to do so for the benefit of mankind, and, vice versa, taking a leading role in the governance of the world implies that America has the rights that go with it.

This justification for a modern military can be seen taking form in the years immediately before and after the Spanish-American War. Before the war, America is presented as a nation that soon will be, and by right ought to be, one of the world's leading trading nations, "perhaps the first".[22] After the war, America's status as one of the world's leading trading nations and its right to that status is taken as given. Thus, for Captain Arthur Williams writing after the war, the issue was how to defend that status:

> The increasing rapidity of ocean travel has made us almost neighbors with all the leading European nations. We have commercial relations with almost every country on the globe, and all our commercial interests must be enlarged if we are to maintain our place among the nations. We cannot afford to lose our assertiveness, nor allow other countries to thrust us aside, or dispossess us of our rightful share in the trade of the world.[23]

Here the globe is a finite space which is rapidly being made smaller by commerce. To maintain her place as a leading nation, America must be able to enlarge its commercial penetration of foreign markets. If America is to ensure that she is fairly treated when her commercial interests conflict with those of other nations, she must have a military capable of matching theirs.

A modern military is needed for America to carry out her global responsibilities

Colonel H.M. Boies in his 1899 essay "The Defence of a Free People in the light of the Spanish War"[24] shows us the other side of the argument: America needs to be a great military power so it can fulfil its duty as a great power to lead humanity. Only a nation with a modern military establishment, Boies claims, will have its voice heard in international affairs. Boies celebrates the Spanish-American War because it has aroused a national consciousness that America is now a great power with world responsibilities:

> A national consciousness has been aroused to the fact that we are no longer a secluded, though a great and powerful people, separated and protected from the other great nations of the earth by the seas which surround us, but standing among them a peer among peers, in close relations, with rights we must maintain and responsibilities we must discharge. The oceans which once were our protection have become the open avenues of international communication and contact, and the necessities of the times require us to constantly prepare to preserve our domestic peace, to defend ourselves from foreign aggression, and to perform our whole duties to humanity among the armed nations of the world. We are not to be permitted hereafter to devote our entire energies to the promotion of our own selfish interests and the enjoyment of prosperity, but are compelled to tax ourselves for security, and the effectiveness of our international influence.[25]

Taken together with the previous statement by Captain Arthur Williams, Boies shows a fateful equation beginning to emerge. It is not completely there yet, but its outlines can be discerned, as can the military progressives' interest in proclaiming it. In this equation, national unity, national prosperity through industrial advance and access to world markets, national prestige through acting as a great power exercising global responsibilities, and national military power are *all* dependent on each other. In a world in which America is locked in military and commercial competition with other nations for finite world resources, a failure in any one part of the circle may prove *irreversible*, resulting in America being permanently relegated to a subordinate status within the international system. This equation presents America as facing a permanent state of emergency requiring the endless modernization of her military system.

In the decades following the foundation of the Military Service Institution the military progressives came to demand a comprehensive transformation of American military policy. This had three main elements:

A general staff

The speed and complexity of modern war meant that the army needed to be organized and directed by a professional general staff, which would bring together military expertise in strategy, tactics, logistics, and intelligence. The German general staff was taken as providing the best model, and when Elihu Root created the army general staff he turned to it for guidance. During peace time the staff should prepare the army for war through the development of war plans, manoeuvres, and other means. To ensure that the army was ready to follow the staff's direction in war it must be given control over the different bureaus of the army. The secretary for war should turn to the chief of staff for advice on military policy. The heads of the bureaus should no longer have direct access to the secretary for war.

The development of military expertise

A war college was vital to ensure that America kept up with the development of military science abroad. Military science should be placed at the centre of officer training at West Point, and new schools for advanced postgraduate training should be set up. Within the army promotions should be based on merit, not seniority or political patronage.

A mass army

Security now depended upon America being able to rapidly field mass armies on the same scale as European powers. This led to two projects. The first, put forward by Upton, argued that modern war demanded, above all, professional officers commanding well-disciplined soldiers. Since large standing armies were not acceptable in the United States, there needed to be a small highly trained professional regular army, capable of expanding rapidly into a mass army. During a war conscripts would be drawn into regular army units. The second project was put forward by the leader of the pre-war preparedness campaign, General Leonard Wood. The first commander of Theodore Roosevelt's Rough Riders, and army chief of staff from 1910 to 1914, Wood argued that it was only if the regular army acted as the instructor of a separate army of citizen soldiers that America could match the mass armies of European nations.[26] The role of regular army officers was to train the mass army of citizen soldiers.

(iii) The masked return of sovereign right

The strategy developed by the military progressives brought about a return of sovereign right. The classic figure of the sovereign is the absolutist monarch whose prerogative allows him to act outside or against the law. The writings of the military progressives show such a figure returning. However, it is no longer a single person, the king, at the apex of a hierarchical society, who occupies the position of sovereign. Instead, sovereign right is fragmented and distributed among the military progressives.

They asserted their sovereign right to intervene in and restructure the American political system by arguing that unless they did so, the republic would be unable to carry out the reforms needed to create the new military system. This was because the political system established by the Constitution, as it had developed, was fundamentally flawed. The president, the secretary of war, senators, and congressmen lacked military knowledge, stood in debt to the interests that had helped them get elected, were at the mercy of an all-powerful, ill-informed and fickle public opinion, and driven by the demands of re-election.[27] The public itself was portrayed as militarily shortsighted, and as we have seen, always forgetting the lessons of past wars.[28] Equally, the people were portrayed as often being unable to put the national interest before their sectional interests. Lieutenant-Colonel Irving Taylor, for example, was frustrated with Midwestern farmers. "It may well be difficult for an inhabitant of the interior," he lamented, "who has perhaps never seen the ocean, to understand the necessity for expending large sums upon the naval establishment. From his viewpoint it is much more desirable to construct federal buildings, improve rivers, or irrigate arid lands."[29] The people were also ignorant of military truths, and largely unaware that there were military professionals whose authority they should heed. They did not comprehend that being a lawyer, doctor, or politician did not give one competence to decide military matters.[30] Worse, the military progressives sometimes wondered whether the people really had the interests of the republic at heart: "The grand promise of equal rights to all has attracted to our shores the down-trodden and oppressed of the world, until we have millions of citizens with but a veneering of attachment for the great democracy which has promised them so much. Would they be an element of weakness in war against their countries?" Lieutenant-Colonel James Pettit wondered in 1906, before suggesting the answer. "I need only ask, How long would you have to reside in Germany to willingly bear arms for her against the United States?"[31]

Located in an America where it was an axiom that military officers should be viewed with suspicion because they might try to take over the state, the military progressives did not explicitly claim that they had a right to intervene in the political system. They did, however, make four claims which together add up to it. And as their position within America strengthened, they made them with increasing force. (1) The study of military science means that they alone have the expertise necessary to understand what kinds of military threats America faces and decide how to meet them. (2) The location of officers at the centre of the general staff and the War College made them, in some respects, better placed in terms of information over the executive and the legislature to decide what threats America faces and what needs to be done about them. (3) The structure of the American political system rendered it incapable of undertaking and carrying through the long-range reforms necessary to prepare America to meet new military threats. (4) The new military threats America faced meant that by the time that the need for action had become clear to the executive, the Congress, and the people it might well be too late.

The military progressives presented themselves, and no doubt largely saw themselves, as operating within the division of power established by the Constitution. They were the servants of the people. They seek to ensure that the president, as commander-in-chief, and the secretary of state for war, as his delegate, get the expert advice they need. They seek to educate the Congress and the American people in the principles of military science and in its application to America in an era of great power rivalry.[32] But implicit in their claim to privileged knowledge about America's military needs is the claim that should their master, the American people and its representatives, jeopardize the nation by seriously misunderstanding their own interests, then America's military officers must temporarily assume the role of master and do whatever is necessary for the safety of the republic.

At the same time as their writings show a return of sovereign right, they also work to erode the clear distinction between order and the state of emergency on which any claim to sovereign right depends. Internally, the military progressives, and even more the patrician reformers, present society on the verge of collapse due to deepening rifts between finance and agriculture, capitalist and worker, immigrant and native American. Externally, they erode the distinction between war and peace. In *The Federalist*, Hamilton and Madison make a clear distinction between periods when America is at peace, periods when she is threatened with invasion, and periods when she is at war. Hamilton presents the president on the one hand, and the Congress on the other, as well placed to see when America is threatened with invasion and when it is not, and able to see when America needs to build up her military forces and when they are no longer necessary. When they detect a danger of invasion there will be time enough to deploy the army as an advance guard, call out the states' militia, and enlist and train volunteers in a citizen army. America's geographical isolation means that like Britain, and unlike European nations, she need not constantly prepare for war. Not so for the military progressives. Technology, industrialism, global commerce, nationalism, global empires, and the fragmentation and decadence of the American nation, they believe, have completely changed the situation. National prestige, national unity, national industrial progress and commercial access to world markets, and national military power are now linked together in a tightening circle; a failure in one could lead to an irreversible failure in the others. The spectre conjured up here was China. Just as Britain, France, Germany, Russia, Japan, and America were devouring a once great civilization, so too might America become the prey of other nations. Militarily, the key factors are now speed, overwhelming force, global vulnerability, and the danger of irreversible defeat. Captain Gilbert Cotton underscores the new reality in his 1896 essay "The Proximity of England to the United States in Reference to Hostilities between the Two Nations". Britain's deployment of a naval squadron in the Venezuela boundary dispute, and rapid development of technology, is taken as a licence for a fantasy about a sudden, unexpected, overwhelming, and catastrophic attack on the United States:

> The very facilities of the highest civilization quicken the transition from a state of peace to one of war; hurry the shifting of the scenery; hasten the catastrophe and the conclusion! . . . War between us will come with a suddeness that will be startling . . . The blows that nations strike will often be bolts from the blue . . . wars ordered by wire will move on steel rails, and great fleets will announce themselves.[33]

Here the image of the lightning bolt is used to convey the idea that America is entering an era in which there will be no warning of impending attacks. This new imagined global geography means that even if no nation actually has the intention of attacking, America must constantly develop its military power in preparation for such an attack, whether on America itself or on its interests abroad. The clear distinction between periods of peace, periods when it is necessary to prepare for war and periods of war, collapses.

(iv) The necessity of covering over incompatible views if the patrician reformers and the military progressives were to forge an alliance

If America was to have a global frontier, she needed a navy and an army like those of European and Asian great powers. There was a natural convergence of interests between the patrician reformers and the military progressives. Yet, if the two were to form an alliance the fact that they held very different views of war had to be suppressed. Roosevelt, Lodge, Root, and Wilson represented the army as an idealized place where young Americans could learn to emulate past military heroes who risked everything for American ideals, and the battlefield as a place of national redemption. The military reformers, by contrast, sought an army that would be capable of fighting a European or Asian great power. This meant conscription, not volunteers. It meant that men would be compelled to fight whether they chose to or not by drill, propaganda, and the threat of the firing squad. It meant that victory would be decided by strategic expertise, numbers, and superior armaments. The patrician reformers also faced another problem in looking to the army to provide it with the ideal models of heroic warfare – the actual history of how the army had won its most recent wars. Grant and Sherman won the Civil War by breaking the Southern will to resist by terrorizing its civilian population and destroying the Southern economy. Following the Civil War, the army used the new railways to attack the Great Plains Indians during the winter. The Indian tribes faced the alternative of starving and freezing to death, or accepting being moved onto reservations.

For the patrician reformers and the military progressives to form an alliance these contradictions had to be suppressed. To this end each side painted a picture of modern war in which incompatibles were reconciled. In his 1900 "Military Preparedness and Unpreparedness", Roosevelt simply denied outright that victory increasingly depended on superior weapons. The Spanish war, he claimed, "completely falsified" any idea that new weapons might "nullify the courage which has always . . . been the prime factor in winning battles".[34] Equally, he painted a romantic picture of the Indian Wars. To emphasize the heroism of the settlers, he claimed the Indians had soon become "accustomed to the new-comers' weapons and style of warfare . . . [and] had become . . . the most formidable savage foes ever encountered by colonists of European stock."[35] The reality of the one-sided Indian Wars and genocide is buried beneath a fantasy of a war between equals.

The military reformers also struggled to reconcile incompatibles. Major James Chester's 1901 "The Invisible Factor" shows a military romantic who was also a military reformer expressing his anguish at the incompatibility between the two sides of his identity. Chester was disgusted by the reduction of command to "mathematics" by military science, while new inventions were no less vile. The Maxim gun was the "embodyment of the spirit of the age": the intellectual ability of mankind was now devoted to "means of killing enemies without running any risk", and war would soon be fought using "traps and poisons".[36] Chester saw these developments as leading to the end of heroic warfare. They were evidence that the moral corruption of materialism had extended to the very place in which the heroic virtues were won. Sounding like an Old Testament prophet, he denounced the new state of affairs:

"The Tool and the Man" . . . have made the wilderness glad and the desert place to blossom as the rose. They have brought the wealth of the world within our reach and said, "Let Wealth be your Salvation: you can buy happiness." And not a few have believed them. But the primal curse remains . . . The Weapon and the Man are the same actors in another part of the drama. They also promise much. They promise, if not to abolish war altogether, at least to make it wageable economically; that is, without running much risk . . . Enemies will be killed as fast as they show their heads above the horizon. Courage will be less essential than keeness of vision. It will be unnecessary to look an enemy in the eye while you thrust him through with a bayonet. This was always unpleasant and even difficult to do. Some men never acquired the knack of it. But Bobadil proposes to abolish all that. Under his system most of the killing will be done by machinery, and at long range, perhaps beyond the range of distinct vision.[37]

Chester struggled to resolve the tension. He argued that while modern warfare made it impossible for the ordinary soldier to be a hero, the commander still could be. By exercising a charismatic power over his men and the enemy, the great commander was still central to deciding which way the battle went. "A forlorn hope led by a hero is almost hypnotized. The men are blind to danger . . . The power of a hero is a spiritual power, and Godlike as it ought to be God given . . . He is a ruler of men by God's own appointment."[38] To back up his case that war would be decided by the "invisible factor", the heroism of the great commander, Chester resorted to theology. Superior inventions, military strategy, and weight of numbers "ought to be successful if there is no God. But there is a God and he takes an interest in the battles of men."[39]

8

The Bankruptcy of Empire
and its Relaunch

Before 1914 Roosevelt, Root, and Wilson all believed that America was, and ought to be, part of the advance guard of civilization. They were clear that the leading countries in this "world movement", to use Roosevelt's phrase in his 1910 address to the University of Berlin, were America, Britain, Germany, and France. Hence the shock produced in 1914 when three of these countries went for each other's throats. The war appeared to break down the key temporal distinction between the "we", the civilized nations, and the "they", the not-yet-civilized countries. Roosevelt's vindication of the conquest of the Philippines by claiming that "until the great civilized nations stepped in there was no chance for anything but such bloody violence", no longer seemed self-evident. As the European slaughter escalated how could the civilized nations claim their conquest and colonization of the world was justified because it ended the cycle of violence in which the not-yet-civilized peoples of the world were caught up?

The avant garde's right to rule was based on the claim, as I show in Part 3, that it alone could see the potential for harmony within society and decide what needed to be done to realize it. Its members imagined a harmonious circle in which science, technology, the study of Greek, Roman and biblical writings, liberal constitutional government, capitalism, the nation, and humanity all reinforced each other. Their task was to detect the threats to this harmony before they became too powerful, and give society the direction it needed to re-establish harmony. In the first months of the war it might be possible to claim that the slaughter did not call this picture into question. The war, after all, might be one of those moments in which there was a temporary departure from harmony. It would be one of those occasions when the avant garde in the different warring nations could demonstrate their right to rule by decisive interventions. They would vindicate themselves by re-establishing the harmonious circle. The war would be a learning experience which would enable mankind to advance further.

This was not what happened. Instead, the war intensified. The elites were as swept up in war fervour as the crowds crying for revenge and national glory. The avant garde's claim that it should rule the world lay in ruins. This was not, of course, the first time that its claims had been discredited. There had always been workers, farmers, women, colonized peoples, and others outside the elite who had seen the modernizing avant garde's rule as reinforcing, not solving, the disasters they suffered. What was different about this occasion was simply that the split within the global avant garde itself made it difficult for it to operate the usual machinery for discrediting such views. So did the Europe-wide scale of the disaster. Whereas previously each national elite had provided alibis for the others, they were now in no position to do so. The smoking guns were clearly in their hands for all to see. Within Germany, even under wartime censorship, Rosa Luxemberg's analysis of how the system had produced the conflict gained a growing readership. While within America the way lay open for women, workers, farmers, African Americans, and other hitherto excluded groups to claim that they had as much right, if not more right, to govern America as the patrician reformers. And, as we have seen from Du Bois' writings, they were quick to assert that right.[1] While outside America Filippinos and other colonized peoples could state that they had every bit as much right to a say in the development of the world as the white races.

In the face of bankruptcy the American elite sought to find a way of salvaging their claim that they should rule the world, and the progressive meta-narrative on which it was based. In the pages that follow I show how they did so by boldly relaunching the world movement under a new name – a global crusade to "make the world safe for democracy". This enabled them to claim that the very war that had called the world movement's claims into question showed how much it was needed. To prevent their project being called into question they completely reclassified international relations. Whereas the German elite had previously been part of the global avant garde, it was now declared to be the enemy of mankind. What is striking is that in doing so the American elite gave itself permission to go ahead with actions that made the war worse. During neutrality America's chemical corporations, funded by the banks, went into overdrive supplying high explosives to Britain and France. Meanwhile America's chemists and chemical engineers entrenched the idea that Germany was uniquely diabolical so as to gain national support for an American artificial dye industry. Far from damping down the fire of war, they poured oil, or more accurately high-explosive, on the blaze. Then, in 1917, Wilson placed his authority as president behind a complete reclassification of international relations. In doing so he was able to relaunch the world movement, with America as its leader, as a completely *new* thing. Through relocating the origin of the world movement in the Declaration of Independence, he presented it as completely different from the "old" world movement of the imperialists. Classifying America as the world's leading democracy, he presented the United States as the natural leader of the new world movement. Classifying France and Britain as democracies in the process of overcoming their imperialism made them America's natural but junior partners in the crusade to make the world safe for democracy. Classifying Germany as an autocratic state hostile to democracy bent on world empire made it the new enemy of the world movement. The need to secure the worldwide victory of the new world movement would now justify America's pouring her entire military and economic might into the war. The irony is that, in doing so, the patrician reformers would be able to use the war to take their programme to make America a great power like Britain, France, *and* Germany a stage further. The American elite rapidly became entrapped in the logic of its own reclassification of states and Wilson's failure to deliver on his promise of "peace without victory" smoothed the way for the rise of National Socialism and for the return of world war in 1939.

The American elite's attempt to revive the corpse of imperial politics whose putrid state and deadly nature had been revealed in the trenches, however, immediately found that it faced competition. Lenin shared the American elite's commitment to the story that mankind was progressing towards the achievement of its sovereignty. However, he followed Karl Marx's argument that, while liberal capitalism had taken mankind a step down the road towards the achievement of its potential by destroying feudalism, its pursuit of profit at the cost of human development meant that it had now become the principal block to mankind's further advance. In exile from Tsarist Russia in Switzerland, Lenin sought to use the war to discredit socialists who believed there could be a parliamentary road to socialism. To show that revolutionary socialism was the only option he argued that the world's leading capitalist nations had reached a point where they could only survive if they could export goods and capital. The nations, such as Britain, which had been first to colonize the non-white world had already grabbed most of the world. This meant that rising liberal capitalist nations faced the option of either fighting to gain a larger share of the world market for goods and capital, or giving up their dreams of national advance. The true origin of the war lay in liberal capitalism itself. Until liberal capitalism had been overthrown by socialism, the world faced an endless cycle of future wars. His conclusion in his *On Imperialism* was that revolutionary socialists, such as himself, were the true avant garde of mankind. Humanity could indeed achieve its sovereignty if it would recognize that its true enemy was liberal capitalism, and join the worldwide communist revolution. Lenin's success in overthrowing the Kerenski government in the November 1917 revolution gave him the platform from which to present this programme to the world as an alternative to Wilson's. America's self-proclaimed liberal capitalist avant garde were now able to complement their claim that they were the only alternative to German autocracy by a second claim that they were the only alternative to Soviet Bolshevism. Revolutionary socialists, for their part, were able to make the reverse argument. By presenting their version of the world movement as a new thing, both were able to make it a sight for fantastic investments. As actually existing things in the world, Wilson's League of Nations and Lenin's Third International became screens onto which mankind could project its hopes and its nightmares. Each would now find in the other the essential enemy it needed to continually defer its allies' and its own people's desire for democracy and liberty.

(i) The production of the world as a battlefield between incompatible principles

How patrician reformers and military progressives sought to use the First World War to complete the takeover of America they had begun in the Spanish-American and Philippines-American Wars can be seen by looking at two addresses by Root. The first, "America on Trial",[2] was given on 20 March 1917 – just prior to America's entry into the First World War – to the Union League Club in New York.[3] To see what was at stake a brief account of the preparedness movement is vital. Root's turn of the century reform of the army gave the military progressives a German-style general staff and a war college. The reformers, however, gained less than they wanted. The staff's control over the army was more nominal than real as, with the help of allies in Congress, the bureaux chiefs were able to retain much of their power. And while the military reformers were able to persuade Congress to authorize an increase in enlisted men to 100,000 the regular army remained far smaller than that of European and Asian great powers. The problem was that Congress simply could not be persuaded that America faced a military threat which required more. When he became chief of staff in July 1910, the former commander of Roosevelt's Rough Riders, General Leonard Wood, and President Taft's secretary for war, Henry L. Stimson, a law partner of Elihu Root, believed they could overcome this difficulty. Their idea was to transform the regular army into a military school. The army would take in, train, and discharge soldiers quickly to build up a reserve of trained manpower. Then, when war occurred, these reserves would become fillers for an enlarged army. Their idea shows the fusion of the patrician reformers and the military progressives' two strategies. The army would be transformed into a permanent version of the

Rough Riders, an embodiment of the nation, and, at the same time, it would give the military reformers the mass army they sought.

This bold attempt to unite the strategies ran into immediate difficulties. Inside the army it was supported by those military reformers who believed that it was the only politically realistic way to gain a mass army, but resisted by others who subscribed to Upton's belief that only many years of training could produce a professional infantryman. Outside the army it faltered due to lack of support by President Taft and a Congress which saw no pressing need for change. To overcome these blocks Wood sought to create a preparedness movement outside the military that could persuade Americans to support the new military system. When Europe went to war in August 1914, the initial steps had already been taken. Wood had encouraged civilian supporters to establish an army league similar to the navy league. Private citizens could agitate in ways indiscreet for generals. He had also begun to enrol the support of the elite by holding two military training camps for college students in the summer of 1913. Camp alumni formed a permanent organization to support preparedness, Wood set up an advisory board of college presidents, and four camps were planned for 1914.

Following the outbreak of the European war, Wood, Roosevelt, Lodge, and Root advanced both strategies by allowing the preparedness movement to become a vehicle through which the supporters of a number of causes could advance their goals.[4] To start with, the movement appealed to other members of America's Protestant establishment. When Stanwood Menken, a leading New York lawyer, sent out letters to prominent New Yorkers inviting them to a meeting to discuss the threat that New York might be attacked, his request met with instant success. The result was the formation of a highly patrician organization, the National Security League, in December 1914 at the Hotel Belmont. When Grenville Clark, also a New York lawyer, his business partner Elihu Root Jr., and Theodore Roosevelt Jr. persuaded Wood to set up military summer camps for businessmen, the idea was a triumph. A special train brought 1300 businessmen, who had all paid $100 for the privilege, to live in pyramid tents and drill at Plattsburg by the waters of Lake Champlain in the Adirondacks. "There, amid simple martial surroundings," historian Finnegan writes, "the upper-class-elite underwent a conversion experience of patriotism, individual responsibility, and collective action."[5] Leading businessmen also believed they had much to gain from preparedness. The National Civic Federation, dominated by big business, and the US Chamber of Commerce, gave strong support. Many businessmen believed that the introduction of universal military training would help improve the efficiency and discipline of the American worker. They also gave strong support to industrial preparedness as a way of achieving existing goals. Howard Coffin of Hudson Motor Car Company, and president of the Society of Automotive Engineers, is a case in point. A dedicated campaigner for standardization in the automotive industry, he saw industrial preparedness as a way of extending standardization to American manufacturing as a whole, and sought to use his membership of the Naval Consulting Board by setting up a Committee on Production, Organization, Manufacture, and Standardization. Prominent progressive social reformers supported preparedness as a way they could achieve key goals, such as central planning, economic regulation, direct taxation, nationalization of natural monopolies, and social insurance against sickness and accidents. They also saw preparedness as encouraging Americans to give up an individualism in which each looked out for himself and the devil took the hindmost, and to see that for patriotism to flourish, there must be an end to injustice and oppression.[6]

The preparedness movement remained confined to America's Eastern, urban upper and middle classes. Most people were not convinced that there was any military threat, and saw preparedness as an enthusiasm of the upper and middle classes. In the words of one commentator, "The big-army sentiment is strong in the clubs and weak in the cheap restaurants."[7] Preparedness was seen as meaning high taxes, militarism, and inefficiency and waste in the armed services. Active opposition came from four overlapping groups: farmers, organized labour, German-Americans, and socialists. The farming bloc was the largest and most important. The geographical divide between urban and rural America was both reflected and intensified by patterns of newspaper readership. The idea that America was defenceless was taken up by East and West Coast urban newspapers. Vivid presentations of the danger of using strong metaphors – such as the *New York Times'* (2 December 1914), question to its readers, "in what direction shall the victor turn for spoils, with their millions of armed men tugging like blood hounds on the leash?" – rapidly overwhelmed rational assessments of the likelihood of foreign invasion. Urban business and professional men, enthralled by daily news reports, analyses, and pictures of the vast scale of the European war, increasingly came to see preparedness as a way America could show national purpose and unity. As a group farmers remained beyond the reach of urban daily papers, and so did not come to see themselves as living in a world in which they might at any moment be threatened by a foreign invasion. Farm leaders saw this as making the farming community more balanced in its assessment of danger than urban America. "Those in the cities who have followed the disastrous conflict across the waters," stated the master of the Ohio Grange, "have more nearly lost their bearings than the man and woman who are on the farm."[8]

President Wilson initially refused to endorse the preparedness movement. It would add credibility to the wild claims of political opponents like Roosevelt, who would then use the movement to attack him for doing too little. But the sinking of the great Cunard liner *Lusitania* by German submarine raider U-20 on 7 May

1915 forced a change of tack. Americans were appalled by the loss of civilian life. Over 1300 civilians drowned, and 100 or so were Americans. Wilson responded by issuing a series of notes to Germany pointing out that the sinking was against international law, and demanding that Germany promise to stop such attacks immediately. When the German government refused to give such a commitment, Wilson realized he was politically exposed to the charge that he had no big stick to threaten Germany with if it did not comply. To take the preparedness weapon out of the hands of his Republican opponents, so that they could not use it to attack him when he stood for re-election in 1916, Wilson now gave his support to a large preparedness programme. He supported 250 per cent increases in the defence budget by the strengthening of coastal defences, legislation to establish a council for national defence, and an immense, accelerated naval programme to build ten battleships and six battleship cruisers in just three years. Wilson's manoeuvres were successful. In the November 1916 elections Democrats and Republicans each sought to prove that they were more neutral than the other. Wilson won by branding the Republican candidate Hughes as a warmonger. This meant that, when Wilson did decide to go to war shortly after in 1917, he did so *directly* against the will of the American people as expressed in the November 1916 election, who had voted for him as the man who had kept America out of the war and promised to keep America neutral.

Let us return to Root's address. In it Root seeks to turn the 18 March 1917 sinkings into a cause for war. He avoids talking about whether Germany had a legitimate reason for sinking these ships because they were supplying Britain and France with war materials. He does not discuss whether a new technology, the submarine, highly vulnerable to attack when it surfaces, makes it unrealistic to expect Germany to follow an international law developed during the era of commerce raiding by surface ships – a point he later thought worth considering.[9] He does not ask whether German attacks may have been motivated by a concern to avoid losing the war rather than by any desire to conquer its neighbours. And he makes no reference to the illegality of Britain's naval blockade of Germany and her intention to bring about German collapse by starving the German people. Instead, Root makes the issue a conflict between principles he presents as absolutely incompatible. The torpedo attacks, he claims, have shown Germany puts her national interest above international law. The war is a battle between a nation which would destroy international law in the interests of its "national evolution" and nations which seek to uphold international law.

To explain Germany's claimed disregard for international law, Root presents Germany and America as having different principles of government. The act of drawing an absolute difference between the political systems of the two countries, and of justifying preparations for mobilization in terms of the defence of individual liberty, forms the centre of Root's speech:

> The present war which is raging in Europe was begun upon an avowal of principles of national action that no reasonable and thoughtful neutral ought to ignore. The central principle was that a state exigency, a state interest, is superior to those rules of morality which control individuals. Now that was not an expedient, an excuse, seized upon to justify the beginning of the war; it is fundamental; The theory of the modern republic is that right begins with the individual. It was stated in the Declaration of Independence, that instrument which it was the fashion to sneer at a few years ago, but which states the fundamental principle upon which alone a free republic can live. It was that individual men have unalienable rights, among which are life, liberty and the pursuit of happiness, and that governments are instituted to secure those rights.[10]

The idea, widely held by patrician reformers like Roosevelt and Wilson before the war, that both are modern nations with constitutions that protect the rights of the individual, is forgotten.[11] Instead, Root draws a sharp line between American modernity and German backwardness. America is a modern republic in which government is instituted to protect the rights of the individual. Germany, by contrast, he now classified with Tsarist Russia as an autocracy in which individuals derive their rights from the state and are subordinate to its exigencies.[12]

Root then paints a picture of the globe in which only *one* of these principles can survive. The colonization of the globe has now been completed. There are no free areas left for expansion. The rapid growth of Germany's population means that, should she defeat Britain and France, her people will have nowhere else to turn but the Americas. The United States will soon find itself threatened by German expansion in the Caribbean, Central America, or South America. In Germany, unlike America, the entire nation's manpower, science, and industry is organized for war. To defend herself, America will have to turn herself into an armed camp. This will be the end of American liberty. Root spells out the consequences. America must win the global struggle between rival principles. Her liberty and security depend upon the "destruction and abandonment of the hated principle of national aggrandizement".[13] Later, Root will follow Wilson and place the emphasis on the incompatibility of democracy and autocracy, stressing that "if you are to maintain your democracy you must kill autocracy".[14]

Root's conclusion is that America must mobilize all its energies to fight a total war. In an earlier address, "America's Present Needs", on 25 January 1917 at the Congress on Constructive Patriotism organized by the National Security League, Root had spelt out what that meant.[15] First, the leaders of opinion must convince Americans they face a deadly threat. The trouble is "the great mass of the people of the country do not believe a word of it". It is vital to "awaken" Americans from their complacency, especially farmers and miners in the Middle Western, North-Western, and Western states. Second, America must transform herself into a nation-in-arms through universal military service. Third, all scientific and industrial power must be organized to support the army.[16] The mobilization of the nation to fight a total war, Root believed, would redeem America from decadence and materialism. This was vitally needed:

> [Americans] assume that liberty and justice come as the air, without effort and need no service and no sacrifice for their perpetuation, a lethargy in which the more material things of life fill the needs and the wants, and to have a fat and increasing income and swell the millions of automobiles in the country, seems to be the mission of the American Republic.[17]

Returning to the early days of the republic, when it was threatened from all sides by foreign powers and every citizen had to serve in his local militia, the preparations for war would be a "re-awakening of the spirit of a free self-governing democracy".[18]

The opponents of universal military service were right in claiming that the idea of a transatlantic invasion of America by Germany was the weak point of the preparedness movement's argument.[19] There was *no* possibility that Germany could have carried out such an invasion even if she was not fighting a war and had wanted to. After analysing the difficulties in his classic work *Against the Spectre of a Dragon*, Finnegan concludes that war department claims that there could be such an invasion were "absolute nonsense".[20] Its calculations were an exercise in "arithmetic, not war". They took no account of the capabilities of the navy, nor of the difficulties of landing armies on open beaches against opposing forces. Neither the American army nor navy had given any consideration to how to defend against such assault, and they completely ignored the logistical problems of how such an army could be supplied. The German general staff, for its part, was well aware that "America cannot be attacked by us", and knew it could not even launch an invasion of Britain without totally new weapons; while the German navy, having been built for use in the North Sea, did not have the bunker capacity to cross the Atlantic and fight.

(ii) Woodrow Wilson's call for an American-led liberal-capitalist world revolution

Wilson developed his rearticulation of the story of civilization in response to events. In the 1912 election campaign the only significant difference between him and Theodore Roosevelt, now running as the Progressive Party's candidate, was that Wilson favoured the lowering of tariff barriers to foreign goods.[21] It was only after he had been elected president that he began to develop a distinctive foreign policy in response to revolution in Mexico, challenges to the open door policy in China, and the war in Europe.

National self-determination. Wilson developed the first element of his programme, national self-determination, in response to the Mexican revolution. To out-manoeuvre Republicans who called on him to place the government behind the interests of particular American businesses, Wilson chose to make his case on 4 July 1914 at Independence Hall in Philadelphia. America had been set up to "vin-dicate the rights of man". Americans must support the 85 per cent of the Mexican people who have "never been allowed to have any genuine participation in their own government or to exercise any substantial rights with regard to the very land they live upon".[22] And "If American enterprise in foreign countries, particularly in those foreign countries which are not strong enough to resist us, takes the shape of imposing upon and exploiting the mass of the people of that country, it ought to be checked and resisted."[23]

Free trade. Wilson set out the second element of his programme in speeches in support of American commerce, and of America's right as a neutral nation to con-tinue trading during the world war. Assured access to foreign markets was vital because "we are making more manufactured goods than we can consume our-selves . . . and now, if we are not going to stifle economically, we have got to find our way out into the great international exchanges of the world".[24] Equally, American commerce had a key role in persuading men that they had a common interest in the peaceful development of the globe, and that the basis for doing this was equal political rights. "America has stood in the years past for that sort of polit-ical understanding among men which would let every man feel that his rights were the same as those of another and as good as those of another, and the mission of America in the field of the world's commerce is to be the same: that when an American comes into that competition he comes without any arms that would enable him to conquer by force, but only with those peaceful influences of intel-ligence, a desire to serve, a knowledge of what he is about, before which everything softens and yields, and renders itself subject. That is the mission of America."[25]

A League of Nations. Before America's entry into the war on the side of the Allies, Wilson believed that both the Central Powers and the Allies had a common interest in the development of the world on the basis of free trade underwritten by international law. This meant that America might be able to use her position as a neutral and as an economic superpower to broker a "peace without victory" and get all the warring parties to join a peace league. In proposing a peace league Wilson was, in part, seeking to take over the ideas of the League to Enforce the Peace. This organization took up Roosevelt's argument in an 8 November 1914 article in *The New York Times* entitled "The International Posse Comitatus", that America needed military preparedness so that it could join with other civilized nations in punishing nations, such as Germany, which broke international treaties. Roosevelt compared the current international situation to the anarchy of the

Wild West. If the law was "defied in an arrogant fashion" the sheriff or marshal summoned a "posse comitatus composed of as many armed, thoroughly efficient, law-abiding citizens as was necessary to put a stop to the wrong doing".[26] Moreover, each man "kept himself ready on emergency to act on his own behalf if the peace officer did not or could not do his duty". In the light of Germany's violation of the Hague Treaty by invading and subjugating Belgium, what was required was "the establishment of some great international tribunal and by securing the enforcement of the decrees of this tribunal through the actions of a posse comitatus of powerful and civilized nations, all of them bound by solemn agreement to coerce any power that offends against the decrees of the tribunal". The public conscience of the civilized nations demanded that there be some method of making the rules of international morality "obligatory and binding among powers". The tribunal would provide a means by which public opinion could become effective. "Force must be put back of justice, and nations must not shrink from the duty of proceeding by any means necessary against wrongdoers."

Wilson set out his full programme for establishing a peaceful liberal capitalist world order in his 22 January 1917 address to the Senate. Claiming that the "world's yearning desire for peace" had not yet found expression because it has been impossible for the citizens of the countries at war to speak out, Wilson proclaimed that it was his task as the leader of the world's leading neutral nation to give them expression. Wilson argued that the old order, with its great power rivalry and its balance of power, cannot guarantee a stable equilibrium. It must be replaced by a new order. "There must be, not a balance of power, but a community of power; not organized rivalries, but an organized common peace."[27] This meant national-self determination, freedom of the seas and of trade, a league of nations, and disarmament. The first step is peace without victory:

> Victory would mean peace forced upon the loser, a victor's terms imposed upon the vanquished. It would be accepted in humiliation, under duress, at an intolerable sacrifice, and would leave a sting, a resentment, a bitter memory upon which terms peace would not rest, not permanently, but only as upon quicksand. Only a peace between equals can last.[28]

As expressed in his earlier writings, he saw the best form of government as constitutional government, of which Germany was an example. This protected liberty and rested on the consent of the governed established through discussion between the governing and the governed. At this point Wilson did not see the war in terms of a fight between democracy and autocracy. The causes of the war were structural:

> Nothing in particular started it, but everything in general. There had been growing up in Europe a mutual suspicion, an interchange of conjecture about what this Government and that Government was going to do, an interlacing of alliances and

understandings, a complex web of intrigue and spying, that presently was to entangle the whole of the family of mankind on that side of the water in its meshes.[29]

Wilson's plea for a peace without victory, then, was an attempt to include the German government in his programme to establish a new liberal capitalist world order. Wilson refused to place the blame for the war on Germany.

(iii) Gentlemen of the Gridiron Club

Before the war the patrician reformers had sought to persuade the American elite that, with the elites of Britain, France, and Germany, they ought to exercise global power on behalf of life. In an after-dinner talk on 9 December 1916 to a select gathering of the elite at the Gridiron Club we see Wilson beginning to persuade the American elite that they should now take the lead in exercising global power on behalf of life. The talk is interesting because it shows that Wilson, often thought of as totally committed to the rule of law, shared Fries' belief that if it was necessary to enable life to fulfil its potential then the law should be set aside. Wilson starts by describing the war as a Hobbesian moment in which men are coming to see their real needs, and to evoke a fantasy in which the United States will step forward as the nation which will enable humanity to leave the state of nature:

> Mr. Chairman, gentlemen of the Gridiron Club . . . Nations are led into war with one another because they do not understand each other, or because the interests of their rulers are not consistent with their own interests in matters of national life and relations. And the thing the world does need is interpretation, is the kind of vision which sees beneath the surface into the real needs and motives and sympathies of mankind.
>
> It is a fearful thing that is going on now, this contest of bloody force, but it is going to do one fine thing. It is going to strip human nature naked, and when it is over, men are going to stand face to face without any sort of disguise, without any attempt to hoodwink one another, and say to one another, "Men and brethren, what shall we do for the common cause of mankind?" And when that question is asked, what answer are we going to make and what contribution is America going to make to that answer?[30]

Like the editors of the *Bulletin of Chemical Warfare*, Wilson understands political vision as similar to artistic vision. This can be seen in a 1909 talk praising Lincoln, where "vision" is described as an imaginative capacity which enables the statesman to hear the voices of the nation not as:

> the accidental and discordant notes that come from the voice of a mob, but concurrent and concordant like the united voices of a chorus, whose many meanings, spoken by melodious tongues, unite in its understanding in a single meaning and

reveal to him a single vision, so he can speak what no man else knows, the common meaning of the common voice. Such is the man who leads a great, free, democratic nation.[31]

The statesman, then, is able to understand what the people say *better* than they can understand themselves. In his post-war bid to gain support for the League of Nations Covenant, Wilson would explicitly use this argument to claim to speak for all mankind.[32]

The key point of Wilson's speech is that the terrible violence has speeded up the development of a world opinion which can see that mankind has a common interest in ending war. The accelerated growth of world opinion means that there is now the potential for the nations to give up the balance of power politics which, Wilson believes, was one of the causes of the war and which must lead to new wars in the future. He seeks to persuade the assembled members of the Gridiron Club that they are the avant garde of mankind who can see that the war has now created the possibility of beginning to achieve world peace, statesmen who can "interpret" the voices of mankind. In doing so, he encourages them to see themselves as having the right to name the enemy of mankind which is preventing it taking this next step towards the realization of its sovereignty. It is vital to understand the full significance of this. By encouraging his audience to see themselves as having the right to name the enemy of mankind, Wilson is encouraging them to see themselves as the *global sovereign*. Wilson's 22 January 1917 address to the Senate shows he believed that the American elite shared this role with European liberals. Yet, as he makes clear the fact that in America liberals controlled the government whereas in European nations they had to share power with conservatives meant that American liberals had to take the lead by speaking for liberals everywhere. Wilson's encouragement of the members of the Gridiron Club to see themselves as part of the global avant garde was part of his redefinition of democracy against Americans who argued that the democratic ideal of equality meant they should participate in decision making. Instead, he defines the "one meaning of democracy" as being nothing other than the naming of the enemies of humanity by those who have an "insight into the essential relation of men to each other" – by which his audience would have understood Wilson to have meant none other than themselves.

Wilson ends by describing the relationship between the Constitution and mankind's realization of its sovereignty. His argument is exactly the same as Fries' argument that law cannot be allowed to stand in the way of humanities' realization of its potential. The American elite's judgement on behalf of mankind is analogous to that shown by a mother in taking care of her children. The re-making of the law is like Jesus's setting aside of the Jewish law in favour of the higher law of love:

That is the reason, among other things, that the movement for woman suffrage is becoming irresistible. Women feel further than we do, and feeling, if it be comprehending, feeling goes further in the solution of problems than cold thinking does. The day of cold-thinking, of fine-spun constitutional argument is gone, thank God. We do not now discuss so much what the Constitution of the United States is as what the constitution of human nature is, what the essential constitution of human society is. And we know in our hearts that, if we ever find a place or a time when the Constitution of the United States is contrary to the constitution of human nature and human society, we have got to change the Constitution of the United States. The Constitution, like the Sabbath, was made for man and not man for the Constitution . . . I have known some judges who seemed to think that the Constitution was a straitjacket into which the life of the nation must be forced, whether it could be with a true regard for the laws of life or not . . . men must be put forward whose whole comprehension is that law is subservient to life and not life to law.[33]

Just as Fries reduces laws which stand in the way of the progress to "arbitrary rules", Wilson reduces the parts of the Constitution which he judges stand in the way of progress to a "straitjacket" which must be broken out of. If the law conflicts with what the avant garde judges needs to be done so that mankind can realise its sovereignty, then it is the law that must give way. If challenged, Wilson would have emphasized that his address was in accord with the Constitution. He would have pointed out that the Constitution acknowledges the people as the constituent power which established it and sets out procedures through which they can revise it. The point is that Wilson presents himself and his audience as an avant garde "we" that knows better than the people themselves what their true needs are and the ways that the law must be changed to meet those needs. The idea that, as the avant garde of humanity, the American elite could act outside the law when the occasion demanded would shortly be put into practice when Wilson declared war on Germany. Since the end of the wars of religion, European states had, with exceptions such as the wars waged between revolutionary France and the surrounding European monarchies, avoided calling into question the legitimacy of states they were at war with. There were good reasons for this. It made it easier to negotiate an end to the war and to restore normal relations. Wilson will set all this aside and brand Germany a nation governed according to unacceptable principles, and he will declare that America is waging war against the German government on behalf of the German people.

(iv) "Masters of the World" – the House of Morgan and America's decision to go to war against Germany

American neutrality was rapidly undermined through the development of a vast trade in war materials with the Allies.[34] Britain's naval blockade of the Central

Powers ensured that no such trade developed with Germany. From the start, the policy of the American government while legally neutral favoured the Allies. The government argued that trade in war materials, including munitions, could proceed as it was not contrary to international law. The British and the French appointed the bank J.P. Morgan & Co. as their commercial agents. The bank's new role promised high war profits, but more than that in the longer run war trade offered America world economic dominance which would inevitably enhance the bank's own wealth and power. At home the bank could carry through plans for rationalizing American manufacturing. The Morgan moved rapidly to organize the purchase, manufacturing, and financing of war materials on a truly massive scale, quickly turning America into the Entente Allies' arsenal. This led to the doubling of American trade during neutrality, and by the end of the war had turned America into the world's leading creditor. The key obstacle the bank faced was Wilson's initial refusal to allow it to finance the Allies through loans. In August 1914 the bank asked the government about the propriety of floating a loan for France. Secretary of State William Jennings Bryan categorically refused, stating privately that money was the worst contraband as "it commands everything else", and publicly that loans to belligerents would be "inconsistent with the spirit of neutrality".[35] This policy was rapidly undermined. By October 1914, State Department Councillor Robert Lansing, acting at the request of Morgan and the National City Banks, gained Wilson's approval for "bank credits of belligerent governments in contradistinction to public loans".[36] Through this accounting fiction, American banks would now finance Allied purchases. The matter was so politically explosive that no official announcement was made until March 1915, and when questioned in the Senate, the administration denied there had been any change in policy.

By mid-1915, however, Britain's voracious demands for war finance made a public loan essential. In August 1915, J.P. Morgan & Company inexplicably halted purchases of sterling. Within days the pound fell sharply, threatening to disrupt the flow of goods from the US to Britain by making American goods too expensive. Treasury Secretary William McAdoo now presented Wilson with a blunt argument in favour of loans. "To maintain our prosperity, we must finance it. Otherwise, it may stop and that would be disastrous."[37] Secretary of State Lansing put much the same point to Wilson in a letter:

> If the European countries cannot find the means to pay for the excess of goods sold them over those purchased from them, they will have to stop buying and our present export trade will shrink proportionately. The result will be restriction of output, industrial depression, idle capital, idle labor, numerous failures, financial demoralization, and general unrest and suffering among the laboring classes . . . Can we afford to let a declaration as to our concept of the "true spirit of neutrality," made in the early days of the war, stand in the way of our national interests which seem to be seriously threatened?[38]

Wilson agreed to let the House of Morgan float a loan for half a billion dollars for the British and French. To raise much of the loan, Morgan turned to those who were benefiting most from the war trade, American manufacturers, and in particular to Du Pont, which underwrote approximately $45 million. Most contracts for war materials went to the North-East, with Du Pont de Nemours Powder Company heading the list, with contracts worth close to half a billion dollars. The booming war trade, and extension of loans meant that almost two years before America entered the war militarily it had entered the war economically on the side of the Allies. The bankers and munitions manufacturers certainly had a hand in the breakdown of neutrality, but as the debate over American prosperity in general within Wilson's cabinet shows, and as Senator Nye who chaired the 1930s Senate Munitions Inquiry which examined the issue in depth concluded, it was the growing dependence of American prosperity on trade with the Allies that was decisive.[39]

The history of how America became Britain and France's arsenal long before it entered the war officially helps us to understand why Germany decided to renew unrestricted submarine warfare in January 1917 when it perceived that American attempts to mediate a peace had failed. By this point the German army and navy believed that America had already entered the war economically and the length of time it would take for America to mobilize militarily meant that Germany had nothing to lose by renewing submarine warfare.

As the war trade swelled, Senior Morgan partner Henry Davison was jubilant: "We are now in a fair way of becoming masters of the world. The more we stimulate [Allied] trade, and the more loans we make to these foreign countries, the more we increase our predominance." But others within the commanding heights of US banking were horrified by what the war trade was leading to. "The carnival of death and destruction has gone far enough," declared the governor of the Federal Reserve Board, W.P.G. Harding, and he went on to argue that America should now use Allied dependency on US finance and manufacturing to help end the war. In addition, he warned that the unending flow of capital to the Allies could be disastrous to the American economy, driving up prices and tightening credit. Opposition to further loans gave Wilson a way of pressing Britain to support his last peacemaking effort in late 1916, so he backed Harding's refusal of a Morgan proposal to use British Treasury Bills to extend Allied credit. By this point Britain was so reliant on American credit and war materials that it was in no position to repeat its earlier intimidation of the administration by cutting back on purchasing. Without American supplies, Britain could not continue the war. Its dependence was total. America's war trade had, paradoxically, given Wilson the opportunity to make a decisive intervention to end the war.

(v) The paradox of Wilson's decision to make the First World War a crusade "to make the world safe for democracy"

Following the 18 March 1917 sinkings of American ships, Wilson and his advisors believed the public outcry meant he now had to decide whether or not to declare war. Earlier in the year, when Germany resumed unrestricted warfare, Wilson had hesitated. Notes by members of his cabinet show him musing about whether to stay out of the war so that the United States could later help maintain the unity of the white race after the war. On the evening of 31 January 1917, Secretary of State Lansing reports Wilson stating that he was increasingly impressed by the thought "that 'white civilization' and its dominance of the world" required the United States to keep itself "intact" for it "would have to build up the nations ravaged by war". At a cabinet meeting on 2 February Wilson's secretary for agriculture reports Wilson stating that if, "in order to keep the white race or part of it strong to meet the yellow race – Japan for instance, in alliance with Russia, dominating China – it was wise to do nothing, he would do nothing, and would submit to . . . any imputation of weakness or cowardice".[40] Then on 2 April 1917 Wilson asked Congress for authority to go to war *militarily* against Germany. Why did he decide to do so?

First, to retain the authority of his administration he had to prevent appearing to lose control over events. He had to show that the presidency continued to represent the sovereignty of the American people. In the spring of 1917 there was an increasing danger that critics could successfully present his administration as adrift, powerless in the face of the growing American trade with and financing of the Allies, the German renewal of unrestricted submarine warfare, and its attempt to draw Mexico into the war if America should join the Allies, and the obstacles raised by the warring governments to Wilson's attempt to mediate a peace.

Second, Wilson believed that the vast contribution America would make to an Allied victory would enable him to set the terms of the peace. This offered him a new strategy for achieving a new world order based on national self-determination, a league of nations, and a liberal-capitalist world order.

Wilson's decision to go to war was not determined by investors and manufacturers interested in maintaining the war trade and ensuring an Allied victory so that their loans would be repaid. Indeed, like other patrician reformers, Wilson was doubtless threatened by the idea that the war showed Americans to be a materialistic people willing to make vast profits out of the war. In the words of one Plattsburger during neutrality America had "turned the other cheek to the buffet, not in weakness but in order to use both hands for grabbing the money".[41] Yet, paradoxically, it was Wilson's need to retain the freedom of action which would enable him, as president, to answer the moral call to ensure that the horrors of the world war would not be repeated which, in the belief that it was the *only* way to retain such freedom, forced him to bow to the economic pressure to maintain the war trade and investor confidence. It was this that led him, first, to enter the war economically by allowing the trade in munitions and by agreeing to allow loans to the Allies, and then, second, to enter the war militarily on their side. Moreover, by alienating other potential sources of political support, he was forced to articulate policies that served the interests of the bankers and munitions makers at the same time that they enabled him to advance his programme to construct a new liberal capitalist world order.

Were there alternative strategies open to Wilson? Could he have continued to maintain American neutrality? Could he have relaunched his existing strategy of using America's neutral position to mediate an end to the war? As the man who had just been re-elected president because he had kept America out of the war, Wilson had a strong mandate had he chosen to make use of it. If he had been willing to reassess the war trade, Britain's strategy of starving Germany into surrender, Germany's response to it by declaring unrestricted submarine warfare, and had admitted earlier failures of judgement in responding to both, he could have used his position to tell Americans a story about the preparedness movement that would have neutralized it as a political force. This story would have focused on the non-existence of any German threat to America and the self-interest of the key groups in the preparedness movement in bringing America into the war. Had Wilson chosen to pursue the latter strategy, however, he would have faced real and perhaps insurmountable difficulties in mediating a "peace without victory". While America's growing war trade with France and Britain had given him an instrument he could use to force them to accept such a peace, he had no such leverage over the Central Powers which now held the military advantage.

This analysis gives us an insight into the intimate relationship between sovereignty and war. A sovereign right has nothing superior to it. It is "superaneus", that which has nothing above itself. The right to war is the most sovereign of all rights, since it allows a sovereign to decide that another sovereign is his enemy and to apply himself to his subjugation or destruction. This is not merely an act of sovereignty, it is the manifestation of its very essence, its assertion of its absolute superiority to everything else. This is the intoxication of going to war. In going to war the people are entranced and intoxicated by the spectacle of themselves as an earthly god. We can sense this intoxication most powerfully in Wilson's 6 April 1918 appeal to Americans to fund the third liberty loan. As America's new 3 million man army began to arrive in France, Wilson sought to evoke the tremendous spectacle of America, and through American leadership humanity, asserting its sovereignty by the victory of its arms over Germany. He presents America as responding to a German challenge that calls into doubt the sovereignty of international law by the complete destruction of that challenge: "There is, therefore, but one response possible from us: Force, Force to the utmost, Force without stint or limit, the right-eous and triumphant Force which shall make Right the law of the world, and cast every selfish dominion down in the dust."[42] By going to war, the president, as the figure who represents the whole nation, proclaims the absolute superiority of the sovereign people. Yet, Wilson's decision to go to war reveals that such absolute sovereignty was an illusion. It reveals the weakness of the state, its lack of sover-eignty, with respect to transnational networks of capital (the war trade and finance), technology (German submarines were an improvement on a largely American invention), and culture (the success of British propaganda in convincing the American establishment, which was already inclined to do so, to see itself as part of a transatlantic Anglo-Saxon culture). Wilson's change of strategy, while not determined, was forced by the perception that his administration would find itself increasingly at the mercy of events if it did not do so. The state's lack of sover-eignty was also present at the heart of Wilson's new strategy. By taking steps to destroy the potential anti-war bloc, Wilson could only execute his new strategy with the support of the groups making up the preparedness movement. His strat-egy could only be successful to the extent that it was compatible with their strategies for realizing their goals: profit maximization, great power militarily, strengthening of elite power through its transformation into a meritocracy, and the organization of American science and the scientific organization of America. There was some room for manoeuvre since the president could, to some extent, rearticulate these strategies to make them compatible with his own. The result is the paradox that, in acting so as to prevent these transnational networks from revealing the illusion of sovereignty, through their capacity to undermine the president's claim to determine events, Wilson's new strategy had to largely fulfill the ends of these networks.

The problem with Wilson's own presentation of his decision to go to war was that it tended to deny its own status as a political judgement, and hence the need for others to make further judgements about its adequacy. (This is because of the aporia of judgement. Since a judgement lacks an absolute ground, further judge-ments are called for to determine its validity. These, in their turn, require further judgements.) Wilson's rhetoric tended to bury his decision's status as a political judgement in two ways. First, by employing theological ideas such as "provi-dence", Wilson ceases to present himself as a statesman making a judgement and becomes an agent of God's plan for mankind. Second, it achieves the same effect using fear to force agreement – if Germany is not defeated, American liberty and democracy will be destroyed. Such rhetoric tends to destroy the political realm itself as an area where there are no certainties and in which we are called to make judgements about what should be done.

A memorandum of a 20 March 1917 meeting to advise the president on whether to go to war by Secretary of State Lansing gives us a unique insight into why Wilson decided to make the need to defend democracy the reason for war. Lansing now stated that it was a political mistake to make the sinking of American ships the reason for going to war as it would "cause debate".[43] It would offer opponents the chance to argue: that the war was being fought to protect the interests of businessmen and bankers who were profiting from supplying the Allies and who stood to lose vast amounts if the Allies lost the war and could not repay loans; that the Royal Navy's blockade of the Central Powers was also against international law and had enabled Britain to manoeuvre America into the war on the side of the Allies; and that the German resumption of unrestricted submarine warfare, while contrary to international law and inhumane, was militarily understandable as America had already entered the war economically against Germany. These were exactly the allegations that the American Socialist Party made when Wilson declared war. "Our entrance into the war was instigated by the predatory capitalists in the United States who boast of the enormous profit of seven billion dollars from the manufacture and sale of munitions and war supplies."[44]

Lansing offered Wilson a strategy for avoiding these dangers. "I said that the revolution in Russia, which appeared to be successful, had removed the one objection to affirming that the European War was a war between Democracy and Absolutism."[45] And when Wilson stated that he "did not see how he could speak of a war for democracy or of Russia's revolution in addressing Congress", Lansing offered him a way of doing so. "I replied that I did not perceive any objection but in any event I was sure that he could do so indirectly by attacking the character of the autocratic government of Germany as manifested by its deeds of inhumanity, by its broken promises, and by its plots and conspiracies against this country."[46] What Lansing was offering Wilson was a causal schema or story for interpreting German actions. The sinking of American ships could now be presented as evidence that Germany was an autocracy, allowing America to go to war on the unifying issue of defending democracy rather than on the divisive issue of attacks on US ships. Wilson could then persuade Americans who had voted for him in 1916 because he claimed he had kept America neutral to support him in a war, and it would help him prevent the country being divided between the North-East which had done so well out of the war trade and the Mid-West and North-West, which were inclined not to see submarine sinkings as an issue that concerned them sufficiently to enter a distant war.

In his speech to Congress on 2 April, Wilson adopted Lansing's strategy. Arguing his own "thought has not been driven from its habitual and normal course by the unhappy events of the last two months",[47] he stated that autocracy made neutrality impossible. In reality there had been a seismic shift in his policy, nothing less than a complete reclassification of international relations. Wilson had changed the test from deciding whether a government could be trusted to uphold international law from constitutional to democratic government, changed

Germany's status from constitutional monarchy to autocracy, and declared that with the March Revolution Russia was now a democracy.[48]

In calling for America to go to war, Wilson declared that submarine warfare was "warfare against all mankind. It is warfare against all nations." In going to war against Germany, America would be fighting to maintain human rights. Wilson's war aims were ambiguous. He started by setting out a limited goal. America's aim was to bring "the government of the German Empire to terms and to end the war".[49] Yet he went on to present the German government as an autocracy which must be destroyed because it would always be a threat to peace, democracy, and liberty. America cannot be neutral, Wilson declared, because the menace to peace and freedom "lies in the *existence* of autocratic governments backed by organized force which is controlled wholly by their will, and not by the will of the people"[50] (my italics). It was therefore necessary to wage a total war whose aim was the replacement of the autocratic German government by a democratic government. It would also be a war in which an old, outdated, principle of sovereignty, in which "wars were provoked and waged in the interests of dynasties or of little groups of ambitious men . . . accustomed to use their fellow men as pawns or tools", would be replaced by the modern principle of the sovereignty of the people. This meant that, strictly speaking, America was not going to war against Germany, but was taking part in a revolutionary struggle by the peoples of the world to overthrow illegitimate forms of government. Wilson repeated the argument he had used to justify intervention in the Mexican Revolution, and which he would use to justify intervention in the Russian Revolution. By excluding alternative interpretations of what the people might want – such as those of German conservatives, Russian Bolsheviks, and Mexicans who opposed American intervention – Wilson was able to present his idea of the Mexican, German, and Russian people as wanting American style liberal democracy as self-evidently true. Having produced the people he wanted, he would then be able to claim to represent them.[51] America, he declared, was fighting for the liberation of the peoples of the world, "the German peoples included".[52]

Wilson now sought to repeat his turn-of-the-century strategy for taming the demands that could be made in the name of democracy. As he had earlier subordinated democracy to its role in the task of the American nation in opening the East, now he sought to subordinate democracy to the demands of America's role as the architect of a new liberal capitalist world order. The meaning of democracy can be determined by its functional role in America's global task. He argued that to defend democracy, America must achieve democratically the degree of organization, discipline, and efficiency Germany achieved through command and scientific organization.[53] Democracy would become the efficient means for achieving the national purpose, it would be the use of "common counsel, for the drawing together, not only of the energies, but of the minds of the nation".[54] Elsewhere, Wilson talks of democracy in terms of "spontaneous co-operation".[55] No dissent is permitted. "If we are true friends of freedom, our own or anyone else's, we will see that the power of this country and the productivity of this country is raised to its absolute maximum, and that absolutely nobody is allowed to stand in the way of it."[56] Wilson placed both legal dissent and law breaking on a continuum, branding both as "mere gradations of . . . the unwillingness to co-operate". His "fundamental lesson" is that "we must not only take common counsel, but that we must yield to and obey common counsel".[57] The effect of Wilson's functional subordination of democracy to economic efficiency and military effectiveness is profound. Placed in the context of this fight for its own survival against autocracy, the possibility of arguing that democracy means the right to call into question the dominant view of America's international task is excluded.

(vi) "The cloud of dread and terror"

Wilson's post-war strategy to gain support for the liberal-capitalist world order, both inside and outside America, repeated and entrenched the depiction of the earth as a battlefield between rival principles.[58] He sought to continue the control over foreign policy he had enjoyed during the war by depicting the wartime state of emergency as not having ended despite the signing of the Armistice on 11 November 1918.

Wilson's policy at the Paris peace talks was made up of two contradictory strands. The first sought the rapid reintegration of Germany into a new liberal-capitalist world order. In his declaration of war speech, Wilson had emphasized that America's quarrel was with Germany's autocratic leaders and not with the German people. His war speeches had sought to drive a wedge between German liberals and the German government by reassuring them that there would be a place for the commerce of a democratic Germany in a liberal-capitalist world order. In seeking to promote revolution in Germany, however, Wilson found that he had contributed to an uprising which called his plans into question. When Germany sought Wilson's help in negotiating an Armistice in October 1918, Wilson's notes to Germany stated he would only negotiate peace with a liberalized Germany in which the military autocrats were subject to democratic control. These notes, by focusing on the Kaiser as the obstacle to peace, helped to set in motion a revolutionary process that quickly threatened the hopes of liberal-nationalist and moderate democratic socialists for a revolution from above. By mid-November 1918 the threat of victory by revolutionary socialists had forced moderate socialists and traditional military groups into a loose alliance.

The unexpected turn of events in Germany alarmed Wilson. As he headed to Europe on the *George Washington* in December 1918, he spoke about the danger that, amidst post-war economic chaos, revolutionary agitation, and starvation, the European masses would turn to the "poison of Bolshevism" as a protest against the "way the world worked".[59] In the midst of the anarchy brought on by war and revolution, Wilson believed that America had an immense opportunity to gain Europeans' support for a new liberal capitalist world system as the *only* path to peace and stability. The trick was to persuade the Allied governments to give up their own imperialist ambitions, and to support the rapid reintegration of Germany into a new liberal-capitalist world order, by convincing them that the alternative might be the spread of Bolshevik revolution to Germany and then to their own countries. In the American delegation to the Paris peace talks, this view was most strongly supported by Secretary of State Lansing, General Tasker Bliss, and Republican Henry White. Speaking to the foreign press club on 11 March 1919, Lansing highlighted the danger: "Like the anarchy which for a year has made an inferno of Russia, the fires of terrorism are ablaze in the states of Germany. Through the ruins of this once great empire the flames are sweeping westward."[60] The idea that a liberal-democratic Germany should quickly be reintegrated found expression in American policies. To shore up Ebert's new German government against the threat of revolutionary socialism, the Wilson administration sought to get immediate food aid to Germany. At the peace talks the American delegation sought to moderate Allied reparation demands, arguing that excessive demands would prevent Germany's economy reviving and maintain the perfect conditions for a Bolshevik takeover of Germany.

Wilson's desire for German reintegration was contradicted by a desire for control and punishment. His concern to maintain control over post-war Germany arose from doubts as to whether the country really had abandoned militarism. His own policy actually helped German militarism survive the German revolution. By backing the moderate socialists and liberal-nationalist's decision to limit the revolution to the area of formal constitution making, Wilson helped ensure that it left largely untouched the social bases of traditionalism in the civil service, the army, Junker landowners, jurists, and large industrialists. His concern that the real power of the militarists had been untouched led Wilson to support the French and British in using the Paris conference to establish post-war military and political control over Germany. "Until we knew what the German Government was going to be, and how the German people were going to behave," he declared in February 1919, "the world had a moral right to disarm Germany, and to subject her to a generation of thoughtfulness."[61] His desire for control was matched by a desire for punishment. The peace treaty should turn Germany into an example, a terrible warning to other nations of the consequences of aggression. "He [Wilson] only looked towards reaching a peace and in doing so putting Germany in the position to build up a commerce which would enable her to pay what she ought to pay in order to make good the robbery and destruction she had perpetrated."[62] Germany's status as a suspected "outlaw" until she had paid reparations and proven she had transformed her character was enshrined in the peace treaty and in the League of Nations. Wilson supported Article 231 of the treaty which attributed all guilt for the war to Germany. In his declaration of war speech, Wilson had argued that only the German government should be blamed for the war. Yet in the Paris peace talks, he appeared unclear about whether it was the state or the nation that should be blamed. The logic of harsh reparations, whose cost the German political and economic elite would certainly try to hand over to the classes below them, necessarily demanded that it was the nation. In responding to a call by Lansing to soften the terms of the treaty, Wilson defended it as hard but just: "It is profitable that a nation should learn once and for all what an unjust war means in itself."[63] For Wilson, the League of Nations Covenant provided the means by which the contradictory goals of reintegration, control, and punishment could be reconciled. Initially, Germany and Russia would be excluded from the League. Through Article 10, in which members promised to preserve the territorial integrity and political independence of all member states against external aggression, the League would be a way in which the wartime military alliance between France, Britain, Italy, and America could be continued into the peace. Through the League they could act together should Germany decide to contest militarily the terms of the peace agreement at a later date. Wilson reconciled the use of the League to maintain a victor's peace through armed force by believing that in the longer run the League would prevent the creation of an inter-Allied trading area, and to promote German integration into a liberal-capitalist world order when she had proved she was no longer an outlaw nation.

Wilson's strategy for gaining American acceptance for the League was the same as the strategy he used to gain British and French acceptance: he presented them as the only sure way in which Americans could protect themselves against Germany and Bolshevik Russia. He reiterated the idea that Germany would continue to pose a military threat to the United States, but because of her crushing defeat he had to cast about for new ways of convincing Americans of this. One way he did so can be seen in his 20 May 1919 special address to Congress sent by telegram from Paris. In it he sought to turn the chemical campaign's propaganda about the terrifying threat the German chemical industry posed to Americans to his advantage. By underscoring the reality of the danger from the German chemical threat, he implicitly emphasized the need for American membership of the League of Nations as a means by which America could share the burden of defending itself with Britain, France, and Italy. At the same time, he wanted to prevent the campaign from claiming presidential authority for its assertions that chemical disarmament was impossible, so he affirmed that America was ready to join in the "programme of international disarmament".[64] When the Senate refused to ratify the League of Nations Covenant without unacceptable reservations, Wilson travelled across the United States stopping in major cities to tell Americans that, despite the end of the war, they continued to be threatened by Germany and now faced a new Bolshevik threat. The best, and perhaps the only way, they could defend themselves against these threats, he tirelessly repeated, was for America to ratify the League of Nations Covenant. What is striking about Wilson's speeches is the number of different ways he sought to convince Americans to accept his new geography in which events in Europe could create world crises that threatened the very existence of America as a sovereign nation. We have become so used to such rhetoric that it is interesting to see the effort that had to be made to begin to persuade Americans to accept it. On 6 September in Des Moines, he argued that modern communications meant that distance is no longer a barrier to the spread of revolutionary ideas:

> And in other parts of Europe the poison spread – the poison of disorder, the poison of revolt, the poison of chaos. And do you honestly think, my fellow citizens, that none of that poison has got in the veins of this free people? Do you not know that the world is all now one single whispering gallery? Those antenna of the wireless telegraph are the symbols of our age . . . And quietly upon steamships, silently under the cover of the postal service, with the tongue of the wireless and the tongue of the telegraph, all the suggestions of disorder are spread through the world.[65]

Here Wilson uses the newness of wireless telegraph broadcasting to constitute it as a site for collective fantasy in the same way that the chemists were doing with poison gas. And he gives shape to that fantasy by using the metaphor of an invisible poison spreading through the body to present it as a means through which Bolshevik propaganda can take hold of America. He goes on to describe the spread of communist ideas as an accelerating process, a poison that will spread "more and more rapidly", until the very existence of America is threatened. Like claims that America was in danger of German invasion it was all pure fantasy. There was no possibility whatsoever that America was in danger of a Bolshevik revolution.[66] On 12 September in Coeur D'Alene, Wilson emphasized the threat of German commerce and linked it to plans for future military domination. Germany's pre-war plan was to open a "line of dominion" between herself and the Far East. She wanted control from:

> Bremen to Baghdad, from the North Sea to Persia . . . [She sought] to crush not only little Serbia . . . but all the Balkan states, to get Turkey in her grasp, take all the Turkish and Arabian lands beyond, penetrate the wealthy realms of Persia, open the gates of India, and, by dominating the central trade routes of the world, dominate the world itself.

He then sketches a nightmare scenario of Germany's new post-war strategy. They are by this time the only people dealing with the Bolshevist government. Their plan was to draw all the finances, commerce, and the development of Russia under their control. And once they had done so they would be able to renew their plans to control the East and extend their domination over the entire world. If America did not support the League, Wilson concluded, she would be leaving the "ground" of Eastern Europe free for Germany to sow it with "dragon's teeth" and its "harvest of armed men". Europeans would once again be under the "cloud of dread and terror" which they had lived beneath ever since Germany's victory over France in the Franco-Prussian War. While in Denver on 25 September, Wilson told his audience that the only alternative to membership of the League was permanent mobilization for war. This would destroy American liberty. To reawaken the fear of attack at a time when Americans wanted to forget the First World War he invoked the threat of new technologies. Their emergence meant that the war just ended could not be taken as a guide to the "next war". To make such a threat credible to inhabitants of Colorado separated from Europe by both a continent and an ocean Wilson made veiled statements about the flying bombs guided by gyroscopes that Elmer Sperry and Charles Kettering were developing for the government and their possible use against cities:

> There were instruments possessing methods of destruction inconceivable, which were just ready for use when the war ended – great projectiles which guided them- selves, capable of one hundred miles or more, and bursting tons of explosives on helpless cities.

The weapons used by the German's were "toys" compared with the weapons that would be used in the next war.[67] In late September Wilson, exhausted from the demands of his speaking tour, suffered a major stroke and was taken back to Washington. He would now direct the final fight to persuade the Senate to ratify the League of Nations Covenant from his sick bed. When Wilson refused to accept amendments which would make the Covenant acceptable to Lodge and Borah the Senate voted against ratification.

9

The Coming Community

Through the League of Nations Woodrow Wilson sought to extend to the world the principles set out in the Declaration of Independence. In 1776 the American people overthrew the "absolute tyranny" of George III and founded a republic to secure their right to "life, liberty, and the pursuit of happiness". In 1918 the world's peoples – including in Wilson's view the German people! – overthrew German autocracy and ended its attempt at world domination and founded a League of Nations which would secure their self-government. Wilson was a second Jefferson, Pershing a second Washington. Indeed, Wilson sought to get all peoples to imagine themselves as first and foremost citizens in an emerging world republic and to see such citizenship as the primary form of community. There is a dark side to Wilson's creation of a world community of republican citizens. For before the world's peoples can become citizens in the emerging global republic they are reduced by the avant garde to a "they" threatened by disaster. This legitimates the avant garde's exercise of unlimited power over the "they" until such time as they can become citizens of the new global republic. In Root's Yale talk this justifies the extension of a global network of power that is more extensive geographically and penetrates more deeply into society than that produced by the Roman republic/empire.

In Wilson's talk to the Gridiron Club he presents the American elite as now having the primary responsibility for developing this network of power over all aspects of life. The result is an ambiguous situation. On the one hand, the earth's peoples can insist that they should, as world citizens, be served by global institutions such as the League of Nations. On the other hand, under the pretext of protecting their lives from the disaster and enabling them to realize their potential, the global avant garde can extend its power over all aspects of human life. In the preceding chapters we have seen how the patrician reformers, and their allies, began to do exactly this. In the immediate aftermath of the war this culminated in Wilson's production of a picture of global relations which justified repeated interventions by the presidency in American and global society so as to save both from disaster. The fact that America had to enter the First World War, he insisted, showed that the globe now formed a complex interdependent whole in which economic, cultural, and military linkages mean that small local crises could rapidly lead to global catastrophes which might reverse the progress of civilization itself.[1] To persuade Americans to see themselves as part of such a whole, Wilson described the relationship between part and whole in terms of vivid metaphors. In order to convince Americans that local events could quickly lead to global catastrophes that might threaten them, he talked about international relations in terms of "quicksand", "forest fires", and the "spread of poison". His endlessly repeated conclusion: the war showed that we cannot rely on a balance of power to avert local crises becoming global catastrophes. The only way that the future of American liberal democracy could be assured would be if America led a worldwide movement in which democracy, liberal constitutional government, science, technology, and capitalism mutually reinforced each other. By creating the institutional machinery needed to enable the liberal democracies to cooperate in carrying out this revolution and to defend it against "outlaw" nations, Americans would ensure that the triumph of liberty over tyranny took place on a world scale. Wilson's rearticulation of the arguments of the military progressives and the patrician reformers, then, made it difficult for Americans to discern whether measures taken to support liberal capitalist world revolution were being smuggled in as reforms needed to secure the very survival of American liberal democracy.[2]

Wilson's attempt to make all the world's peoples citizens of a universal republic was based on both consent and terror. Through the presentation of the League as a new way of ordering international relations, Wilson secured widespread consent for it by making it a blank screen upon which the world's peoples could project their hopes. To middle-class Europeans and Americans who projected their worst nightmares on to Lenin's proclamation of a worldwide communist revolution, it appeared as a way of avoiding both socialist revolution and a return of world war. The element of terror was no less important. Internationally the victorious powers imposed a punitive peace which sent a message to all other nations: "Accept our government of the globe, or we will do to you what we did to Germany." They also hoped that the isolation of Russia, which Wilson believed would lead to the collapse of the November Revolution, would send a similar message to any people tempted to follow the communist path.[3] Through endorsing the chemical campaign, as we have seen, Wilson also supported the development of a giant industrial capacity for manufacturing poison gas which could be used as a means of exercising terror against Germany or Russia in the future. Nationally, Wilson told the American people that, because the world was now a tightly linked, interconnected whole, the failure to ratify the League Covenant would lead to America's very existence being threatened by communist revolution, business depression, and the resurgence of German autocracy. To forestall any widespread challenge to the patrician reformers' account of why America had had to go to war, Wilson and the Republican opponents of ratification made anyone who dared to make such a challenge the object of public hostility by identifying them with Russian Bolshevism or German autocracy. This sent the message: "Challenge our account, and we will silence you." In the light of Wilson's use of terror to support the liberal capitalist world revolution it is entirely appropriate that, as well as naming an aircraft carrier the *Theodore Roosevelt*, the US Navy has named a ballistic missile submarine the *Woodrow Wilson*.

(i) The community to come

I have started to call into question the idea that we are, primarily, citizens of a global republic by beginning to articulate an alternative idea of community. I call this "the coming community", following Georgio Agamben's book of that name.[4] This idea of community takes as its starting point the fact that what we share first of all is our shared concrete existence, an existence that becomes concrete precisely in the address from one to another. That is to say, each of us exists through voicing personal pronouns such as "I" or "we" as we take up and rearticulate the languages of religion, art, science, liberty, democracy, socialism, the nation, and so forth. Yet we do not already know *how* we should rearticulate these languages nor will we ever achieve a transparent grasp of any stable criterion telling us how to do so. What we have seen is that the experience of struggling to find the right words to say what needs to be said is suppressed by the avant garde's claim that it already knows what needs to be said. Thus, in Part 1, we saw how Fries and West confronted the reader of *Chemical Warfare* with the horror of the poison gas cloud so that he or she would, for a brief moment, not know what he or she should do or say. Once the reader is embroiled in this perplexed and vulnerable state, Fries and West are in a position to "reassure" them once more, telling them that what is demanded is the rapid development of America's chemical warfare capability. We do not already know what to say in response to such events because we do not know the full context of past usage. That is to say we do not know how the current use of words has been established and hence what is at stake in continuing to use them in this way. Thus, as we have seen, current usages of the word "democracy" have been shaped by a struggle that most Americans know nothing about and they therefore have little idea of what is at stake in repeating such usages. This means that, each time each one of us speaks, he or she has to make a judgement about how to take up and rearticulate the ways of speaking that have been bequeathed to us. It is a question of searching for the right words to apply in this case. The investigation I have carried out into the inadequacies of the language used by the chemical warfare officers to speak about research into new poison gases is an example of what this can mean in practice. What is more we can never know with certainty whether we have made the right judgement. This is because of the aporia inherent in judgment itself: in order to know whether the criteria used by a first judgement are authoritative, a second judgement is needed. Yet this second judgement in turn requires a third judgement to assert that the criteria it uses are themselves authoritative. Indeed, the demand for certainty leads to an infinite regress of authorizations. This logical point can be expressed more poetically. Animals immediately know how to speak. The cricket chirps in the grass, the owl hoots as it passes over the wood beneath the stars. By contrast, human beings are born without knowing what to say and have to struggle to find the words they need. What we all have in common is that we are first and foremost "in-fans" (etymologically, someone who does not yet know how to speak). This does not stand in opposition to our being a member of a particular national community, a class community, or any other kind of community. What it does do, however, is to call into question any attempt to give a final determination of the boundaries of such communities. This can be seen by looking at how the patrician reformers sought to use the war to determine the boundaries of the American community. They argued that the war showed that German-Americans had to choose between being loyal to Germany or to America. They could not be both. It was a question of either/or. If they wanted to be Americans, they had to prove that they were "100 per cent American". The patrician reformers defined being American as being not German. They believed they had the right to make a final determination of what it was to be an American because they were the avant garde of America, an avant garde that was enabling the national community to achieve its sovereignty. What I have discovered in my analyses calls this determination of the boundaries of the American community into question. As I have shown, the definition of Germany as an autocracy hostile to American democracy, far from being in the universal interests of Americans, was in fact part of the (largely Anglo-Saxon) patrician reformers' evolving strategy to take over America. Ironically, that strategy involved turning America into a state similar to the reformers' caricature of the "German enemy". This example places us in a position to define the relationship between the coming community and Wilson's emerging global republic. The coming community is not the logical opposite of the global republic. Instead, it is the community of human beings who seek to find the right words or actions to respond to contemporary events. They do so by being attentive to whether the currently dominant criteria for responding to such events really do justice to what is at stake in them; when they sense that these criteria have become problematic, they search for new ways of speaking about them. This, as I argue in the introduction to Part 1, is not achieved through creation ex nihilo but by searching among marginalized or subordinated languages to find the fragments of language which can be combined to form new ways of speaking. In the aftermath of the investigations I have carried out into how the avant garde excluded alternative ways of talking about terror and democracy the reader now has some examples of what this actually means in practice. The result is the articulation of new ways of speaking about war, democracy, science, and so forth which call into question the self-proclaimed global avant garde's determination of the sense of these terms and the communities associated with them. The avant garde, by contrast, is constantly seeking to control the coming community by dividing it into a part which it claims is logically consistent with its idea of the global republic and a part which is opposed to it. The patrician reformers' use of the Washington Conference to split the post-war disarmament movement is a case in point. The avant garde's attempt to domesticate the coming community, as I have documented, is imposed on it through the creation of fantastic points of identification, such as the League of Nations, and the direction of community hatred against those whom the avant garde identifies with groups already believed to be a danger to society.

(ii) Reconsidering the foundation of the American republic in the light of the global republic/empire's use of violence to impose a liberal capitalism order

Today the presidency and its advisors' repeated production of states of emergency to justify the use of violence to impose the continuous transformation of America and the world by science, technology, and capitalism makes it difficult to see any essential difference between it and its wartime depiction of German autocracy. The use of violence on behalf of law becomes indistinguishable from the use of violence against law.

It is in the ruins of the burnt-out building that its original structure can be most clearly discerned. What we see is the use of violence to impose a liberal-capitalist order at the centre of the foundation of the American republic emerging into full view. The Declaration of Independence presents itself as a moment when a "we", gives itself a state to defend all men's equal rights to life, liberty, and happiness against "absolute Tyranny". There was no such moment. Instead, if we look at the contemporary meanings of the words used in the Declaration what we see are elements of the colonial commercial, landowning, and slaveowning elite seeking to persuade artisans, labourers, and farmers to fight for them against the British while giving them as little real power as possible. On the one hand to reinforce the support of the colonial elite, Jefferson speaks a language of liberty which they understand to mean protection of their property and a representation in government to ensure it continues to be protected. On the other hand, he speaks a language of equality which the elite understand narrowly to mean an end to the exercise of hereditary power over them by an English nobility and the "mob" understand more broadly to also mean they will have an equal representation in government with the wealthy.[5] Both parties are clear, however, that the language of liberty and equality does not apply to Indians, black slaves, black freemen, and women. To cement the unequal alliance, Jefferson's Declaration of Independence presented a paranoid Whig interpretation of British rule as a vast conspiracy to deprive Americans of their liberty. Everything was read as evidence of what Jefferson had earlier described as a "deliberate, systematical plan of reducing us to slavery".[6] The result was the paradox that despite the fact that Americans knew they were probably freer than any other people many were convinced they had to break free from the British state before their liberty was destroyed.[7] Those that were not convinced were brought into the struggle through conscription whose imposition meant, since the wealthier citizens could either buy themselves out or provide a substitute, that the elite was able and in many cases did escape the full burden of fighting while artisans, labourers, and farmers could not.[8]

The elite's urgent need for popular support in fighting the War of Independence led them to agree to the setting up of state legislatures which, in some cases, gave artisans, labourers, and farmers a larger share in government than they had previously enjoyed. Once the war was over, however, the assertiveness of their representatives led the elite to seek a way of taming democracy. There was a danger that the people might use their votes to challenge the elite's right to the unlimited accumulation of wealth. A Privates Committee advice to voters electing representatives to the 1776 convention to frame a constitution for Pennsylvania urged them to oppose "great and overgrown rich men" and argued that great wealth was incompatible with republican government. "An enormous proportion of property vested in a few individuals is dangerous to the rights, and destructive of the common happiness of mankind; and therefore every free state hath a right by its laws to discourage the possession of such property."[9] The device the colonial elite eventually settled on to prevent such laws being enacted was to claim that the very existence of the republic was threatened internally by political and commercial disorders and externally by foreign invasion. This could only be cured by a Constitutional Convention to establish a federal government. The resulting Constitution, as Madison famously reveals in *The Federalist* no. 10, was created to ensure that the actions of the majority could not interfere with "the rights of property". By proclaiming the need to exercise of power on behalf of life

Hamilton, as we have seen, justifies the Constitution giving the federal government unlimited power to tax, raise credit, and establish military forces so as to be able to meet all the contingencies that may threaten Americans.

The claim that the Constitution's checks and balances will prevent the misuse of this power is a myth that enables the proliferation of elite power to go unchecked.[10] The system of checks and balances, which gives each branch of the government a power to intervene in the decisions of the others, makes it difficult for Americans to see who was really responsible for particular decisions, and hence to hold its elected representatives accountable at elections. The system of representation was deliberately established to ensure that the national elite would predominate in all parts of the federal government, and hence the interests of this class would be supported by the executive, the legislature, and the courts. To prevent the majority of the people from controlling the government through the legislature it is split into two parts. To give the people a sense of democratic governance there is a House of Representatives in which a large number of congressmen are elected for short terms. To prevent the majority from exercising power in ways which are against the interests of the national elite, however, legislation has to also be agreed by the Senate. The small number of senators and their long term of office ensures that it is dominated by the national elite. Should these checks and balances fail to ensure that nothing is done against the interests of the national elite, the president has the power to veto legislation. Where the interests of the national elite are threatened, the knowledge that neither the courts nor the legislature is likely to oppose the executive in taking actions which defend the interests of the national elite, allows it a free hand to extend its power without fear of being checked. The same is true for action by the courts or legislature.

Today the patrician reformers' strategy for taming democracy has succeed in persuading many to give up the struggle for democracy within America in return for the intoxication of being represented as heroes in a story about humanity's realization of its potential on a global scale through science, technology, and the market. The United States is properly described as a post-democratic spectacular society.[11] The majority of Americans, for whom democracy has been reduced to a meaningless choice between identical parties in elections, should not see the Declaration of Independence and the Constitution as a moments when a people, of which they are part, gave itself a state so as to realize their aspirations. Instead, they should see the government structure they have inherited as to a greater or lesser extent violently imposed on their ancestors through force and fraud and as designed to maintain inequality by limiting democratic challenges to wealth created through economic exploitation. It suggests they should go beyond asking that the Constitution's system of checks and balances should be respected and either demand fundamental changes in its structure – such as the American Socialist Party's demand that the

Senate be abolished as an anti-democratic instrument for defending wealth based on exploitation – or withdraw legitimacy from the Constitutional system and devote their energies to setting up more democratic institutions.

(iii) Hiding the convergence between the American and the Prussian military and attempting to redeem war as a glorious and heroic activity

The patrician reformers and the military progressives used the First World War to transform America into a world power. In doing so they transformed the United States into a state with many features in common with Wilhemine Germany. One area in which this was most apparent was the development of a military capable of projecting its power throughout the world, and which was planned to be a centre for indoctrinating young Americans in the patrician reformers' idea of democracy. Since the German army's system of discipline and indoctrination had been presented as the very paradigm of the autocratic system America had gone to war to defeat, the patrician reformers and military progressives' plans to continue the development of such a military after the war were highly questionable. Such a military was essential to Wilson's plans for a post-war liberal-capitalist world order. This demanded an American military which, with the forces of Britain, France, and League of Nation states, would be capable of deterring an attack on a League member. As two of the great powers, Germany and Russia, were excluded from the League the task called for a large expansion of the army and navy compared with their pre-war level. When the war ended Secretary of War Newton Baker and Chief of Staff Peyton March sought to create such an army while enthusiasm for the military still remained strong. They needed to move fast as opponents of universal military service, which formed the heart of their plan, had been very successful in 1916 in persuading Americans it was an illegitimate attempt to extend German militarism over America in 1916. By introducing universal military service they would finally fulfil the military reformers' dream of creating a mass army. Baker and March also saw universal military service as a way of turning the army into a place in which young Americans would learn to be ideal democratic citizens. This can be seen in Baker's 1920 address to the graduating class of the staff college:

> A successful democracy . . . is a society in which co-ordinations and subordinations are automatically effected, and where they are complete, spontaneous, recognized, and, though resting on consent, are accepted . . . Therefore we have in the Army a type of democratic organization which, because of the circumstances under which it is formed and the singleness of its purpose, always has an opportunity to be a complete and persuasive example of the efficiency of democracy actually organized and working.[12]

Baker concludes with a statement designed to turn the heads of the assembled officers. "America is, therefore, the leader of the world, and you gentlemen represent the highest type of democratic co-ordination and efficiency." Baker's address sought to enrol new members of America's elite in Wilson's "democratic" rearticulation of the patrician reformers' and military progressives' projects and to teach them the redefinition of democracy. By contrast, a March 1920 address by Major General Silbert seeks to explain to scientists and businessmen how universal military service will get Americans outside the elite to accept that democracy means subordinating themselves to its idea of what America ought to be:

> I know nothing which . . . will do more to create a spirit that will solve the serious industrial questions ahead of us, all on account of the democracy that comes from the association forced by such training. This training, however, should be coupled with a system of instruction extending from the kindergarten to the university, instilling into the youth of the land the precept that a nation must be just in order to play its predestined part in the world, and must be strong and ready to exert its strength in order to do its part in maintaining fairness and justice among the peoples of the earth. Modern science is too potent in the hands of selfish natures to permit any other course, and selfishness will last until the millenium comes.[13]

We are now well placed to understand what Baker and March were doing when they ordered the dissolution of the Chemical Warfare Service. The decision was taken at the very same conference which decided to press for universal military service.[14] Within this political context the decision to dissolve the Chemical Warfare Service did three things. First, it was a way of differentiating Baker and March's proposals for universal military service, and the creation of a nation in arms, from German militarism. Second, conscription and mass slaughter in the trenches had called into question the very idea of the battlefield as a place where citizens could demonstrate their commitment to America by voluntarily risking their lives for the nation. As James Chester's 1901 "The Invisible Factor", shows, this had already been highly questionable well before the war. This meant that there was a deep tension between the military progressives' goal of a professional army capable of fighting a modern war and the patrician reformers' goal of turning the army into an ideal place where young Americans can learn to be citizens. By singling out chemical weapons, and by then excluding them from the army, March and Baker were creating the illusion that this tension could be removed from their ideal army. Third, March and Baker were well aware of army preparations to use chemical weapons on a massive scale in 1919. In this light, the reason March later gave for dissolving the Service, that gas could not be controlled and would inevitably lead to civilian deaths, was undoubtedly a factor in their decision. The speed with which the war had grown to encompass the entire world, and the way in which the incorporation of civilians into the war economy made targeting them one way of securing victory, however, suggests that this was also a way of attempting to re-establish the idea that war itself could be controlled by military professionals and that it would not inevitably spread to civilians.

The decision to dissolve the Service was a declaration that chemical warfare officers would not be part of Baker and March's ideal army. The officers responded by presenting the chemical weapons laboratory as the new ideal place of heroic warfare. The officers who directed the laboratory were military heroes, like Caesar, Napoleon, Grant, and other military innovators, who were pushing forward new methods of war which would decide the fate of civilization. In their eyes the Service was an ideal community which represents America as the Rough Riders had. They did this by weaving together the patrician reformers' idealization of the frontier and scientists' and engineers' presentation of researchers as pioneers exploring and colonizing a scientific and technological wilderness. Faced with the danger that the endless slaughter in the trenches would lead to a permanent withdrawal of legitimacy, the idea that the crucial battles would now be fought between scientists and engineers in rival laboratories was one way of attempting to restore the legitimacy of the military and war making. The idealization of a new high-technology warrior was another. Fries and West declared that chemical warfare was just as much a "matching of wits" as warfare was "in the days when the Knights of the Round Table fought with spears on horseback".[15] Elsewhere the officers drew on race pride to present the white soldier using chemical weapons as showing superior courage to the savage warrior. The white man's rationality enables him to deal with the terror of modern weapons whereas the "superstitious instincts of semi-civilized men" leads them to break and run.[16] The romanticization of the high-technology warrior is even more powerfully stated in Billy Mitchell's post-war presentation of the air service. They require "moral qualities" which have never been demanded before. Unlike the soldier in the trenches who can rely on others, they are alone. At each moment "they know that if a flaming bullet comes through their gasoline tank it immediately becomes a burning torch and they are gone".[17]

(iv) Du Bois' interruption and rearticulation of Wilson's story about America's war to create an global republic modelled on the United States

The coming community, I have argued, is not the opposite of the emerging global republic. Instead, it exists through the interruption and rearticulation of the avant garde's determination of the boundaries of the global republic and of other communities. The post-war disarmament movement provides one example of this.

The African-American seizure of Wilson's proclamation of a war to make the world safe for democracy as an opportunity to call into question the boundaries of both American democracy and Wilson's new global republic is a second. Wilson sought to establish a League of Nations that would enable liberal democracies to work together to develop the world. Though not explicitly stated it would also enable the white domination of the world to continue by allowing those coloured nations which had become too powerful to be simply excluded (Japan) from participating in world government, while providing a forum in which the leading white nations could legitimate their continued domination of the rest to continue by agreeing with each other that their colonial subjects were not yet ready for self-government. All this is well known. What is not well known is that the coloured world sought to use a split between the Americans and the French over whose country was the ideal democracy to challenge the Paris talks' reinscription of race domination. The history of how they did so remains to be written. Here I outline Du Bois' role in setting up the Second Pan-African Congress and in using it as a platform to argue that Wilson's League of Nations could only claim to represent humanity if it was based on race equality.

We pick up the story at the point when Wilson decided to enter the First World War. In May 1917 Du Bois, with other African-American leaders, had come out in support of Wilson's war. Du Bois now suppressed his analysis that there is no sharp distinction between Germany and America, that both are democratic despotisms in which white big business and labour are allied to exploit coloured men. The war was a political opportunity. By risking their lives in battle for America, blacks could demonstrate that they placed the nation above their own self-interest. This would prove, using the patrician reformers' own favourite criterion, that there was no politically relevant difference between whites and blacks justifying disenfranchizement. If America was to maintain her international credibility as the leader of the democratic nations, she must now enforce African-Americans' constitutional right to the vote. There were other advantages. Officer training would give some African-Americans leadership experience, while training and warfighting would give a larger number the confidence and skills to defend themselves. Many rural African-Americans were already escaping southern oppression by going north. Now larger numbers would be able to move north to fill jobs left vacant by white conscription or created by the wartime boom.[18] There was also a degree to which African-Americans had little choice except to support the war. Nationally, failure to support the war would result in their being branded as traitors and set back the struggle to regain the vote. Locally, any lack of patriotism would mean an intensification of lynching and riots against black communities.

There followed a series of struggles. The army had to be persuaded not to relegate African-Americans to labour battalions but let them fight; to train more black officers; and to stop the abuse and harassment during training. The war saw a continuation of lynching and mob attacks. On 1 July 1917 a white mob carried out a pogrom in East St Louis. Causes of the pogrom included the Aluminium Ore Company which was seeking to keep white wages down by hiring black workers, and the American Federation of Labour's exploitation of white fear that this would be repeated at other plants to build a coalition between skilled and unskilled white workers. The NAACP organized a silent parade of 8 to 10,000 African-Americans down Fifth Avenue on Saturday 28 July to demand presidential action. The marchers held banners reading "MR. PRESIDENT, WHY NOT MAKE AMERICA SAFE FOR DEMOCRACY". In August a black military police-man, Corporal Baltimore, was shot at, arrested, and beaten by a city policeman in Houston. After further insults, assaults, and Jim Crow trolleys and cinemas his unit, the 3rd Battalion of the 24th Infantry, decided they had had enough. Attacking the nearest police station, they shot dead sixteen whites, including five police, while suffering the loss of four soldiers themselves. The army responded with secret court-martials of the soldiers, hanging the first batch without right of appeal in December. Secretary for War Baker persuaded Wilson to reduce the total number to hang from twenty-four to nineteen, despite pressure from southern senators who believed there should be more not fewer object lessons.[19]

In 1918 Du Bois came to believe, its seems, Wilson's story that Americans were in the midst of a democratic revolution which would spread democracy to all mankind. This led him in his May 1918 editorial "Close Ranks" to urge African-Americans to set aside "their special grievances" and give total support to the war,[20] whereas in the eyes of other leading African-Americans such as Bryon Gunner, Trotter, Harry Smith, and Archibald Grimké, he should have insisted that if white America wanted black American support in the war the government must immediately stop lynching and riots.[21]

Du Bois' domestic campaign to use the war to gain the vote was matched by an international campaign. Internationally, he sought to play on the French belief that *their* democracy was the best example for mankind to put pressure on the American government. The French had sought to enrol their colonial subjects in their war with Germany, and had turned to Blaise Diagne, a Senegalese. In one year, Diagne raised 680,000 African troops and 240,000 African labourers for France. When the Pan-African movement asked Diagne to help them establish a Pan-African Congress to coincide with the Paris Peace Conference, Diagne used Clemenceau's indebtedness to him to gain official French support for the Congress. This gave Du Bois an international platform to demand that if the vic-tors meant to show they were better than German autocracy, it was time to deliver on claims that they had only colonized the coloured world so as to lead it towards self-government. He insisted that when "any State deliberately excludes its civilized citizens or subjects of Negro descent from its body politic and cultural, it shall be the duty of the League of Nations to bring the matter to the attention of the civilized world".[22]

These tactics met with mixed success. African-Americans were but one of a number of groups who used Wilson's endorsement of democracy to demand the extension of democracy. Workers called for industrial democracy and women for the vote. Wilson responded by giving the American Federation of Labour a part, albeit a minor one, in government, and urging Congress to legislate women's suffrage. By contrast, African-American demands for the vote were left out in the cold. Yet, there were gains. The large numbers of African-Americans who had made the trip north to work in industry were now wealthier, while military service had given African-Americans both the ability and the will to use arms against lynch mobs and white rioters. Speaking for the returning troops, Du Bois sought to capture their refusal to return to race oppression and insistence on democratic rights:

> We return from the slavery of uniform . . . to look America squarely in the face and call a spade a spade. We sing: This country of ours, despite all its better souls have done and dreamed, is yet a shameful land.
>
> It <u>lynches</u> . . . It <u>disenfranchises</u> its own citizens . . . It encourages <u>ignorance</u> . . . It steals from us . . . It insults us . . .
>
>
>
> We <u>return</u>
> We <u>return from fighting.</u>
> We <u>return fighting.</u>
>
>
>
> Make way for Democracy! We saved it in France, and by the Great Jehovah, we will save it in the U.S.A., or know the reason why.[23]

The war had indeed changed African-Americans, and in the race riots that broke out across America in the summer of 1919 they were increasingly ready to fight in their own defence.

PART 3

10

The Gyroscope

In Part 1 we saw how the leaders of the chemical campaign present American chemical warfare research as a key element in a larger harmony. Through its defeat of Germany, America had crushed the principal threat to world peace. Now chemical warfare research would enable her to defend civilization against a resurgence of the German threat. It would lead to the achievement of man's sovereignty in other ways as well: the conquest of diseases through new drugs; an end to famine through pesticides and fertilizers; and the suppression of riots and strikes by new tear gases. This story was central to their attempt to manage the political field. If the middle ground believed this story, then they would not support critics inside and outside the elite who called it into question. Without such support, these critics would not be able to make use of the rights they enjoyed as citizens of a democratic republic to lift the veil on the chemical campaign. The wider public would remain unaware of the interests that lay behind it, or of the weaknesses in its arguments. In fact, the chemists were only partially able to manage the national debate. They persuaded the government that a large science-based chemical industry was essential for the development of American military power, and that chemical tariffs and embargoes in support of an American dye industry were the right way to achieve it. They were also able to persuade the government that the Chemical Warfare Service ought to be kept as an independent branch of the army. They were not, however, able to stop the 1921 disarmament movement's confronting the elite with the threat that if it supported the development of a large chemical warfare establishment, then it would be seen to be no different from the German autocrats and militarists America had gone to war to defeat. In these circumstances, the Republican Harding administration decided the prudent course at the Washington Conference was to reiterate the Hague Convention's ban on the use of chemical weapons. In this way Secretary of State Hughes, and Senators Root and Lodge, were able to present themselves as dealing with the threat of a chemical arms race.

This history shows how the elite sought to defend its self-assigned status as the guardians of a harmonious whole when confronted by the 1921 disarmament movement. In the next three chapters I continue to read history against the grain. I am interested in American scientists' argument that they should be regulators of the whole. In mechanical terms, that they could and ought to act like a gyroscope in a plane or ship which corrects its controls when it begins to wander off course. I will argue that the history of American science in the First World War shatters the idea that America was such a whole and that America's scientists were a regulator of that whole. I also argue that it called into question American scientists' ideas about their role in progress. The scientists' ideas about humanity in many ways repeated their ideas about the nation. Humanity was evolving into a harmonious whole, and the scientists of the civilized world could and ought to act as its regulator. The scientists fitted the two levels together by arguing that the competition between scientists in the world's leading civilized nations was the engine of human progress.

Chapter 11, "The Bomber/Poison Gas Combination", takes aim at the proposition that in the long run it does not matter what direction scientific research takes. The idea is that natural phenomena are governed by a single set of principles, and that no matter in which direction scientist's research proceeds over time their investigations will unearth this same set of principles. All the investigations undertaken by scientists into this or that bit of nature are useful as they provide clues for uncovering the fundamental architecture of the universe. These ideas are summed up, and reinforced, by the metaphor of the expanding circle. The movement of such a circle has no direction. It does not matter which direction individual scientists take, the collective work of scientists will lead to the circle being expanded to cover more and more ground. The idea that in the long term it does not matter which direction a scientist's research takes presupposes a harmonious relationship between the part and the whole. The work of individual scientists are part of a greater whole whose research is converging on the ultimate laws of nature.

The first part of the argument takes issue with this idea through a study of post-war chemical weapons research. It uses the concept of "heterogeneous engineering" to show how scientists and engineers built a system whose survival and expansion depended on continuous research into poisonous chemicals. As this system grew, it acquired increasing momentum so that it became increasingly difficult to change this research direction. In a world of finite resources commercial and state support for research in this direction meant that support was not available for research in other directions. The result is that our knowledge of toxic compounds, and the means available to extend that knowledge and use it, has developed at the expense of other areas of knowledge and technology. At the same time, our society has been reshaped so as to ensure we continue to give support to further research in these directions. Tear gas has come to be seen as a preferred solution to civic unrest, chemical pesticides as an integral part of dealing with the threat of insects to food production, and chemical weapons as a militarily useful weapon. The case study shows that it matters whether we decide to advance our research in this direction rather than that. Over time such choices are locked in place as alternative directions research could have taken are forgotten and alternative means of solving key problems we face are pushed to the margins.

Why did scientists believe that it made no long-term difference which direction scientific research advanced in? Why do we find it difficult to talk about the need for society to make a choice about which direction research should proceed in today? To answer these questions Chapter 12, "The Mind Which is Destined to Govern the World", takes a step back in time to look at the origins of the American pure science movement in the decades after the Civil War. The pure science movement sought to renegotiate the place of the scientist in American society. Its leaders argued against the idea that scientists should have to demonstrate that their research would lead to useful results if they were to be given large resources. They argued that once the true nature of science was understood, Americans would appreciate that research undertaken for the sake of discovering the ultimate principles of nature would be the most useful for society. Such research was a quicker and surer way of discovering such principles than research undertaken to solve practical problems. Once the master principles had been discovered, they would provide the key to solving all sorts of practical problems facing society. These scientists presented America as a nearly harmonious whole which just needed a series of small adjustments by the scientist to progress towards perfection. At they same time, they argued that in the absence of support for pure science society faced a catastrophic collapse. Society was held together by the willingness of its members to put the good of the whole above their own self-interest. The rise of commercial society meant that this was now threatened as Americans increasingly made material satisfaction their highest good. By supporting scientists in pursuing truth for its own sake alone, however, the Protestant establishment could overcome the danger. Like the military heroes beloved by the patrician reformers, the scientists would prevent the corruption of American youth by presenting them with living or dead exemplars whose actions showed the pursuit of high ideals was all-important.

The best thing for the national community to do, then, was to give scientists a large blank cheque. The nation should give scientists all the resources they needed for research and leave them free to use them to investigate the problems that interested them. The pure science movement has bequeathed us a conception of scientific research and the scientist which makes it very difficult for society to have a discussion about the direction of scientific research. Indeed, the concepts developed by the pure science movement make it a pointless to even discuss the long-term consequences of carrying out research into one direction rather than another. Contrary to its own claims that the best science and scientists were non-political, the pure science movement's account of science and the scientist was a highly political rearticulation of earlier concepts. Its claims did not rest on a systematic investigation of scientific practice, but on a rearticulation of a theological idea that God had created the world so that scientific activity undertaken with a concern for truth alone would be of the greatest benefit to the community. The fact that research which the pure science movement claimed had been undertaken solely to discover the truth about nature, such as Faraday's research into electricity, had led to so many useful inventions was a magnificent example of God's providential ordering of the world. It bore witness to the goodness of the creator.

The pure science movement's rearticulation of earlier ideas about science and theology was highly interested. The leaders of the pure science movement offered America's Protestant establishment a deal. The Protestant establishment would support pure science by encouraging its sons to take university courses in science and by providing funds for pure science research. In return, the pure scientists would support the establishment's claim to be a meritocracy whose knowledge gave it the right to govern America and the world. The deal was to the advantage of both parties. The Protestant establishment needed to renew its right to govern America as it came under pressure from other groups, Catholic, Jewish, Socialist, Populist, German-American, and Irish-American, who believed that, as citizens of a republican democracy, they should have a full share in the government of America. Coming at the high point of European colonial expansion, the pure science movement also reinforced the Protestant establishment's claim to a share in governing the coloured world. Within the United States it reinforced its claim that the conquest and subjugation of native Americans was right. Outside America it reinforced its right, in its own eyes, to direct imperialism (the Philippines) and indirect imperialism (Latin America, the Caribbean, the Pacific, and China). The scientists, for their part, needed the establishment's support. To take just one example, they were locked in a battle with the independent inventors over who should take credit for the telegraph, the telephone, and many other new technologies which Americans were coming to see as the glory of the age. They needed the support of the establishment to enforce their claim that their discoveries were the ultimate origin of these inventions.

In the decades before the First World War, I argue in "Permanent Mobilization", the claims of the pure science movement were themselves rearticulated by applied scientists on the one hand, and pure scientists carrying out large-scale research on the other. These groups argued that America had become a modern complex society, which now depended on organized research for both its very existence and its future progress. In doing so, they took over the pure science movement's idea that society just needed a small adjustment by the scientists to be a harmonious whole, and that in the absence of that adjustment, it would suffer catastrophic and perhaps irreversible collapse. The difference was that now the principal danger was a series of threats to America's ability to protect and enhance the material life of its citizens. Modern society was a complex whole in which the nation's health, its industrial and commercial advance, its social stability, its security from attack, and the conservation of its resources were all vital to each other. To ensure that a failure in any one area did not lead to disaster what was required was the national organization of science, and the scientific organization of the nation. This would enable America to keep up with Europe in solving the key problems facing mankind. Failure to do so would mean that America would lose its sovereignty as it became increasingly dependent on Europeans for its development. It would become "like China". The relationship between high and low values was now inverted. For the pure science movement, the pursuit of high values – in the case of science truth for its own sake – would providentially lead to the improvement of material life as scientific discoveries were turned into useful inventions. For these scientists the pursuit of low values, such as commercial advantage, security from attack, and the enhancement of bodily health, would equally providentially lead to the advance of high values. Most of all they stressed that improvements in communication technologies would bring the whole of mankind into a discussion which must lead to its moral, intellectual, and political advance. In the years immediately before the First World War, these scientists increasingly argued that they should participate directly in governing America. They presented their training as giving them a disinterested concern for humanity and truth, and a scientific method, which would enable them to identify threats to society and to determine how these could be corrected. They could act as a gyroscope which could identify when society began to head towards destruction, and then act as a guide which would direct it back on to the path to progress.

The First World War gave these scientists their opportunity. Led by pure scientists involved in large-scale research, they came together to form an organized research movement and to create a national institution, the National Research Council, to carry through the organization of applied science begun by corporations like General Electric and the organization of pure science begun by the Carnegie Institution. In their own eyes the key role that organized research played in the defeat of Germany provided a thorough vindication of their claim that scientists should act as the gyroscope of society, pointing the way for its political leaders to take it.

Read against the grain, the history of the First World War reveals the bankruptcy of the key concepts of both the pure science and the organized science movements. In Part 1, we saw that far from leading international society towards peace, American chemists and chemical engineers rationalized the trade in high explosives by depicting Germany as seeking to dominate the world, and then after the war sought to consolidate their new status by portraying America as locked in a continued state of war in which she might be attacked at any moment. Far from acting as a gyroscope which corrected the drift away from international harmony, the chemists had contributed to making the war worse and to its future return. In Chapter 13 I take this story a stage further. I show that the organized research movement seized advantage of America's entry into the First World War to form a symbiotic though conflictual relationship with the presidency. This was institutionalized through the establishment of the National Research Council. The scientists and big business supported the president's claim that a state of emergency, or near emergency, existed that only the presidency was in a position to deal with. The president lent a measure of his authority to the scientists by making them his advisors. Under the guise of acting as advisors the scientists and their allies in big business could exercise considerable power over large areas of policy. The second part of the history is the account of how the organized research movement used the war to consolidate an alliance between America's scientists, engineers, big business, and the military. They used the war to turn the National Research Council into a machine through which big business could influence the direction of American scientific and technological research. In return, big business promised to give large funds to support the National Research Council's national organization of pure and applied research. This reinforced the ability of America's giant corporations to use their own industrial research laboratories to protect capital they had invested in technological systems, and to make superprofits through market manipulation and monopoly.

Independent inventors were pushed to the margins. It became more and more difficult to create alternative technological systems. Equally, it seems likely that the new deal between the scientists and big business favoured pure science research programmes which were already well established, or which promised results useful to the military or to big business. Scientists who had already achieved national prominence were more likely to be elected to the National Research Council, and these scientists were more likely to fund research programmes that were already well established. After the signing of the Armistice the leaders of the organized research movement sought to defend their wartime gains. They adopted the same strategy as the leaders of the chemical campaign. They argued it was vital for America to continue the organization of science begun during the war as this was the only way it could defend itself against a continued German threat. American science had to be permanently mobilized for war. At the same time, the organization of science was no less essential if America was to survive in the industrial and commercial struggle with other nations that would follow the war. The scientists sought to reinforce and extend the power they had acquired during the war, in short, by turning the temporary wartime state of emergency, which they themselves had helped create, into a permanent state of emergency.

The history of American science and the First World War makes it difficult to defend the twin claims that the nation should be seen as almost in a state of harmony, and the scientists as acting as a gyroscope that could detect the extent to which the nation was beginning to deviate from the path it ought to take. Instead, both claims are revealed to be part of a strategy through which scientists sought to use the First World War to advance their position within American society. They were a means by which scientists managed to capture an element of state authority for their production of a permanent state of emergency which, they claimed, only they could guide America past. Through doing so the scientists were able to develop new networks of power both nationally and internationally.

Why this all this matters can be seen from a troubled editorial in the November 1921 edition of *Scientific American* entitled "The Control of Atomic Energy".[1] This starts by deploying the standard argument used by the leaders of the movement for organized research to gain support. Modern society is presented as threatened by a catastrophe, albeit a slowly unfolding one. As civilization progresses, it uses up energy at an ever more rapid rate. At an unspecified point in the future, there must come a point when mankind runs out of coal, oil, and other sources it needs to sustain modern life. Having painted a picture in which mankind is faced with disaster if it continues on its present course, the editors canvas the available solutions. They acknowledge that if the sun could be harnessed there is more than sufficient energy available, but argue that the really promising source is atomic power. The potential of atomic energy is described with religious awe. Science is the saviour of mankind which has "revealed" the presence of a "a storehouse of energy so vast and so intensive that he who shall first unlock the door will be possessed of a power in the presence of which all the vast potentialities of the world's store of coal, oil, water power will shrink to insignificance". In their closing paragraphs, however, the memory of the world war leads the editors to adopt a different tone. They now present it as fortunate that it may take scientific research a long time to develop this new energy source. "When we survey the happenings of the past twenty years, and see to what base uses the best products of science and invention have been put, we may be reconciled to the slowness with which we approach the ultimate goal of unlimited free power."

The editors, then, are fully aware that it is likely that research into nuclear physics will be used to produce weapons of unprecedented power. Their problem is that their conception of the scientist and scientific activity makes it impossible for them to talk about mankind deciding *not* to pursue this line of research. The scientists had become entrapped in the very net they had themselves woven. They were snared in a conception of science in which the only problem can be the abuse of scientific discoveries. Despite the fact that the organized research movement has created means for deciding in which direction the nation's science should proceed, they remain caught in the pure science movement's conception of science as inevitably leading to the discovery of a single set of principles which give mankind power over nature. This is because the organized research movement's rearticulation of the ideas of the pure science movement never fully called into question the latter's claim that in the long run it does not matter which direction research takes because the same principles will be discovered anyway. Even though they have argued that solar energy offers an alternative solution to future energy demands, they cannot talk about the need for society to decide whether it should support research into nuclear physics *or* into those areas of physics useful for solar power. Nor can they talk about the politics of nuclear physics research. While the editor of any serious daily newspaper sees it as his business to probe the interests that lie behind projects in any other area of human activity, the editors of *Scientific American* do not ask the same question about nuclear physics research. They are prevented from doing so because they have inherited the pure science movement's claim that the true scientist is motivated by a concern for truth and humanity alone. The problem of motives can only arise after the principles of nuclear physics have been discovered. This leaves the editors in a desperate position. Their conception of science and scientists is such that they can only take a passive stance as they contemplate the likelihood that nuclear energy will be used for weapons which will give those who wield them a power close to God's. Their passivity and pessimism contains an element of self-interest: it enables them to go on reporting science without having to bestir themselves to challenge its current directions. The editors are, ultimately, left with a completely passive hope that the future will turn out to be radically different from the past. The editorial weakly concludes:

> So enormous is this energy that it will confer upon the man, or the race, which learns to release and control it, a power only less than that of the Omnipotent. Before that day arrives let us hope that a way will have been found to put more of the human in what we are pleased to call the human race.

There is no scientific basis for such a stance, only the idea that God has providentially ordered the world so that it will all turn out for the best. The theological roots of the scientists' passivity in the face of the horrors they see ahead, however, must be kept out of sight by an avowedly secular science. Thus, the possibility of actively creating hope through political action to end nuclear physics research and to support research into solar energy is foreclosed. We must utterly break with this view of science and the institutions which support it and which it supports. It offer us nothing but a world of repeated violence and intimidation. Like Dante's Hell, above whose gate is written, *"LASCIATE OGNI SPERANZA VOI CH' ENTRATE!"*[2] it is a world without hope.

Air power: a visual essay

List of illustrations

1. Vickers-Vimy-Rolls Bomber used by Alcock and Brown for first flight across the Atlantic. *The Aircraft Journal*, 21 June 1919, front cover.
2. US Army Air Service Martin bomber over Washington. *The Aircraft Journal*, August 1919, p. 5.
3. Martin bomber silhouetted against clouds. *The Aviation and Aircraft Journal*, 21 March 1921, front cover.
4. Glen Martin Company advertisement for commercial air transport. *The Aircraft Journal*, 26 July 1919, inside front cover.
5. The R-34 airship on test flight over the English coast. *The Aircraft Journal*, 5 July 1919, front cover.
6. Arrival of R-34 at Roosevelt Field, Mineola. *The Aircraft Journal*, 12 July 1919, front cover.
7. New German airship, *The Bodensee*. *The Aircraft Journal*, 20 September 1919, front cover.
8. Aerial photograph of New York skyscrapers. *The Aviation and Aircraft Journal*, 3 January 1921, front cover.
9. Aerial photograph of the area of New York "attacked" by the air service on 29 July 1921. *The Aviation and Aircraft Journal*, 22 August 1921, front cover.
10. Announcement of RAF defeat of Somali rebellion with photograph of Dakka, Afghanistan, "captured . . . after extensive air operations". *The Aircraft Journal*, 24 April 1920, p. 3.

The author gratefully acknowledges *Aviation Week & Space Technology* and the British Library for permission to republish the above images from *The Aircraft Journal* and *The Aviation and Aircraft Journal*.

AIRCRAFT JOURNAL

June 21, 1919   *Every Saturday*   *Price Ten Cents*

Airplane That Flew Straight Across the Atlantic

The Vickers-Vimy-Rolls Bomber

First Machine to Make a Non-Stop Flight Across the Atlantic—Pilot, Capt. John Alcock, an Englishman; Navigator, Lieut. Arthur Whitten Brown, R. A. F., an American—Time, 15 Hrs. and 57 Min.

This photograph of the Vickers-Vimy-Rolls Bomber in which Captain John Alcock and Lieutenant Arthur Brown, RAF, crossed the Atlantic on 14–15 June 1919 depicts an incontestable fact around which the readers of the *Aircraft Journal* can form a many-layered pearl of dreams and nightmares.

Trans-Continental Flight Further Delayed

Captain Francis' Martin Bomber Wrecked in Hangar by Storm After Fast Flight from Dayton to Mineola

Another delay was caused in the trans-continental flight of an Army Martin bomber, piloted by Capt. Roy N. Francis, last Monday when a violent storm, with the characteristics of a tornado, struck Hazelhurst Field in its eccentric course and wrecked the Martin bomber housed in the large iron hangar at the north end of the field. A bolt of lightning hurled iron plates and girders on the plane, and the twisting wind, entering through the torn roof, completed the destruction.

Captain Francis had only a few days previously arrived from Dayton, ready for the first great hop from Mineola to North Platte, Neb., a distance of about 1500 miles.

Captain Francis' flight from Dayton to Mineola was made July 25 in six hours and 52 minutes, considerably better than 90 miles an hour for the 650-mile journey. The flight was made against a north-east wind for almost the entire distance. Inspection of the plane and testing of the engines was immediately begun.

Details of the preliminary route surveys made public by the Navy Department show that the Martin Bomber to be used carries 710 gallons of gasoline and consumes about 36 gallons an hour at a speed of 90 miles an hour. It is believed the plane will make from 1,600 to 1,700 miles without refueling.

It is probable that the stop will be made in the vicinity of North Platte, Neb., which is 1,502 miles by air route from New York.

Unless unusually strong cross-currents prevail, Captain Francis will be able to maintain his course between latitude 37 and 42 north. Winds which would blow him off his course would be offset by favorable winds from the east to be found at certain altitudes.

The route proposed over the Allegheny Mountains starts from Bellefonte, the highest peak being 2,350 feet, and the average height 1,700 feet. This average extends to Clarion, and then begins to slope down gradually toward Cleveland.

Across Nebraska the altitude runs as high as 4,849 feet. The Platte is crossed west of Waterloo, the line of flight being some twenty miles south of the railroad until Central City is reached, thence the route is to North Platte, 1,592 miles. Continuing westward, the line of the railroad is followed close to the Colorado boundary, and Wyoming crossed at Pine Bluffs. The land elevation is there above 5,000 feet, and the distance from New York 1,650 miles.

Passing Cheyenne (6,058 feet), the aviator will be close to Pole Mountain (10,000 feet), and cross the Laramie River at the city of that name (7,145 feet.) A safe flying altitude should be from 2,000 to 3,000 feet higher than the land elevation, and air currents moving around the mountains may call for a higher altitude to avoid the side drifts. Carter, Wyo., on the Muddy River, is 2,000 miles from New York, at an elevation of 6,507 feet.

Utah is entered at Castle Rock. Salt Lake is a little south of the direct route, but a good objective on account of the variable winds from off the Wasatch Mountain range. Crossing Great Salt Lake and continuing west, Nevada is entered at Shafter and the Thousand Springs Valley followed, the route passing north of the Ruby range and between the Elko and River ranges to Carlin and Winnemucca; thence to the Humboldt River Valley and Reno. An alternate route west to Ogden may be taken that will cross Lake Tahoe (6,225 feet), and California entered at Truckee.

An altitude of 11,000 feet is necessary to insure a safe crossing of the Sierra Nevadas.

"As the trans-continental flight is to be one upon which valuable data and photographs will be made, the weather conditions will be a considerable factor and will determine the exact time of starting after arrangements have been completed," says the War Department's statement.

Captain Francis' trip will be the longest non-stop flight made in this country.

The storm that wrecked the Martin bomber also smashed the giant Caproni triplane, which was frequently seen over New York, and a great Handley Page machine weighing eleven tons. These were three of the largest planes in the country. Two smaller machines were also wrecked.

Bombing in Mexico

Americans at El Paso, Texas, from Chihuahua, Mexico, have brought reports of the accidental bombing of Gen. Pablo Quesnga's federal infantry by government airplanes scouting for Villa bands. The soldiers were marching overland from Jiminez to Parral, the Americans said, when they were sighted by the airplanes and bombs were dropped among the infantrymen.

No estimates of the casualties was known to the Americans.

Breaks Altitude Record

In a test flight, Roland Rohlfs, test pilot for the Curtiss Engineering Corp., Garden City, L. I., broke the American altitude record by reaching a ceiling of 31,100 ft. This is 2200 ft. better than record made last year by Major R. W. Schroeder of the U. S. Air Service in a Bristol with a Hispano-Suiza motor. Schroeder still holds the official world's record, although Casale, a Frenchman, in a Nieuport, is accredited with an unofficial record of 33,100 ft. made early this year.

Rohlfs' record was made in a Curtiss Wasp, a triplane designed and built by the Curtiss company for the United States Army. It is equipped with one of the new Curtiss 400-hp. motors. Early this year, in a test flight under the auspices of the government, it made a speed record of 160 m.p.h. and a climbing record of 16,000 ft. in ten minutes. Rohlfs expects to make his official test early next week, and, according to the performance Thursday, he anticipates no difficulty in setting a new world's record.

Rohlfs stated that the temperature at the highest point in his flight was 25 deg. below zero. In making the flight Rohlfs traveled more than 200 miles.

Airplane Linen Bids

Bids for 120,732 yards of airplane linen are invited by the Bureau of Aircraft Production, the New York district office of which is at 350 Madison avenue. All bids for the purchase of the goods must be submitted by 12 m., August 2.

Long Seagull Flight

From New York to New Orleans and possibly to South America in a flying boat by way of the Hudson, St. Lawrence, Ohio and Mississippi rivers, with a jump by rail from Buffalo to Cincinnati, is planned by the Curtiss Aeroplane and Motor Corporation, to be started early in August by Majors W. E. Parker and G. Talbot Willcox, formerly members of the Royal Air Force, in a Curtiss Seagull, a three passenger flying boat, equipped with a 150-horsepower motor and wireless telephone and telegraph. Reports of the progress of the flight will be made to the American Flying Club Radio service.

Major Willcox served with the Sixth Highland Light Infantry during the early part of the war, taking part in the Dardanelles campaign. He went to Egypt and joined the air force, and was sent to France as a member of the first night bombing squadron.

MARTIN BOMBER OVER WASHINGTON
(C) Underwood & Underwood

MARCH 21, 1921   Issued Weekly   PRICE 15 CENTS

AVIATION
AND
AIRCRAFT JOURNAL

The New Martin Bomber of the U. S. Army Air Service

VOLUME X
Number 12

Four
Dollars
a Year

SPECIAL FEATURES

WHO'S WHO IN AMERICAN AERONAUTICS
THE AVELINE AUTOMATIC AIRPLANE CONTROL
THE B. M. W. 6-CYL. 185 HP. ENGINE
GROUND ENGINEERING
CANADIAN AIR PROGRESS, 1920

THE GARDNER, MOFFAT CO., INC.
HIGHLAND, N. Y.
225 FOURTH AVENUE, NEW YORK

Entered as Second-Class Matter, Nov. 22, 1920, at the Post Office at Highland, N. Y.
under Act of March 3, 1879.

The Martin bomber seen from below blackly silhouetted against the sky. This evokes a fantasy of the absolute power of the bomber pilot and the powerlessness of the civilian population below. Through science and technology the world is now divided into masters and victims.

Advertisement for the Martin Company. This presents the bomber as part of mankind realizing its sovereignty. Through air transport the world's peoples will trade goods and ideas and see they share an interest in using science, technology, liberal democracy, and capitalism to develop the earth. The development of an American civilian aircraft industry will give her the advanced aircraft needed to defend this global revolution.

AIRCRAFT JOURNAL

July 5, 1919   *Every Saturday*   *Price Ten Cents*

Photo Keystone View Co.

R-34 in a Test Flight as Photographed from an English Airplane 3,000 Feet in the Air

The new R-34 rigid airship over the English coast. The dark menacing profile of the airship reminds the reader of the First World War German Zeppelin raids on Paris and London. And it points towards a future in which the tourist or businessman will be lifted across continents and oceans in luxury and comfort.

AIRCRAFT JOURNAL

July 12, 1919   *Every Saturday*   *Price Ten Cents*

(C) International Film Service.

Striking View of the British Airship R-34 as She Landed at Roosevelt Field, Mineola, L. I., July 6—The Picture Shows a Close-up of the Stern

Arrival of R-34 at Roosevelt Field, Mineola. The *Aircraft Journal* editorialized: "Foremost perhaps the voyage of R-34 spells the doom of America's splendid geographical isolation. The sea barrier of the Atlantic is no longer inviolable . . . The warning is obvious." (Editorial, *The Aircraft Journal*, 12 July 1919, p. 8.)

AIRCRAFT JOURNAL

September 20, 1919   *Every Saturday*   *Price Ten Cents*

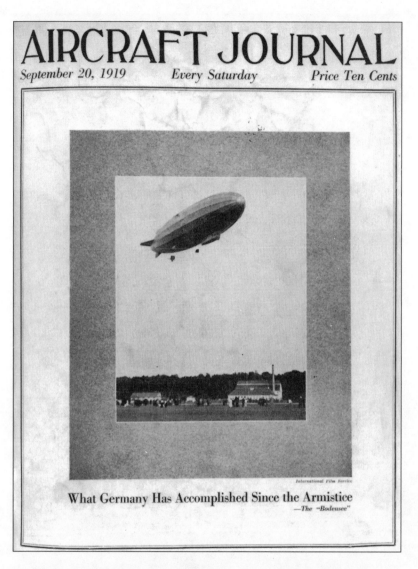

International Film Service

What Germany Has Accomplished Since the Armistice
—The "Bodensee"

Photograph of a new German airship, *The Bodensee*. According to Francis Garvan, the very same week that the Atlantic was crossed by airship "the Department of Interior exhibited in a little vial a new gas that they had discovered but had not put into the war, and it was asserted by our army officials that five aeroplanes could carry over New York enough gas in one night to annihilate the 5,000,000 inhabitants of that city" (Francis Garvan, "Washington Letter", *JIEC*, 12.1, January, 1920, p. 91).

JANUARY 3, 1921   Issued Weekly   PRICE 15 CENTS

AVIATION
AND
AIRCRAFT JOURNAL

The Skyscraper District of New York from the Air

VOLUME X
Number 1

Four
Dollars
a Year

SPECIAL FEATURES

U. S. NAVAL AIRCRAFT CONSTRUCTION
A STABILIZED CAMERA
OPERATION OF A RIGID AIRSHIP
A REMOTE CONTROL COMPASS
THE ANSALDO A-300C

THE GARDNER, MOFFAT CO., INC.
HIGHLAND, N. Y.
HARTFORD BUILDING, UNION SQUARE
22 EAST SEVENTEENTH STREET, NEW YORK

Entered as Second Class Matter, May 19, 1920, at the Post Office at Highland, N. Y.
under Act of March 3, 1879.

Aerial photograph of New York. Contemporary Americans had never seen such pictures.
The spectacle of the skyscraper district invited them to see themselves as part of a nation
whose scientific, technological, and industrial power was enabling mankind to realize its
potential on a world scale. The Roman lettering superimposed on a Roman eagle evoked
the idea that America was creating a new, greater, Roman republic/empire.

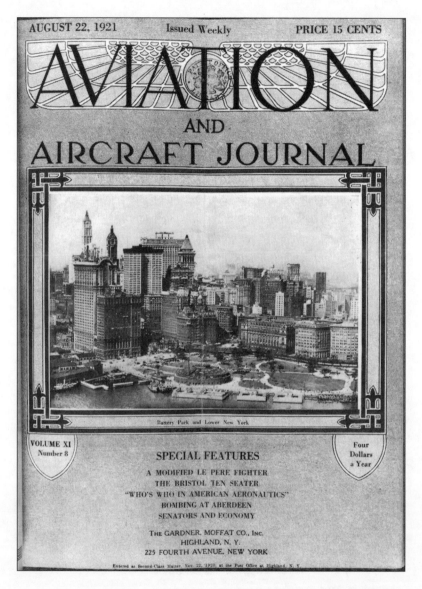

AUGUST 22, 1921   Issued Weekly   PRICE 15 CENTS

AVIATION
AND
AIRCRAFT JOURNAL

Battery Park and Lower New York

VOLUME XI
Number 8

Four
Dollars
a Year

SPECIAL FEATURES

A MODIFIED LE PERE FIGHTER
THE BRISTOL TEN SEATER
"WHO'S WHO IN AMERICAN AERONAUTICS"
BOMBING AT ABERDEEN
SENATORS AND ECONOMY

THE GARDNER, MOFFAT CO., INC.
HIGHLAND, N. Y.
225 FOURTH AVENUE, NEW YORK

Entered as Second-Class Matter, Nov. 22, 1920, at the Post Office at Highland, N. Y.

Photograph of the area "attacked" by the air service on 29 July 1921. To ensure Americans got the picture General Mitchell ordered that the "photographic section . . . will have sufficient airplanes, properly equipped with personnel and both moving and still cameras to secure photographs and moving pictures of the simulated attack upon New York" ("Bombing Raid on Eastern Cities", *The Aircraft Journal*, vol.11, no.6, August 8, 1921, p. 160). The left of the photograph shows the place where the World Trade Centre will later be built.

I. D. GARDNER
PRESIDENT

W. D. MOFFAT
VICE-PRESIDENT

W. I. SEAMAN
TREASURER

AIRCRAFT
JOURNAL

LADISLAS D'ORCY
EDITOR

GEORGE NEWBOLD
BUSINESS MANAGER

H M. WILLIAMS
GENERAL MANAGER

VOL. VI   APRIL 24, 1920   No. 17

The First Decisive Air War

British Aircraft, Acting as Main Striking Force,
Ends Mad Mullah's Power in Three Weeks

For the first time in the history of the world, aircraft have acted as a main striking force in a campaign and have proven a decisive factor in the defeat of the enemy. The first air war, properly speaking, took place in British Somaliland, and was directed against Mad Mullah, a native chieftain, who for twenty years had defied the administration of that protectorate. Many costly campaigns were conducted by the British against the Mad Mullah during this period, but the wild country behind the coast had offered well-nigh insurmountable difficulties to ground troops, so that the power of the natives was never really broken and the British practically abandoned half of Somaliland to the rule of the Mad Mullah.

After the armistice, however, it was decided to finally break the power of the fanatic chieftain. The campaign was opened on January 21 by the Royal Air Force and in less than three weeks the power which had threatened the colony for two decades was destroyed, the Mad Mullah losing, according to official information, "the whole of his force, all his stocks and all his belongings."

The brief, but telling campaign which has reestablished peace in Somaliland, is worth more than passing notice, for it affords the first illustration of how warfare will be conducted in future conflicts. In the Great War aircraft acted on the main as auxiliaries to ground troops and fleets, the aerial observation, bombing and fighting work being necessary to insure the success of the operations planned by the senior fighting services, that is, the armies and the navies. As a striking force, aircraft were, it is true, employed in independent capacity towards the close of the war, but their action was never powerful enough to be decisive without the active cooperation of the land and sea forces.

THE SIGNIFICANCE OF THE CAMPAIGN

Not so, however, in the recent Somaliland campaign. There the air force contingents were actually running a war of their own, in which aircraft formations acted as a primary striking force and played a decisive role in terminating hostilities. Ground troops were merely employed as auxiliaries for the purpose of "mopping up" the scattered forces of the enemy and for occupying the country after the air power had asserted itself.

This is then the main lesson to be drawn from this cam-

DAKKA, AFGHANISTAN, CAPTURED BY BRITISH TROOPS AFTER EXTENSIVE AIR OPERATIONS

(C) International

Announcement of the RAF's defeat of a Somali rebellion with photograph of Dakka, Afghanistan, "captured by British troops after extensive air operations". This shows the fantasy of an annihilating attack on New York turned the real relations of force upside down. The limitations of all aircraft made this impossible. This page, by contrast, shows the actual use of bombers by civilization to exercise imperial control through terror.

11

The Bomber/Poison Gas Combination

I now turn to look at the attempt of chemical warfare officers to create a chemical/air warfare system. I am interested in the long-term consequences: how, as the system grew, it became increasingly difficult to stop its further development; how it contributed to the development of further systems – bomber aircraft for the terrorizing of cities and colonial control, tear gas for the internal suppression of dissent, and pesticides and herbicides for capital-intensive agriculture; and how it reshaped science and technology so that not only were new weapons developed, but the possibility of inventing such weapons became easier in the future.

(i) Heterogeneous engineering and the chemical warfare system

By the end of the First World War, the American chemical warfare system had become the world's largest research programme prior to the Manhattan project, the Second World War programme to develop the atomic bomb. The impetus for its creation came from civilian scientists at the Bureau of Mines. By May 1917, just one month after America entered the war, the Bureau had established chemical warfare research laboratories in twenty-one universities, three industrial companies, and three government agencies.[1] As the war progressed, however, the military decided to bring all chemical warfare research under its direction. To do so, the general staff copied the Germans and established a single military organization coordinating all aspects of chemical warfare. This led to the foundation of the Chemical Warfare Service on 28 June 1918. The system bound together a diverse collection: laboratories (the Bureau of Mines, the Chemical Warfare Service field laboratory in France, the cluster of laboratories at the American University, and over thirty university laboratories across America); factories (Edgewood Arsenal, Zinsser and Company, the National Aniline and Chemical Company); military units (the First, Second, and Third Gas Regiments); sciences (chemistry, physiology, etc.); technologies (phosgene, mustard gas, gas masks, gas shells, gas cylinders, etc.); publications (the *Chemical Warfare Bulletin*, the *Journal of Industrial and Engineering Chemistry*); and a range of professions (engineers, chemists, physiologists, medical doctors, soldiers, chemical manufacturers).

To capture the fact that system building involves the reshaping of science and technology on the one side, and society on the other, sociologists have coined the term "heterogeneous engineering". So far we have seen one side: the remaking of society by rearticulating the ideas and interests of social groups in order to persuade them to support the system – or, more radically, forming new social groups with an interest in the growth of the system. Thus, we have seen how the leaders of American chemistry sought to convince chemists, engineers, manufacturers, and soldiers that they had a common interest in both chemical preparedness and an artificial dye industry.

The other side of system building is the remaking of science and technology. To gain and keep the support of social groups, the system builders had to make scientific discoveries and develop technologies which fitted their new perception of these groups' interests. To maintain the army's interest, for example, science and technology had to advance in particular directions. Chemists and physiologists had to discover more deadly poison gases, and ways of filtering out new enemy gases. Chemical engineers had to work out how to manufacture safely vast quantities of poison gas, combine it with weapons such as artillery and trench mortars, and ship it safely and quickly in quantity to the battlefield.

There is more to heterogeneous engineering. Technology can be shaped to shift the balance of power between social groups. Take the gas mask. The first gas masks came in two pieces: goggles to protect the eyes and a mouthpiece for breathing in filtered air. Soldiers took advantage of this. By taking off the goggles they could expose their eyes to mustard gas without the danger of inhaling the gas, giving themselves an injury serious enough to ensure evacuation from the trenches and a period of hospitalization, yet not so serious that it led to permanent blindness. This shifted the balance of power in the trenches from the officers towards the troops. In *Chemical Warfare* Fries and West tell us how heterogeneous engineering was used to shift the balance of power back. They start by reasserting the right to exercise coercion over such troops by labelling them as malingerers and cowards, then describe the technological adjustment made to counter the reversal of power relations. The gas mask was reconstructed as a single unit. Now the eyes could not be exposed to gas without exposing the lungs.[2] The exercise of coercive power by officers over men is made less liable to provoke resistance by being invisibly built into technology; when presented with a military gas mask today, who would guess that its shape is part of a technique to prevent troops escaping the front line?

Heterogeneous engineering is the art of building machines. A machine is, first of all, a machination, a stratagem, a form of cunning, in which both social and technological/scientific forces keep each other in check and all contribute to the goals of the machine builder.[3] Systems start fragile. The groups that support a system are only weakly attached to it. At any moment they may decide that their real interests lie elsewhere. Equally, the system builders have only an imperfect mastery of the science and technology on which the system depends. Notoriously, in the early stages of building a system, key pieces of technology break down at the worst moment. To ensure the survival of the system, the system builders seek to identify its weakest element and strengthen it. In the chemical warfare system, the first gas attacks were dependent on the vagaries of the wind which could suddenly reverse. The chemists quickly realized this was a potentially fatal weakness which might lead the army to reject poison gas and concentrate on artillery. To overcome it, they experimented with filling artillery and mortar shells with gas. The result was that cloud gas attacks were soon supplemented by artillery and mortar gas attacks.

As a system develops its weak points change. The chemical warfare system now showed weaknesses in other areas that hindered its universal adoption by the warring armies. One such weakness was that gas masks made attacks ineffective, so the chemists searched for a gas that would penetrate them. The result was the introduction of gases, such as chloropicrin, that went through existing gas masks. What is a weakness of a system is relative. A strength may become a weakness as other elements of the system develop or rival systems are built. To point this out Thomas Hughes has taken the term "reverse salient", which emphasizes the relative nature of weaknesses, rather than the usual term, "bottleneck", which suggests their absolute nature.[4] The term comes from trench warfare. When attacks were launched some troops advanced further than others, meaning that in places the enemy trenches penetrated behind the general line of advance. The danger was that the enemy could use such reverse salients to launch a successful counterattack. For this reason it was considered vital to remove such reverse salients quickly.

(ii) The growth of the system and the development of momentum

Through heterogeneous engineering, system builders seek to persuade more and more social groups that the growth of a system is in their interest, and to tie them ever more strongly to its development. Social groups come to see themselves as having multiple interests in the development of the system. Thus, American chemists were persuaded to support the chemical warfare system not only as a way of defending America, but also as a way of gaining an artificial dye industry. At the same time, as we have seen in the case of the gas mask, mechanisms are created that make it more and more difficult for groups to break away from their allotted role in the system. One of the most effective ways of tying social groups to a system is to destroy alternative systems. If the chemical warfare officers had persuaded Congress not to fund the alternative system, a mass infantry supported by artillery firing high explosives, then the army would have had no alternative except to rely on chemical weapons.

System builders can become trapped in their own creations. As they persuade more and more groups that the system is in their interests, and some groups that they have multiple interests in it, it becomes difficult to stop its expansion. The system acquires *momentum*. The need for these groups to achieve a return on their investments leads them to reproduce the picture of the world which originally justified the development of the system – even when this picture no longer fits the world. Of course, whether or not the picture fits the world will always be a matter of dispute. But, the analogy with physical systems suggested by the term "momentum" must not be carried too far. There is no autonomous technology. The system is never independent of the actions of the social groups that make it up. At each stage more heterogeneous engineering is required to ensure that the groups that support the system continue to perceive that it is in their interests to do so.

An interesting light is cast on these issues by a 19 April 1919 telegram Du Pont was forced to release to a 1930's Senate investigation into the wartime munitions trade. The telegram is from Francis Garvan, then a key figure in the Office of the Alien Property Custodian, the body that seized German dye patents when America declared war. Garvan was also president of the Chemical Foundation, which led the chemical manufacturers' campaign for an American artificial dye industry. The telegram is to a Bradley Palmer who was with the American delegation at the Paris peace talks. In tones of extreme urgency, "*this most important*", Palmer is urged to persuade Wilson to endorse a British amendment to the Treaty requiring Germany to surrender all war materials in excess of specified levels. The amendment required the Germans to "put the Allies in effective possession of all chemical processes used during the war . . . or for the productions of substances from which such things can be made".[5] Clearly, if accepted this would be a great boost to the American and Allied chemical industries in post-war competition with their German rivals.

The telegram shows that while the Chemical Warfare Service was seeking to enrol leading chemical corporations and chemists in support of its system, these groups were themselves seeking to enrol the Chemical Warfare Service in the construction of a larger system, the creation of an American coal tar dye industry. They needed the Service's support to give military authority to their claim that America had to have such an industry. The chemical warfare system would be a sub-system nestling within the larger system like one Russian doll within another. In these circumstances it was ambiguous who was enrolling whom.

The telegram shows how the system builders seek to capture presidential support for their system. The president is to be presented with a picture of a system on which the very existence of America as an independent nation depended, and with the support of so many powerful interests that it would be politically foolish to oppose it. Garvan telegraphs:

> There must be no possibility of injuring the industry on which rests, first, our defence against the explosive, gas and germ future offensive of Germany; second, five hundred millions invested in the dye industry itself; third, the independence of all textile, paint, varnish, and other industries dependent upon the American dye industry; fourth, destruction of present espionage system, only partially destroyed by the war, through the German dyers' agents and representatives in America; fifth the general chemical development upon which modern industry so greatly relies; and sixth, the future of chemical medicine in America.

Garvan then used German authority to underscore the vital importance of Americans subordinating themselves to the development of industrial systems. He ends by quoting Dr. Albert, the German government's financial advisor in America, whose papers he had seized soon after America entered the war:

> I have just come across a report by Albert to the home office to the effect that Germany has nothing to fear in America in the coal tar industry as we lack the moral power for the creation of such an industry, that in America nobody keeps the whole in mind, that the problem can only be solved through regard for all points of view to which belong scientific training, development of first-class chemists, cherishing the dye industry with wisdom and provision while it is still in its infancy, patience, persistence, and willingness to sacrifice. This is impossible in America, says Albert.

The telegram gives us further insight into how the chemists attempted to capture the federal government. It shows us the key place of the idea of an efficient system in the tactics they employed to do so. The nation is reconceptualized as a single industrial, capitalist, military, scientific, and technological system. Though Germany has been militarily defeated and is in social and economic chaos, the chemists claim its chemical industry makes it a continued threat. Through the deferral of an end to the war, the chemists transform the wartime state of emergency into a permanent state of emergency. Through their production of a permanent state of emergency the efficiency of the nation, now conceived of as a single system, becomes the sole criteria for state action. Under the mask of being the servants of the elected head of state, the chemists assert a sovereign right to decide what should be done. On the basis of their expertise and privileged locations in the laboratory, industry, and the military, the chemists act as master, telling the president what he must do. The Germans, through the quotation from Dr. Albert, are imagined as the world's leading systems builders which the American nation must now surpass. Here American liberal democracy converges with its imagined opposite, German autocracy, to the point where the two become difficult to distinguish.

(iii) Defending the system by recruiting new allies, both technological and human

The officers, scientists, engineers, and manufacturers building the chemical warfare system reacted to the general staff and disarmament movement's hostility by seeking new allies. In some cases, these allies were people, such as the police and the National Guard. In others, they were scientific and technological, such as the science of entomology and the technology of aerial crop or poison gas spraying. To recruit new allies, the chemical warfare officers attempted to enlarge the chemical warfare system by creating new sub-systems.

The bomber/poison gas system

The First World War saw American and Allied plans to bomb German cities with gas in 1919. Under General Hugh Trenchard, head of the Royal Air Force, they assembled a force of thousands of bombers to launch a massive attack in 1919 on German "industry, commerce and population", using incendiaries and a new American poison gas.[6] The British contracted for 250 four-engined Handley-Page bombers capable of delivering 7500 pounds of bombs. These could reach Berlin, a planned target. The United States "devised, manufactured and filled" bombs each containing one ton of mustard gas to be used against Metz.[7] The target was German morale. "I would very much like it if you could start up a really big fire in one of the German towns," Trenchard was instructed by his superior, "I would not be too exacting as regards accuracy in bombing railway stations . . . The German is susceptible to bloodiness, and I would not mind a few accidents due to inaccuracy."[8]

These plans marked a further stage in city bombing. German Zeppelin airships had carried out the first raids on Paris and London, and the British had followed suit with bomber raids on German cities. The initial reason given for bombing was to attack the factories, railway lines, and other facilities which the armies depended on. This was soon followed by the idea that a terrorized civilian population might lead to the collapse of the enemy's "will" to fight. The demands of domestic propaganda, however, may have been more important. "The target of attack," according to Michael Sherry, "was not so much the enemy as the flagging spirits of one's own compatriots. Air war, like no other weapon in the modern arsenal, satisfied yearnings for blood and punishment among peoples deeply wounded by war and deprived of decisive victories."[9]

With the end of the war, talk about planning to win wars by bombing cities with gas might have led to a backlash against chemical preparedness. Instead chemical officers stressed the enormous potential of attacking military targets with gas from the air. However, as set out in the conclusion to Part 1, in a key article by General Fries entitled "CHEMICAL WARFARE INSPIRES PEACE" and subtitled "Carrying of Horrors to Doors of Entire Populace a War Deterrent", the 1919 strategy of bombing cities with poison gas re-emerges.[10] To understand the full significance of these moves, it is essential to look at the attempt to build the bomber/chemical weapon system from another angle, the view-point of supporters of the bomber aircraft inside and outside the post-war air service. After the war the supporters of an American strategic bomber force, like the supporters of a large chemical warfare establishment, were trapped by the general staff's claim that the *actual* fighting in the war had proven that these weapons should have a subordinate role. The infantry and artillery were the crucial military arms. Aeroplanes had a vital, but subordinate, role as the army's "eyes". All efforts must be devoted to an escalating battle to observe without being observed. This meant masses of reconnaissance and fighter aircraft. Strategic bombing was an ineffective diversion from this critical task. Poison gas, for its part, had been shown to be a substitute for high explosives that the artillery could use in special circumstances, though in general artillery was more effective. Acting separately, neither service had sufficient authority to contest the staff's interpretation of the war. Acting together, however, they might have sufficient combined authority to claim that the war that was about to have been fought in 1919 was a better guide to the future. It was thus the virtual reality of the air bomber/chemical weapon combination at the end of the First World War which must be taken into account.

Within the administration, Assistant Secretary for War Benedict Crowell led the battle. In an argument that paralleled that of the chemists, Crowell argued that support for civil aviation was the cheapest, most effective way of developing America's military power.[11] After the war, American aircraft manufacturers were unable to find buyers because vast numbers of military aircraft had been dumped on the market. To encourage investment in civil aviation, Crowell argued, the government must initially provide a secure market through military orders. This would soon lead to a self-supporting civil aviation industry. Such an industry was vital to America's security as future war would be decided by air power. "The aggressive nation will be prepared to launch an attack upon the shipping, munitions, manufacturing and even cities of its opponents. Unless the opponent is ready to meet or anticipate such attack vital victories will early be accomplished."[12]

Crowell saw military and civil aviation as part of a single system. Through its coordinated development America could lead the world in both civil and military aviation. The government should concentrate all air activities under a single head and form a united air service. Early action was vital if America was to prevent Britain from exercising the same stranglehold over commercial aviation she already enjoyed over the rest of the "world's communication system – with her merchant marine, cables, and radio".[13]

Within the army air service, Brigadier-General William Mitchell was the leading advocate of a "strategic" or "independent" air force. Faced with general staff opposition to an independent air force as opposed to a subordinate air service, he sought to force the staff's hand by appealing directly to the American public. To do so, as we have seen in the Introduction, he mounted a series of spectacular demonstrations to show that an air force could defend America more cheaply and better than the navy and to demonstrate that American cities were vulnerable to attack by bombers carrying poison gas. There was, then, a convergence of ideas, interests, political strategy, supporters, and technology between the supporters of chemical weapons and of bomber aircraft. The idea of fusing the two systems was actively canvassed by the scientists and engineers of the National Research Council in a 1921 pamphlet "Chemistry and War". This underscored the enormous potential of the bomber/poison gas combination. It would be a far cheaper way of developing American military power than its current attempt to build a fleet of battleships equal to that of Britain. The cost of a single battleship, $30 million, "would endow an establishment for chemical research such as the world has never seen".[14] The bomber/gas combination made the battleship obsolete. Equally, the bomber/gas combination was effective against armies: "The airman of the next war will not need a machine gun or even bombs to attack the enemy underneath . . . All he needs to do is to attach a sprayer to the tail of his machine and rain down poison on the earth beneath as the farmer kills the bugs on his potato field."[15] It cited Chemical Warfare Service testimony before the House Appropriations Committee claiming that had the Germans developed this technology, "the entire American army would have been annihilated in 10 or 12 hours". It concluded that the bomber/gas combination was a new technology which made existing military policy outdated. "We are in the midst of a revolution in warfare as great as that when guns and cannon supplanted the bow and spear."[16] Acting as bridge builders between the chemical warfare soldiers and the airmen, scientists and engineers at the National Research Council saw the potential to create a single system.

The other side of building the chemical/bomber system was the Chemical Warfare Service's effort to develop the knowledge and technology necessary to deliver poison gas by air. This led to three new technologies: (1) a pressurized sprinkling apparatus which dispersed large droplets of gas; (2) a non-pressurized spraying apparatus which dispersed a fine mist; and (3) gas bombs.[17] The air service, for its part, sought the development of a long-range heavy bomber. Frustrated in the 1920s, it succeeded in the 1930s with Boeing's development of the B-17 "super-fortress" bomber.

Colonial control

The Chemical Warfare Service saw the bomber/gas system as an ideal weapon to use against "not-yet" civilized peoples. It showed a keen interest in "Great Britain's secret experiments with poison gas and aircraft in Mesopotamia". The Service had already argued that:

> If the United States must clean up Mexico or is forced to put down uprisings in the Philippines, in San Domingo or in any other place among peoples not thoroughly prepared with masks, it can be done with the use of gas at a less expense and with far less loss of American lives than any other method of Warfare put together.[18]

It now argued that Britain's experiments showed that by "marking time", America was falling behind as other nations moved rapidly ahead. Supporters of the Air Corps officer's campaign for a strategic air force were equally interested in the Royal Air Force's new strategy. Under the banner headline "THE FIRST DECISIVE AIR WAR: BRITISH AIRCRAFT ACTING AS MAIN STRIKING FORCE, END OF MAD MULLAH'S POWER IN THREE WEEKS", *The Aircraft Journal* pointed out the historic importance of Britain's actions. "For the first time in the history of the world, aircraft have acted as a main striking force in a campaign and have proven a decisive factor in the defeat of the enemy."[19] Just as the Chemical Warfare Service saw Mesopotamia (the area of modern Iraq) as a place for experimenting with aircraft and poison gas, the supporters of strategic air power saw Somalia as a laboratory in which the British had proved the critical importance of strategic air power in future wars. They believed aircraft could help America maintain hegemony in its sphere of influence. Their success in influencing policy led to the bombing of Ocotal and other Nicaraguan towns in 1927.

These editorials and articles point to the Royal Air Force's post-war bid to demonstrate its value as an autonomous organization. Aircraft and chemical weapons, it claimed, could save money. Britain's strategy for maintaining hegemony over regions she did not directly rule was as old as empire. Hegemony over the majority of local powers could be maintained by using bribes, isolating the few remaining resisters who should be destroyed in the most spectacular way.

This would provide an example to the others of the futility and cost of resisting. In the aftermath of the First World War, Secretary of State for War and Air Winston Churchill sought to reduce the cost of this strategy. The power of rebel leaders in remote areas, he believed, could be more rapidly, spectacularly, and economically destroyed by aircraft dropping gas bombs to terrorize their followers than by slow-moving and difficult to supply ground troops.[20] For Churchill, this was all part of a larger game. Maintaining control of Mesopotamia was critical to ensuring privileged British access to the developing Mosul oil fields, whose importance grew as the Royal Navy converted from coal to oil-fired ships. The Royal Air Force, for its part, saw colonial control as a way of justifying its existence as an independent force at a time of savage budget cuts. This power-play meant that the Royal Air Force was soon engaged in colonial control through aerial terror not only in Iraq but also in Somalia, India, and Afghanistan.

Combining "Zeppelin" airships with poison gas

An alternative to the bomber/gas combination was the rigid airship/gas combination. After the war, *The Aircraft Journal* promoted government support for the development of rigid airships. It pointed out the advantages they enjoyed. The cost per pound of transport by airship was one half that of the aeroplane, while the economic limit of airship transport was 1000 miles against 500 miles for the airplane.[21] It noted scientists' view that aeroplanes faced fundamental limitations in the amount of weight they could carry. It reported Signal Corps Chief Major-General Squier's enthusiasm for the possibilities opened up by replacing hydrogen with helium as the lifting agent, opening "a new era for the dirigible balloon. With a non-inflammable gas, not only comfort and expeditious, but also safe transcontinental and transatlantic travel, in dirigibles will, it is believed, become common place."[22] Following the crossing of the Atlantic by the British R-34 Airship on 6 July 1919, the editors claimed that this completely changed America's relationship to Europe:

> Foremost perhaps the voyage of the R-34 spells the doom of America's splendid geographical isolation. The sea barrier of the Atlantic is no longer inviolable since an aircraft carrying thirty men succeeded in reaching these shores from Europe. What today seems but an experimental flight achieved in the face of great difficulties will in a brief time seem quite a common occurrence.

The editorial concluded with a statement which could apply equally to its military or the commercial potential. "The warning is obvious. Its high time the United States took a hand in the development of lighter-than-air craft of great size, and particularly of large rigid airships."[23]

The military significance was not lost on contemporaries. Whereas fixed-wing aircraft might someday cross the Atlantic, rigid airships already had. During the

First World War the Germans had used Zeppelins to bomb Paris and London. In testimony to the Dye Subcommittee of the Senate Finance Committee, Garvan, now the Alien Property Custodian, noted the danger America now faced:

> Gentlemen, this thing has burnt into our minds throughout the past two years, but I do not think anything brought it to my mind so clearly and distinctly as did the fact that after the armistice airships flew over the sea; and during the same week that those ships flew between England and America, the Department of [the] Interior exhibited in a little vial a new gas that they had discovered but had not put into the war, and it was asserted by our army officials that five aeroplanes could carry over New York enough gas in one night to annihilate the 5,000,000 inhabitants of that city.[24]

He concluded that America had to build its own fleet of airships equipped to bomb European cities with poison gas. "Where are we going to get our protection from such gas in the future? There is only one protection possible. That is for a country that might send some airships over here with that gas to know that we can send back ships the next night and annihilate the people or the city that manufactured it."[25]

Tear gas

During the war all sides had used tear gas. Even in small amounts it greatly reduced efficiency by forcing troops to wear gas masks.[26] After the war chemical warfare officers campaigned for its use as a way of controlling protests, strikes, and riots. Its regular use by police, they hoped, would help allay the public's aversion to chemical war. Tear gas would also provide the Chemical Warfare Service with a peacetime role training police forces and National Guard units in its use, a consideration which became urgent when the general staff forbade the service to train army troops in chemical warfare.

General staff opposition and the fear that the use of tear gas might backfire against them, led the Chemical Warfare Service to adopted a double strategy. On the one hand, they sought to introduce tear gas in a way which least risked provoking public outrage. The public was not to learn that a war gas was being prepared as a means of controlling them. Chemical Warfare Service work adapting a tear gas they had discovered during the war, chloroacetophenone, for use within America by developing a special tear gas grenade, was kept secret. This had a non-fragmenting celluloid and paper body so that it did not cause visible injury. Tear gas could now be presented as a less violent and more effective alternative to the use of firearms and clubs to control riots or mobs. Equally, concern about public reactions led the Chemical Warfare Service to first float the idea of using tear gas for "police work" in the Philippines and in Central America in 18 June

1919 Senate hearings.[27] Later, when it discussed the use of tear gas within the United States, the Chemical Warfare Service sought to legitimate its use by emphasizing its use against "mobs" or "criminals".

On the other hand, the officers sought to bypass general staff opposition by helping former chemical officers establish private companies to manufacture tear gas grenades and provide training in their use. Through these companies, the service sold the idea of using tear gas to the police and national guard. The first such company was set up by Major Stephen J. DeLanoy, an ex-chemical warfare officer. On 6 July 1921 Fries allowed DeLanoy to interview researchers on the civilian chemical weapon project. The service also supplied him with 100 tear gas grenades for demonstration purposes. DeLanoy then staged demonstrations of the efficiency of tear gas for the New York and Philadelphia police departments. The *New York Times* gave a graphic account of the first demonstration on 19 July 1921. It told how six men had three times driven back "weeping violently" 200 Philadelphia policemen who had been sent to capture them. "[An] Official asserted," it concluded, "it was likely the gas would replace means hitherto used to subdue mobs and criminals."[28] When the Philadelphia Police Department agreed to adopt tear gas, DeLanoy set up a company to manufacture tear gas grenades, Stephen J. DeLanoy, Chemical Protection.

Subsequently, two other former officers established similar companies, Lawrence Company, (later Federal Laboratories) established by Captain Ruben B. Lawrence, and Lake Erie Chemical Company, established by Lieut.-Colonel C. Gross. The Service helped these companies extensively: it provided them chloracetophenone for research purposes, gave them technical information about tear gas grenades and a testing service, and referred requests from police departments and national guard units for tear gas grenades and training to them. These companies then helped spread tear gas use by marketing it internationally. These tactics led to rapid adoption of tear gas by police forces and national guard units. By the end of 1921, more than 600 cities had been equipped and there were already several reports of its use. Tear gas was a powerful police weapon. Forces equipped with tear gas seldom needed the help of federal troops to handle disorders, and there was an abrupt drop in local authority requests for federal troops or national guard forces.[29]

Using poison gas to control insects

During the war the army was concerned that lice might spread typhus to American troops. This led to research by the Chemical Warfare Service and Department of Agriculture's Bureau of Entomology into the use of gas to kill lice. The idea was that troops wearing masks would enter a room filled with gas and this would kill lice infestations.[30] Though unsuccessful, this research led to an expanded programme in which war gases were tested on dozens of insects. It was eventually discovered that the poison gas chloropicrin killed insects effectively.

As with tear gas, after the end of the war the Chemical Warfare Service saw research and development of insecticides as capable of providing it with a peace-time role. At the height of hostility to chemical weapons in 1922 such research enabled it to claim it had beaten "the sword into the ploughshare".[31] There was another, not publicly mentioned, advantage of such research. Chemicals which poison one species frequently poison others – research into insecticides might lead to the discovery of new poison gases.

The Bureau of Entomology, for its part, saw a war against insects as a way of underscoring the national importance of its work. In his December 1921 address "The War Against Insects" as retiring president of the American Association for the Advancement of Science, the head of the Bureau, Leland Howard, proclaimed that the end of the war in Europe set the stage for the escalation of a war against insects. Earlier in his career Howard had stressed the benefits insects provide. This was now forgotten. They were simply an enemy threatening civilization's survival. Insects, he said, seemed to have a quality "born of another planet, more monstrous, more energetic, more insensate, more atrocious, more infernal than ours". Federal entomologists were portrayed as a heroic force of "four hundred trained men" waging a "defensive and offensive campaign" against these hordes.[32]

At the Department of Agriculture such statements entrenched the idea that insects threaten human survival. After quoting Howard's remarks to a 1935 meeting of exterminators, the chief of the Insecticide Division, R.C. Roark, continued: "People must be taught that insects are enemies of man; and as the public becomes insect conscious the opportunities for service by the entomologist, the insecticide chemist, the chemical manufacture and the exterminator will increase."[33] Subsequently, Roark was the key person in selling dichlorodiphenyltrichloroethane (DDT) to the US army during the Second World War.

Actual attempts to show the value of chemical weapons against a key insect pest were unsuccessful. After the war, concern about boll weevils was at an all-time height. Boll weevils had entered Texas from Mexico in 1892 and created havoc through the cotton belt, reaching Virginia in 1922. The Bureau of Entomology had sought a biological method of control without success. The boll weevil was an unlikely candidate for biological control as it had spread gradually from its native land, making it unlikely that effective natural enemies in Mexico that had failed to follow it would be found.[34] The Chemical Warfare Service now collaborated with the Bureau of Entomology and state experimental stations in trying to find a suitable insecticide, but after seven years research it had not succeeded.[35]

The Chemical Warfare Service, however, saw the project as valuable from a chemical weapon point of view. In its 1927 report it claimed that the project had:

"Extended our knowledge of the fundamental facts concerning the toxicity of compounds which will prove beneficial to certain investigations undertaken with a view to the solution of specifically Chemical Warfare problems."[36] The war against insects was also a way of developing the technology needed to spread chemical weapons from the air. The Army Air Service collaborated with the Bureau of Entomology and the Huff-Danland Corporation to develop a special plane for crop dusting. Given the close collaboration between the Bureau of Entomology and the Chemical Warfare Service, it seems likely this helped the Chemical Warfare Service develop the means to disperse chemical weapons from the air.

The Chemical Warfare Service alliance with the Bureau of Entomology helped tip the balance in favour of chemical control, and against biological control (using natural enemies, for example importing the Australian ladybird known as vedalia to control the attack of cottony-chusion scale on Californian citrus fruit) and cultural control (destroying the conditions an insect needs to prosper, for example draining the water malaria mosquitoes need to breed).[37] Its intervention came at a critical time. The failure of projects to achieve biological control of the gypsy moth and the boll weevil had weakened support for biological control within the Bureau of Entomology. Equally, wartime developments had boosted support for chemical control. During the war it had been discovered that para-dichlorobenzene (PDB) was effective against peach tree borer and calcium arsenate was effective against boll weevil. Further, cutting off German supplies had led to American production of the coal-tar intermediaries needed to produce para-dichlorobenzene, and the wartime demand for lead shot, signal flares, plate glass, and the poison gas diphenylcholoroarsine had boosted its capacity to manufacture arsenical insecticides. The closure of wartime markets now led chemical manufactures to put their weight behind insecticides so as to develop a market that would employ this new capacity.

(iv) How the chemical warfare system changed scientific research

Knowledge is a social product. It consists not only in what is known, but in who has authority to say what is known, how disputes about what is known are decided, what instruments are used for investigation, what range of issues it is believed possible to have knowledge of, and so forth. The development of the chemical warfare system not only added to the content of our knowledge, it also led to a small but significant shift in how knowledge is produced.[38] To see this a list of some of the elements that go into the social production of knowledge is helpful:

1. The set of propositions regarded as possibly true or false;
2. The instruments that can be used for investigation;

3. The set of materials or objects available for investigations;
4. The way investigations are organized;
5. Long-term research programmes;
6. Which people have authority to undertake investigations;
7. The social groups which give support for investigations.

Before continuing, two points about the above list need to be clarified. First, the concept of a set of propositions regarded as possibly true or false, and the idea that this can change, is best illustrated by an historical example.[39] Before 1890 scientists believed that it was the cell as a whole that carried out chemical transformations. They formed hypotheses about living protoplasm and conducted investigations to determine how it worked. A decade later, all this had changed. Scientists now believed that all chemical transformations could be traced to the action of specific enzymes. The reactions carried out by enzymes were no different from actions carried out in the chemical laboratory. The set of propositions that scientists regarded as possibly true or false had changed. Second, the idea of a long-term research programme, taken from the philosopher of science Imre Lakatos.[40] Newtonian physics or ecology are such research programmes. They are made up of a "hard core" of ideas about how the world is, which remain unchanged as research proceeds. These are surrounded by a "protective belt" of assumptions believed to be true, which may be changed as research continues. Finally, there is a set of problems to be solved.

The development of the chemical warfare system does not seem to have had any detectable influence on the first element of my list. A look at some of the other elements, however, is revealing. During the war the Chemical Warfare Service was able to spend, by contemporary standards, very large funds on the development of new instruments for research into new poison gases. The Chemical Warfare Service's interest in developing poisonous particulates led it to support the work of Wells and Gerke to develop an improved ultra-microscope capable of measuring the size of smoke particles.[41] Scientists could now carry out investigations into smoke particles. In other words, the new instrument changed the set of propositions which scientists could investigate. It opened up new areas for research. There was, however, only a limited pool of public and private resources available to build new scientific instruments. This means the government's decision to devote large resources to building the instruments needed for chemical warfare research meant that other instruments for investigating other phenomena were not built.

Chemical warfare research also influenced the organization of research. In the years before the war leading scientists had called for the organization of inter-disciplinary teams of scientists and engineers equipped with the latest scientific instruments. Only this, they argued, would allow America to solve key problems in pure and applied science. The wartime chemical warfare research effort enabled the organized research idea to be developed, tested, and refined, and through its employment of over a thousand scientists and engineers at its height, it gave researchers throughout America a working knowledge of organized research in practice. After the war the National Research Council supported Charles Herty, the editor of the *Journal of Industrial and Engineering Chemistry*, by providing a forum for an address in which he claimed that chemical warfare research had shown the value of organized research.[42] Herty argued that chemical weapon research had shown what "tremendous speed and progress can be made in research" when chemists, pharmacologists, biologists, and physicians are organized into teams. As such, wartime chemical warfare research provided a *paradigm* for how research should be organized in other fields. If philanthropists would step forward with funding, it would lead to "the solution of the intensely intricate problems connected with the health of our people". When that day came it would show that the new method of research developed at the American University Experimental Station was "the greatest peace asset we have gained from the recent war". Through the "higher utilization of chemistry . . . America will make the world its debtor, not in dollars but in blessings bestowed".

The history I have recounted in this chapter shows how the building of the chemical warfare system had a large impact on both research programmes and the social groups that support them. The alliance between the Bureau of Entomology and the Chemical Warfare Service helped tip the balance in favour of chemical control, and against biological and cultural insect control, promoting biochemical research, while marginalizing ecological research. At the same time, the construction of the chemical warfare system strengthened the coalition between chemical corporations, chemical scientists and engineers, the military, and capital-intensive farming, while weakening an alliance between entomologists, small-scale farmers, and other groups.

It is difficult to evaluate the full impact of the chemical warfare system on the production of knowledge. What is needed are historical studies that consider how it tilted the balance against alternative directions that knowledge production could have taken. Questions that need to be asked include: To what extent did the use of large government funds to develop instruments useful for the study of toxins deny funds to the development of instruments for the study of other aspects of nature? To what extent did the development of organized research close off other lines of research? And, to what extent did the shift in favour of chemical and against biological and cultural control change the way in which the science of ecology developed?

What my study does show is that the construction of the chemical warfare system had a long-term consequence: it shifted the production of knowledge in ways that made further chemical warfare research easier. This means that while chemical weapons may be destroyed by international agreements, it will not be difficult to reinvent them. Thus, it is not simply the weapons that have been produced by scientific research that we have to worry about, but, as philosopher of science Ian Hacking has underscored, that such research reshapes the way our society produces knowledge to make it increasingly easy to research and develop new weapons in the future.[43] Though further investigation is needed, the importance of appreciating this point is suggested by German research and development of new nerve gases in the late 1930s and early 1940s. It was because Dr Gerhard Schrader had already been carrying out research into organophosphorus insecticides that Germany was rapidly able to develop a research programme into how organophosphorus compounds could be used as poison gases.[44] At the same time, the failure to dismantle German militarism after the First World War meant that it was not difficult to reactivate social support for continued chemical weapon research. The result was the discovery, development, and production of the new deadlier nerve gases Tabun and Sarin.

12

The Mind which is Destined
to Govern the World

The need for society to decide the direction of research is underscored by the history of chemical and air weapons.[1] The decision to direct research into the discovery of more toxic substances, and the reshaping of society to support such research, had massive consequences. The very form of science and technology was changed. Through directing their research into toxic substances – such as toxic chlorine and phosphorous compounds and technologies which use them – such as pesticides, herbicides, poison gases, tear gases, and the means to use aircraft to spray or drop these substances from the air – it became easier for scientists to make further discoveries about toxic substances and to develop new toxic technologies. And by reshaping society to support such research and development, it becomes easier to gain support for such research and development in the future. Indeed, society may reach the point where it is believed that it has no choice except to continue, as alternative directions for research and development no longer exist and have been forgotten. Yet the very idea that society needs to make judgements about the direction of research is obscured by the very concepts scientists use to think about research. I now explore how these concepts were formed by scientists in their struggle to advance their position within American society.[2]

(i) The use of story and metaphor to change America's conception of science and scientists

The second half of the nineteenth century saw a bid by leading American scientists to increase their control over the direction of scientific research.[3]

Previously, investigators or natural philosophers (the contemporary terms for scientists) sought funds by claiming that specific investigations would provide solutions to critical problems facing the military, business, farmers, and other groups. Investigators, for example, claimed the national government should fund research at the naval observatory because it would lead to better techniques for determining the position of ships, a practical problem of great concern for both commercial and naval shipping. This way of getting funds had a price. In return for funding, the investigator had to largely accept other people's views of the direction his research was to take. Of course, the cunning servant could manipulate the master. Then as now, an investigator could negotiate a measure of control over the direction of research by explaining to the groups who funded him what the key problems that faced them were, and by telling them how his investigations could solve them. The fact remained, however, that the direction of research, the expenditure of money on equipment, the timetable for its completion, the explanation for failure to produce useful results all had to be negotiated from a position of relative weakness. In competition with other investigators, the scientist largely had to accept the terms set by more powerful groups. Such groups often had other ways to solve their problems. Scientists needed them more than they needed scientists.

The alternative to calling for funds on practical grounds was to justify it on religious or political grounds. Investigators claimed that their work revealed the majesty of God in his natural works, or that science should be supported in a democratic republic because it helped prevent citizens from being manipulated by special interests. By teaching them how to test opinions for logical consistency and against observed fact, science taught Americans how to form their own judgements. In using religious or political justifications for science funding, however, the position of the investigator in negotiating control over funds was no better than justifying science in terms of its practical utility. The investigator had to demonstrate that time and money spend on investigations into natural phenomena would be of greater value than time spent studying the bible or the Constitution.

Leading scientists such as Benjamin Gould and Henry Rowland sought to dramatically alter the terms on which scientists received funding. They used the power scientists had already acquired within the nation, the university, and the laboratory to establish the credibility of a new conception of science, the pure science idea. Power was used to acquire more power. The campaign for pure science sought to renegotiate the place of the scientist. Its leaders wanted to form all American scientists into a united bloc, and to form a series of alliances with other groups. To see how they did so, I now look at how these scientists formed the idea of pure science, deployed new tactics, and developed a series of alliances. While the scientists did all these things simultaneously in their attempt to rearticulate power relations, for analytic purposes it is helpful to treat each separately.

The leaders of the movement for pure science sought to change America's idea of what science is. They claimed that scientists are, and ought to be, driven by a concern for truth alone. In the long run, the search for truth for its own sake is a more effective way of promoting mankind's material and moral progress. To establish these claims, scientists told two sets of stories. By repeating these stories they sought to consolidate an idea of the ultimate nature of the scientist and of scientific research – in philosophical terminology, to establish the "ontology" or being of the scientist and of research.

The nature of the scientist

The first set of stories sets out to establish the nature of the true scientist. He is presented as being driven by a concern for truth alone. This can be seen in the ex-president of the American Association for the Advancement of Science Benjamin Gould's 1869 address to the Association:

> At all times and places there have been some in whom the divine fire burned; and so it doubtless ever will be. Such could no more be turned from their high instinct to discover causes and laws, than the mountain torrent from its course toward the sea. Yet how few are these, although they have never failed to pass the torch from age to age! Even in the days of Roman dominion Africa nursed the embers of the sacred flame; and swarthy Arabs and Moors, with here and there a silent monk, guarded it through the dark ages; ages replete with classic lore, with wondrous art, with barbaric luxury, yet devoid of science, except in the secret guardianship of those who dared not betray their priceless yet mysterious possession . . . These are the men who toil in their lofty studies, seeking the truth for its own sake, drawn by some resistless magnetism, and working even better than they know.[4]

To convince his audience that true scientists are driven by a concern for the truth above all else, Gould presents his claim as a repetition of a series of stories it already believed. These stories depict particular men as having been ready to die for the truth, the most famous being Socrates and Christ. At the same time, however, the implicit repetition of these stories varies them to make a precise intervention. Gould seeks to consolidate the idea that there is a type of person, the scientist, who is driven by an overpowering instinct, the instinct for truth. By using the terminology of instinct, Gould conveys the idea that the willingness to make sacrifices for truth is not a momentary thing, but a continuous and powerful drive that can be depended on to work at all times. It can be relied upon even where it is opposed by strong material temptations. The idea that the scientist is driven by such a force is reinforced with metaphors evoking the forces of gravity, fire, instinct, and magnetism. Gould notes that he himself had first coined the term to designate the kind of person who is driven by the instinct for truth to investigate nature: "Twenty years ago I ventured to propose . . . the word *scientist*."[5]

The scientist is presented as having a special ability to understand nature through stories about the origin of this ability.[6] Take Johns Hopkins physicist Henry Rowland's classic statement of the pure science idea, his 1883 address "A Plea for Pure Science". Initially, the student of nature tends to base his ideas on established opinions or his own imagination. Through education he is taught to test his ideas against a standard of "absolute truth".[7] By bringing his mind into "direct contact" with nature, he is "convinced of its errors again and again". The student learns to form new hypotheses and to test them until he finds one which fits the observed facts. After repeated trials, he finally discovers the "proper method of reasoning". The result is a mind which is neither in thrall to received ideas nor so arrogant that it cannot learn from others. Such a mind is able to overturn existing ideas and initiate a new era:

> He has a longing for truth and is willing to test himself, to test others and to test nature until he finds it. He has the courage of his opinions when thus carefully formed, and is then, but not till then, willing to stand before the world and proclaim what he considers the truth. Like Galileo and Copernicus, he inaugurates a new era in science, or like Luther, in the religious belief of mankind.[8]

The final product is a mind whose strength lies in the fact that through direct contact with nature it is able to correct its own errors and to know the truth. Or, to use the analogy I used as the title to Chapter 10, the scientific mind is like a gyroscope which is able to correct its own deviations. Through his self-formation, the scientist acquires a right to govern both the social and the natural world:

> This is the mind which has built up modern science to its present perfection, which has laid one stone upon the other with such care that it to-day offers to the world the most complete monument to human reason. This is the mind which is destined to govern the world in the future and to solve problems pertaining to nature as well as politics.
>
> It is the only mind which appreciates the imperfections of the human reason and is thus carefully able to guard against them. It is the only mind that values the truth as it should be valued and ignores all personal feeling in its pursuit.[9]

The nature of science

The second set of stories present the nature of scientific discovery. These stories present five propositions:

1. Through experiment or observation the scientist is able to discover a set of internal principles which govern all natural phenomena.

2. It is impossible for the scientist to say in advance exactly what his investigations will discover, yet once carried out these investigations give the scientist privileged knowledge of whole areas of nature.

3. All scientific observation and experiment contribute to the discovery of such principles. This means that no investment in research is ever wasted.

4. These principles form a unified structure. As research continues, scientists are coming closer and closer to discovering the set of principles that govern all natural phenomena.

5. Knowledge of the principles of nature gives the scientist power over nature; modern inventions are based on scientists' discovery of such principles. The path, however, from a scientific discovery to the invention that makes use of it may be a long one. It is not possible to say in advance which discoveries will lead to important new inventions.

These propositions are conveyed by stories about Michael Faraday. His research into electricity is presented as an example of the selfless drive to discover the truth, and the discovery of a set of principles that have resulted in unforeseeable inventions which have created the new electricity industries. "A Plea for Pure Science" provides a typical example:

> For generations there have been some few students of science who have esteemed the study of nature the most noble of pursuits. Some have been wealthy, and some poor; but they have all had one thing in common – the love of nature and its laws. To these few men the world owes all the progress due to applied science, and yet very few ever received any payment in this world for their labors. Faraday, the great discoverer of the principle upon which all machines for electric lighting, electric railways, and the transmission of power, must rest, died a poor man, although others and the whole world have been enriched by his discoveries.[10]

A second story about Faraday emphasizes the indirect and unpredictable way in which research leads to invention. The article "Original Research as a Means of Education" from *Nature* of 23 October 1873 tells how Faraday's discovery of benzole led Zinin to the preparation of aniline. For many years this was regarded as no more than a "chemical curiosity". Eventually, however, it led to the artificial dye industry.[11]

These stories are precisely targeted. They seek to give pure science the ultimate credit for the new electrical and chemical industries, displacing claims of inventors such as Thomas Edison. Minimally, they present the pure scientist as the co-creator of these industries; maximally, they reduce the inventor to a mere applier of pure scientists' discoveries.[12] The stories emphasize that it is research to discover the principles of science, and not research to solve some immediate practical problem, that has provided the basis for these industries, and that it is not possible to say in advance what future research will lead to the development of new industries. The stories are packed with powerful metaphors that provide guidance as to how they are to be understood. As we have seen, the idea that the scientist is driven by an over-powering concern for truth is buttressed by describing it in terms of the forces of gravity, magnetism, and instinct. Other metaphors make other points. The idea that pure scientific research will inevitably provide a return is reinforced by metaphors of sowing and harvesting.[13] To emphasize that science is a collective enterprise it is likened to the building of a temple. Even the smallest discovery is significant as it adds to the development of the temple.[14] The claim that the scientist cannot predict what his investigation will discover, yet once his investigation is completed he will have a privileged knowledge of a whole area of nature is supported by describing research as like the exploration and charting of an unknown territory:

> We are exploring a new country, and our outlook must therefore be doubly sharp; we must be prepared for every possible event, and ready to meet every change of fortune. We must, like a traveller, not be discouraged by reverses, but patiently persevere in our course, feeling convinced that the path, which for a long time may be a thorny one, must in due course lead us to a point from which we shall enjoy an extended view of the surrounding country, and be able to trace the tortuous paths by which the elevation has been reached.[15]

This metaphor conveys two different claims. The first is that the scientist cannot know in advance what he is going to discover. Only the actual exploration of nature can discover its principles. The second is that once the scientist has carried out his investigation, he has a privileged knowledge of a whole area of nature.

A third metaphor is that of the expanding circle of knowledge. Gould again:

> The activity and energy of scientific inquiry at the present moment are intense beyond all precedent in history . . . An important fact, noted but unpublished by one man, speedily manifests itself to others; so that suppressed discoveries are in fact abandoned ones, and the most important are very frequently made in duplicate. This is simply because the limit of our knowledge spreads like a great circular wave, emanating from a center. The advancing lines have access only to what lies upon the margin before them, and the throng who press forward tread in contiguous paths, the divergence of whose radiation is overbalanced by the continually increasing number in the ranks.[16]

Finally, the idea that through their discovery of the principles of nature, scientists can obtain control over the production of natural phenomena is conveyed through the use of military metaphors. Gould gives a colourful example, drawing on recent memories of the Civil War:

Scientific progress in these days is like that of a besieging army. Little by little miners work beneath the surface; slowly the entrenchments grow to right and left, approaching always, however indirectly; gradually the long circumvallations close around the citadel . . . At last a point is secured whence the artillery may begin its work. Under cover of this, new approaches are effected, until at last, in the fullness of time, the final charge is made. One brilliant dash, and the stronghold falls.[17]

This metaphor emphasizes the collective activity of conquest and that the discovery of principles gives power over nature.

(ii) The tactics used by scientists to advance their position within the nation, universities, and in government laboratories

These stories and metaphors formed the linchpin of a series of tactics to advance the position of scientists. These tactics were based on the power that American scientists had already acquired. Power is the basis of acquiring more power. Scientists already held positions as investigators in government laboratories, and as teachers in universities. They were already employed by manufacturers, albeit on an occasional basis, to help them with the development of technology. At the same time, with other white Americans, they exercised power over the American Indians, and after the Philippines-American war, over Asian people. It is on the basis of their existing power that these scientists were able to rearticulate stories about science, with a good chance of preventing them from being effectively challenged by those outside the scientific community. Equally, it is on the basis of their power over non-white people that they were able to rearticulate stories about white civilization, without non-white people being able to mount an effective challenge. I now look at how they did so in three locations: the nation, the university, and the government laboratory.

The nation

How the scientists rearticulated the story of America can be seen in Benjamin Gould's 1869 and Henry Rowland's 1883 addresses to the American Association for the Advancement of Science. There are three key steps. First, Gould and Rowland present America as a great civilizing nation. Speaking shortly after the Civil War, Gould stresses America's technological achievements. America has "given to the world many a masterwork in the arts of peace and the arts of war: the steam boat, the cotton gin and sewing machine; the practical application of the electric telegraph . . . the most powerful ordinance and the most impregnable vessels".[18] Both emphasize America's political achievements and her conquest of the American Indians. Gould tells how the American people have vanquished "the forest, the desert and the redman".[19] Speaking in Minneapolis, Rowland underscores how the extension of the frontier and the colonization of new land has made America a great power. The American people are like the force of nature itself:

> This magnificent country of ours has rivalled the vigor of spring in its growth. Forests have been levelled, and cities built and a large and powerful nation has been created on the face of the earth. We are proud of our advancement. We are proud of such cities as this, founded in a day upon a spot over which but a few years since, the red man hunted the buffalo.[20]

Like Roosevelt and Wilson, then, Rowland sought to enthral his audience with the spectacle of themselves as members of a great nation engaged in conquest and colonization.

Next, they present a fundamental stumbling block to America's claim to be a great civilizing nation. Focusing on the many advances they had made in science, Americans were blind to the true state of affairs. By comparison with Europe, America lagged far behind. At the same time, Americans confused science with the application of science. In reality, America was heavily indebted to Europe for the scientific discoveries which were the origin of her inventions. This confusion, Rowland argued, meant that America was in danger of following the path of China:

> To have the applications of science, the science itself must exist. Should we stop its progress, and attend only to its applications, we should soon degenerate into a people like the Chinese . . . By contenting themselves with the fact that gunpowder will explode . . . they have fallen behind the progress of the world.[21]

In claiming that science was the origin of inventions, the pure scientists faced opposition from America's independent inventors who believed they were the creative force behind invention. To deal with this challenge, the pure scientists used their model of the nature of scientific research to either dismiss the inventors as mere appliers of scientific knowledge, or to incorporate them as really, in part, pure scientists. Rowland's barely veiled attack on Thomas Edison in his 1883 address "A Plea for Pure Science" shows the use of the first technique. Rowland almost certainly suspected Edison of bribing scientists at the 1881 Paris International Electrical Exhibition to support the claims he had made for his electric lighting system. In tones of high moral outrage, he thundered:

> It is not an uncommon thing, especially in American newspapers, to have the *applications* of science confounded with pure science; and some obscure American who steals the ideas of some great mind of the past, and enriches himself by the application of the same for domestic uses, is often lauded above the great originator of the idea, who might have worked out hundreds of such applications, had his mind possessed the necessary element of vulgarity.[22]

By contrast, the 9 February 1883 editorial of the first number of *Science*, funded by inventor of the telephone, Alexander Graham Bell, shows the attempt to incorporate the inventor. The editors argue that good inventors are actually scientists:

> It may readily be conceded that the man who discovers nothing himself, but only applies to useful purposes the principles which others have discovered, stands on a lower plane than the investigator. But when the investigator becomes himself the utilizer; when the same mind that made the discovery contrives also the machine by which it is applied to useful purpose – the combined achievement must be ranked as superior to either of its separate results.[23]

Finally, having called into question America's claim to be a great civilizing nation, Gould and Rowland show what America must do to make good her claim. They propose a new deal between the national community and its scientists. This is based on the proposition that pure scientific research is the origin of all inventions, yet because a long time often separates the original discovery from its application there is no reward for the discoverer. The pure scientist is not rewarded, while the inventor grows wealthy through patents. Only the national community can redress the imbalance. Either the state or wealthy philanthropists must ensure that scientists get the resources they need for pure research. This is an equitable exchange: the national community provides the resources, the scientist gives his talents and sacrifices of his material interests. Equally, this will enable America to deal with the debt it owes to Europe for discoveries Americans have used in their inventions. America will "do its share", rather than being "the almshouse of the world".[24] Their conclusion: if America is to make good her claim to be a great civilizing nation, she has to compete with European nations in funding pure science. Rowland pressed for a great national academy like "the Royal Society or the great academies of science at Paris, Berlin, Vienna, St. Petersburg, Munich and indeed, all the European capitals and large cities".[25] Proper funding of pure science will bring true national glory. It will, Gould concludes, "hasten the time when the land of the setting sun shall become the Orient by leading the science of the world, aweing the nations rather by her intellectual achievements than by her material power."[26]

The university

The second half of the nineteenth century saw a convergence of interests between America's Protestant established elite and its leading universities. On the one hand, as we have seen, the established elite felt threatened by rising social groups. In response it sought to reassert its right to govern America by renewing its claim to be a meritocracy which governed in the interest of the nation as a whole. On the other hand, private universities like Harvard, Princeton, and the new Johns Hopkins claimed that their expansion should be supported as crucial to the formation of a national consciousness. Through training in the humanities, young Americans from all parts of the United States would learn to see problems from a national point of view. They would learn to see America as engaged in a rivalry with other civilized nations, Britain, Germany, and France, and as the successor of the great civilized nations of the past, Greece and Rome. The study of the classics was at the centre of this programme. Through the study of Plato's *Republic* young Americans would see the importance of government by a meritocracy and the limits of popular democracy. Through the study of Virgil's *Aeneid* they would see themselves as nation builders and imperialists who had a duty to extend civilization.

The leaders of American science crafted the pure science idea to win a place for scientists within this programme. In his 1869 address, Gould emphasizes that American scientists should stop attacking the classics for their lack of utility. By attacking classics, he argues, they undermine their own claim that science should be primarily valued for its revelation of God's natural laws. Scientists and classicists should realize they are both under attack from the supporters of utility and profit: "The crusade is not in behalf of this or that form of intellectual progress; it is against such intellectual culture as has not some tangible end, capable of being represented by dollars, or finding expression in some form of physical well-being."[27] America is threatened by an "outburst of utilitarianism" combined with the "worship of Mammon". In language which echoes that of Plato's *Republic*, he warns that the "age of gold" has degenerated first to the "age of iron" and ultimately to that of "tinsel". This demanded a united response from the scientist and the classicist. "To save our country from the abyss, on the verge of which it stands, will require all the energy which can be summoned."[28] Gould concluded by underscoring the value to the classicists of an alliance with scientists: "Would that the prospects of classical culture and refinement were one-half as good as those of scientific progress; for the proper mutual relations once established, these could not fail to reinforce and supplement each other."[29]

The leaders of the pure science movement also sought to renegotiate the position of the scientist within the university. Scientists must be given long periods away from lecturing when they can work in the laboratory, and laboratories with the latest equipment to keep up with the current state of science. Both original research and laboratories, they argued, were necessary if they were to give their students the character they needed to govern in the interests of the nation and mankind. The movement for pure science, then, offered America's established elite an exchange. In return for their supporting scientific research laboratories within the universities and the scientific training of the next generation of the elite, scientists would support the elite's claim to be a meritocracy with the right to govern both America and, with other great civilized nations, the world.

The government laboratory

By the turn of the twentieth century, the American government was probably the largest backer of scientific research in the world. Congressmen demanded that the government only fund scientific programmes shown to be in the public interest. They insisted scientists be held accountable for the efficient use of government funds. At the same time, leading government scientists sought to go beyond the survey work – such as charting the coastline or mapping geological resources – they had originally been charged with and discover underlying principles. This led to conflict with legislators. The paleontological work of the Geological Survey and its work to reconstruct the geological history of America were attacked as going beyond its mandate to uncover the nation's mineral wealth, as was all but the most obviously useful work of the Naval Observatory. With the establishment of the Allison Commission (a Congressional committee appointed to study the administration and organization of scientific agencies), cuts in appropriations for scientific bureaus in the 1880s, and in some cases the firing of research-oriented scientists, the conflict emerged into public view.

In the course of this struggle scientists sought to develop and use the picture of science and the scientists produced by the pure science movement to renegotiate the terms of their funding. To make the case for scientists' control over scientific programs, the editors of *Science* pointed to the navy's failure to make efficient use of a national resource, the Naval Observatory at Washington:

> There has been no unity, no continuous plan of work, and few of the results which might have been gained by organized action . . . The published observations of the thirty-five years are of every possible character, from the refined discussions of the accomplished astronomer to the vain efforts of the tyro working in the dark, and the confused records of careless men who did not know what to do, and cared for nothing except to draw their pay – all put in without discrimination.[30]

To make the case that scientists should be allowed to use public money for research into the principles of nature, the editors of *Science* argued that was the most efficient way of solving agricultural problems:

> Shall the experiment-station seek to reach an *empirical* solution of one problem after another as it may be presented to it, or shall it search into the elementary conditions of the most important of those problems, and thus endeavour to work out a *rational* solution? . . . We believe that work of the latter class should be held in the higher esteem, and that the constituency of the station should, if possible, be brought so to regard it, because its results are of vastly more permanent value.[31]

In his examination by the Allison Commission, the head of the Geological Survey John Wesley Powell insisted that scientists must be allowed flexibility in the use they made of public funds:

> Now, the work of the Survey is of such a character that it cannot be fully specified and planned in advance, from the fact that to a large extent it is research for facts and principles not yet discovered . . . Only the general object in view and the general line of investigation to be pursued can be designated.[32]

Equally, the editors of *Science* insist that scientists must only be held accountable for the aggregate success of scientific programmes in the long term:

> If knowledge is to be advanced, if better methods of work are to be discovered, if greater accuracy is desired, if unknown facts are to be ascertained and recorded and discussed, and, in short, if there is to be real progress, the methods of free-dom are to be employed, not those of petty regulation . . . discretion must be given to the chiefs of bureau, and they must be held accountable for the aggre-gate success of their work . . . Somebody who has all the facts in mind must make the determination, and he must not be too quickly condemned, because the immediate results of the investigations which he has undertaken are not yet apparent.[33]

Finally, the editors of *Science* supported Alexander Agassiz' call to end the situation where the work of heads of government science bureaus could be submitted to "a clerk in the auditor's department" and for the government to consult the National Academy of Sciences to reorganize government science.[34] In short, they argued that for the efficient and effective solution of key problems scientists must be assured of a continuous flow of funds; they must not be dependent on success or failure in annual appropriations battles; they must be allowed to redeploy resources in response to new discoveries and advances in scientific method or technique; and they must have a say in the organization of the federal govern-ment's scientific programmes. It added up to a plea for large public funding with few strings attached.

Scientists' attempt to renegotiate the terms on which they received government support met with resistance. Critics saw it as a manoeuvre to subordinate demo-cratic government to a special interest. In 1885, in response to an investigation of alleged corruption and inefficiencies in the Coast Survey by the Treasury Department, the editors of *The Popular Science Monthly* put the case against the expansion of government science:

> The "scientific politician" has made his appearance in Washington, and the political element in him will dominate the scientific. That he will be a lobbyist and intriguer, and become skilled in the art of getting favors and appropriations from Congress, is

but to say that he will work according to his opportunities, objects and the nature of the materials to be manipulated. An unsupervised and irresponsible scientific department at Washington would be run in the interest of its sharpest managers, would be filled with sinecures, give the least results at the greatest expense, while these results would be aggravated by the sense of exemption from criticism.[35]

In response to the claim that scientists could be trusted to use public funds without direct government oversight, the editors charged that "political scientists" formed an interest group like any other. "Like other men, they are self-seeking, ambitious, and have their personal ends to gain."

(iii) Reconsidering the ontology of science

In recent decades the idea that scientists "discover" the fundamental principles through "direct contact" with nature has been called into question by sociological studies of scientific practice. The starting point for many of these studies is a logical point: observations of nature are insufficient to tell us whether or not a particular principle is true. There is always more than one theory of how natural phenomena are connected which fits the observed facts. Theory is underdetermined by observation. That this is not merely a logical point can be seen from studies of scientific controversies. Take Barnes, Bloor, and Henry's analysis of the controversy between the American physicist Robert Millikan and the Viennese physicist Felix Ehrenhaft over the measurement of the electric charge on the electron.[36] Millikan believed that electricity came in the form of electrons. To determine the size of the charge on the electron, he looked at the behaviour of oil drops between two oppositely charged electric plates. The oil drops were given an electric charge when they were formed. A radioactive source was used to ionize the air, so that the oil drop could acquire a further charge when it encountered an ionized air molecule. Millikan assumed that the amount of this charge was some multiple of the charge on an electron. The mass of the oil drop could be calculated by determining the velocity of its fall when the electric plates were switched off and no electric field was present. This was done using Stokes' law which relates the viscosity of air, the size and mass of the falling object, and the velocity of its fall. The charge on the electron could then be calculated by seeing how fast the oil drop rose once the electric field was switched on, and how its velocity changed when it acquired a further charge through contact with an ionized air molecule. As a result of the observation of numerous oil drops, Millikan calculated that the charge on an electron was 4.7×10^{-10} esu.

The examination of Millikan's notebooks, however, showed that he arrived at this figure by not considering results that would have given a substantially different figure. For example, if Millikan had used oil drop number 41 to calculate the charge on an electron he would have estimated that the charge was one tenth the size. In some cases, he rejected the use of particular measurements because his knowledge of the experimental apparatus led him to suspect an aberrant result, for example that the electric field was not constant or that air currents were present. In other cases it appears he rejected particular measurements because they did not agree with his prior belief that the charge on an electron would be in the region of 4.7×10^{-10} esu. In fact, if some latitude is allowed for experimental error, any list of numbers representing a range of observed values for the charges on the oil droplets can be represented as integral multiples of a supposed unit value, provided the unit is made small enough. This means that Millikan's result was not the result of observation alone. It depended on the prior belief that electricity was made up of small particles, that is electrons, rather than being a fluid; and that the charge on each electron was in the region of 4.7×10^{-10} esu. Theory was underdetermined by observation.

The fact that observation alone was insufficient to determine Millikan's conclusions is shown by the work of Felix Ehrenhaft, a renowned Viennese physicist. Ehrenhaft had sought to determine the charge on the electron using a similar technique. But whereas Millikan used oil drops Ehrenhaft used small particles. Initially, Ehrenhaft had determined that the charge on the electron was 4.6×10^{-10} esu. However, the existence of results like those that Millikan rejected, which could only be accounted for by postulating a much smaller charge, led him to change his mind. He concluded that experimental observations neither supported the idea that electricity was made up of electrons nor Millikan's figure for the charge on an electron. Faced with challenges by Millikan that his results might be due to problems with his equipment, Ehrenhaft introduced improvements to remove possible sources of error, checking that his particles really were spherical and using a modified version of Stokes' law to remove errors which might arise from the small size of his particles. At the same time, Ehrenhaft pointed to weaknesses in Millikan's experiment. His own apparatus could handle a greater range of particle sizes and pressures than Millikan's could, and thus provided a larger window on to nature. The controversy was never settled by experiment. Instead, as other physicists like Bohr adopted Millikan's figure in their research, Ehrenhaft's research became regarded as an anomaly.

This shows that observation and experiment are not sufficient to explain why a scientist designed an experiment the way he did, deduced a particular result from his observations, and persuaded other scientists of his conclusions. We also need to take account of social factors. In Millikan's case, one social factor was the existence of a particular physics tradition which believed in the existence of electrons and that their charge was in the region of 4.7×10^{-10} esu. Millikan's design of his experiment, his selection of observations to base his calculations on, and his presumption that colleagues would accept his conclusions all depended on these prior shared beliefs. Millikan's actions, in other words, only make sense when placed in the context of a particular physics tradition. Ehrenhaft's search for the charge on an electron shows he initially shared this tradition. Later, however, when he changed his mind his research results were appreciated by a different tradition, the anti-atomists and empiricists surrounding Ernst Mach.

The fact that the credibility of an experiment is based on a particular tradition reveals a key problem. How does a scientist turn an experiment which has the support of a particular group of scientists into a result which has the support of all scientists?

Social studies of science have shown the key importance of technology, large resources, and recruiting powerful social groups. As the Millikan–Ehrenhaft controversy reveals, when both sides have access to more or less the same technical resources, it is difficult for one side to prove the other is wrong. When one side claims that observations made using an experimental apparatus decisively shows the validity of their theory, the other side can try to manipulate the apparatus to show that observations made using it also supports other conclusions. The result is a stalemate like that soldiers experienced in the trenches of the Western Front. However, if one side has access to much greater resources, it can make it impossible for the other side to sustain its challenges. Thus, in microbiology a claim that the rat tibia cartilage assay shows the presence of a hormone GHRH is brought in to question by a rival group who show that the same assay can also indicate the presence of a variety of other chemicals. By creating a new assay which is much more sensitive, the radio-immunoassay, the second group is able to remove this line of challenge to their own research.[37] The ability to invest in new technology is central to winning scientific disputes. Indeed, it is essential even to participate in many scientific disputes in the first place. To acquire and maintain the new technologies they need for experiments scientists must persuade powerful social groups to back their line of investigation. The process requires scientists and engineers to carry out the kind of heterogeneous engineering we have looked at in the previous chapter. On the one hand, the scientists must choose a line of investigation whose likely results will interest such groups. On the other hand, they must redescribe the interests of social groups so that they see the necessity of supporting such research.

This analysis reveals two factors regarding judgements about the direction of research. First, the underdetermination of scientific theory by observation shows that scientists do indeed make judgements about the direction of research. Second, the central importance of technology and large resources in winning scientific arguments shows that deciding which direction to take in research is also a decision on which social interests to enrol. A judgement about what research direction to pursue is simultaneously a judgement about how nature is likely to be, and a judgement about what alliance of social interests it may be possible to construct. There is a short- and a long-term side to this. In the short term, an alliance with a powerful social group may enable a group of scientists to win a scientific dispute, and thereby alter the content of science. In the long term, pursing a particular direction of science and recruiting interests to support it changes the very form of science: it alters the set of statements that scientists believe may be true or false, and which they have ways of investigating.[38]

(iv) The pure science movement reconsidered

We are now in a position to see why the ontology of pure science makes it difficult for scientists to make judgements about the direction of their research. The idea that scientists are motivated by truth alone prevents questions being asked about their motivation. It places the burden of proof on the questioner, who has to prove that the scientists are not motivated by truth alone. The laboratory becomes a magic place, absolutely unlike the rest of society. While it is normal to ask what motivates a politician or businessman, for example, as soon as a scientist goes into his or her laboratory, he or she is presumed to behave quite differently. Within the laboratory they are presumed to be primarily motivated by a desire for truth. If it is shown that a particular scientist is principally motivated by other desires, this is presented as an anomaly. This has a peculiar effect on journalism. The very same editors who would question any journalist who submitted a political story which did not probe beneath what politicians say to examine the interests that lay behind their words are quite content when their science correspondent hands them a story which largely repeats the claims of scientists themselves.

Equally, the idea that science is uncovering a unified set of fundamental principles that govern all natural phenomena makes it senseless to ask about the direction of research. As the metaphor of the expanding circle makes plain, this view means that science has no long-term direction. Or, which is the same thing, science advances in all directions at once. The way this blunts the demand for judgements about the direction of research can be seen in Gould's address. He acknowledges that the military interest in the exercise of power through violence has been a major force in the advance of particular sciences:

> More than any other art, war has stimulated physical science; and those branches which have been made to contribute most abundantly to military ends are those which have thriven most among military nations. Applied mathematics and the departments of physics useful to the engineer, the topographer and the artillerist have specially flourished in France.[39]

The history of American science provides ample evidence for Gould's claim. In the early years of the republic the surveying of the American continent and its adjacent seas was the major scientific enterprise.[40] Starting with the Lewis and Clark expedition survey work, and the topographical science on which it relied, science was strongly supported by the army and navy. Equally American scientists actively pointed out the military advantages to the republic of supporting such work.[41] This research enabled the Republic to reverse the military advantage enjoyed by the indigenous peoples through their knowledge of local geography. As such it laid the basis for their defeat and colonization. The marriage between science and the military goes both further back and deeper. The mechanical world-view which found its greatest expression in Newton's 1687 *Principia Mathematica* is deeply influenced by its origins in Galileo and Descartes taking a military view of reality as made up of forces impinging on each other and making it the model for understanding reality as a whole, while vice versa, the supporters of this model of the world actively sought and gained support from the state by promising to provide it with increased military power by solving key problems in ballistics, fortification, and other aspects of military power.[42] It is not for nothing that Galileo's 1638 *Two New Sciences* is set in the heart of Venetian military power, the Arsenal, or that he promises his patrons, the Florentine Medici princes, "secrets" which will enhance their power. Gould thus suggests the need for judgement about the direction scientific research should take. The scientist needs to consider whether he should be aiding his country's army through research in applied mathematics or ballistics. This calls for investigations into how research in these areas will enhance his country's military capacity. Will it improve his country's capacity to defend itself without threatening its neighbours? Will it contribute to an arms race? Will it help his country to carry out wars of aggression and colonization?

Ultimately, however, Gould's address blunts our sense of the need for judgement about motives and directions by arguing that all scientific research leads mankind towards peace:

> The magnificent discovery of the correlation of physical forces weaves the physical sciences into harmonious relationship, and opens to our vision glimpses of still grander generalizations beyond. Recognition of the equivalence of these different forces entails the introduction of absolute units which command universal acceptance . . . Thus the nations are entering into more intimate intellectual relations with each other, at the same time that, by the progress of the arts of life, the physical barriers which separate them are broken down, and the sharpness of the dividing lines softened.[43]

The progress of science is breaking down the "prejudices" that divide mankind. At the same time, the progress of communication is breaking down the distances that separate nations. The result is that mankind is coming to see its unity, leading to an end to war. This means there is no need to be concerned about the direction of research: in the long run every investigation will contribute to peace. The metaphors used by Gould also work in opposite ways. Thus, while Gould's description of science in terms of an expanding circle presents science as having no long-run direction, his description of science advancing like an army to take a strong point presents it as a highly directed activity.

The idea that we don't need to worry about the interests that drive scientific research and the direction it takes presumes a harmony between the part and the whole. All pure scientific research is believed to ultimately contribute to human progress. There is no scientific basis for this idea. No observation we can make or experiment we can perform would show whether it was true or false. We can look at past scientific research and argue about whether it did or did not contribute to human progress. But what is demanded here goes far beyond that. The idea that pure scientific research will always contribute to progress is a secularization of the idea of divine providence. God has so ordered the world that all pure scientific research will contribute to human progress. Today science claims that it has nothing to do with religion and this is all kept out of sight. However, the initial founders of the pure science movement actively sought to enlist the support of theology. This can be seen in Gould's address:

> I do claim, first, that we have reached a stage at which it behoves us to acknowledge a higher aim, as much beyond the commercial and technological as the intellect is beyond the body: that the aim is dictated to us by the Creator through intellectual incentives and opportunities and that its pursuit is unfailingly rewarded by material recompense.[44]

Here the need to pursue the truth for its own sake is presented as nothing less than the divine command. At the same time, by presenting the instinct for truth as an example of God's providence, Gould gives theological support to the idea that scientific research ought to be supported because in the longer run it will benefit the community. New technologies such as the steam engine and telegraph are God's reward to the community for the virtue of its scientists in following God's command to pursue the truth for its own sake. The supporters of pure science soon distanced themselves from theology, asserting that theology and science had no more to do with each other than "jurisprudence and astronomy".[45] Stories about the role of scientific discovery in making possible contemporary invention now stood on their own, the original use of theology to support the credibility of the idea of pure science was forgotten.

In contrast to the ontology of the pure science movement, its history sharpens our sense of the need for scientists and society to make judgements about the direction of science. It shows that the ontology of science and the scientist developed by the pure science movement was not, in fact, disinterested. To the contrary, it formed the centre of a series of tactics to renegotiate the position of scientists within America. By arguing that all research ought to be funded because it all contributed to the discovery of the same set principles of nature, they sought to end divisions between scientists and to form them into one power bloc. They sought to persuade American scientists that they had a common interest in arguing for increased funding for science as a whole, and sought to improve their position within America's elite. They offered the elite a new exchange: in return for increased funding for pure science, the elite could present themselves as supporters of mankind's intellectual, moral, and material progress. Equally, through their alliance with classicists in America's elite universities, they contributed to the elite's claim to be a meritocracy. By presenting themselves as in no way political, because they were simply searching out the truth, they could be of *greatest* political value to the Protestant establishment in legitimating its right to govern America. The scientists demonstrated the paradox at the heart of modern science. In the words of historian Steven Shapin "the more a body of knowledge is understood to be objective and disinterested, the more valuable it is as a tool in moral and political action. Conversely, the capacity of a body of knowledge to make valuable contributions to moral and political problems flows from an understanding that it was not produced and evaluated to further particular human interests."[46]

13

Permanent Mobilization

The leaders of the pure science movement claimed that training in science would give students at Johns Hopkins, Harvard, Princeton, and other East Coast private universities the right type of mind to govern mankind. In doing so they, like the classicists, sought to renew the claim of America's Protestant establishment, of which they were themselves members, to be a meritocracy to whom Americans could entrust the task of governing the nation. In return, the pure scientists looked to the Protestant establishment to support scientific teaching and research in the universities, and pure scientific research in the government's scientific bureaux. In renegotiating the relationship between American scientists and the Protestant establishment, the leaders of the pure science movement were able to draw on ideas about science and scientists already well suited to their purpose. This was no accident. These ideas had themselves been crafted by an earlier generation of scientists in their own efforts to make themselves indispensable to the English state.

The pure science movement, whether or not it was aware of it, was rearticulating the deal that the founders of the Royal Society had made, with varying success, with Charles II and Anglicanism.[1] The English Civil War had seen Protestantism transform the English political landscape. The idea spread that just as Protestantism asserted every man should judge for himself in religion, so should every man judge for himself in politics. The mass of the people began to assert a right to participate in their own government, becoming a force that could not simply be excluded from politics. "[E]very man born in England," insisted the

Levellers, "cannot, ought not, neither by the law of God nor the law of nature, to be exempted from the choice of those who are to make the laws and for him to live under, and for him, for aught I know, to lose his life under."[2] With the fall of the Protectorate and the restoration of the monarchy following the return of Charles II in 1660, these new claims were suppressed, but the crown faced the danger that they would re-emerge and sweep it away. At any moment religious dissent could become the basis for revolution. In these circumstances the idea that every man's individual judgement could be a legitimate ground for decisions about society was politically dangerous. The king, reportedly, "always lamented" that Englishmen of all classes now had access to the bible. "This liberty was the rise of all our sects, each interpreting according to their vile notions and to accomplish their horrid wickednesses."[3]

Finding themselves in the midst of this crisis of political legitimacy, the founders of the Royal Society sought to insert themselves at the heart of the relationship between Anglicanism and the monarchy. The ministers of the Anglican Church reinforced the legitimacy of the king by affirming that he was God's representative on earth, while the king reinforced Anglicanism's claim to be the true Church by placing the weight of royal authority behind it. To insert itself into this relationship, the Society presented its activities as offering support to Anglicanism and the king against the threat of radicalism. Most of all, the Society offered Anglican ministers a defence against the charge, made by Hobbes on one side and religious radicals on the other, that they shaped their doctrines to suit their interests. The Society presented itself as, by nature, free from any such charge. As gentlemen of independent means they had no interest at stake in their investigation of nature. No less importantly, the Society's findings did not rest on individual judgement, but on the consensus of all its members who had witnessed the outcome of experiments. Paradoxically, it was by presenting themselves as non-political that they were most politically effective in supporting the state and the religion of the state. The society of gentlemen experimenters would support Anglicanism through accounts of nature which showed it could only be the creation of an all-powerful God (the argument that if nature was an intricate clock there must be a clockmaker), and by showing that the proper model for deciding difficult question in other areas, such as the interpretation of scripture, was the consensus of gentlemen who recognized that the crown was the source of all order in society. In soliciting and accepting the support of the king, the Royal Society showed that Charles II was the earthly origin of its endeavours and that its achievements were a reflection of his glory. The Society, in short, would pull the very ground from under radicals by discrediting the idea that each individual should decide questions about God and nature by their own unaided judgement. In doing so they were able to shore up the claims of both Anglicanism and the monarchy to represent the whole of society at the very time when these claims were being called into question by political/religious radicals who asserted the right of the common people to participate in government.

Yet, while the leaders of the Royal Society presented themselves as supporters of the king and established religion, they were already beginning to invest themselves with a sovereignty like that of God. When the leaders of the pure science movement claimed training in science produces the mind that ought to govern mankind, they were rearticulating earlier presentations of the scientific mind by members of the Royal Society such as Newton and Boyle.[4] They went beyond the idea that the scientist was recovering the knowledge and mastery over nature that Adam had enjoyed before the fall, and began to present the scientist as occupying a position like that of the Christian-Platonist God. By setting aside religious and political prejudices, the scientist occupied a neutral position outside and above society, while by experiment he discovered the laws of nature which God had laid down at the creation. This meant that the scientist both knew the world from the same position as God, and came to share in God's knowledge of it. As well as sharing a part of his omniscience, the scientist shared something of God's omnipotence. Through his knowledge of the principles of nature the scientist created technologies which had never existed before. By creating something that would not have come into being had he not willed it, he acted like God when he created the world *ex nihilo*.

The first decades of the twentieth century saw the emergence of a rival to the pure science movement. Its leaders called for "organized research". Initially, many of the arguments later deployed in favour of organized research were advanced in favour of applied science and engineering.[5] In the 1890s men like John Johnson and Victor Alderson argued that America's technical schools need to become centres for the teaching of applied science. After 1900 America's leading electrical, chemical, and communications corporations developed a new kind of laboratory, the industrial research laboratory, in which scientists did original research aimed at the solution of major industrial problems. It was after America's new industrial research laboratories had been successful that a self-conscious national movement for organized research began to take form.[6] This can be seen in articles appearing in *Science* and *The Journal of Industrial and Engineering Chemistry* around 1910. To a large extent, the new movement was created by rearticulating the ideas of the pure science movement, though the reassertion of the older and still vibrant tradition of Benjamin Franklin which stressed the utility of science was as important.

First, the scientist is presented as driven by a desire to aid mankind as well as by a desire for truth. This point is conveyed by stories of great scientists setting aside pure for applied research. Newton, Watt, Franklin, Rumford, Faraday, and Henry are all described as unselfishly working for the benefit of mankind. Thus Michael Faraday is described as having given "many of the best years of his life" to the improvement of lighthouses, and as being "delighted" when he saw a huge dynamo, whose principles he had first discovered, being used illuminate the tower of a lighthouse and save human lives.[7]

Second, the charting of nature is described as having already reached a point where research is most efficient if organized. This is supported by metaphors which emphasize that nature has already been mapped. John Johnson likened applied scientists to the Puritan Fathers who colonized the New World once the initial work of exploration had been carried out.[8] In 1913 Arthur Little used the same metaphor to argue that "modern progress can no longer depend upon accidental discoveries". The charting of nature has reached a point where scientists know enough to decide where it will be profitable to do further research. "Today . . . having learned how to read the stars, organized, equipped, they set sail boldly on a charted sea in staunch ships with tiering canvas bound for new El Dorados."[9]

Third, to convey the idea that a leading scientist can see how scientists in different fields should be organized, James Rowland Angell, Chairman of the National Research Council, presents nature as like the well-known English countryside. "The world of science has thus come to present somewhat the appearance of an English landscape with its checker-board effect of small fields set off from one another by high, impenetrable hedges. To one who toils inside such a field, the universe is limited by his own bit of hedge-row."[10]

Fourth, organized research is therefore a more *efficient* way of solving the problems facing mankind than that of the pure scientist, the mechanic, or the inventor. The applied scientist, John Johnson argues, combines knowledge of the state of research in several fields. To this he adds the mechanics' knowledge of how things work and the man of affairs' knowledge of trade and commerce. Finally, he cultivates his "inventive faculty". The result is a man who can solve practical problems better than either the pure scientist, the mechanic, or the inventor:

> The duplication or copying of old methods or appliances is the work of the mechanic. The solution of a new problem by the ignorant inventor will bring a long and expensive line of failures and if success is reached it is by a sort of happy accident. But our applied scientist should be able to find the successful solution, if there is one, and know before he embodies his ideas in wood or metal or stone, that his project will be a success . . . With such men to lead, our industrial progress would be marvellous. For such men the world has infinite need, and they could command inexhaustible capital.[11]

The applied scientist will be able to ensure a tremendous acceleration in the rate of industrial progress, then, because they can "know" in advance when a proposed solution to a problem will succeed, and hence whether it is worth investing in.

Fifth, organized research is now essential to solving problems in pure science. In 1905 William Ritter argued that scientists were now beginning to encounter a fundamental obstacle. "Progress in science leads to ever greater, more multifarious minutiae of knowledge, and at the same time to ever clearer revelation of the close and vital independence among different sciences. This characteristic of progress tends inevitably, for the individual investigator towards unyielding paradox. On the one hand, he is confronted by an ever-increasing mass of detail, which dictates ever narrower specialization, while, on the other hand, he is required to fit himself ever more thoroughly in an increasing number of sciences."[12] Organization, he concluded, is now the *sine qua non* to scientific progress in many fields of science.

Sixth, there is no real problem subordinating the individuality of individual investigators to the demands of organization. Ritter again: "For observe, it would not be a system of forcing investigators into work, for which they should have neither taste nor fitness, but rather of *selecting* them for tasks for which they would have both, and then of giving them facilities and opportunities for following their bent that they could not generally secure through their individual, unaided efforts."[13]

In this chapter I look at how the pure science movement's rearticulation of earlier ideas about the scientific mind was itself rearticulated by the movement for organized research. The movement for organized research thereby intensified the pure scientists' claim to a sovereign right to intervene to reshape the political system. They distinguished their exercise of sovereign right from earlier exercises of sovereignty, and indeed hid the very fact that it was one, by asserting that they were merely acting as the servants of society in using their knowledge of nature's laws to reveal the outcome of different courses of action. The organized research movement broke with the pure science movement's claim that scientific activity should primarily be directed to discover the truth for its own sake. Instead, it should be directed towards helping humanity realize its potential. Guided by scientists and engineers, organized research, big business, and the state could act together harmoniously to realize man's sovereignty. The close relationship between German universities, banks, manufacturing firms, industrial research laboratories, and government showed what could be achieved and provided a model for America. The other side of the organization of American science was, therefore, the scientific organization of America.

I then turn to look at how the leaders of the organized research movement seized advantage of the First World War to gain presidential authority and support for a new institution, the National Research Council, to promote the new alliance between organized research, big business, and the state. The Royal Society had sought to insert the scientist into a relationship in which Anglicanism supported the legitimacy of the king, and vice versa. Now American scientists and engineers used the First World War to occupy the position that Anglicanism had held in England. The National Research Council would legitimate presidential power, while presidential power would legitimate the National Research Council and the alliance between the state, big business, and organized research it promoted.

What is at stake in this history is an intolerable negation of democracy. The alliance between organized research, big business, and the state supports the growth of technological systems in which large capital is already invested and which favour the power of the American state. Alternative technological systems have either been strangled at birth or kept in a subordinate position. The consequences are hard to underestimate. In the field of energy, for example, the result has been the world-wide domination of nuclear power and oil at the expense of alternatives such as wind, solar, and energy saving. Just as the Royal Society sought to help Anglicanism and the king deny Englishmen's demand for participation in government, so the organized research movement on the one side, and the presidency on the other, have sought to convert American demands for active participation in their own government into satisfaction with choosing between members of the power elite at elections. The outcome is a politically immature population – in Tocqueville's telling phrase, "Greater than kings, and less than men" – whose passive acceptance of the dominant technologies makes them appear as fate. If we are to realize the potential of science and technology, this must be overcome. Where science has been used to blunt the demand for democratic participation, we must now extend democratic participation to include scientific research.

(i) The assertion of scientists' sovereign right

In the years before the First World War, leading American applied scientists and engineers began to rearticulate the strategy developed by the pure science movement. Their first step was to paint a picture of a world in which America's place as a world leader and its survival as an independent nation increasingly depended on the rapid development of its scientific establishment. To persuade America the threat was real, they pointed to Germany. German artificial dye manufacturers' success in using scientific research to dominate the world artificial dye market showed the shape of things to come. Germany was now in a position to repeat her success in other markets. Other leading nations had to grasp the fact that they were now locked in a "race" or "war" in which national survival depended on the ability of their manufactures to utilize science. "No nation," Victor Alderson, dean of the Armour Institute of Technology, argued in 1902, "can successfully resist this world wide movement."[14] The difficulty in making the threat convincing was that America's vast natural resources gave her manufacturers an alternative strategy for dominating world markets. Through large-scale production they could produce manufactures more cheaply than other nations without using science. American scientists therefore argued that what had succeeded in the past would not succeed in the future. America was now a complex modern society and national commercial success now depended on using science to identify and find solutions to a whole series of problems. Three examples from the pages of *Science* and *The Journal of Industrial and Engineering Chemistry* illustrate the general form of argument: apparently unlimited raw materials would soon be exhausted unless science made production more efficient; the growing labour force in America's great cities would be ravaged by disease unless scientists identified the necessary sanitary reforms; the social inequalities created by rapid industrialization meant that, unless she carried out reforms based on scientific research, American democracy would be destroyed by class warfare.

How scientists sought to close off the idea that America could dominate world markets by using large-scale production can be seen in a 1910 address "The Chemist's Place in Industry" by Arthur Little, a Boston-based chemical consultant who was rapidly becoming one of America's leading applied scientists. Little presents the scientist as engaged in a struggle for human life against the forces that threaten it. In this struggle there is a potential harmony between the scientist's pursuit of truth, the manufacturers' need to seek the highest rate of return on investment, and the life of the spirit, the intellect, and the body. Little starts by acknowledging the value of the pursuit of the truth for its own sake, but rejects the idea that as an applied scientist he is any less "valiant for the truth" than the pure scientist merely because the particular truth he seeks has an obvious and immediate application to the development of life. The applied scientist is right to devote himself to industry, being "well aware that before the hunger of the spirit or the hunger of the mind can be appeased, the hunger of the bodies moving in their millions through the world must first be satisfied". He then presents modern industry as essentially engaged in a titanic battle to satisfy this hunger, and in doing so producing a disaster which the applied scientist must correct:

> In its effort to satisfy this hunger modern industry has developed a complexity of organization, a magnitude of operation, a scale of expenditure and a drive and pressure of production far beyond anything which the world has seen before. Men and machines have alike been speeded up, worn out and cast aside. The march of progress has been over a continuous battlefield upon which the old was ever struggling with the new ... Accompanying it all in our own country at least has been a riot of waste lighting up the back ground with the flame from forest fires, burning oil wells, wasted gas and beehive coke ovens; cumbering the field with forest litter,

piles of culm and slag, scrapped machinery and abandoned plant; poisoning our water course with wastes which bore away a profit.[15]

Little goes on to argue that the coming exhaustion of what once seemed limitless raw materials means that American industry itself has an interest in abandoning its strategy of seeking to maximize profits through the large-scale exploitation of cheap raw materials. "To those who read the signs the watchword of the future is even now clearly outlined," he concludes, "it is no longer 'increased production' but 'increased efficiency of production'."

At the heart of Little's argument is the production of America as facing a crisis that only the applied scientist can find the solution to. This is done by a slight rewriting of the story told by the pure scientists. He accepts their division of the life of mankind into a higher part, the mind and the spirit, and a lower part, the body. Through talk of hungry millions, he transforms the earth into a battlefield in which mankind's achievement of its sovereignty is threatened by mass starvation. The applied scientist can correct industrial progress so that it will be able to overcome the threat of starvation without exhausting the earth's resources or destroying the environment. This can be achieved by working with the "growing sentiment for conservation" so as to convert American industry from its commitment to "increased production" to "increased efficiency of production". Through this adjustment the applied scientist will be able to bring truth, humanity, profit, and efficiency into harmonious they already potentially have.

(ii) The scientists' claim that they were better placed to solve key problems facing society than elected representatives

The scientists asserted their claim to a sovereign right to remake America's political system by drawing a favourable contrast between themselves and "politicians". This term summed up a picture of the typical elected representative as corrupt, short-sighted, incompetent, or in thrall to opinion. Thus in an attack on federal legislators for not giving the Forestry Service sufficient funds, the editors of *The Journal of Industrial and Engineering Chemistry* describe "our politicians" as "chips on water, bobbing any which way a chance wind may blow them".[16] Their lack of understanding makes them incapable of leadership or exercising judgement, the prey of selfish interests and petty politics. In his 1910 lecture "Science and Industry", Leo Baekeland, chemist, inventor, and industrialist, argues for scientists and engineers' exercise of sovereign power. Instead of legitimating the power of scientists and engineers by contrasting them with current politicians, which would raise the problem that they are elected while scientists and engineers are not, Baekeland legitimates their exercise of sovereign power by contrasting them with past rulers:

The two most powerful men of our generation are the scientist and the engineer. Society at large is far from realizing this fact, simply for the reason that the scientist and the engineer manifest their power not as despots, not as cruel tyrants. Their might is not put in evidence by the amount of chattel-slaves they hold in bondage, nor by the barbaric splendor of their lives; it is not marked by the devastation wrought by armies; their work does not consist in conquering and subjugating weaker nations . . . no artists have had to record their triumphant homecoming, greeted as saviors and heroes while marching over the mutilated corpses of their fallen enemies . . . No, the masses are unaware of the immense power of the scientist and engineer because both of them modestly play the role of the "servant in the house".[17]

For Baekeland the power of the scientist and engineer is more legitimate than that of past rulers because they exercise it anonymously as "servants" whose knowledge of the laws of nature is enabling mankind to realize its full potential. By contrast, past rulers exercised arbitrary rule based on their power to threaten their subjects with death and their ability to defeat other nations in war. Baekeland left no doubt that the scientist and engineer had a duty and a right to overcome those who resisted his efforts to realize mankind's potential:

Society has been pushed ahead, against the will of the masses, by a few active, daring, restless men who forced the others to follow; just like a herd of sheep is unwillingly driven forward by the shepherd and his dogs. Many people among whom we live have truly been prodded into progress; they may properly be called remnants of bygone times, symptoms of mental atavism of the race; they do not properly fit in our age.[18]

Since mankind's realization of its sovereignty is the sole value, there can be no reason for limiting the scientists and engineers' power. The scientists and engineers' exercise of power is based on the law of nature itself; they simply enable mankind to realize its own natural potential. Baekeland's argument is interesting in the light of later events. We see that the place that the Kaiser and German autocracy will come to occupy was already prepared before the First World War, and that it is through the production of the figure of the autocrat as its opposite that American science and engineering side-steps the problem of their own lack of democratic legitimacy as they seek to exercise power over larger and larger areas of American life.

We now have a picture of how pure and applied scientists began to see themselves as exercising a sovereign right to remake national and international society before the First World War. This framework of ideas would be rearticulated, in different ways, by both sides of the debate over chemical weapons after the war. The pure and applied scientists saw their authority as resting on their knowledge of the laws of nature, and on the fact that they were driven by a concern for truth and for humanity. They thus hid the role of their judgement in the exercise of sovereignty, and diverted attention from the biases that always attend the exercise of judgement. Their sovereign right is set off from that of earlier sovereigns: whereas past rulers showed their sovereign power through executions and wars, the scientist and the engineer display their sovereign power through their enhancement of life based on a knowledge of its laws. There is an awareness that science and engineering could lead mankind to disaster, but this is suppressed. Aspects of science that are problematic, such as the development of high explosive, are not talked about – or, if they must be talked about, they are prevented from calling science and engineering itself into question by the idea that progress is unstoppable.[19] The scientist and engineer's research is the origin of mankind's realization of its possibilities on a world scale, and through their role in improving communications there is a developing harmony between the nations and between all aspects of human culture. The sovereignty of the scientists and engineers has its own specific space and time. Spatially, they are drawing all mankind into a common process of development through the abolition of distance. Temporally, they are inaugurating a new era in which mankind will overcome the obstacles to its potential. This, however, has not yet been achieved. This means that at present mankind is involved in a war with both those men who would hold it back and with the forces of nature. As the end of this war is deferred until an unspecified date, this means that mankind now dwells in a permanent state of emergency. In this state of emergency, the sovereign right of the scientist and engineer is without limit.

(iii) The convergence between the strategies of the organized researchers and big business

So far I have looked at scientists and engineers who supported organized research strategy. I now want to shift the perspective. I am interested in how organized research fitted into the strategy being developed by American big business to accumulate capital by operating on a world scale.[20] This involved a refinement of an old strategy. From the merchants of the Venetian Republic operating in the Mediterranean, to the agents of the Dutch East India Company operating in Europe and Asia, to the transnational corporations of our own time, we see refinements of the same strategy. Through their place at the centre of an extensive intelligence network, a small number of big businessmen are able to identify opportunities for extraordinary profits. Their privileged access to finance enables them to rapidly mobilize the very large capital needed to take advantage of these opportunities, and their flexibility allows them to abandon ventures where the rate of profit is falling and concentrate on these new opportunities. Lastly, they are able to draw on the power of the state to overcome obstacles to their operations. The privileged location of these businessmen, and their experience in taking advantage of it, then, enables them to pursue a strategy that is simply not available to the great number of ordinary businessmen. They are able to generate super-profits through the achievement of monopoly, whereas greater or lesser degrees of competition force the rest to be content with far smaller returns. Where merchants, financiers, and industrialists of one city or nation have succeeded in pushing their competitors aside, they have placed their city or nation at the centre of world power. This is what was achieved by the merchants of Venice, then Antwerp, and finally Genoa in the sixteenth century, Amsterdam in the seventeenth century, England in the nineteenth century, and lastly America in the twentieth century. In doing so they have relied on, and helped build up, a symbiotic relationship with the state: a portion of the super-profits going to the development of the state's capacities, and the development of the state's capacities enabling business to overcome obstacles to the achievement of further super-profits. Once created, such a strong state enjoys considerable autonomy from business, but its continued reliance on a share of these profits sets limits beyond which it cannot go without destroying its conditions of existence.

The operations of business in the world economy – which for the Venetian meant the Mediterranean, but for the Dutch had extended north to the Baltic, west to the Americas, and East to Asia and Pacific, before becoming a truly global economy for the English in the later half of the nineteenth century – besides creating a single "core" state also created a set of states which shared in the profits of worldwide trade, the "semi-periphery", and an area of extreme exploitation in which the local state was either extremely weak or collapsed completely, the "periphery". The semi-periphery is a reflection of the need of the core state to gain its security at least expense. To do so core states have pursued a balance of power strategy, shifting their support so as to ensure that they are never without powerful allies and to isolate their enemies. The result is that in the semi-periphery the ability of the core-states' merchants, financiers, and industrialists to use their superior information, capital, and access to political power is limited by the need to avoid making too many enemies. Things are far different in the periphery. Here these advantages can be pushed to the limit, and the local state completely subordinated to the demand for maximum profit. As well as leading to the juxtaposition of spaces in which very different rules apply, the strategy pursued by business also leads to the production of different times. This can be seen by looking at sixteenth-century Dutch capitalism. At its centre is the world's most liberal state, with laws supporting religious toleration and a degree of freedom of speech. At the periphery, however, the operations of Dutch merchants actually drive things backwards. In the Baltic, Dutch grain merchants allied themselves with Polish landowners to reintroduce feudalism on their estates. Seventeenth-century English and French merchants went one stage further. To fill the void left by native peoples killed by European weapons and disease, African slaves were imported to work on plantations. Most of the profits flowed to the merchants who pushed the planters into a subordinate position through their control of the price of slaves, credit, and sugar, to which the planters responded by intensifying exploitation on the plantation. By the end of the eighteenth century, the products of slave labour in the Americas constituted one third of the value of European commerce.[21] Through their creation of intelligence networks, systems for rapidly mobilizing very large resources, and states capable of projecting power on a world scale, then, big businessmen found a way to generate super-profits which, in turn, gave them the ability to generate yet further super-profits. In the process of doing so they continually refined their basic strategy to overcome the obstacles they met, both from each other and from monarchs, state officials, aristocrats, priests, medium and small businessmen, tradesmen, craftsmen, labours, and peasants in Europe, and from native rulers, merchants, agriculturists, and tribesmen in Asia, Africa, the Americas, and the Pacific.

In the late eighteenth and nineteenth centuries European and American big business began to discover that science and invention offered a way of refining big business's basic strategy. Here I look at the American story. The scientific revolution led to a changed idea about human invention and its relationship to God's providence. God had made the universe like a clock. Through discovering the parts of the clock, and the way that they operated on each other, the scientist could come to see the world as God saw it. The difference being that while God saw the whole of his creation, the scientist only saw a small part of it. Only God had made the world in the full sense of creating it out of nothing, but the inventor could now come to have a part in God's creation. Through his knowledge of the elements of the world and the principles they obeyed, the inventor could assemble the parts of the clock into new combinations. While this was not creation out of nothing it did resemble it. Without the inventor's synthesis of the different elements of the machine into one whole on the basis of his knowledge of the principles they obeyed, there would be no such machine. Just as the scientist came to be like God by seeing the world as God saw it, the inventor came to be like God by creating it. According to this view the scientist and the inventor had a key part to play in God's providence. Through their discoveries and inventions they improved man's mastery of nature, showing that God had indeed ordered the world providentially. And by carrying out further investigations and making new inventions they had a key role in the fulfilment of providence. As part of the workings of God's providence, the results of science and invention could only be good. Hence the proliferation of optimistic scenarios about the results of invention. In the short term a new invention might lead to unemployed weavers, but in the longer run everyone would benefit as man's wealth was increased and full employment restored. Equally, the invention of new weapons might lead to increased bloodshed in the short term, but in the long term it would lead to universal peace.[22] The work of the inventor was an unequivocal good which ought to be encouraged by the community by being rewarded for his work. In the United States the victory of a providentialist view of scientific progress at the Constitutional Convention meant that the inventor alone was given a legal monopoly on the sale of his invention. Having rejected a proposition that would have empowered Congress "to establish public institutions, rewards and immunities for the promotion of agriculture, commerce and manufactures", the Convention authorized Congress "to promote the progress of science and the useful arts, by securing for limited times to authors and inventors the exclusive right to their respective writings and discoveries".[23] Subsequent American law granted inventors of a patentable invention a monopoly on its sale for seventeen years. This formed the legal basis for America's golden age of invention, during which many of the technological systems which dominate our lives today were developed. Samuel Morse developed the telegraph, Alexander Graham Bell the telephone, Thomas Edison electric lighting and the gramophone, the Wright brothers the aeroplane, Elmer Sperry the gyroscopic compass and gyroscopic stabilization, and Hiriam Maxim a machine gun.

The history of the development of these inventions shows big business adapting its basic strategy for generating super-profits to take advantage of the right of the inventor of a patentable device to a legal monopoly.[24] Big business's incorporation of science and invention into its strategy had three stages. In the first stage the key figures are the inventor and the businessman who decides to back his not-yet-proven invention. Typically, once an inventor had secured a patent, he entered into a partnership with a businessman. The inventor contributed patents, and the businessman the finance necessary to develop the invention into a saleable commodity. If further finance was needed the company issued stock. It was a high-risk business, and many such companies failed.

In the second stage, the key figures are the big businessman, such as financier J.P. Morgan, who played a leading role in the formation of General Electric in 1892, and the patent lawyers, such as Frederick P. Fish, who rose to become president of American Telephone and Telegraph through his handling its patent cases. Such men saw companies with the core patents of new technological systems as the key to dominating the new electrical and communication industries. To this end they developed a series of tactics which combined access to large capital with a mastery of the intricacies of patent law. Where an inventor developed a new invention that either threatened the company's profits because it offered an alternative to the system it was selling, or offered a way of developing that system, they could simply buy it by outbidding the competition. When the inventor refused to sell, they could employ patent lawyers to attack his patent in the courts by arguing that his patent infringed patents already held by them. To maintain the monopoly the company had enjoyed because it held the key patents of a new technological system after these had expired, they could acquire patents on new devices needed for its further development. On a larger scale, they could either orchestrate the takeover of rival companies or, where that was not possible, negotiate mergers.

In the third stage we see the arrival of the research director, the applied scientist, and the engineer. The successful employment of the tactics set out above meant that, by the turn of the twentieth century the electric power, lighting, and communications industries were dominated by just three companies: General Electric (GE), Westinghouse, and American Telephone and Telegraph (AT&T). These giant companies, however, were threatened by the expiry of patents that were central to their business, the success of smaller companies, and the invention of superior technologies. Their reliance on buying up patents on inventions that might threaten their business increasingly appeared both costly and risky. Profits might be reduced by inventors who demanded very large sums, and their market dominance might collapse if the inventor sold to a rival. In these new conditions the new technological giants, led by the General Electric Company, turned to a German development, the industrial research laboratory, to reinforce their market dominance.[25] In taking the lead, GE was motivated by international developments. Through his invention and patenting of a high-resistance carbon filament lamp, Thomas Edison created an electric light and power system which could compete with gas lighting. Edison's patents formed the basis of GE's empire. At the turn of the twentieth century, German and Austrian scientists were patenting superior lamps which threatened General Electric's dominance of the American market. The Austrian Carl Auer von Welsbach had invented a osmium-tungsten filament lamp, while Walter Nernst and Werner von Bolton, German physical chemists, had invented superior metallic-filament lamps – both decidedly superior to GE's carbon filament lamp. The danger that customers would be prepared to pay more for European lamps which used less high-cost electricity was brought home by Westinghouse obtaining the rights to manufacture the Nernst lamp in the United States. Faced with this threat, GE accepted the arguments of its in-house inventor, Charles Steimetz, and established America's first industrial research laboratory under the direction of MIT physical chemist Willis Whitney. Other high-technology companies soon followed: Du Pont in 1902 and AT&T in 1907.

In the new industrial research laboratory, a leading scientist focused the research of a large number of scientists and engineers on the "reverse salients" of the technological systems being developed by the company and by its rivals. The vast costs of running such a laboratory meant that only the giant companies which already dominated the market could afford them. Only such companies could make rapid improvements in existing technological systems and receive the full financial benefits from such improvements by incorporating them into the systems they managed. Through this research, these companies could now use patents to reinforce their market dominance without having to rely on outside inventors. This had a number of advantages. They could now deliberately set out to integrate recent scientific advances made in the university into the development of their systems. AT&T decided that the development of a long-distance repeater would be crucial to reinforcing and extending its dominance of the telephone communication market, and turned to scientists familiar with electron theory to develop Lee De Forest's three element vacuum tube into a working long-distance repeater. No less vitally, research into the reverse salients of the systems being developed by other giants could provide a corporation with bargaining patents. These could be used as bargaining chips in negotiations in which the giants divided up the national market among themselves. Lastly, through research into the reverse salients of radical new technologies that were appearing on the horizon, the giants could defend their investments in existing technologies by determining the pace at which rival systems were developed or whether they were developed at all.[26]

This history shows a new refinement of the centuries-old strategy through which leading merchants, financiers, and industrialists have developed information networks, access to large capital, and a measure of control over state power to identify and take advantage of opportunities to dominate markets and reap extraordinary profits. This strategy is written into the very fabric of the industrial research laboratory. Through his supervision of teams of scientists and engineers, the research director is able to spot technological opportunities for the development of the system. These may arise from work being carried out inside the laboratory itself, or from the laboratory scientists and engineers' awareness of work being done by university scientists, independent inventors, or craftsmen employed in the company's factories. Through his connections to the company's board of directors, the research director has access to the capital he needs to take advantage of such opportunities. He can immediately secure funds to hire the new specialists he needs to take advantage of a new scientific discovery that might dramatically improve in the system's profitability. Lastly, through his access to the company's patent lawyers and political contacts, he can enlist the power of the state to defend the company's market dominance. The company's deep pockets mean that it can wear down independent inventors who seek to go it alone by mounting repeated legal challenges to their patents, while its political contacts can ensure the passage of legislation which allows the most profitable development of the company's technological systems.

A 1911 article "Research as a Financial Asset" in *The Journal of Industrial and Chemical Engineering* by Willis Whitney, who as director of GE's industrial research had pioneered industrial research in America, shows what was at stake. Whitney emphasizes that at the heart of the industrial research laboratory is the enormous potential of cooperation and access to new instruments:

> The mathematics of cooperation of men and tools is interesting . . . Separated men trying their individual experiments contribute in proportion to their numbers, and their work may be called mathematically additive. The effect of a single piece of apparatus given to one man is additive only, but when a group of men are cooperating, as distinct from merely operating, their work raises with some higher power of the number than the first power. It approaches the square for two men and the cube for three. Two men cooperating with two different and special pieces of apparatus, say a special furnace and a pyrometere, or a hyraulic press and new chemical substances are more powerful than their arithmetical sum.[27]

The activity of the industrial research laboratory showed the enormous potential of cooperation that brings together a diverse collection of types of people and kinds of things. To solve key problems for GE, Whitney brought together individuals whose knowledge and talents complemented each other. Theoreticians worked with experimentalists. Experts in particular areas of chemistry worked with physicists. Scientists cooperated with engineers and technicians. As Witney's mention of furnaces, pyrometers, and other equipment indicates, new instruments were no less important. In their research, scientists, engineers, and technicians make discoveries and inventions which they rapidly incorporate into new instruments. These in turn made for yet further discoveries and inventions. In this the research director's role was largely to act as an enabling and directing element. Through bringing different expertise, talents, and equipment together, he enabled the potential of the whole to be realized. Whitney was a master of the indirect touch, a word of encouragement at the right moment, a deployment of a senior researcher to quietly suggest to a colleague that a line of research was unprofitable and his talents might be best employed in another direction. He was no less brilliant at creating informal mechanisms, such as the laboratory seminar and joint publication, through which a spirit of cooperation could be both created and guided in the right direction.

The industrial research laboratory, in short, showed the potential of cooperation to remake our world. Yet, the guiding force behind this cooperation was to generate high returns on capital invested in existing technological systems. Where research into new systems was carried out, it was for the purpose of stopping or retarding their introduction to protect investments in existing systems, or of ensuring that the corporation would be able to dominate the development of the new system as it had the old.

(iv) The supporters of organized research and big business take advantage of the First World War to consolidate their alliance

The applied scientists' calls for organized research were matched by some pure scientists.[28] The applied scientists, as we have seen, argued that only through the organization of applied science could mankind overcome a series of threats to human life. The pure scientists, for their part, argued that science had reached a point where continued progress could only be made through organization. The first such claim I have found is marine biologist William Ritter's 1905 "Organization in Scientific Research". Ritter called on wealthy Americans to extend the funding they were already providing for prestigious astronomical observatories to other areas. If the case was strongly presented, he urged scientists, it was "pretty sure to have a relaxing effect upon purse strings . . . particularly in our country where wealth is so abundant and the general spirit of giving for the promotion of learning so much abroad".[29]

In seeking to open up a new area for philanthropy, such pure scientists were aided by the powerful personality and vast wealth of steel magnate Andrew Carnegie. In 1902 Carnegie established the Carnegie Institution to "encourage investigation, research and discovery".[30] Carnegie gave the Institution $10 million in US Steel Bonds, throwing the full force of his wealth behind Gould's and Rowland's claim that, compared with Europe, American science was a national disgrace which must be rectified. Emphasizing America's "national poverty in science", Carnegie set out to do nothing less than "change our position among the nations". It was a spectacular gesture. In one swoop the Institution had an endowment equal to that of Harvard, and larger than the research endowment of all American universities combined. Carnegie's gift issued a direct challenge to other wealthy Americans, who must now match his generosity or admit their inferiority. Manoeuvring within the board of the Institution led to a decision that it would seek, wherever appropriate, to substitute "organized for unorganized effort". By 1910 the Institute was putting six times the amount it gave out in small grants to just ten large projects.

Carnegie's gift helped legitimize his steel empire. This was vitally needed. The capital required by J.P. Morgan to launch US Steel in 1901 was sufficient to run the federal government for two years. To many such a concentration of money power was incompatible with free market principles and threatened to undermined republican government. They expected the government to use the Sherman Anti-Trust Act to break up the giant. Many were also shocked by the violence Carnegie had used to build up his fortune in the first place. They remembered how he had made an example of steel workers at his steel plant at Homestead, Pennsylvania, on the Monogahela river. In 1892 Henry Frick, almost certainly backed by Carnegie, decided to break the steel workers' union and reduce wages. He built a three mile long twelve foot high fence, topped with barbed wire, with peepholes for rifles. Then when workers refused a pay cut he laid off the entire workforce. Supported by the local townspeople, strikers and sympathisers now surrounded the plant. To break the blockade on 5 July hundreds of Pinkerton's guards came up the river by barge, and when they insisted on disembarking, a gun battle ensued. When the guards surrendered to the strikers, men had been killed on both sides. The state governor now brought in militia armed with rifles and Gatling machine guns to escort strike breakers into the plant. The strike leaders were charged with murder, and others with lesser crimes. No jury, however, would convict them. The entire Strike Committee was then arrested for treason against the state. Again a friendly jury refused to convict them. The strike remained confined to one Carnegie plant, and with the use of strike breakers production was able to continue. After four months the strikers lacked resources to continue. They agreed to return to work, and their leaders were blacklisted. The defeat enabled Carnegie to stop unionization in other plants until well into the twentieth century. Workers had to accept pay cuts, and to agree increases in already long working hours.[31] In these circumstances Carnegie needed the support of America's Protestant establishment. Funding pure science enabled him to present himself as driven by a concern for higher values, and as a patriot concerned that America should lead in making the discoveries on which the future of mankind depended.

Led by astrophysicist George Elery Hale, director of the Carnegie Institution's Mt. Wilson Solar Observatory and editor of *The Astrophysical Journal*, and aided by chairman of the board of the Institution, none other than Senator Elihu Root, the pure science supporters of organized research took advantage of the First World War to gain presidential support for the national organization of American science. A brief chronology of events shows the same symbiotic relationship between the presidency and its "advisors" we have seen in the case of the Council of National Defence – itself very much a Root creation – and the War Industries Board. We see Hale and Root attempting gain the presidential authority they needed to organize science while escaping presidential control. At the same time, we see Wilson seeking to make use of Hale's and Root's organization of American scientists and engineers without having his agenda dominated by them.

April 1916

Following the sinking of the *Sussex* by a German submarine, the National Academy unanimously endorses Hale's resolution offering its services to the government. The resolution marks the maturation of plans laid in the preceding years. When Hale was first elected foreign secretary to the National Academy of Science, Root had drawn his attention to the Academy's chartered role as a semi-government body and the official advisor to the government in scientific matters. The moribund Academy offered a vehicle for enlisting state support for organized science. To gain the support of America's scientists – and perhaps more subtly to strengthen Root's support – Hale then wrote a short history of science which presented national academies, supported by their government, as the force behind Europe's great achievements in science. This echoed Ritter's seductive 1905 plea to wealth with a similar plea to power: "To accomplish great results in this field, an academy must enjoy the active cooperation of the leaders of the state . . . What was done by Alexander the Great and the Ptolemies for Egypt, by the house of Medici for Italy, by Richelieu, Colbert and Napoleon for France, can be done by living statesmen to-day."[32] Having used the *Sussex* incident to consolidate the support of the scientists, Hale moves rapidly to secure the support of the president. A delegation from the Academy meets with Wilson at the White House a week later. After Academy President William Welch has outlined its special relationship with the government, Hale argues it can plan an arsenal of science. Wilson, however, has been expanding his role as president by presenting himself to Americans as the only person who can mediate a peace between the Central Powers and the Allies. He is not yet prepared to lend his authority to the preparedness movement since this would undermine his policy of neutrality. He asks the Academy to set up a committee, but to keep it confidential. German–American relations are at a delicate stage, he cautions, and the public might misinterpret an open request for military help from its official scientific advisor. After the meeting Hale is ecstatic: "I really believe this is the greatest chance we ever had to advance research in America."[33]

July 1916

Hale and Root's plan is in trouble. After the meeting with Wilson the Academy has responded to Wilson's request by quietly forming a National Research Council (NRC). The problem is that this immediately faces absorption or marginalization by an existing organization, the Naval Consulting Board (NCB), set up by Secretary of the Navy Josephus Daniel and led by inventor Thomas Edison who believes that inventors, not pure scientists, are best placed to organize American technology for war. In a deliberate snub, Edison has refused to have any pure scientists on the Board, making an exception for mathematicians to help with calculations. The Board has already been operating for almost a year and has already drawn America's engineering societies and leading directors of organized research into its web. With the open support of Daniels the Board is in a strong position. When Hale meets with Ingersoll Rand director and NCB board member William Saunders, he is told so in no uncertain terms. Saunders brushes aside talk about cooperation. The scientists, he says, might possibly work with

Edison's group in a subordinate capacity. Hale and Root face the danger that Edison will use the war to strengthen American's belief that it is inventors *not* pure scientists who are the force behind modern technology, and that pure scientists are impractical eccentrics.

To trump the Board's secretary of the navy, Hale and Root decide the Council must have the president's *public* approval. To get it they take advantage of the fact that Wilson is facing re-election. Hale's first move is to persuade Republican presidential candidate Charles Evans Hughes to endorse the NRC at his speech accepting the Republican nomination. He then tells Wilson's close advisor, Colonel House, who is sympathetic to the NRC, what Hughes is going to do. The colonel immediately advises the president to publicly endorse the NRC. "I think one of the best things that has been done in the way of preparedness is the work of these men and I would hate to see the Republicans get any benefit from it."[34] On 24 July the White House sends a letter to the Academy and telegraphs its contents to Hale. It includes everything Hale wants: presidential approval for the NRC, the assurance of government cooperation, and the promise of presidential appointments from government departments.

New York 20 March 1917

In an address to the Union League Club of New York, as we have seen, Root uses his authority as senior statesman to transform the 18 March sinking of the American ships *Illinois*, *City of Memphis*, and *Vigilancia* into a cause for war.[35]

Washington 1917–18

America enters the war on the Allied side. The NRC occupies offices close to the White House. It organizes research into the detection of submarines, the manufacture of optical glass, sight and sound pin-pointing of artillery fire, and poison gas and gas masks. Once the Council is firmly established, Root and Hale seek to turn it into a permanent body and to shift its emphasis from military to industrial research. They face a choices: the Academy could ask Congress to revise its charter, or, on the basis of its existing charter, it could ask the president for an Executive Order. Congress is dominated by Democrats. Hale has contempt for Democratic senators who, he believes, tend to be against all "organizations for advanced study". They decide to by-pass Congress and go directly to the president. On 27 March 1918 Hale sends a draft Executive Order to the president through Colonel House. In a covering letter, he argues that the United States will not be able to "compete successfully with Germany, in war or peace, unless we utilize science to the full for military and industrial purposes". Hale asks the president to give the NRC sweeping powers to organize science inside and outside the government.

Root presses Colonel House to ensure that Wilson endorses the order quickly. Wilson, however, is cautious and sends the draft to the Committee for National Defence. The Committee reacts badly. Secretary of Agriculture David Houston warns the president that he might find it "embarrassing" to approve, in any manner, industrial research activities by an "agency over which the Government has very slight control".[36] The president now writes to Hale: does the NRC want the "authority" to coordinate the scientific work of the government? Wilson doubts whether he has the "right" to give any outside body such authority and the "practicability and wisdom of doing so".[37]

Root and Hale now face a dilemma: if they ask for authority Wilson may ask them to go to Congress, and Congressional support is likely to come at the price of government oversight. Oversight is what they have manoeuvred to avoid. Throughout the war Hale later wrote he had taken "great precautions" for the NRC to "act as a department of the [Council for National Defence] . . . without becoming a part of it and without surrendering any authority to it".[38] The structure of the NRC had been set up to ensure this. The government might appoint representatives to the Council, but it could not control it because nominations to the Council lay in the hands of the Academy. This meant that the Council had all the advantages of government cooperation, but it retained "the freedom of action which Government Departments could not enjoy". To maintain this status, Hale and Root decide to push for an Executive Order giving official recognition without official authority.

After an encouraging meeting with Colonel House, who promised to push the Order through, Hale replies to Wilson. The Council has "no desire for authority to coordinate the . . . scientific agencies of the Government". It merely desired "such official recognition as will give it the influence which it needs to secure co-operation".[39] The president now sends the revised order back to Houston but, apparently after Colonel House's intervention, Wilson simply asks the agriculture secretary to make sure it expresses Hale's "real purpose". When Wilson issues the Executive Order on 11 May 1918, Hale declares "We now have precisely the connection with the government we need, and . . . it will be our own fault if we do not make good use of it."[40] The cost of avoiding government control is the absence of government funding. After the end of the war, Root will ensure that the programme can continue none the less by securing a $5 million grant from the Carnegie Corporation and a half million dollar grant from the Rockefeller Foundation. Additional funds are secured from members of the NRC's Industrial Advisory Committee (see below) and from other big businessmen such as Henry Ford. At the same time that Hale and Root gain presidential support for a permanent NRC, they also shift its purpose from being primarily military to industrial. The groundwork for doing so had been laid right at the start. In its statement of purpose the Council was charged with organizing research for industrial as well as military purposes. In the spring of 1918 Hale takes advantage of this to form an Industrial Relations Division, made up of the leaders of America's industrial research. To support it, he also forms an Industrial Advisory Committee made up of some of the most powerful men in America's banking, steel, chemical, electrical, and communications industries.[41] "Strong men," in the words of a Council report, "with the imagination to foresee the general benefits" of science.[42] Following the receipt of Wilson's Executive Order, Hale officially launches the new division on May 29 1918 with a formal banquet at the university club in New York.

London and Paris 1917–18

On 10 September 1918 Hale meets with Wilson at the White House to discuss an Inter-Allied Research Council. Hale wants to exclude German scientists from international science after the war. He knows he must proceed indirectly if he wants to get Wilson's support as the president is publicly committed to the proposition that it is the German government and not the German people who are to blame for the war.

Hale's desire for such a Council follows a change of heart. In the early years of the war, Hale had dismissed German scientists' statement of support for the German army's burning of the library at Louvain as a temporary departure from scientific internationalism due to the heated atmosphere created by the conflict. Now, under the influence of French mathematician Emile Picard, he believes that they share their government's responsibility for the war. To achieve the post-war exclusion of German scientists from international science, Hale has proposed that each of Germany's enemies ought to form their own NRC, and then federate together for form an Inter-Allied Research Council. This will be officially set up to encourage cooperation on war problems between the Americans and the Allies. When Germany is defeated, it can be extended to pure and applied science generally, and neutral nations invited to join. Thus the problem of how to get neutral scientists to side with America and the Allies is deferred until after the end of the war. Equally, by setting up the new Council solely for war purposes he gives opponents in the Academy no grounds for challenging it as opposed to the spirit of scientific internationalism. Most important of all, he can get the presidential support he believes is absolutely vital to the new project. By masking its real purpose of excluding German scientists from international science from the president, Hale can present the Inter-Allied Research Council as in accord with Wilson's declaration that America is only at war with Germany's rulers and is a friend of the German people. Wilson can be persuaded to support the Council as a temporary measure to strengthen the war effort.

But if Hale is a fox, so is the president. Hale has twice tried to get the president's endorsement by asking for his comment on the plan, and while the president has not objected to it, neither has he approved it.

Now Hale uses his imminent departure for London to set up the Inter-Allied Council to force the president to make a decision. Hale tells Wilson that the danger is that, unless America takes a lead, French, Belgian, and some British scientists are likely to use the October meeting to issue sweeping denunciations of Germany. Wilson reacts strongly. The president was, in Hale's words, "very emphatically opposed to any resolution directed against German men of science". Such attacks would be "the best possible way to play Germany's game . . . [adding credibility to] the claim that Germany is surrounded by vindictive enemies". Hale now argues that an organization for war purposes would avoid exactly these problems, but Wilson objects to the very idea of joining the Allies in a formal organization. "France and other European nations have felt the war much more than we have, and are therefore likely to take drastic action that might bind us to do things contrary to our natural intent."[43] All the president would agree to was inter-Allied scientific conferences of a strictly informal nature. Hale is not deterred and sets out for England to see what he can do. When he arrives in London in October he believes he sees a way round Wilson's objections. The president had only objected to formally conjoining with the Allies while the war lasted. American scientists could work with the Allies informally while the war lasted to establish the foundations of the new organization, and postpone its formal establishment until after the defeat of the Central Powers. To prepare the way for this Hale persuades the conference to pass a declaration of principles in line with Wilson's position that a reformed Germany could enter the League of Nations, and squashes Belgian and French moves to denounce German scientists. When the war is over the new International Research Council is formally set up in July 1919 at the Palais des Académies, Brussels. The result, never endorsed by Wilson, was that the National Research Council became a member of an international organization, the International Research Council, which continued the wartime division of international science after the war had ended.

(v) A machine for controlling the direction of American scientific and engineering research

Manoeuvring through the corridors of power, Hale, guided by Root, used the war to create a national institution for the organization of American science. He thus gave big business a further means of using science to obtain super-profits through market manipulation and monopoly. Positioned at the heart of the NRC, the American big businessman's privileged access to the three vital elements, intelligence, capital, and power, was considerably enhanced.

Intelligence

Through the NRC Research Information Service he had an intelligence service which enabled him to spot new opportunities to use science for profit both inside and outside America. "Properly regarded," Hale claimed, "the Information Service may be considered the pioneer corps of the Council, surveying the progress of research in various parts of the world, selecting and reporting on the many activities of interest and importance . . . and disseminating it to men and institutions which can use it to advantage."[44] The enormous value of the information service was shared by men at the heart of the new corporate giants. "Knowledge is Power," observed Charles Rees, head of research at Du Pont. "Information and knowledge are so closely related that it might be said that information is power and coordinated information is power plus."[45]

Capital

Through the Industrial Relations Division and the Divisions that succeeded it, the big businessman had contacts to launch large-scale research projects necessary to take advantage of such opportunities at minimal cost to himself. In this way, America's leading scientific corporations could use their own industrial research laboratories to greater advantage. By using the NRC to coordinate research in federal, university, private foundation, and industrial research laboratories, they could reduce the cost of such research to themselves. Through their dominance of key markets and their industrial research laboratories, America's corporate giants were in a better position than smaller firms to use such research to generate super-profits through market manipulation and monopoly. No less important than giving big business a way to direct the nation's research, the NRC provided it with a means to direct the nation's production of scientists and engineers. Through the NRC, it could seek to ensure that, a minimum cost, the nation's universities and technical schools provided it with scientists and engineers who were already trained and conditioned to do the kind of research it needed.

State power

In the NRC, the big businessman acquired a forum in which he could meet with federal officials, military officers, and scientists and engineers to direct American research and education. Formulated by a body "recognized" by the president's Executive Order, and presented as being in the national interest, such plans would enjoy a legitimacy they would lack if they came from a private body. They could form the starting point for campaigns in which big business could use its money power and political contacts to break down any opposition to their realization. The

NRC was by no means unique. The end of the war saw the establishment of a number of other bodies, such as the Brookings Institute, which provided business with semi-private fora to which it could invite representatives of social interests, gain consensus for reforms based on scientific research, and launch campaigns to influence policy.[46] As a body set up by Executive Order and not reliant on Congress for its core funding, the NRC's actions were not subject to Congressional oversight or control. This meant that it provided big business with a means by which it could gain state support for its plans without being subjected to democratic control. This was no accident. In a confidential memorandum entitled "The Origin and Purpose of the NRC" circulated within its executive council in May 1919, Hale spelled out his anti-democratic intention:

> The Academy organized the National Research Council . . . with a view to stimulating the growth of science and its application to industry and particularly with a view to the coordination of research agencies for the sake of enabling the United States, in spite of its democratic, individualist organization, to bend its energies effectively toward a common purpose.[47]

In return for their supporting its strategy for producing super-profits, big business supported Root and Hale's plans for the organization of scientific research. Prompted by them, the leaders of American industry emphasized their interest in supporting pure research as the basis of future industrial advance. Hale and Root argued that the new arrangement was entirely beneficial for pure science. They told a story in which everything was harmony and concord.[48] Big business's new-found appreciation of the debt they owed to pure science as the foundation of their industries, they claimed, meant that pure science would now enjoy an unprecedented flow of funds. More than that, big business was awakening Americans to the fact that pure science should be funded because it was nothing less than the "advance guard of civilization".[49] The organization of science was in no way hostile to the spirit of scientific inquiry. It could not be as it was only the application of the scientific method to deciding how scientific investigation should itself be carried out. "Scientific men are only recently realizing that the principles which apply to success on a large scale in transportation and manufacturing and general staff work apply to them," Root argued in a passage later quoted by Hale with approval. The senator continued, "The effective power of a great number of scientific men may be increased by organization just as the effective power of a great number of labourers may be increased by military discipline."[50] There was, in their eyes, no conflict between the organization of science and the freedom of the individual investigator. Organization did not limit the investigator in any way but gave him the means to pursue research that he would otherwise be unable to carry out. It enabled him to make sure it was well directed by providing him with information about research already carried out. It stimulated him by bringing

him into contact with other scientists, and it enabled him to carry out investigations that could only be undertaken by large numbers of scientists working
together according to a common plan and requiring expensive instruments. While
in Germany the organization of research had been carried out by autocratic diktat
to a "docile and submissive people", Root averred, in America scientists would
spontaneously organize themselves because they recognized the need to so if the
nation was to carry out the pure and applied scientific research needed to lead
human progress and to survive in future military and commercial struggles.

To reinforce and extend the new links between science, business, the military
and the presidency in the post-war era, the leaders of the NRC employed the same
strategy we have seen used by the leaders of the chemical campaign to secure a
high chemical tariff. They emphasized that despite the signing of the Armistice
and the negotiation of the Paris Peace Treaty, America continued to be faced by
threats to its very existence as a nation that only the continued organization of
research could protect against. Thus in his 13 November 1919 "Address to the
Association of Land-Grant Colleges" as the post-war slump took hold, the new
chairman of the NRC James Rowland Angell echoed Root's wartime call for post-
war perpetuation of the NRC. The lesson of the war, he underscored, is that there
must be a "permanent mobilization" of scientific ability. This must be "instantly"
available in case of war. "Nothing can be more certain" than that national development in industry, agriculture, public health, and "the preservation of the
physical framework of our civilization" will be "dependent" on the "quality and
quality of sound research". The truth of this, he claimed, becomes more apparent
when one recognizes the fact that "every modern nation stands in relations of
industrial and commercial competition with other nations; and in the measure in
which this is true, to fall notably behind the others in scientific development is to
precipitate a trend of events which spells national depression and disaster".[51]

14

Manifesto for a Global
Deep Science Movement

I have traced the emergence of a strategy to enrol Americans in building an imperial republic surpassing Rome. Before 1914 groups within the elite – patrician reformers, scientists, military progressives, and big business – presented themselves as part of a global avant garde which was linking the forces of science, technology, capitalism, the nation-state and constitutional government in a harmonious circle. With each revolution mankind took a step further towards bringing the forces of nature and society under its direction. Time itself would be commanded. Progress would be made irreversible. Unlike its Roman predecessor the new empire would be truly eternal.

At the heart of the strategy was fear. To convince Americans to forgo the struggle for democracy and to support the transformation of the United States into a "great civilizing nation", these groups claimed that they alone were able to spot the signs that the forces of nature and society were beginning to spiral out of control and take the decisive measures necessary to restore the harmonious circle. In addition, they claimed that the United States was already part of an interdependent world system in which it was threatened by a series of potentially irreversible disasters – disease, war, labour strikes, stock market panic – unless Americans supported the total mobilization of society necessary to become a global power. Through the creation of a permanent state of emergency they justified, in their own eyes, their intervention in every aspect of American life and their creation, with their European counterparts, of a network of power which encompassed the globe and all its peoples.

They sought to realize Francis Bacon's vision on a world scale. In the *New Atlantis,* the Jacobean Lord Chancellor and natural philosopher described how man could realize his sovereignty by using science to bring the natural and social worlds under his control. "The end of our foundation," proclaims one of the scientists who govern Bacon's imagined utopian island located somewhere in the Pacific, "is the knowledge of causes, and the secret motions of things; and the enlarging of the bounds of human empire, to the effecting of all things possible." It was an intoxicating idea. Yet events soon suggested that the attempt to realize Bacon's vision has unintended consequences that challenge its foundations – the idea that the world is the kind of thing that can be mastered.[1] The attempt of European governments to master a local contingency, the 28 June 1914 assassination of Archduke Franz Ferdinand in Sarajevo, quickly led to a European-wide war *beyond their control.*

The American elite's actions unintentionally helped to transform this into a truly worldwide disaster, firstly, by bringing the whole of America's economy into the war on the side of the Allies, and then in 1917 by bringing America into the war militarily. To justify these actions they gave the war a single cause, Germany's alleged desire to master the world, and then placed that cause outside the harmonious circle. This enabled Woodrow Wilson to relaunch the project of empire under the cover of an anti-imperialist crusade to "make the world safe for democracy". In doing so, Wilson implicitly denied that the war had called into question the very idea that the world was the kind of thing that can be mastered. Yet the fact that the rationalization for their actions used by these groups was partially motivated by their own special interests shows that the problem of mastering contingency cannot be removed by first locating it outside the elite program, and then creating vaster forces to overcome it. The project is flawed because the men who would exercize control do not stand outside the forces they seek to control, but are themselves partially determined by them.

The argument here should not be confused with the Marxist argument that capitalism inevitably leads to world war. My thesis is both weaker and perhaps ultimately more disturbing. It is that as a matter of fact the build up of immense military, industrial, state, and other forces did lead, because of unforeseen chains of events, to a world war that none of the contending parties wanted. The military experts who designed the mobilization timetables did not foresee that, once the order for mobilization had been given, the rigidity of these timetables would make it difficult to avoid war. Equally I doubt many American businessmen fully understood the long term consequences of wartime trading with Britain and France alone, and the growing pressure to rationalize that trade by demonizing Germany. The difficult of foreseeing how chains of events will interact is not the only problem. As those who would bring the world under control are always in part determined by the very forces they would control, and their knowledge of the world is necessarily limited, the build up of such immense forces will continue to produce global contingencies.

The failure to acknowledge the bankruptcy of the imperial project and its return under other names has been tragic. After the end of the First World War Wilson sought to create a League of Nations which would enable the civilized nations to cooperate together in spreading the liberal capitalist revolution to all mankind and in defending it against "outlaw" nations. To persuade Europeans and Americans to support his renewal of the imperial project under a new name, he emphasized that this was the only way they could protect themselves against the German and Russian "outlaws". The result was that the opportunity for a "peace without victory" which would have consolidated the power of a Liberal–Social Democrat alliance within Germany was lost. This cleared the way for an alliance between the militarists and the Nazis to take advantage of the Great Depression to seize state power, and meant that far from mitigating the global contingency created by European powers' different interpretations of how to respond to the assassination of Franz Ferdinand, Wilson's efforts cleared the path for a return of that global contingency in the Second World War and subsequent Cold War.

Since then other events have added to the appreciation that the imperial project is fatally flawed. The attempt to overcome industrial society's projected energy shortages through nuclear power leads to disasters like Chernobyl, and leaves nuclear waste which will threaten men, women, and children with cancer for hundreds of thousands of years. The attempt to conquer disease through drugs without changing local power relations leads to the rise of new forms of drug-resistant tuberculosis and other diseases . . . The list is easily continued. We are living in a late-modern era in which the attempt to control all local contingencies has led to the emergence of what William Connolly calls "globalized contingencies" which appear to resist all efforts to bring them under control.[2] The modern idea that mankind can achieve its sovereignty through the central direction of ever greater forces to control nature and society increasingly appears to be inherently flawed and tragically counter-productive.

The Baconian dream is over. "The fully enlightened earth", Adorno and Horkheimer underscore in their reply to Bacon, "radiates disaster triumphant."[3] This means that in responding to contemporary events, we need to rethink how the Enlightenment's promise to liberate men from fear and to establish their sovereignty might now be realized. Today the idea that the world should be governed by an imperial republic is returning in new forms.[4] Many leaders of institutions like the International Monetary Fund or the World Health Organization, of universities like Toronto or Cambridge, and of non-government organizations like Amnesty International or Oxfam, increasingly see themselves as part of an international system which is enabling mankind to realize its sovereignty through the global extension of liberal capitalism. In doing so they find themselves in complex relations of both support and opposition to the resurgence of old empires (China, India, Russia and the United States) and new regional empires (the European Union). All these forms are governed as much or more by the cynical meta-narrative, with its emphasis on the construction of a fortress and pre-emptive attack, as by the progressive meta-narrative.

The dilemma that confronts opponents of the avant garde's claimed right to determine what republic/empire should be, and whether it should have priority over other institutions, is that they find themselves in the middle of a history in which republic/empire is both discredited, and is being relaunched in multiple versions under different names. Therefore they must be sensitive to the conjuncture in which they find themselves. Before the Great Depression, the elite's attempt to enrol Americans in supporting empire by pointing to the threat presented by Germany and Russia was fraudulent. After it, the rise of German National Socialism meant that it was better to support British, Russian, and American empires against Fascism. The Cold War offered similar moments of hard choice. The situation that confronts us after the end of the Cold War is analogous to that in the years after the First World War. National and international institutions can be remade so that they serve the majority of the world to secure fair trade, an end to terrorism and war, the rule of law, robust health, and a sustainable environment. Yet what we are seeing is an attempt by the national elites of the world's more prosperous nations to deny that there are such opportunities by producing new enemies that justify the extension of cultural, scientific, commercial, and military empire.

Here I focus on the resurgence of American empire alone, though the need to resist other forms of imperialism is equally urgent. Its origins go back to the end of the Second World War when the Truman administration's use of atomic weapons announced to the world that the United States would now ensure that the benevolent circle of science, technology, capitalism, the nation-state and liberal democracy would be extended to all mankind, and that should communists or third world peoples attempt to oppose the process, the United States had both the capability and the will to do to them what it had done to the people of Nagasaki and Hiroshima. It justified this to Americans and to its Allies, however, by announcing that its use of terror was militarily necessary to defeat Japan. In doing so the administration repeated the strategy of enrolling Americans in the task of empire, as I show in the following section, by claiming that this was the only way that America could be defended. The fantasy that American science and technology would enable it to combine global control with humanity, however, did not last long. The attempt to achieve security through increasing the forces of science, technology, capitalism, and military power, already discredited by the First World War, was now further discredited as the world faced the prospect of total annihilation through atomic war. This new intractable global contingency was further exacerbated as the nuclear arms race between the super-powers led to the spread of atomic weapons to a wider circle of nations.

The end of the Cold War gives us a unique opportunity to remake international law. I teach Montesquieu against Hobbes.[5] What is called for is not a new system of laws, but rather the enforcement of laws that are not applied, the reinterpretation of existing laws, and the creation of new laws. This remaking of the laws is driven by hitherto excluded groups seizing the principles of equality and liberty and insisting they apply to them.[6] Thus the non-nuclear weapon states have to insist that the legally binding obligation of the declared nuclear weapon states under the Nuclear Non Proliferation Treaty (NPT) to carry out nuclear disarmament is carried out and does not become a dead letter. In the years since the end of the Second World War it has become increasingly apparent that the spread of nuclear weapons is but one of the global contingencies being created by the liberal capitalist world revolution. The result has been the rise of a series of global movements which seek international agreements to set limits on science, technology, capitalism, and the nation state. The disarmament movement seeks treaties which limit the development of both nuclear and conventional military force. The environmental movement seeks treaties which limit the emission of ozone layer destroying chemicals and of green house gases that cause global warming. And the world development movement seeks fair trade treaties that limit the operations of trans-national corporations and banks which have led to an increasing gap between the affluent one billion and the excluded five billion.[7]

The growing evidence that the liberal capitalist revolution is producing further global contingencies shows the need for yet further global movements. Thus the combined effects of the attempt to contain communism by "winning" the Cold War and to increase the profits of transnational corporations by the removal of all barriers to trade, has created the perfect conditions for the growth of a global trade in heroine, cocaine, and other narcotics. A new global movement against the drugs trade and transnational crime is needed, powerful enough to counter-balance the short term interests of transnationals in market access and create real international and national barriers to both narcotics and organized crime. Existing movements have had important successes. Thus the NPT and the Comprehensive Test Ban Treaty (CTBT) are significant steps towards ending the nuclear arms race, while the United Nations Framework Convention on Climate Change (UNFCCC) is a step towards bringing climate change under control.

The post-Cold War attempt by the new global movements to remake international law now finds itself in fundamental conflict with the American relaunch of empire. The situation is analogous to that after the First World War when the patrician reformers, and their allies, sought to convince Americans that they had no alternative to empire by producing a series of "enemies" which they claimed only the transformation of America into *the* world power could protect them against. The difference is that, under the Bush presidency, the collapse of the distinction between America's claim to exercize violence on behalf of law, and "outlaw" nations' exercize of violence against the rule of law, has grown to the point where it has become impossible to ignore.

In other ways the situation is analogous to the German militarists' and Nazi Party's total and unremitting saturation of society with depictions showing the populations' complete vulnerability to attack by bombers dropping poison gas, as described in Chapter 3. Today, however, global television networks, and a news cycle driven by competition which leaves reporters little time for reflection, are so ubiquitous that there is no longer any need to rely on such clumsy devices as mock up bombs suspended from street lamps to achieve the desired effect, and the reach of the strategy can now extend beyond the boundaries of a nation to encompass the globe.

Just as was the case for the leaders of the chemical and air campaigns after the First World War, and with the Truman administration after the Second World War, the key has been the denial that there is any alternative path forward except planetary control through global military terror. This denial was already manifest under the Clinton administration. It accepted, as I set out in conclusion to Part 1, the argument of the leaders of its nuclear weapons laboratories that the CTBT should be signed if and only if, through investment in super-computers and other technologies to design new atomic bombs without the need to test them, it could become a way of ensuring that America retained its ability to threaten nuclear destruction while denying other nations the right to acquire such an ability. And it supported continued work on a nuclear missile defence shield (NDM) which would give America the ability to launch nuclear missile attacks on other nations without their being able to reply in kind.

The result was that America would be able to realize, with a different set of technologies, Billy Mitchell's original vision that air power would enable a single nation to dominate the globe through being able to instantly destroy any place on earth without fear of retaliation. Clinton's policies opened the way for George Bush to come forward as the more robust exponent of peace through nuclear terror. Tests of the nuclear missile defence shield were the key. Through the repeated firing of "enemy" missiles on test ranges and attempts to shoot them down, Americans would see themselves as still living at the height of the Cold War when they believed they were in immediate danger of a world-destroying Russian missile attack.

The 11 September terrorist attack was immediately integrated into this strategy for renewing global empire. The situation is complex, riven with tensions, and ambiguous. This means the following paragraphs are no more than first suggestions as to how the awareness of the way empire constructs our experience of space and time, which the reader has gained throughout the book, gives us the means to identify opportunities to resist both American state and Al Qaeda terrorism. Firstly, the role of empire itself in overseeing the liberal capitalist revolution as a central cause of Al Qaeda is pushed into the background. This is done by replacing the search to understand the multiple causes that have come together to create these disasters by a focus on a single cause. This cause is then placed outside of the policies pursued by empire. Thus the fact that the rise of Al Qaeda is, in part, a "blow back" of US imperial polices in Saudi Arabia and Afghanistan is covered over.[8] Anyone who draws attention to such facts and the need to discuss their implications is attacked as unpatriotic. The American state's own use of terror as an instrument of policy is pushed firmly out of sight.[9]

Secondly, the right of empire to either remake the laws in its own interests or to act outside them is asserted by depicting these causes as the kind of threat that demands such actions. The key to this is the reinvocation of exactly the fantasies about total vulnerability that I have focused on in this book. These fantasies are there to be reinvoked because they have been repeatedly evoked by the presidency and the weapons laboratories for over a century. Thus by presenting the terrorists who attacked the world trade centre as a *new* phenomenon, a "global terror network", the Bush administration made Al Qaeda a blank screen for Americans' fears. At the same time, by suggesting that they were a threat like other earlier, at the time new, phenomena such as atomic weapons and before that the bomber/chemical weapon combination, the administration was able to suggest that the terrorists had the power to destroy American society. Equally, the magnitude of the effect produced by Al Qaeda's attack was taken as proof that there must be an equally large cause: the shocking collapse of the World Trade Centre towers was taken as showing the existence of a new kind of terrorist network with the power to threaten civilization itself.

Thirdly, the American people, and other peoples, are asked to give up their own struggles to extend democracy and exercize power to solve problems facing them in return for having the intoxication of being represented as heroes in a global struggle. This is done by organizing spectacular displays of the vast forces generated by the circle of science, technology, capitalism, the nation-state, and liberal democracy. These displays give the citizens the opportunity to imagine themselves as the heroes of a story in which mankind is realising its sovereignty on a world scale, or alternatively defending their own national sovereignty against outside forces bent on their destruction. Thus we are shown aerial footage of a hill side on which it is claimed Al Qaeda fighters are firmly dug in, a B-52 US Air Force bomber flies over and drops a daisy cutter bomb. Under the immense force of the explosion the hill top is blown sky high. It is clear that no human being could have survived the blast.

The dramatic exercize of force hides the fact that the national elite can no longer solve key problems facing Americans because it is itself, to a large extent, under the influence of the very forces it claims to control. Thus it cannot provide Americans with economic security by improving the rights of workers because it relies on corporate funding to get elected, and has been intoxicated with the idea that the stock market offers it unlimited opportunities for profit. Thus like its First World War predecessor it is itself as much, or more, swept up in the terrifying fantasies of terrorists and outlaw states, and intoxicating visions that new weapons will enable it to combine control, revenge, and humanity, as the wider citizenry it seeks to enthral.[10]

International law is in crisis.[11] It is an open question whether the NPT, which forms the cornerstone of all other nuclear disarmament and non-proliferation treaties will survive. Moreover Bush's decision not to ratify the Kyoto Protocol on climate change and allow increased emissions of greenhouse gases lays the axe to the roots of international attempts to limit environmentally destructive activity. Finally the president's June 2002 statement that the United States has the right to use pre-emptive military force, including nuclear weapons, against any state that it sees as hostile or as making moves to acquire weapons of mass destruction repudiates the core idea of the United Nation's Charter, which prohibits any use of international force that is not undertaken in self-defence after the occurrence of an armed attack across an international boundary or pursuant to a decision by the UN Security Council.[12]

The attack on international law is paralleled by an attack on domestic law. The federal government has used fear of terrorism to circumvent Constitutional rights and create a vast grey area in which the secret state can operate.[13] Thus the US Patriot Act gives the government the means to use the fear of terrorism to curtail the right to free speech and to political association protected by the First Amendment and the right of the people to be "secure in their persons, houses, papers, and effects, against unreasonable searches and seizures . . . but upon probable cause" protected by the Fourth Amendment. The government is also using claims of an immense terrorist threat to enrol citizens in a vast expansion of the secret state. The Justice Department's Terrorism Information and Prevention System (TIPS), means the US will have a higher percentage of citizen informants than the former East German Stasi secret police. A pilot project, scheduled to start in August 2002 in ten cities, will involve no less than one million informants out of a total population of 24 million, or one in 24 people. At the same time, it has sought to use fear of terrorism to create a zone outside domestic and international law where it can operate without regard for law. Thus through a 13 November 'Military Order' the executive gives itself the right to indefinitely detain any non-citizen accused of terrorism, and for military commissions to try defendants with no provision for judicial review.

The 1921 disarmament movement succeeded in blocking the emergence of a strong alliance between the chemical and air weapon systems. It also shattered the alliance built up by the chemical campaign. This success shows that there is *no* necessity which makes the development of terror technologies inevitable. We will live in a world full of such weapons if, and only if, the heterogeneous engineering needed to build them is successful. Yet, the disarmament movement's success was an ambiguous one. Through endorsing the elite's claim that it had gone to war to save American democracy it laid the way open for the Harding administration to use the Washington Conference to tame the movement. The administration translated its call for disarmament into a call for arms control which would enable the war's victors to maintain their dominance over the vanquished. The chance to get all the leading powers to carry through both chemical and aerial disarmament was lost, as was the opportunity to reverse the victor's peace imposed at Versailles. This meant success was local and temporary. By the early 1930s the development of chemical weapons and strategic bombers in Europe, Asia, and America was once again well underway.

This history shows that – even if it is successful at other levels – any movement which does not successfully challenge the way modern empire has reshaped our experience of space and time *will* lose – a point underscored by one of Fascism's greatest critics, Walter Benjamin, in his 'Theses on the Philosophy of History.'[14] *In this book I have sought to sharpen the reader's sensitivity to the singular features of time and space which empire's construction of history and geography leaves out, and which reveal opportunities to respond to current dangers without bringing about the repetition of violence on a larger scale.* The cultivation of such a sensitivity frees us from our entrapment in one particular viewpoint and reminds us that to an infinite intellect, such as God, the world looks very different than it does to our finite mind.

In terms of space it is a question of constructing a counter-geography. I have shown how, in the first part of the twentieth century, the claim used to justify empire – that America was threatened by foreign attack – was based on the manipulation of fantasies about technology. In fact the Atlantic ocean made both a sea invasion and an annihilating air attack on a city impossible. Today such details are as important. America's oceanic isolation still matters and makes it impossible for Iraq to launch a missile attack on America. This security could be increased through treaties halting research and development of missile technologies and guidance systems.[15] Equally, it means recognizing that Al Qaeda's success in destroying the World Trade Centre was in part due to flaws in the building design and to inadequate airport security; that in the absence of a supporting population within America Al Qaeda's previous failure to launch a successful major attack on America over a decade is probably a better guide to the future than 11 September; and that Al Qaeda was largely the product of America's own policies in Saudi Arabia and Afghanistan. Equally, when the threat of bioweapons is evoked to justify pre-emptive war abroad and the secret state at home, it means noticing that the peculiarities of biological weapons – extreme difficulty of distributing the agent, need to make the particles exactly the right size, problems with cultivating the right strain and maintaining virulence – make it extremely difficult for a state let alone an organization like Al Qaeda to use them as weapons of mass destruction.[16] Just as we have seen is the case with the vital importance of tacit knowledge in making functioning nuclear weapons, these details mean that the Biological and Toxic Weapons Convention, which prohibits these weapons, can be effective if it is strengthened by a strong verification protocol.

In terms of time it is a question of constructing counter-memories. These prevent the struggle against empire being coopted by multiplying and strengthening resistance.[17] In this book I have taken marginalized images – the young American conscripted to fight in the trenches drowning in agony in a sea of poison gas, the black family fleeing Tulsa after the mob has used air planes dropping gasoline bombs to burn them out of their homes – as a starting point for constructing such memories. They are complex, double, memories. They are, firstly, memories not only of what happened but of what was prevented from happening through violence. They are memories of the happiness which might have been, but which was not allowed to be because its realization threatened the interests of the powerful. Through reading history against the grain I have constructed a series of such memories. I have unearthed the hidden history of how the patrician reformers, military progressives, big business, pure scientists, and organized researchers, conscripted a generation to fight in the First World War. They would face high explosives, poison gas, and the other horrors of the trenches so that a series of interests – in relaunching empire so as to tame democracy within America, in justifying the vast profits from munitions trade, in securing an artificial dye industry, in gaining a mass army and a modern navy, in the organization of American science and the scientific organization of America – would be advanced.

Some who fought were caught up in the dream of America exercising its power on a world scale and had "a good war". Others were less fortunate. My great aunt's father, Dr. John H.W. Rhein, a Philadelphia pioneer of neuro-psychiatry, may have been one of them. His early death a few years after the war was attributed by my great aunt, Florence Bird, who loved him very much, to the "whiff of gas" he received while serving in France as a lieutenant-colonel in the second Army of the American Expeditionary Force.

I have begun to uncover the history of how political struggles opened up a series of opportunities to make a better world, and of how the patrician reformers and their allies completely or partially prevented these opportunities being realized. There was the wartime struggle to keep America neutral so she could help mediate a "peace without victory". There was the African-American struggle to use America's entry into the war to "make the world safe for democracy" to advance their struggle for democracy within the United States. There was the opportunity created by the post-war disarmament movement to reverse the verdict of Versailles through engaging Germany and Russia in world disarmament talks. And there was the opportunity to direct research away from the nuclear physics which it was known might lead to an atomic bomb and towards physics useful for solar power.

These memories are, secondly, memories of how the victors of political struggles have sought to prevent their victory being called into question by erasing memory. They attempted to make their control total by wiping out the memory that there had been an opportunity for a different outcome, and hence that there may be such opportunities today. I have focused on the return of the Roman argument that empire is the way to achieve peace. Indeed, it seems little except the scale of the violence has changed since Tacitus nailed the lie at the heart of Roman propaganda by writing "they make a slaughter and call it peace". Thus during the Philippines–American War the patrician reformers' argued that just as Americans had been justified defeating the Indian peoples, America was now justified in defeating the Filipino nationalists. "Every expansion of civilization makes for peace", Theodore Roosevelt wrote, "The rule of law and order has succeeded to the rule of barbarous and bloody violence. Until the great civilized nations stepped in there was no chance for anything but such bloody violence."[18] Equally, they argued, Americans had to support the war because it was only by accepting the mission to become a great civilizing nation that Americans could maintain their own freedom in an increasingly interdependent world.

The argument that empire meant peace was repeated to justify America's economic and then military entry into the First World War. The war had revealed the bankruptcy of the claim that empire meant peace. This was covered over, as we have seen, by placing the causes of the war's violence completely outside civilization and by relaunching the project of empire under the new slogan of making the world safe for democracy. Through a bold reclassification, the Germans were shifted from being one of the leading civilized peoples, and placed with the Filipinos and the Indians as pre-civilized people. The patrician reformers and their allies could then employ the same logic they had used to justify the Indian Wars and the Philippines–American War as necessary for peace to justify war against Germany. Finally, after the war, the same argument was used to deny there ever had been any opportunity for worldwide disarmament. Thus the Harding administration denied there ever had been such an opportunity by using the Washington Conference to reassert its depiction of America, Britain, and France as the global sovereign and Germany and Russia as "outlaws". Through reiterating these arguments the patrician reformers and their allies attempted to bury memories that there ever had been opportunities for anything other than peace through the extension of empire, and in doing so helped smooth the way for a century of total war.

These memories change our relationship to the present. We no longer see it as simply one moment in a series of similar moments in which we have to advance the cause of peace through the expansion of empire. Instead, the present is transformed into a site of struggle in which, if the imperial project is not defeated, the post-Cold War opportunities for the liberty and democracy we need to secure health care, demand creative and sustaining work, stop race violence, and an end to world war will, once again, be suppressed and the memory that there ever has been such opportunities erased.

Other images and dates provide the reader with alternative starting points for the construction of counter-memories. Such work is vitally needed if the struggle against the resurgence of empire is to be broadened and deepened. Thus the official story of American action in Afghanistan is called into question by the revelation that on 3 July 1979 President Carter, who had been told by National Security chief Zbigniew Brzesinski that doing so was a way of entrapping Russia in a Vietnam-type war, signed the first directive for secret aid to the opponents of the pro-Soviet regime in Kabul – six months before the Soviet military intervention in Afghanistan.[19] Or again, the elite's claim that the Americans must support the liberal capitalist world revolution seems doubtful when we understand the role played by the Reagan administration's attempt to arrest America's decline as the world's number one economy by raising interest rates, cutting tax, and allowing corporations freedom to do what they wanted has, along with its promotion of structural adjustment policies by international institutions, ended in denying South America and Africa the capital they needed to develop. This has contributed to an Argentinean economic collapse in which families face destitution after their life savings have been wiped out and to creating an African tragedy whose horror and scale rivals that of the Nazi holocaust.[20] In the pages that follow I look at recent historiography which calls into question the official account of Hiroshima and Nagasaki and the start of the Cold War.

(i) "It is not an explosive. It is a poisonous thing that kills people by its deadly radioactive reaction"

With the August 1945 dropping of the atomic bomb on Hiroshima and Nagasaki, America made its own the strategy for exercising world power through the global terror Billy Mitchell had warned Americans that an autocratic nation might be tempted to try. To prevent Americans calling this strategy into question the Truman administration managed the news very carefully to ensure that the American people would see it as absolutely different in kind from the German initiation of poison gas warfare in 1915.

There was no military necessity to drop the atomic bombs.[21] It is now clear that the Truman administration knew from the decoding of Japanese radio transmissions and other sources that the Japanese were already seeking to surrender. The supreme commander of the Allied Forces in Europe, General Eisenhower, and Chief of Staff Admiral Leahy, told Truman they were opposed to the atomic attack.[22] After Hiroshima other officers at the very top of the air force, navy, and army declared there had been no military necessity to use the atomic bomb.[23] The main Japanese concern was the retention of the emperor as the symbolic figurehead of the nation. This was clearly not an insuperable obstacle to Truman, as America did finally agree to let the Japanese retain the emperor. It is less clear why Truman did decide to drop the atomic bomb. If we ask the question why America decided to make German and then Japanese cities the targets of vast air raids then one part of the answer is the air service's interwar bid for independence from the army by developing the idea of strategic air power, while another part of the answer lies in the process of escalation whereby attacks on civilian targets by one side were used to justify further such attacks by the other.[24] If we ask the more limited question of why Truman decided to drop the atomic bomb the key important factor was most likely his belief that the bomb would give him a winning card in negotiating with Stalin. Truman delayed his July 1945 Potsdam meeting with Stalin and Churchill until after the atomic bomb had been tested. On the ship crossing the Atlantic to the Big Three meeting he told an associate: "If it explodes, as I think it will, I'll certainly have a hammer on those boys."[25] Following the testing of the atomic bomb on 16 July 1945 in the New Mexico desert, the American stance changed from regarding cooperation among the Big Three (America, Russia, and Britain) as essential to managing world relations to one in which America and Britain would manage and contain Russia. Next day at Potsdam Truman took the "offensive" and demanded "free and unfettered elections" in Bulgaria and Romania. In the months that followed Truman actively sought to delay the Soviet declaration of war against Japan until after the atomic bomb could be used.[26] Finally, America no longer sought Soviet cooperation so as to ensure Germany was never again a threat and antagonized the Soviets by blocking the large-scale reparations they believed had been agreed at Yalta.

We will never know key parts of the story of why the bomb was dropped. The significance of the atomic attack, by contrast, for the communist and colonized world was clear. The United States presented itself as the global sovereign who has the power to suspend international laws and customs banning the use of terror when it judges it necessary to defeat outlaw nations. The atomic attacks were a clear contravention of international law. The first atomic bomb was dropped on the city of Hiroshima which contained 350,000 people. The attacks broke the Hague Convention's Article 22 which prohibits military attacks on unarmed civilians. They were also acts of terror. Through the instant annihilation of entire cities their people were transformed into examples. The world's peoples then became hostages in the American government's hands which it could use to coerce or blackmail their governments into accepting its orders. The press release announcing the atomic attack underscored the impossibility of resisting. It identified American power with the force of nature itself. "It is an atomic bomb. It is a harnessing of the basic power of the universe. The force from which the sun draws its powers had been loosed against those who brought war to the East."[27] The attacks sent a clear message: "Accept our right to act as the global sovereign, or we may do to you what we did to them." Through carrying out these attacks at the end of the war, when Japanese militarism was already defeated, America blurred the boundary between the use of terror to restore the rule of law and the use of terror so as to carry out a liberal-capitalist world revolution which would enable mankind to realise its sovereignty. The horror of Soviet, Chinese, and German use of camps and extermination against their own citizens, was now matched by American willingness to use violence abroad on behalf of the liberal-capitalist world revolution.

The fantasy that science and technology would give America control soon collided with reality. The London Council of Foreign Ministers a month after Hiroshima saw the beginning of the Cold War. Before the meeting Secretary of State Byrnes was, according to Secretary for War Stimson, "very much against any attempt to cooperate with Russia. His mind is full of problems with the coming meeting of the foreign ministers and he looks to have the presence of the bomb in his pocket, so to speak, as a great weapon to get through the thing."[28] The Soviets, however, responded to the threat implicit in America's actual use of atomic weapons by declaring that America's atomic monopoly could not last long. On 6 November 1945 the Soviet foreign minister, Molotov, warned against using the bomb as an instrument of power politics: "At the present time there can be no large-scale technological secrets that can remain the property of any one country or any one narrow group of countries. Therefore the discovery of atomic energy must not encourage . . . enthusiasm for using this discovery in a foreign-policy power game."[29] Stalin made Soviet acquisition of the atomic bomb the top priority. He told Igor Kurchatov, the head of the new Russian bomb programme, "If a child doesn't cry, the mother doesn't know what he needs. Ask for whatever you like. You won't be refused."[30] The Russians exploded their first atomic bomb in 1949 and their first thermonuclear bomb in 1953.

The Truman administration carefully managed the media's reporting of the atomic attacks. It was vital to do so to ensure that the atomic attack was not seen to blur the distinctions on which its right to govern the world depended. There was the danger that the initiation of atomic warfare against civilians by America would appear worse than Germany's initiation of chemical warfare against military troops in 1915. Truman's chief of staff, Admiral William Leahy, opposed the use of the atomic bomb because he saw too great a similarity between the two weapons. "'Bomb' is the wrong word to use for this new weapon. It is not a bomb. It is not an explosive. It is a poisonous thing that kills people by its deadly radioactive reaction."[31] Fleet Admiral Chester Nimitz held the same view: "It is [an] indiscriminate killer and I am hopeful that it will be dropped as an inefficient weapon. Poison gas and bacteriological weapons are in the same category."[32] To prevent the American public drawing the same conclusion, the Truman administration press release announcing the Hiroshima attack described the bomb as like conventional high explosives except more powerful. "It had more than two thousand times the blast power of the British 'Grand Slam' which is the largest bomb ever yet used in the history of warfare."[33] It did not mention that the bomb also killed through radiation. The press release also described Hiroshima as "an important Japanese Army base",[34] hiding the fact that the bomb was dropped on a city full of civilians. In the months that followed no effort was spared to prevent Americans learning about how Japanese men, women, and children were dying a painful and lingering death from radiation poisoning. When America occupied Japan General MacArthur immediately barred all reporters from travelling to Hiroshima and Nagasaki. When Australian war correspondent Wilfred Burchett did reach Hiroshima and reported the scenes he found in hospitals there in the *London Daily Express* on 5 September 1945, MacArthur ordered all reporters out of Tokyo to Yokohama were it was easier to keep an eye on them. Japanese photographs and film showing the human suffering that followed the bomb were seized by the military authorities, and only released many years later. The government also sought to prevent scientists and doctors carrying out a full assessment of what radioactivity had done, and was doing, to the people of these cities. In America the statements of those few scientists who raised questions about radiation deaths met with official denial and then, when that could not be maintained, statements minimizing the extent of radiation poisoning. In Japan America assembled an official team of scientists, led by General Thomas Farrell, who carried out a superficial survey and then trivialized the extent of the disaster. One researcher later revealed that Farrell had told him that "our mission was to prove there was no radiation from the bomb". MacArthur then smothered all scientific discussion about Hiroshima. Japanese scientists studying the effects of radiation had to submit all papers to a censorship board for review, where they would then be held indefinitely.

(ii) Rethinking the categorical imperative to treat others as ends-in-themselves in the wake of war and terror

The return of empire reiterates the progressive meta-narrative. This the reader will recall claims that there is a "we", the elites of the world's liberal-capitalist nations, which sees that science, technology, liberal-democracy, and capitalism can form a harmonious circle. All that is needed is to overcome the immediate block to the realization of that whole by organizing the good-willed but ignorant majority against the malicious minority. The result will be that mankind will be able to achieve its sovereignty. The progressive meta-narrative should be rejected. It tends to convert the call to help others into an opportunity to exercise control over them. In Part 1 and Part 3 we have seen how it led American scientists to do this. Horrified by the slaughter, American scientists and engineers searched for what they could do about it. At the same time they were part of a chemical industry that was making vast profits out of the sale of munitions. Through rearticulating the progressive meta-narrative they were able to reconcile the two. They rescued the idea that science, technology, liberal democracy, capitalism, the nation, and humanity form a harmonious circle by placing the blame for the war completely outside it. Whereas American scientists had previously taken Germany as the model for America to follow, they now claimed that German autocracy had turned scientists and technologists away from their goal of truth for its own sake and human material well-being. They then relaunched the project of empire under another name. It was now America which provided a model of how the harmonious circle could enable mankind to achieve its sovereignty. By defeating Germany, America would now make possible a worldwide revolution in which the rest of humanity would copy the American model. In any cases where they did not America, as the global sovereign, had the right to act outside international law to defeat any deviation in case it threatened the entire system. The military case is not exceptional. Instead as Root's 1907 talk to Yale students shows, it is best seen as providing a *window* through which we can look at other areas in which scientists' desire to answer a moral imperative addressed to them by other people ends up being converted into a relationship of control over them through a rearticulation of the progressive meta-narrative. We need to go in the opposite direction. The world war showed the bankruptcy of the idea that, because they have a mind which can correct its own prejudices scientists and engineers can correct deviations away from the harmonious circle. It needs to be replaced by an acceptance that the scientific mind may not be able to correct its own prejudices, and hence scientists and engineers must listen to those outside science who point out ways in which they may be in danger of converting the imperative to aid others into relations of control. In other words, there must be a total rejection of the ontology of science and the scientist which enables Rowland to claim that the mind trained in the physics laboratory is "the mind which is destined to govern the world" and which lies at the centre of both the pure science *and* the organized research movements.[35]

The scientists and engineers, of course, were only one of the elite groups which rearticulated the progressive meta-narrative to justify their use of the war to improve their position within America. The same points I have made about the scientists and engineers can be made about statesmen, military officers, and big business. And they can be put in terms of how we should take up the philosopher whose ideas about history, more than any other, are increasingly providing the justification for the global extension of liberal capitalism today, Immanuel Kant. At the centre of Kantian ethics is the idea that other people are ends-in-themselves. This part of the Kantian legacy provides a starting point we can build upon.[36] There is also a part of the Kantian legacy which must be rejected. This is the idea that we can look at human history *as if* the events in it showed a progression towards a federation of republics which had renounced war between themselves. This part of Kantian philosophy was rotten from the start. The problem is not with the goal. It is with the idea that history should be looked at *as if* events were tending towards that goal. This justifies elites in colluding with a whole range of forces . . . capital, science, technology, the nation . . . which treat people as means by allowing them to imagine ways in which it would eventually contribute to them being treated as ends-in-themselves. In the course of doing so political opportunities to forge alliances with groups outside the elite to resist injustice in the present were passed over, and elite rule legitimated. This can be seen in Kant's own essay *Perpetual Peace: A Philosophic Sketch*. In it Kant recognizes the vicious nature of the fiscal-military state being developed by England to exercise worldwide empire, and being copied by contemporary continental states:

> This ingenious system, invented by a commercial people in the present century, provides a military fund which may exceed the resources of all other states put together. It can only be exhausted by an eventual tax-deficit, which may be postponed for a considerable time by the commercial stimulus which industry and trade receive through the credit system. This ease in making war, coupled with the warlike inclination of those in power (which seems an integral feature of human nature), is thus a great obstacle in the way of perpetual peace.[37]

It is worth pausing a moment to describe exactly what Kant was referring to by the "ingenious system". Following the Glorious Revolution, England led the development of a new fiscal-military state which drew together a number of distinct elements into a system: taxation. The development of a relatively uncorrupted taxation bureaucracy, with an intelligence system that determined the most efficient rate of taxation, and special tax courts that rapidly settled disputes, gave the British state a lead over European rivals in raising taxes without provoking a tax payers' revolt.

Credit and the City of London

This tax gathering power, the creation of the Bank of England, the pioneering of new methods of deficit financing, and the security given to Britain by its insular situation, enabled the British government to raise money at a far lower rate than France.

Parliamentary oversight and military power

The idea that Protestant Britain's very existence was threatened by Catholic France created a political consensus between the Court and Country parties in parliament. The Country party had no trouble with the government funding professional soldiers and raising armies provided they were for use abroad, while the perception that the navy could never be used domestically as its element was the sea meant the Country party had even less trouble with the build-up of the Royal Navy. Further, the bipartisan consensus about the need to fight France meant that the competition between the Court and Country parties helped the taxation, banking, and military system to grow. It ensured that parliamentary scrutiny of the government's expenditure prevented corruption from growing so large that it brought a halt to the further growth of the system.

World empire and the national market

This system gave Britain the edge in its century-long fight with France to decide who would be the globally hegemonic power. It enabled the British government to meet the exponentially increasing costs of war without collapse. It created a system of government in which respect for the liberty of wealthy Englishmen at home was matched by aggressive military operations abroad to destroy all competitors in Europe, the Mediterranean, North America, the Caribbean, and India. The British lead in creating a unified national market meant that British merchants were increasingly able to ensure that international trade passed through them by offering foreign merchants the tempting carrot of the British market, and to do so on advantageous terms by threatening them with the stick of withdrawing the help they needed to gain access to that market if they were not compliant. This combination of world commercial empire and the world's greatest domestic market meant that increasingly the world's wealth flowed through London and the stage was set for England's rise to world hegemony in the nineteenth century.[38]

But what does Kant do when confronted by the fiscal-military state in the process of conquering and colonizing the world? He does not engage in a detailed analysis which would reveal the opportunities that exist to oppose it. Instead he imagines how history could be looked at *as if* war itself is contributing to the progress of human culture, and in doing so preparing the way for its own dissolution by forcing the development of mankind's reason to the point when it will come to see the irrationality of war. Whereas the categorical imperative's insistence that we should always treat people as ends-in-themselves suggests an absolute opposition to war, Kant's now adopts a God's eye-view of human history which enables him to endorse war because it contributes to mankind's advance. This is most clearly stated in his *Critique of Judgement*:

Though war is an unintentional human endeavour (incited by our unbridled passions), yet it is also a deeply hidden and perhaps intentional endeavour of the supreme wisdom, if not to establish, then at least to prepare the way for a lawfulness along with the freedom of states, and thereby for a unified system of them with a moral basis.[39]

In "Perpetual Peace" Kant argues that war has contributed to mankind's advance by dispersing people throughout the world, and that the spirit of commerce will eventually lead to an end to war – ignoring his own observation that it is precisely a commercial people, the English, who have developed the fiscal-military state and who are bent on using it to dominate the world. The extraordinary escalation of aggression between European states in the eighteenth century as they competed for world empire made Kant's passive relationship to his times incompatible with the categorical imperative he so sharply described. He avoids confronting the fact that, to a large extent, politics is a field of forces in which he must take the risk of deciding who the enemy is, in this case the fiscal-military state, and then calculate how to defeat it before it defeats him. Faced with the evidence that the fiscal-military state, and its use of violence, was growing, Kant's failure to look for political forces capable of combating it makes him complicit in its brutality through adopting a moralistic apolitical stance which collapses into fatalism:

The god of morality does not yield to Jupiter, the custodian of violence, for even Jupiter is still subject to fate. In short, reason is not sufficiently enlightened to discover the whole series of predetermined causes which would allow it to predict accurately the happy or unhappy consequences of human activities as dictated by the mechanism of nature; it can only hope that the result will be as it wishes.[40]

To maintain such a stance after the First World War requires a blunting of any ethical sensibility to the point of killing it. The avant garde's idea of a harmony between science, technology, liberal-democracy, the nation state, and humanity is a secularization of the theological idea of providence. This presented God as making the world so that it was suitable for mankind's moral progress. The opposite of a harmonious relationship between parts of a community is that one part is master and the other part is the slave. Yet, we have seen that American scientists thoroughly intertwined the two. To create the harmony that would enable mankind to realize its potential, it had to dominate the human and natural enemies of mankind. The idea that the human and natural worlds are the kind of thing that can be mastered is also a secularization of the idea of providence.[41] It is based on the idea that God has made the world for man as the kind of thing that he can master. The way that empire has amassed ever greater means to enable the avant garde to master the world, and in doing so has transformed ethical desires to respond to the need of other people into domination over them, means this is as discredited as the idea of harmony. Faced with the bankruptcy of empire, it becomes vital to develop the idea of a coming community that is neither a great machine (master/slave relations) or an organic whole (harmony between part and whole).[42]

(iii) Notes for a deep science movement to redirect science, engineering, and invention

A striking *Scientific American* editorial "The Control of Atomic Energy" (see Chapter 10) shows that in 1921 scientists were confronted by a clear choice between the different research directions and had a clear idea of the likely consequences. They could investigate those areas of nature most useful for developing solar power. This would be unlikely to lead to new weapons. Or, they could investigate areas of nature useful for nuclear power. They saw this could very well lead to a weapon of unprecedented destructive power. Writing immediately after the First World War, the editors clearly saw the horrendous possibilities. Yet they were so strongly caught up by the ideas propagated by the pure science movement, and reiterated by the organized research movement, that they did not believe it really was possible to stop the development of such knowledge. In the end the best they could come up with was a hope that by the time mankind had acquired it, humanity would have risen to a higher moral level.

The partial success of the 1921 disarmament movement in opposing the development of the bomber/chemical weapon combination shows that such fatalism and such passivity was mistaken. The leaders of the chemical and air campaigns, as we have seen, had been trying to get Americans to support this direction of research. They had sought to convince them they were in immediate danger and that this was the only way they could protect themselves. At the same time they sought to discover new poison gases and to develop the technology to deliver them from the air. The disarmament movement successfully used the Washington Conference to prevent the chemical campaign allying itself with the air campaign, and to partially fragment the coalition between chemical manufactures, chemists, chemical engineers, and chemical warfare officers. In the years following the army general staff was able to marginalize the Chemical Warfare Service and starve it of funds. Research and development of the air/chemical combination was, if not altogether stopped, greatly slowed down. Stopping it would have required a disarmament treaty. Yet, as the later German research into nerve gases shows, the success of the disarmament movement remained limited in time and space. In Part 2 I explored one reason for this. In *The "Next War": An Appeal to Common Sense*, Will Irwin sought to gain a hearing for the movement among the elite by giving a twist to the elite's own story of America's entry into the First

World War. America had gone to war to defeat German autocracy. Now, Irwin argued, America's pursuit of naval superiority and the bomber/chemical combination showed she was in danger of repeating Germany's drive to dominate the world. If America was to continue to lead the world she had put her weight behind disarmament. The problem was that by endorsing the elite's own story of America's role in the world war, this prepared the way for the Harding administration to lead the public in a slightly different direction. This was done by making the Washington Conference an arms control conference, and by only inviting the victors of the First World War. The disarmament of Germany's chemical weapons and war planes imposed by America and the Allies at Versailles was not matched by America, France, Britain, Italy, and Japan. Instead, Root's Treaty on chemical weapons and submarines was a reiteration of the claim that Germany was to blame for the war. No actual chemical or air disarmament took place. More significantly, by inviting only the winners of the First World War, an opportunity to reverse the victors' peace imposed on Germany at Versailles was lost. Both failures smoothed the way for the Nazi Party, in the midst of the Great Depression, to play on German fear of attack by bombers carrying poison gas and the one-sidedness of the Versailles Treaty to gain and consolidate their grip on state power. The result was that the strong social coalition in support of the chemical/air weapon research which had been, partially, taken apart in the United States in the early 1920s was now reassembled in Germany in the early 1930s – and the discovery and industrial production of nerve gases followed.

The investigation into the pure science and applied science movement I have carried out in Part 2 places us in a position to see the second reason why the disarmament movement's success remained limited in time and space. Once again Will Irwin's The "Next War" (see Chapter 1) provides a good starting point. In it Irwin seeks to gain a hearing for chemical/air disarmament among scientists, engineers, and inventors by retelling the pure science and the organized research stories. The pure science story claims that scientists are driven by a concern for truth for its own sake. The applied science, or organized research story, adds to that a claim that scientists are also driven by a concern to aid humanity. I have used the word "drive" to underscore their claim that these are strong forces that will prevail unless other, equally strong forces, are at work. Irwin argues that 22 April 1915, when Germany first used poison gas, is as important in human history as 12 October 1492 or 4 July 1776. This is because it is the date when the forces of German autocracy and militarism turn scientists towards destruction and away from their natural tendency towards the discovery of truth for its own sake or for the sake of human betterment. The danger, Irwin underscored, is that as the wealthiest and most powerful nation American post-war research into the poison gas/bomber combination is repeating Germany's distortion of science's natural tendency. The result will be an arms race leading to a war in which the new forces of science may very well destroy civilization itself. To stop this happening American scientists, engineers, and inventors should absolutely opposed continued chemical/air weapon research and insist that America takes the lead in disarming these weapons. Through retelling the scientists' and engineers' own story, then, Irwin directs their hostility against a particular direction of research. The problem is that this tactic also limits the capacity of the imperative to end terror to call into question scientific and technological practice. This is because the scientists' and engineers' own story about science exempts, from the start, the possibility that the *main* directions of scientific research and technological development have been established by scientists', engineers' and inventors' interests in religious, state, military, and commercial power, and their collaboration with priests, statesmen, military officers, and businessmen with the same interests. It forecloses the possibility that far from turning scientists away from truth, or inventors and engineers away from technical creativity, it is the alliances they have actively forged with these groups which have enabled them to discover the key truths of modern science and to make the key inventions of modern technology. And that it is these truths and inventions which, in turn, have enabled them to reinforce their alliances with statesmen, priests, military officers, and businessmen. This would mean that the story that pure science was temporarily diverted from the search for the truth for its own sake, and that applied science was temporarily diverted from its search for human betterment, has the world turned upside-down. It would mean that what the war showed was not a diversion from the main tendency of science and technology, but one of the main tendencies themselves. The post-war focus on poison gas would fit in with this upside-down world. It makes it easy to suggest that the war showed that science and technology had been recently and temporarily diverted from their main aims. This is not so easy to do with artillery and high explosives. There is a strong case to be made that the incredible violence of the artillery barrages on the Somme, at Ypres, and elsewhere on the Western Front did not happen because science had been recently and temporarily diverted towards war, but took place because for hundreds of years some of the main directions of science, such as mechanics and chemistry, have been driven by a concern to solve artillery problems. This arose because many scientists, like Galileo, actively sought out military support by promising solutions to artillery problems, just as many military officers, like Napoleon, actively sought scientists' help to solve artillery problems.

The dominance of the story that war showed a recent deviation from the central tendencies of science and technology had large consequences. It meant that the imperative to end the repetition of terror was solely focused on correcting the alleged deviation. There could be, clearly, from this point of view no need to investigate the main tendencies to see whose interests they served nor any need to redirect them. We can now understand the problem posed by Irwin's retelling of the pure and applied/organized science stories. On the one hand, it was an effective way of turning scientists', engineers', and inventors' hostility against a particular direction of research. On the other hand, through appealing to the dominant ontology of science and scientists to gain a hearing among these groups, Irwin prevented the imperative to end terror calling into question the main directions of science and technology. This left the way open for Elihu Root to carry out a further restriction of the imperative. He did this through his Treaty reiterating international law banning the use of chemical weapons, and tightening international law forbidding submarines to sink civilian ships. Through framing the Treaty in this way Root reiterated the American scientists' story that Germany was the origin of the First World War, and that it was Germany's desire for world domination which had turned science from its natural tendency to contribute to progress. This had two effects. The first related to the present. It ensured that hostility to poison gas did not lead to Elihu Root's and George Hale's own efforts to use war to strengthen the links between science, engineering, the state, the military, and capital being called into question. It covered over the convergence between the American and the German national organization of science, and scientific organization of the nation. The second effect relates to the past. It ensured that hostility to poison gas did not lead Americans to begin to question the pure science and organized research movements' story that science had its origins in drives for the truth for its own sake and in desires for human betterment. There would be no alternative history which examined how modern science and technology may have grown out of collaboration between scientists, inventors, and engineers on the one hand, and the state and capital's interest in power and profit on the other hand.

Both Irwin and Root take up and rearticulate the story that American scientists and engineers had developed in a way which forestalls, in advance, any claims that poison gas, high-explosives, submarines, machine guns, bomber aircraft, and other First World War weapons showed the bankruptcy of the claim that science was part of a harmonious circle that was leading to human progress. The scientists and engineers did so by using precisely the same moves that the patrician reformers used to prevent the war calling into question the project of empire – placing the blame entirely outside the main directions of scientific research and technological development by making Germany the scapegoat, and then claiming that such science, invention, and engineering was now more urgently needed than before to defeat Germany. As the case of Henry Rowland shows for the pure scientists, and George Hale and Elihu Root shows for the organized researchers, the moves to rescue the two projects to some extent coincided and can only be separated for analytic purposes.

The years after the atomic attack on Japan saw a similar use of the pure science and applied science stories to prevent the main research directions of contemporary science from being called into question. In 1921 scientists already knew that research in nuclear physics would very likely lead to weapons of unprecedented power. This meant they could have decided to concentrate on other areas of research, such as solar power, so that nuclear physics did not develop to the point where a bomb was no longer a theoretical conjecture but something that very likely could be made. After the atomic bomb pure science ideology was retrospectively invoked to suggest that there never had been such an opportunity.[43] This was done by giving a false origin for the atomic bomb. It was presented as being an application of the fundamental principles of relativity discovered by Einstein's pursuit of truth for its own sake. In pursuing this research Einstein did not know that it might have such applications. This meant that responsibility for the atomic bomb lay with Nazi Germany because it had forced physicists to work out how to apply relativity to the building of an atomic bomb, and with the Truman administration which decided to use the atomic bomb. This story makes the abuse of scientific knowledge look as if it is the whole problem. In fact the scientific origins of the atomic bomb did not have much to do with relativity at all. Instead its beginnings lay in Rutherford and Soddy's 1903 calculation of how much energy was released by radioactive decay. Rutherford immediately saw that the very large amount of energy released might form an explosive. "Could the proper detonator be found," Rutherford remarked, "it was just conceivable that a wave of atomic disintegration might be started through matter, which would indeed make this old world vanish in smoke."[44] It was through continuing to pursue experimental investigations into nuclear fission over forty years that nuclear physicists, well aware that they might be creating the knowledge needed to build a weapon of unprecedented power, transformed the idea of an atomic bomb from a theoretical conjecture, to a probability worth investing in, to a working nuclear explosive. The fact that they continued to pursue this research in the wake of the First World War testifies to the extraordinary grip of the idea that all scientific research is good because it contributes to knowledge and to human progress, and to the success of the scientific community in preventing the First World War calling these beliefs into question by locating the main cause of modern weaponry outside of science – in the American case by locating it in German autocracy's turning of science towards destruction.

If the imperative to resist terror is not to be tamed as it was after the world wars, scientists, engineers, and inventors must break with the ontology of science and the scientist at the heart of the pure science and the organized research movements. We are, I believe, in a moment when it is clear that many of the existing directions taken by scientific research and technological development are disastrous for the majority of mankind, and when new social movements are appearing to challenge them. A new world is in the process of coming into being. Yet the enormous power built up by the groups that support the existing directions, their sense that they have that power as a right, and their knowledge of how to use that power means that, unless we act decisively, that new order will be destroyed before it can establish itself. At the centre of such action must be an alliance between scientists, engineers, and inventors who see the need to change the direction of research and development, and rising social movements who are challenging the return of empire in the name of liberty and democracy. What is at stake is the enormous potential of scientific curiosity, engineering efficiency, and inventive creativity identified by Willis Whitney when scientists, engineers, and inventors cooperate together and have the instruments and machines they need. Whitney underscored what could be achieved in such circumstances in his experience as director of America's first industrial research laboratory at General Electric. He claimed that, given intelligent cooperation, as more elements came together what was achieved increased exponentially. What could be achieved by two people was not twice but four times what could be achieved by one. I will end by setting out some ideas for a global deep science movement which, in the same way that the deep ecology movement is committed to identifying and challenging the fundamental causes of environmental destruction, is committed to changing the directions of science and technology where, in seeking to answer human needs or satisfy human curiosity, they are actually leading to relations of control.

First, scientists, engineers, and inventors must take responsibility for the direction of scientific research and technological development
This means appreciating that scientists, engineers and inventors are first and foremost heterogeneous engineers who actively establish a direction for their research and development. As I have shown by looking at the history of the poison gas/bomber aircraft system, this involves scientists and engineers persuading social groups to support one direction rather than another, looking for discoveries and trying out technical possibilities that fit these social groups' ideas of their interests, and developing mechanisms that make it difficult for both the social and natural elements they have brought together to oppose the direction they have chosen.

Second, scientists, engineers, and inventors must seek to discover what is at stake in the direction of research and development they are pursuing by looking either at past, or at marginalized, science and technology
It is not always immediately clear what social interests are supported by a particular line of research and development. Does an investigation in Newtonian astronomy supports one set of social interests rather than another? At first sight it is not clear that it does. It appears to be an example of the pursuit of knowledge for its own sake. Equally it is not always clear that there are alternative directions that research and development could take. Is there any alternative to research into

new antibiotics as a way of curing new antibiotic-resistant tuberculosis? A look at history shows that scientists and engineers have actively persuaded powerful social groups to support research into the kind of problems that Newtonian astronomy claims it can provide answers to. Thus Galileo sought to gain the support of the Medici princes for his investigations into the laws governing matter in motion by suggesting it would lead to improvements in ballistics. Equally, Newton's own claims that the solar system needed to be constantly corrected by God ensured it received warm support from an English monarchy concerned to argue that the king was essential to correct societies' constant tendency to depart from equilibrium.[45] More recently the pure science movement persuaded the American elite to provide support for such research by offering to vindicate the elite's claim to be a meritocracy which should govern mankind. Vice versa, discoveries in fields such as astronomy do, indeed, continue to contribute to the stock of knowledge useful for improving military weapons. Today star sighting gives the submarine-based Trident nuclear missile the potential to hit a target the other side of the earth with amazing accuracy. Looking at marginalized science and technology can provide similar insights. In Europe and America the idea that phages, viruses that live on bacteria, could provide a cure for disease was abandoned in the interwar period. It continued to be funded, however, in the Soviet Union. The result is that it now provides an alternative approach to dealing with diseases that have become resistant to antibiotics. This is because the virus that lives on a bacteria, and can be used to kill it, is a living organism that mutates as fast as the bacteria it lives off does.

Third, the state's development of nuclear weapons as instruments of terror shows the vital necessity of scientists, engineers, and inventors making use of their skill as heterogeneous engineers to aid the disarmament movement
Changing the directions of research and development means, first and foremost, blocking currently dominant directions. This is because the momentum that has been built up by existing scientific research directions and associated technological systems with them means that their supporters are well placed to strangle at birth any alternative. What opposing such systems means in practice can be seen from the leading role played by dissenting scientists, engineers, and inventors in the struggle for nuclear disarmament. They have helped form and strengthen the nuclear disarmament movement. They have used their scientific and technological expertise to show that deterrence is no guarantee against a nuclear war. They have used research into geophysics and seismology to argue that a Comprehensive Nuclear Test Ban Treaty (CTBT) could be monitored. Their knowledge of nuclear physics has been essential to showing why a CTBT would be an effective step towards nuclear disarmament. More recently the social scientist Donald McKenzie has reinforced this argument by pointing out the key role of tacit knowledge in nuclear weapon construction, and also shown that a CTBT

could be strengthened by further treaties banning the testing needed if the military is to be certain that long-range missiles can be accurate enough to be used in a nuclear first strike.[46] The speed and force with which the nuclear weapons laboratories, and their allies in the presidency and the Congress, have moved to prevent the movement for nuclear disarmament achieving a CTBT is instructive. It underscores the fact that unless scientists, engineers, and inventors on the one side, and their allies in the nuclear disarmament movement on the other, drive the debate by anticipating the competition we will continue to have a world dominated and divided by nuclear terror.

Fourth, it is just as vital to contest big business's use of patents, industrial research, and other means to determine the direction of research and invention so as to secure the maximum return on capital invested in existing technological systems

The significance of big business's ability to control the direction and pace of technological advance has been huge. Thus in recent decades, as Zygmunt Bauman in his pathbreaking book on globalization has shown, business has been able to combine jet travel and telecommunications so as to take its strategy-making super for profits by taking advantage of opportunities to manipulate the market to new heights. The other side of big business's development of its own global mobility has been the development of new ways to keep the world's poor in their ghettos. The logical conclusion of this strategy of spatial confinement can be seen in the emergence of America's free enterprise prison system as a way of containing the largely African-American underclass.[47] Here, however, I will concentrate on the corporate takeover of world agriculture. The post-First World War transformation of chemical weapons into pesticides contributed to the emergence of a far wider strategy to remake every aspect of world agriculture. The patrician reformers seized advantage of war to block the emergence of the Populists, who argued farmers' interests should not be subordinated to the banks, as a national political force. America's chemical manufacturers then used the huge profits they had made from high-explosives to take over agriculture. Supported by chemists like Arthur Little they claimed that if America was to feed a growing population, an agricultural revolution was essential. Large-scale capital-intensive agriculture based on scientific knowledge must replace the family farm. The same technologies which had been used to wage war on man, high explosives, tanks, and fertilizers, would now be transformed into fertilizers, tractors, and pesticides to wage war on famine. The result has been a global takeover of agriculture based on an alliance between the nation-state, big business, and scientists and engineers developing the appropriate knowledge and technology. The application of biotechnology to agriculture is simply the latest phase of this takeover. So successful has this been that it is now difficult for us to imagine that agriculture could have developed in any other way. What we need to imagine is how agriculture might have developed if there had been an alliance between the Populists, scientists, engineers, and independent inventors. The rise of organic farming within America, and the emergence of farmers' movements opposed to the corporate takeover of the world's food supply, shows that the struggle is by no means over.

Fifth, scientists, engineers, and inventors should ally themselves with disarmers, environmentalists, workers, and other groups outside the power elite in their demand for an equal say in which directions scientific research and technological development should proceed

All areas of our lives are now deeply affected by scientific knowledge and technological systems. This means that liberal democracy no longer has any meaning unless the citizens can determine the directions of research and development. There is no liberty unless the citizens can ensure that their freedoms are not taken away through false claims that this is the only way that society can deal with threats to life. The citizens can only be sure that this will not happen if they themselves, or associations they trust to act for them, can participate in decisions about the direction of scientific research and technological development. There is no democracy if such decisions are taken by scientists, engineers, and inventors on the one side, and elite groups on the other side, behind closed doors. Such decisions determine what the range of choices open to society are going to be. If the citizens are not included in making these decisions, then their role is reduced to deciding between a set of choices already determined by others. Scientists, engineers and inventors face a choice: whether or not to ally themselves with groups outside the elite who are seeking to extend liberty and democracy. If they do nothing they are, as I have shown in the preceding chapters, by the very fact of their position within the structure of society reinforcing the patrician reformers' programme for taming demands for liberty and democracy. In these circumstances vitally needed alternative directions of research and technological development will only be successful if scientists, engineers, and inventors join with groups outside the elite to break open the closed spaces where decisions about the direction of research are taken in the name of liberty and democracy.

Notes

Introduction

1 Burke Davis, *The Billy Mitchell Affair*, Random House, 1967, p. 115.
2 William Mitchell, *Winged Defence*, Putnam, 1925, p. xiv.
3 Mitchell, *Winged Defence*, pp. 25–26.
4 William Mitchell, *Skyways*, Lippincott, 1930, p. 187 and p. 308.
5 Mitchell, *Skyways*, p. 263.
6 Mitchell, *Winged Defence*, p. 26.
7 Bruce Franklin, *War Stars: The Superweapon and American Imagination*, Oxford, 1988, p. 95.
8 Quoted in Franklin, *War Stars*, p. 98.
9 Quoted in Franklin, *War Stars*, p. 98.
10 Quoted in Franklin, *War Stars*, p. 99.
11 Michael Sherry, *The Rise of American Air Power: the Creation of Armageddon*, Yale, 1987.
12 David Holloway, *Stalin and the Bomb*, Yale, 1994.

1 The Infant Stage

1 Amos Fries and Clarence West, *Chemical Warfare*, McGraw-Hill, 1921, pp. 11–12.
2 On fantasy and technology see Susan Buck-Morss, *The Dialectic of Seeing: Walter Benjamin and the Arcades Project*, MIT, 1989; for historical works on fantasy, technology, and weapons see Bruce Franklin, *War Stars: The Superweapon and the American Imagination*, Oxford, 1988, and Thomas Leonard, *Above the Battle: War-Making in America from Appomattox to Versailles*, Oxford, 1978, and Michael Sherry, *The Rise of American Air Power: The Creation of Armageddon*, Yale, 1987.
3 Fries, *Chemical Warfare*, p. 383; See also Fries, "Chemical Warfare Inspires Peace", *Bulletin of Chemical Warfare*, (Henceforth *BCW*), vol.6, no.5, 5 March 1921, p. 4.
4 Amos Fries, "Sixteen Reasons Why the Chemical Warfare Service Must Be a Separate Department of the Army", *BCW*, vol.2, no.7, 1 January 1920, p. 2.
5 "Editorial", *BCW* vol.6, no.12, 20 June 1921, p. 1.
6 *An Atlas of Gas Poisoning*, Medical Research Committee, British Government, 1918.

7 Their use of statistics is shown to be highly selective by William Irwin in the 9th edition of his book, *The "Next War": An Appeal to Common Sense*, Dutton, 1921, p. 37.

8 Norris Hall, *The Next War*, Harvard, 1925, p. 34.

9 Editorial. *BCW*, vol.7, no.9, 21 November 1921, p. 1.

10 Sherry, *The Rise of American Air Power*, p. 30.

11 William McNeill, *The Pursuit of Power: Technology, Armed Force, and Society Since AD 1000*, Blackwell, 1983, pp. 262–299; Paul Rogers, *Losing Control: Global Security in the Twenty-first Century*, Pluto, 2000; and R.N. Lebow and J.G. Stein, *We All Lost the Cold War*, Princeton, 1994.

12 The full history can be found in Robert Cuff, *The War Industries Board: Business-Government Relations during World War 1*, Baltimore, 1973; Cuff, "American Mobilization for War 1917–1945: Political Culture vs Bureaucratic Administration", in *Mobilization for Total War*, ed. N.R. Dreisziger, Wilfred Laurier University Press, 1981; Paul Koistinen, *Mobilising for Modern War: The Political Economy of American Warfare, 1865–1919*, Kansas, 1997, p. 114–136; and M.W. Coulter, *The Senate Munitions Inquiry of the 1930s: Beyond the Merchants of Death*, Greenwood, 1997.

13 Elihu Root, "The Organization of Research", *Bulletin of the National Research Council*, Hereafter, *BNRC* vol.1, no.1, October, 1919, p. 10.

14 Ibid.

15 Peyton March, *The Nation at War*, Doubleday, 1932, pp. 331–336.

16 See Judith Butler's discussion of authority and speech acts in her *Excitable Speech: A Politics of the Performative*, Routledge, 1997, especially pp. 127–163.

17 Fries, *Chemical Warfare*, pp. 364–365.

18 For an account of the 1921 disarmament movement see Leonard Hoag, *Preface to Preparedness: The Washington Disarmament Conference and Public Opinion*, Washington: The American Council on Public Affairs, 1941. On the Washington Conference more generally see Harold and Margret Sprout, *Toward a New Order of Sea Power*, Princeton, 1940, and Thomas Buckley, *The United States and the Washington Conference*, Tennessee, 1970.

19 Harriet Brown, "Women to the Rescue", *The Nation*, vol.112, no.2902, 16 February 1921, pp. 261–2.

20 Irwin, *The "Next War"*, p. 37.

21 Ibid., p. 27.

22 Ibid., p. 28.

23 Ibid., p. 17.

24 Ibid., p. 145.

25 Ibid., p. 137.

26 Ibid., p. 151.

27 Ibid., p. 161.

28 Fries, "Extracts from the Annual Report", *CWB*, vol.10, no.12, 15 December 1924, p. 9.

29 See Butler, *Excitable Speech*, and Jean-Francois Lyotard's *The Differend*, Minnesota, 1989.

30 Lyotard, *The Differend*, p. xi, 9.

31 On the naval arms race see McNeill, *The Pursuit of Power*, pp. 262–306, and Eric Hobsbawm, *The Age of Empire 1875–1914*, Pantheon, 1987, pp. 302–327.

32 Frederick Brown, *Chemical Warfare*, Greenwood, 1968, pp. 61–72. The general account of the Conference is from Hoag's *Preface to Preparedness*.

33 P. Fritzsche, "Machine Dreams: Airmindedness and the Reinvention of Germany", *The American Historical Review*, vol.98, no.3 June 1993, pp. 685–705.

34 Lyotard, *The Differend*, p. 11.

2 The Marked Leaders of the World

1 Editorial, *BCW*, vol.7, no.7, 20 October 1921, p. 5.

2 Jean-Francois Lyotard, *The Postmodern Condition: A Report on Knowledge*, Minnesota, 1989, pp. 18–37; and Lyotard, "Missive on Universal History", in *The Postmodern Explained*, Minnesota, 1993, pp. 26–27.

3 C. Herty, "The Reserves of the Chemical Warfare Service". *Reprint and Circular Series of the National Research Council*, 16 February 1921, pp. 4–5.

4 For full details see Stanley Cohen, "A Study of Nativism: The Red Scare of 1919–1920", *Political Science Quarterly*, vol.79, March, 1964.

5 Editorial. *BCW*, vol.2, no.12, 5 February 1920, p. 2.

6 The dominance of the liberal meta-narrative of progress is shown by the fact that during the war Theodore Roosevelt on one side of the elite debate, and Woodrow Wilson on the other, made their case for different policies by rearticulating this story in different ways.

7 Lyotard, "Missive on Universal History", pp. 26–27.

8 Editorial. "Do Not Lose the Perspective", *BCW*, vol.5, no.7, 5 April 1921, p. 1.

9 Editorial. "Snap Out of It", *BCW*, vol.5, no.8, 20 October 1920, p. 1.

10 Ibid.

11 Fries, *Chemical Warfare*, pp. 438–439.

12 Fritz Haber, *The Poisonous Cloud*, Oxford, 1986.

13 Frederick Brown, *Chemical Warfare*, Greenwood, 1968, p. 29.

14 Haber, *The Poisonous Cloud*, p. 256.

15 Ibid., p. 135.

16 Brown, *Chemical Warfare*, p. 31.

17 Benedict Crowell, *Hearings on HR* 8078, 1804, quoted in Brown, *Chemical Warfare*, p. 32.

18 Haber, *The Poisonous Cloud*, p. 168.

19 Ibid., p. 167.

20 Article 171 of the Treaty of Versailles stated: "The use of asphyxiating, poisonous, or other gases and all analogous liquids, materials, or devices, being prohibited, their manufacture and importation are strictly forbidden in Germany. The same applies to materials specially intended for the manufacture, storage, and use of said products or devices."

21 Quoted in Brown, *Chemical Warfare*, pp. 75–76.

22 The Chemical Foundation was set up during the war to organize the sale of German chemical patents seized to American manufacturers.

23 Addison, J.T. "Address", *BCW*, vol.7, no.9, 21 November 1921, p. 6.

24 On the classic republic and the role of those who have died risking their lives for its ideals see Lyotard, *The Differend*, pp. 99–100 and 20–21.

25 I owe this insight to Dimitri D'Andrea.

26 Fries, *Chemical Warfare*, p. 365.

27 Editorial. *BCW*, vol.7, no.9 21 November 1921, p. 1.

28 Ibid., p. 1.

3 The German Outlaw

1 Editorial, "A Time for Gathering", *JIEC*, vol.13, no.8 August 1921, p. 670.

2 G.F. Whittemore, "World War 1, Poison Gas Research, and the Ideals of American Chemists", *Social Studies of Science*, vol.5, no.2, May, 1975.

3 E.L. Nichols, "Science and the Practical Problems of the Future", *Science*, vol.29, no.731, 1 January 1909, pp. 8–9; William Walker, "The Spirit of Alchemy in Modern Industry", *Science*, vol.33, no.859, 16 June 1911, p. 918; Leo Baekeland, "Science and Industry", *Science*, vol.31, no.805, 3 June, 1910, p. 848; Arthur Little, "Natural Resources and Manufacture", *JIEC*, vol.1, no.2, February, 1909, p. 62; V.C. Alderson, "Technical Education at Home and Abroad", *Nature*, vol.67, no.1737, 12 February 1903, p. 356; E.L. Nichols, "Science and the Practical Problems of the Future", *Science*, vol.29, no.731, 1 January 1909, p. 5; F.B. Raymond, "The Value of Research to Industry", *Science*, vol.40, no.1042 18 December 1914, p. 873; D.M. Grosh, "What's the Matter with the American Chemist?" *JIEC*, vol.5, no.8, August 1913, p. 692; G.A. Mayer, "Our Universities and Research", *Science*, vol.32, no.817, 26 August 1910, p. 260; D. Kinley, "Democracy and Scholarship", *Science*, vol.28, no.720, 16 October 1908, p. 497; Arthur Little, "The Chemist and the Community", *Science*, vol.25, no.643, 26 April 1907, p. 648.

4 Little, "Natural Resources and Manufacture", p. 62.

5 Kinley, "Democracy and Scholarship", p. 497.

6 Alderson, "Technical Education at Home and Abroad", pp. 356–357.

7 A. Prill, "Campaign for American Dyestuff Industry", *JIEC*, vol.6, no.11, November 1914, p. 45.

8 Editorial, "The Seattle Meeting", *JIEC*, vol.7, no.10, October 1915, pp. 818–819.

9 The uneasy conscience of chemists can be seen in James Withrow's December 1915 address to the American Association for the Advancement of Science. This combines remarks about the horrors of war with a lyrical account of the construction of explosive plants on an "undreamed of scale" now "mushrooming" across America. James Withrow, "The American Chemist and the War's Problems", *JIEC*, vol.8, no.5, May 1916, p. 455.

10 Francis Garvan, "Washington Letter", *JIEC*, vol.12, no.1, January 1920, p. 91.

11 Editorial, "A Victory of Arms, Not Yet of Ideals", *JIEC*, vol.10, no.12, December 1918, p. 66; Editorial, "Preparations for After the War", *JIEC*, vol.10, no.11, November 1918, p. 878; Editorial, "Future Arms", *JIEC*, vol.11, no.6, June, 1919, p. 506; Editorial, "A New Declaration of Independence", *JIEC*, vol.11, no.8, August 1919, p. 718.

12 Francis Garvan, "Industrial Germany – Her Methods and Their Defeat", *JIEC*, vol.11, no.6, June 1919, p. 574.

13 Ibid.

14 Francis Garvan, "Washington Letter", p. 91.

15 Francis Garvan, "Report of the Alien Property Custodian on the Chemical Industry", *JIEC*, vol.11, no.4, April 1919, p. 355.

16 Editorial, "A Call to Service", *JIEC*, vol.13, no.6, June, 1921, p. 503.

17 Lefebvre was on the staff of the British dyestuff corporation and therefore had an interest in painting a picture of a German threat which would gain British government support for its dye industry, see Haber, *The Poisonous Cloud*, p. 287.

18 Victor Lefebvre, *The Riddle of the Rhine*, 1921, Collins, pp. 255–256.

19 Giovanni Arrigi, "Three Hegemonies of World Capitalism", *Gramsci, Historical Materialism, and International Relations*, Stephen Gill ed. Cambridge, 1993, p. 176; Eric Hobsbawm, *The Age of Empire 1875–1914*, Pantheon, 1987, pp. 302–327.

20 Nicholas Stargardt, *The German Idea of Militarism: Radical and Socialist Critics 1866–1914*, Cambridge, 1994, pp. 141–147.

21 Haber, *The Chemical Industry 1900–1930: International Growth and Change*, Oxford, 1971, p. 181.

22 For an excellent account of Social Democratic Party opposition to German militarism see Stargardt's *The German Idea of Militarism: Radical and Socialist Critics*.

23 R.D. Zucker, "Germany's Industrial Position", *JIEC*, vol.11, no.8, August 1919, p. 777.

24 Haber, *The Poisonous Cloud*, Oxford, 1986, p. 287.

25 Haber, *The Chemical Industry*, Oxford, 1971, p. 283.

26 Editorial. "A Dyestuff Section of the American Chemical Society", *JIEC*, vol.10, no.9, September 1918, p. 674.

27 These difficulties were later emphasized by the Chemical Warfare Service itself. See Augustin Prentiss, *Chemicals in War*, McGraw-Hill, 1937, pp. 515–523.

28 This is Barraclough's view in *The Origins of Modern Germany*, Blackwell, 1949, p. 446, where he asserts that: "the die was, as early as 1919, already cast".

29 A.J.P. Taylor, *The Origins of the Second World War*, Hamish Hamilton, 1981, p. 59.

30 This was the starting point for Wilson's argument that the war had to end in a peace without victory. See Arthur Link, *Woodrow Wilson, Revolution, War and Peace*, Harlan Davidson, 1979, p. 23.

31 Marc Ferro, *The Great War 1914–1918*, Routledge, 1973, p. 226.

32 W. Haynes, *American Chemical Industry*, vol.2, Nostrand, 1945, pp. 18–19.

33 Haber, *The Chemical Industry*, p. 214.

34 Haynes, *American Chemical Industry*, vol.2.

35 A.W. Coulter, *The Senate Munitions Inquiry of the 1930s: Beyond the Merchants of Death*, Greenwood, 1997, p. 42.

36 Haber, *The Chemical Industry*, p. 256.

37 The story can be found in G. Meyer-Thurow, "The Industrialization of Invention: A Case Study from the German Chemical Industry", *ISIS*, vol.73, 1982, pp. 363–381; and J.J. Beer, "Coal Tar Dye Manufacture and the Origins of the Modern Industrial Research Laboratory", *ISIS*, vol.49, 1958, pp. 123–131.

38 Haber, *The Chemical Industry*, pp. 179–180.

39 Michael Palmer, "Report of the Alien Property Custodian on the Chemical Industry", *JIEC*, vol.11, no.4, April 1919, p. 357; see also Editorial. "A Time for Gathering", *JIEC*, vol.13, no.8, August 1921, p. 670.

40 Palmer, "Report of the Alien Property Custodian on the Chemical Industry", p. 357.

41 Cable, Garvan for Bradley, Palmer, 19 April 1919, no sub, Exhibit 4874D, U.S. Senate, *Hearings, Special Committee Investigating the Munitions Industry pursuant to S 206*, 74th Cong., 2nd. Sess., 1936, Part 39, p. 13456. Quoted in Brown, *Chemical Warfare*, Greenwood, 1968, pp. 54–55.

42 Report of the Activities of the Chemical Industry, n.d., Exhibit 913, U.S. Senate, *Hearings, Special Committee Investigating the Munitions Industry pursuant to S 206*, 74th Cong., Sess., 1936, hereafter, *Nye Committee*, 11, 2400–01, 2563; quoted in Brown, *Chemical Warfare*, pp. 57–58.

43 Exhibit 914, *Nye Committee*, 11, 2564–68; quoted in Brown, *Chemical Warfare*, p. 59.

44 On "underdetermination" see Barry Barnes, David Bloor and John Henry, *Scientific Knowledge: A Sociological Analysis*, Athlone, 1996, pp. 18–45.

45 I take the term from Judith Butler. See her *Gender Trouble*, Routledge, 1990, p. 65. The locus classicus for this analysis is the first volume of Michel Foucault's *The History of Sexuality*.

46 Peter Fritzsche, "Machine Dreams: Airmindedness and the Reinvention of Germany", *The American Historical Review*, vol.98, no.3, June 1993, pp. 685–705.

47 Ibid., p. 700.

48 Ibid., p. 709.

49 Ibid., pp. 708–709.

4 A New Declaration of Independence

1 Jefferson's use of the word "independence" in *The Declaration of Independence* comes from the neo-Roman theory that royal prerogative and freedom are incompatible. The neo-Roman theory proclaimed that freedom means not only the enjoyment of rights, but also the certainty that these rights cannot be taken by the ruler's exercise of prerogative. The neo-Roman theory proclaimed that without the latter certainty men were no more than slaves. See Quentin Skinner, *Liberty before Liberalism*, Cambridge, 1998. The Constitution does not explicitly rule out the president's exercise of prerogative. The way is left open for the president, as commander-in-chief, to act against the law when he knows that his actions are likely to be agreed to by the other branches of the federal government because they will agree with him that there really was a danger that required such action. In leaving the Constitution vague on this point, while making a great noise about the Constitution's checks and balances, its authors were able to present it to the public as designed to prevent the return of royal prerogative while at the same time allowing the president wide scope to act against threats to the rule of the national elite. I discuss the structure of the Constitution further in the conclusion to Part 2. On the Constitution and presidential power to deal with emergencies see Bernard Manin, "Checks, Balances, and Boundaries: The Separation of Powers in the Constitutional Debate of 1787", in *The Invention of the Modern Republic*, ed. Biancamaria Fontana, Cambridge, 1994.

2 On sovereignty see Reinhart Koselleck, *Critique and Crisis: Enlightenment and the Pathogenesis of Modern Society*, Berg, 1988; Carl Schmitt, *Political Theology: Four Chapters on the Concept of Sovereignty*, MIT, 1985; Georgio Agamben, *Homo Sacer: Sovereign Power and Bare Life*, Stanford, 1998; John McCormick, *Carl Schmidt's Critique of Liberalism: Against Politics as Technology*, Cambridge, 1999, pp. 149–152; Jean-Luc Nancy, "War, Law, Sovereignty – Techné", in Verena Conley, ed., *Rethinking Technologies*, Minnesota, 1993; Michael Hardt and Antonio Negri, *Empire*, Harvard, 2000, pp. 69–136; and Cynthia Weber, *Simulating Sovereignty: Intervention, the State, and Symbolic Exchange*, Cambridge, 1995.

3 John Locke, *Second Treatise of Government*, Cambridge, 1989, pp. 374–375.
4 Alexander Hamilton, *The Federalist Papers*, no.23, Mentor, 1999, p. 121.
5 Hamilton, *The Federalist Papers*, no.23., p. 123.
6 Hamilton, *The Federalist Papers*, no.26, p. 141.
7 James Madison, *The Federalist Papers*, no.41, p. 226.
8 The history Burke Davis, *The Billy Mitchell Affair*, Random House, 1967.
9 Fries, "Chemical Warfare – Past and Future", *BCW*, vol.8, no.7, 15 July 1922, pp. 2–5.
10 Fries had, in fact, gone a long way towards undermining the chain of command. Not only had he been active outside the army in Congress and as a leader of the post-war chemical campaign, but he had also sought to foster rebellion within the army to the general staff and War Department. In a memorandum of 2 July 1919, circulated to the chiefs of service branches, almost certainly from Fries, the War Department general staff had been accused of taking the attitude that "every officer appearing before them, whether from a Staff Department or from another department of the Army, is overenthusiastic, incompetent, or purely deceptive in his statements". "The memo", according to chemical warfare historian Frederick Brown, "was a frank appeal for revolt against the General Staff." (Brown, *Chemical Warfare*, pp. 80–81). By arguing that the nation which does not develop new military technologies will inevitably be defeated, Fries gives the military commander who is in charge of the development of new weapons a sovereign right to by pass, break, or undermine the Constitutionally established authority when he judges that it is vital to the nations security to do so.
11 Fries, *Chemical Warfare*, pp. 437–438.
12 Ibid., p. 433.
13 Quoted in J. Paxman and R. Harris, *A Higher Form of Killing: the Secret Story of Gas and Germ Warfare*, 1982, Chatto and Windus, p. 43. Whether Britain actually did use aircraft dropping poison gas bombs to terrorize Afghan rebels is a disputed point, as records were either not kept or destroyed.
14 Fries, "Chemical Warfare Inspires Peace", *BCW*, vol.6, no.5, 5 March 1921, pp. 3–4.
15 Editorial, "Vision", *BCW*, vol.7, no.7, 20 October 1921, p. 5.
16 Fries, "Chemical Warfare Inspires Peace", p. 3.
17 Lee Lewis, "Is Prohibition of Gas Warfare Feasible?" *The Atlantic*, 1922, pp. 834–840.
18 Jean-Francois Lyotard, *Just Gaming*, Minnesota, 1989, pp. 107–109.
19 Bernard Manin, "Checks, balances and boundaries", p. 58.
20 Editorial. "A New Declaration of Independence", *JIEC*, vol.11, no.8, August 1919, p. 718.
21 The leaders of the campaign's own logic led them to themselves begin to call into question any sharp distinction between German autocracy and American liberal democracy. The logic of Fries's argument is that the only difference between Germany on the one side, and France, Britain, and America on the other, is that the Germans showed superior insight in developing and using chemical weapons, while Lee Lewis argues that the continued condemnation of Germany's use of chemical weapons is an irrational continuation of wartime propaganda which seized on her initiation of chemical weapons to demonize Germany. Fries, "Chemical Warfare Inspires Peace", p. 3; and Lewis, "Is Prohibition of Gas Warfare Feasible?" p. 840.
22 Michael Klare, *Rogue States and Nuclear Outlaws*, Hill and Wang, 1995, pp. 1–64.
23 Mary Kaldor, *The Imaginary War: Understanding the East–West Conflict*, Blackwell, 1990.
24 Donald MacKenzie and Graham Spinardi, "Tacit Knowledge and the Uninvention of Nuclear Weapons", *Knowing Machines: Essays on Technological Change*, MIT, 1998.
25 Quoted in J. Cabasso, "The Hidden Agenda of Nuclear Weapons Development in the United States", Paper read at Conference "Our Unsecure World", Stockholm, 27–28 October, p. 10.
26 J.H. Nuckholls, "The State of the Laboratory", *Energy and Technology Review*, July / August 1991, pp. 1–3.
27 "Why Are Nuclear Weapons Important? The Los Alamos Perspective", Remarks by Dr Stephen Younger, Associate Laboratory Director for Nuclear Weapons, June 21, 1999. Video obtained by Greg Mello, the Los Alamos Study Group.
28 H. Kristensen, "Targets of Opportunity", *Bulletin of the Atomic Scientists*, September–October, 1997, p. 22–28.

29 US Joint Chiefs of Staff. "Doctrine for Joint Theater Nuclear Operations", Joint Pub 3–12.1, 9 February 1996. Quoted in Kristensen, "Targets of Opportunity", p. 26.
30 W.S. Cohen, "The Military Requirements of Defense Strategy", *Annual Report to The President an Congress 2000*, Chapter 2. Quoted in Cabasso, "The Hidden Agenda", p. 6.
31 Nuckholls, "The State of the Laboratory", pp. 1–3.
32 Cabasso, "The Hidden Agenda", p. 14.
33 Air Force FY98 Space and Missile Technology Area Plan. See Cabasso, "The Hidden Agenda", p. 14.
34 Kristensen, "Targets of Opportunity", p. 27.
35 Kurt Goltfried, "Sowing Nuclear Misconception", *Nature*, vol.404, 13 January 2000.

5 Democratic Despotism

1   Cartoon, *The Crisis*, March 1916, p. 236.
2   Herbert Shapiro, *White Violence and the Black Response*, Massachusetts, 1988; and Stewart Tolnay and E.M. Beck, *A Festival of Violence: An Analysis of Southern Lynchings, 1882–1930*, Illinois, 1992.
3   John Thompson, *Reformers and War: American Progressive Publicists and the First World War*, Cambridge, 1987, pp. 91–93.
4   Alex De Tocqueville, *Democracy in America*, vol.2, bk. 4, ch. 5, Wordsworth, 1998, p. 356.
5   W.E.B. Du Bois, "The African Roots of War", *The Atlantic Monthly*, 1915, p. 711.
6   Ibid., p. 711.
7   Ibid., p. 708.
8   Ibid., p. 709.
9   Ibid., p. 709.
10 Ibid., p. 713.
11 Ibid., p. 712.
12 Ibid., p. 712.
13 Du Bois, "The Battle of Europe", in *The Crisis*, September 1916, pp. 216–217.
14 Ibid., pp. 216–217.
15 William McNeill, *The Pursuit of Power*, Blackwell, 1983, p. 143; see also Anthony Giddens, *The Nation-State and Violence*, Campus, 1987, pp. 222–223.
16 Ernesto Laclau and Chantal Mouffe, *Hegemony and Socialist Strategy: Towards a Radical Democratic Politics*, Verso, 1985, pp. 149–193.
17 Herman Melville, *Moby Dick*, ch. 26, Bantam, 1984, p. 113.
18 Ida Wells Barnet, quoted in Shapiro, *White Violence and the Black Response*, p. 121.

6 The Striking and Stupendous Spectacle

1   E.D. Baltzell, *The Protestant Establishment: Aristocracy and Caste in America*, Yale, 1987; Michael Pearlman, *To Make Democracy Safe for America: Patricians and Preparedness in the Progressive Era*, Illinois, 1984; Thomas Leonard, *Above the Battle: War-Making in America from Appomattox to Versailles*, Oxford, 1978; David Burton, *Theodore Roosevelt: Confident Imperialist*, Philadelphia, 1968; Richard Leopold, *Elihu Root and the Conservative Tradition*, Little Brown, 1954; William Widenor, Henry Cabot Lodge and the Search for an American Foreign Policy, California, 1980.
2   Baltzell, *The Protestant Establishment*, pp. 87–225.
3   Quoted in Pearlman, *To Make Democracy Safe for America*, p. 15.
4   Theodore Roosevelt, *The Winning of the West*, Putnam, 1889, p. 17.
5   Quoted in Pearlman, *To Make Democracy Safe for America*, p. 16.
6   Quoted in Pearlman, *To Make Democracy Safe for America*, p. 20.
7   Quoted in Pearlman, *To Make Democracy Safe for America*, p. 18.
8   Roosevelt, "Expansion and Peace", *The Strenuous Life*, Duckworth, 1911, p. 34.

9 Ibid., p. 30.

10 On John Locke and the Enlightenment production of the absolutist monster, see Koselleck's *Critique and Crisis*, pp. 53–61.

11 Alexis de Tocqueville, *Democracy in America*, book 2, part 4, Fontana, 1968; Georgio Agamben, *Homo Sacer: Sovereign Power and Bare Life*, Stanford, 1998.

12 Agamben, *Homo Sacer*, pp. 71–115.

13 Elihu Root, *The Yale Lectures on the Responsibility of Citizenship*, Yale, 1907, pp. 5–31.

14 Ibid., pp. 5–6.

15 Ibid., p. 9.

16 Ibid., p. 8.

17 Ibid., p. 10.

18 Ibid., p. 13.

19 Ibid., pp. 19–20.

20 Wilson shared Root and Roosevelt's belief in the value of the Roman ideal of sacrifice for the nation as a model Americans should emulate. Interestingly he tended to fuse it with Christ's sacrifice to redeem man from sin. See Wilson "Notes for a Religious Talk", *PWW*, Vol.10, 2 November 1899, p. 273, and Report of a Religious Talk, "Vital Morality", *PWW*, Vol.10, 3 November 1899, pp. 274–275.

21 Ibid., p. 13, and p. 20.

22 Ibid., p. 25.

23 Kenneth Grahame, *The Wind in the Willows*, Penguin, 1994, p. 43.

24 Ibid., p. 207.

25 Ibid., p. 219.

26 Agamben, *Homo Sacer*, pp. 104–111.

27 Woodrow Wilson, "The Modern Democratic State". 1 December 1885 *Papers of Woodrow Wilson*, (hereafter *PWW*), vol.5, Arthur Link, ed., Princeton, 1966, pp. 80–85.

28 Woodrow Wilson, "Democracy and Efficiency", 1 October 1900 *PWW*, vol.12, p. 10.

29 Ibid., p. 10.

30 Ibid., pp. 11–12.

31 Wilson, "Democracy and Efficiency", p. 12–13.

32 Woodrow Wilson, "The Ideals of America", 26 December 1901 *PWW*, 12, p. 208.

33 Ibid., p. 214.

34 Richard Welch, *Response to Imperialism*, Chapel Hill, 1979, pp. 45–47.

35 On Wilson's pre-war classification of states see Ido Oren, "The Subjectivity of the 'Democratic' Peace", *International Security*, vol.20, no.2 Fall 1995, pp. 147–184.

36 In the words of Thomas Paine: "As war is the system of government on the old construction the animosity which nations reciprocally entertain, is nothing more than what the policy of their governments excites, to keep up the spirit of the system . . . Man is not the enemy of man, but through the medium of a false system of government", in Thomas Paine, *Rights of Man* (1791) Citadel Press, 1974, p. 147.

37 R.L. Hanson, *The Democratic Imagination in America*, Princeton, 1985.

38 Oren, "The Subjectivity of the 'Democratic' Peace", pp. 169–171.

39 Wilson, "The Modern Democratic State", p. 63.

40 Aage Thorsen, *The Political Thought of Woodrow Wilson 1875–1910*, Princeton, 1988, gives the best account of Wilson's programme to remake democracy. The development of Wilson's program can be seen in: "The Modern Democratic State", pp. 61–92; "The Study of Administration", 1 November 1886, *PWW*, vol.5, pp. 359–380; *The State*, 3 June 1889, *PWW*, vol.6, pp. 253–266; "The Reconstruction of the Southern States", 2 March 1900 *PWW*, vol.11, pp. 459–479; "Democracy and Efficiency", 1 October 1900 *PWW*, vol.12, pp. 6–20; "The Real Idea of Democracy", 31 August 1901 *PWW*, vol.12, pp. 175–179; "The Ideals of America", 26 December 1901, *PWW*, vol.12, pp. 208–227; "A Memorandum on Leadership". 5 May 1902 *PWW*, vol.12, p. 365; "Education and Democracy". 4 May 1907 *PWW*, vol.17, pp. 131–136; "The President of the United States", in "Constitutional Government", *PWW*, vol.18, pp. 104–123.

41 Wilson, "Democracy and Efficiency", p. 17.

42 Ibid., p. 18–19.

43 Wilson, "Democracy and Efficiency", p. 10; see also Wilson, "Constitutional Government", *PWW*, 18, pp. 104–123.

44 Wilson, "Democracy and Efficiency", pp. 9–10; see also Wilson, "The Study of Administration". 1 November 1886 *PWW*, 5, pp. 359–380.

45 Thorsen, *The Political Thought of Woodrow Wilson*, pp. 176–177.

46 Wilson, "Democracy and Efficiency", p. 20.

47 Wilson, "Education and Democracy", pp. 131–136.

48 Ibid., p. 136.

49 Wilson, "Reconstruction of the Southern States", p. 475.

50 Wilson, "The Real Idea of Democracy", p. 178.

51 Wilson, "Democracy and Efficiency", p. 8.

52 Wilson, "The Modern Democratic State", p. 85.

53 Wilson, "Democracy and Efficiency", p. 19.

7 Bolts from the Blue

1 On the military progressives see: Russell Weigley, *History of the US Army*, Indiana, 1984, his *Towards an American Army*, Columbia, 1962, and his *The American Way of War*, Indiana, 1977; Samuel Huntington, *The Soldier and the State*, Harvard, 1985; and John Finnegan, *Against the Spectre of a Dragon*, Westport, 1975. For a history of great power politics and the origins of the First World War see Marc Ferro, *The Great War 1914–1918* Routledge, 1995; Eric Hobsbawn, "From Peace to War" in his *The Age of Empire 1875–1914*, Pantheon, 1987; Giovanni Arrigi, "Three Hegemonies of World Capitalism" in Stephen Gill, ed., *Gramsci, Historical Materialism, and International Relations*, Cambridge, 1987; and Giovanni Arrigi, *The Long Twentieth Century*, Verso, 1994.

2 J.B. Fry, "Origins and Progress of the Military Service Institution", *Journal of the Military Service Institution* Hereafter *JMSI*, vol.1, no.1, 1880.

3 J.M. Schofield, "Inaugural Address", *JMSI*, vol.1, no.1, 1880, p. 3.

4 Ibid., p. 6.

5 Ibid., p. 9.

6 Ibid., p. 11.

7 Fry, "Origins and Progress", p. 29.

8 J. Gibbon, "Danger from Lack of Preparation for War", *JMSI*, vol.11, no.1, 1890, p. 22; see also W.C. Sanger, "The organization and training of a national reserve for military service", *JMSI*, vol.10, 1889, p. 36.

9 Weigley, *History of the US Army*, p. 168.

10 Emory Upton, *The Military Policy of the United States*, 1904, Washington, p. VIII.

11 Arthur Wagner, "Popular Military Education", *JMSI*, vol.7, no.28, 1886, p. 397.

12 A.C. Redwood, "Democracy and Our Armies", *JMSI*, vol.38, no.140, 1906, p. 361.

13 Wagner, "Popular Military Education", *JMSI*, vol.28. 1886, p. 397. See also I. Rodic, "Military Conditions in the United States and Japan", *JMSI*, vol.41, no.148, 1907, pp. 12–27; P.D. Bunker, "What measures taken in time of peace will secure the best results in time of war through joint action of the Army and Navy", *JMSI*, vol.47, no.166, 1910, p. 11.

14 Upton, *The Military Policy of the United States*, p. XIII.

15 Ibid., p. XIV.

16 G.F. Price, "The Necessity for Closer Relations between the Army and The People", *JMSI*, vol.6, no.24, 1885, p. 319.

17 I. Taylor, "America and the Next World War", *JMSI*, 1917, p. 351.

18 G.F. Price, "The necessity for closer relations between the army and the people, and the best method to accomplish the result", *JMSI*, vol.6, no.24, 1885, p. 320. See also Arthur Wagner, "The Military Necessities of the United States and the Best Provisions for Meeting Them",

JMSI, vol.5. 1884, pp. 234–239; G.P. Cotton, "The proximity of England to the United States considered in reference to hostilities between the two nations", *JMSI*, vol.19, no.84 1896, pp. 441–442; G.M. Blech, "The Problem of our National Defence", *JMSI* vol.55, no.191, 1914, p. 259; H.R. Hickok, "Our Greatest National Need: A Rational Military Policy", *JMSI*, vol.55, no.191, 1914, p. 209.

19 William Mitchell, *JMSI*, vol.46, no.163, 1910, p. 25.

20 F.V. Green, "The Important Improvements in the art of war during the last twenty years", *JMSI*, vol.4, no.13, 1883; G.F. Price, "The necessity for closer relations between the army and the people", *JMSI*, vol.6, no.24 1885; Wagner, "The Military Necessities of the United States", *JMSI*, vol.5. 1884; T.M. Woodruff, "Our Northern Frontier", *JMSI*, vol.9, no.33, 1888; W.C. Sanger, "The Organization and Training of a National Reserve for Military Service", *JMSI*, vol.10. 1889; J. Gibson, "Danger From Lack of Preparation For War", *JMSI*, vol.11, no.1, 1890, p. 21; J.B. Bachelor, "A United States Army", *JMSI*, vol.13, no.55, 1892; S.E. Stuart, "The Army organization, best adapted to a Republican form of government", *JMSI*, vol.14, no.62, 1893; W.C. Sanger, "The Army organization, best adapted to a Republican form of government", *JMSI*, vol.14, no.66, 1893; G.P. Cotton, "The proximity of England to the United States", *JMSI*, vol.19, no.84, 1896; J.S. Pettit, "How far does democracy affect the organization of our armies, and how can its influence be most effectively utilized", *JMSI*, vol.38, no.139, 1906; C.E. Hampton, "The experiences of our army since the outbreak of war with Spain", *JMSI*, vol.36, no.135, 1905; P. Bunker, "What measures taken in time of peace will secure the best results in time of war through the joint action of the Army and Navy", *JMSI*, vol.47, no.166, 1910; W. Mitchell, *JMSI*, vol.46, no.163, 1910; G.M. Blech, "The problems of our national defence", *JMSI*, 1914; H.R. Hickok, "Our greatest national need: a rational military policy", *JMSI*, vol.55, no.191, 1914; and I. Taylor, "America and the Next World War", *JMSI*, 1917.

21 Price, G.F. "The necessity for closer relations between the army and the people", p. 321; Sanger, "The Organization and Training of a National Reserve", p. 37; Bachelor, "A United States Army", p. 55; S.E. Stuart, *JMSI*, vol.14, no.62, 1893, p. 238.

22 G.P. Scriven, "The Nicaragua Canal in its Military Aspects", *JMSI*, vol.15, no.67, 1894, p. 19.

23 A. Williams, "Readiness for War", *JMSI*, vol.21, no.79, 1897, p. 249.

24 H.M. Boies, "The Defense of a Free People in the Light of the Spanish War", *JMSI*, vol.24, no.97, 1999.

25 Boies, "The Defense of a Free People in the Light of the Spanish War", p. 17. On responsibilities as world power demanding a modern military see also E.R. Stuart, "The Organization and Function of a Bureau of Military Intelligence", *JMSI*, vol.32, no.121, 1903, p. 158; and T. Schwan, "The Coming General Staff", *JMSI*, vol.34, no.12, 1903, p. 9; Blech, "The Problem of our National Defence", p. 259; Hickok, "Our Greatest National Need", *JMSI*, vol.55, no.191, 1914, p. 209.

26 Weigley, *Towards an American Army*, pp. 199–217.

27 J.S. Pettit, "How Far does Democracy Affect the Organization of our Armies", *JMSI*, vol.38, no.139, 1906, pp. 3–9.

28 A.C. Redwood, "Democracy and Our Armies", *JMSI*, vol.38, no.140, 1906, p. 361.

29 Taylor, "America and the Next World War", p. 353.

30 I. Rodic, "Military conditions in the United States and Japan – A comparison", *JMSI*, vol.41, no.148, 1907, pp. 12–27.

31 Pettit, "How Far does Democracy Affect the Organization of our Armies", p. 32.

32 Bunker, "What measures taken in time of peace", pp. 11–12.

33 Cotton, G.P. "The proximity of England to the United States", *JMSI*, vol.29, no.84, 1896, p. 442.

34 Roosevelt, "Military Preparedness and Unpreparedness", *JMSI*, vol.26, no.103, 1900, p. 59.

35 Roosevelt, *The Winning of the West*, Putnam, 1889, p. 17.

36 James Chester, "The Invisible Factor", *JMSI*, vol.28, no.111, May, 1901, p. 360.

37 Ibid., pp. 360–361.

38 Ibid., p. 358.

39 Ibid., p. 360.

8 The Bankruptcy of Empire and its Relaunch

1 W.E.B. Du Bois, "The Battle of Europe", *The Crisis*, September, 1916, p. 216.
2 Elihu Root, "America on Trial". in Elihu Root *The War, Russian and Political Addresses*, Harvard, 1918, pp. 27–38.
3 For an account of the background to Root's speech see: Gabriel Kolko, *The Triumph of Conservatism: A Reinterpretation of American History, 1900–1916*, New York, 1977; John Finnegan, *Against the Spectre of a Dragon: The Campaign for American Military Preparedness, 1914–1917*, Westport, 1975; Michael Pearlman, *To Make Democracy Safe for America: Patricians and Preparedness in the Progressive Era*, Illinois, 1984; John Thompson, *Reformers and War: American Progressive Publicists and the First World War*, Cambridge, 1987; Emily Rosenberg, *Spreading the American Dream*, Hill & Wang, 1982; William Widenor, *Henry Cabot Lodge and the Search for American Foreign Policy*, University of California, 1980; David Burton, *Theodore Roosevelt: Confident Imperialist*, University of Pennsylvania Press, 1968; and R.W. Leopold, *Elihu Root and the Conservative Tradition*, Little Brown, 1954.
4 Finnegan, *Against the Spectre of a Dragon*, and Pearlman, *To Make Democracy Safe for America*.
5 Finnegan, *Against the Spectre of a Dragon*, p. 66.
6 Thompson, *Reformers and War*, pp. 139–140.
7 Quoted in Finnegan, *Against the Spectre of a Dragon*, p. 92.
8 Quoted in Finnegan, *Against the Spectre of a Dragon*, p. 124.
9 Root, "The Conditions and Possibilities Remaining for International Law after the War", in R. Bacon and J.B. Scott *Men and Policies*, ed. Freeport, 1968, pp. 427–428.
10 Root, "America's Present Needs", in *The War, Russian and Political Addresses*, p. 19.
11 On the American Protestant establishment's pre-war classification of states see Ido Oren, "The Subjectivity of the 'Democratic' Peace", *International Security*, vol.20, no.2, Fall, 1995.
12 Root, "America on Trial", p. 31; and Root, "America's Present Need", p. 19.
13 Root, "America on Trial", p. 26.
14 Root, "A Federated Union of the American Bar", *The War, Russian and Political Addresses*, p. 60.
15 Root, "America's Present Need", pp. 11–26.
16 Ibid., p. 18.
17 Ibid., p. 11.
18 Ibid., p. 11.
19 Lucia Ames Mead, "Compulsory Military Service", reprinted from *The Public* by the New York City Branch of the Women's Peace Party; H.A. Garfield, "The Attitude of the US towards Preparedness". March, 1916, British Library Catalogue number i.9608028; Oswald Villard, "Universal Military Service", 1916, leaflet published by Women's Peace Party, Boston, British Library number 08425g.9, p. 3; and G. Nasmyth, "Universal Military Service", 1916 leaflet from the Women's Peace Party, British Library number 08425g.9, p. 10.
20 Finnegan, *Against the Spectre*, p. 50. See also John Thompson, "The Exaggeration of American Vulnerability: The Anatomy of a Tradition", *Diplomatic History*, vol.16, no.1, Winter 1992, pp. 23–28.
21 The secondary works on Wilson I have found most useful in understanding his politics are Arthur Link, *Woodrow Wilson: Revolution, War and Peace*, Arlington, 1979; Gorden Levin, *Woodrow Wilson and World Politics: America's Response to War and Revolution*, Oxford, 1968; and Frank Ninkovich, *Modernity and Power: A History of the Domino Theory in the Twentieth Century*, Chicago, 1994.
22 Wilson, "A Fourth of July Address", 1914, PWW 30, p. 252.
23 Ibid., p. 251.
24 Wilson, W. in Stannard, R. and Dodd, E.W. (ed.) *The Public Papers of Woodrow Wilson*, (hereafter PPWW) vol.2, New York, 1925–27, p. 375. Quoted in Levin, *Woodrow Wilson and World Politics*, p. 14.
25 Wilson, PPWW, vol.4, p. 323.
26 Theodore Roosevelt, "An International Posse Comitatus", *The New York Times*, 8 November 1914.
27 Wilson, "Address to Senate, 22 January 1917", p. 536.

28 Ibid., p. 538.
29 Quoted in G. Levin, *Woodrow Wilson and World Power*, p. 32.
30 Woodrow Wilson, "After-Dinner Talk", *PPW*, vol.40, 9 December 1916, p. 194.
31 Woodrow Wilson, "Abraham Lincoln", *PPW*, vol.19, 12 February 1909, p. 42.
32 Woodrow Wilson, "An Address in St. Louis", *PWW*, vol.63, 5 September 1919, p. 33.
33 Wilson, "After-Dinner Talk", p. 196.
34 Paul Koistinen, *Mobilising for Modern War: The Political Economy of American Warfare, 1865–1919*, Kansas, 1997, pp. 114–136; M.W. Coulter, *The Senate Munitions Inquiry of the 1930s: Beyond the Merchants of Death*, Greenwood, 1997, pp. 107–125; P. Birdsall, "Neutrality and Economic Pressures". *Science and Society*, vol.3, 1939.
35 Quoted in Koistinen, *Mobilising for Modern War*, p. 127.
36 Ibid.
37 Ibid., p. 129.
38 Quoted in Birdsall, "Neutrality and Economic Pressures".
39 Mathew Coulter, *The Senate Munitions Inquiry of the 1930s*, Greenwood, 1997, p. 114.
40 Quoted in Buehrig, *Woodrow Wilson and the Balance of Power*, p. 143.
41 Pearlman, *To Make Democracy Safe for America*, p. 60.
42 Woodrow Wilson, "An Address", *PWW*, vol.47, 6 April 1918, p. 270.
43 Woodrow Wilson, "A Memorandum by Robert Lansing, 20 March 1917". vol.41, *PWW*, p. 441.
44 "Resolution on War and Militarism". *International Socialist Review*, vol.17, no.11, May 1917, p. 671.
45 Wilson, "A Memorandum by Robert Lansing", p. 440.
46 Ibid., p. 441.
47 Woodrow Wilson, "An Address to a Joint Session of Congress, 2 April 1917", p. 523.
48 On Wilson's pre-war classification of states see Ido Oren, "'The Subjectivity of the 'Democratic' Peace", pp. 147–184.
49 Wilson, "An Address to a Joint Session of Congress", p. 521.
50 Ibid., p. 523.
51 On Wilson and sovereignty see Cynthia Weber, *Simulating Sovereignty*, pp. 61–91.
52 Wilson, "An Address to a Joint Session of Congress", p. 525.
53 Woodrow Wilson, "An Address in Buffalo to the American Federation of Labor, 12 November 1917", *PWW*, vol.45, p. 16.
54 Ibid., p. 11.
55 Woodrow Wilson, "Remarks to the Labor Committee of the Council of National Defense", *PWW*, vol.42, p. 297.
56 Wilson, "An Address in Buffalo to the American Federation of Labor", p. 14.
57 Ibid., pp. 16–17.
58 For further analysis on this point see Ninkovich's discussion of Wilson and the origins of the domino theory in his *Modernity and Power*, pp. 37–68.
59 Quoted in Levin, *Woodrow Wilson and World Politics*, p. 131.
60 Ibid., p. 138.
61 Ibid., p. 157.
62 Ibid., pp. 158–159.
63 Ibid., p. 161.
64 Woodrow Wilson, "A Special Message to Congress", *PWW*, vol.59, 20 May 1919, p. 289.
65 Woodrow Wilson, "An Address in Des Moines", *PWW*, vol.63, 6 September 1919, p. 77.
66 See Stanley Cohen "A Study of Nativism: The Red Scare of 1919–1920", *Political Science Quarterly*, vol.79, March 1964.
67 Woodrow Wilson, "Address in Denver", *PWW*, vol.63, 25 September 1919, p. 495.

9 The Coming Community

 1 Frank Ninkovich, *Modernity and Power: A History of the Domino Theory in the Twentieth Century*, Chicago, 1994, pp. 44–69.

2 John Thompson's, "The Exaggeration of American Vulnerability", *Diplomatic History*, vol.16, no.1, Winter, 1992, shows that this is an enduring pattern in American foreign policy.

3 Woodrow Wilson, "Notes on the meeting of the council of four", *PPW*, vol.56, 27 March 1919, pp. 328–329.

4 Georgio Agamben, *The Coming Community*, Minnesota, 1993, and *Infancy and History: Essays on the Destruction of Experience*, Verso, 1993.

5 Celeste Michaelle Condit and John Louis Lucaites, *Crafting Equality*, Chicago, 1993, pp. 19–40.

6 Quoted in Gordon Wood, *The Creation of the American Republic, 1776–1787*, University of North Carolina Press, 1998, p. 34.

7 Ibid., p. 3.

8 Howard Zinn, *People's History of the United States*, Harper, 1995, pp. 76–78.

9 Quoted in Zinn, *People's History of the United States*, p. 62.

10 Bernard Manin, "Checks, balances and boundaries: the separation of powers in the constitutional debate of 1787", in B. Fontana, ed. *The Invention of the Modern Republic*, Cambridge, 1994, pp. 27–62; John McCormick, *Carl Schmitt's Critique of Liberalism*, Cambridge, 1999, p. 222; and Negri, *Insurgencies*, pp. 154–174.

11 The classic statement of the argument is Guy Debord's *The Society of the Spectacle*, Zone, 1994.

12 Newton Baker, "Address to the Graduating Class of the General Staff College", *BCW*, vol.5, no.4, 20 August 1920, pp. 4–5.

13 William Silbert, "Dedication of the New Chemistry Hall", *BCW*, vol.3, no.5, 18 March 1920, pp. 7–8.

14 Peyton March, *The Nation in Arms*, Doubleday, 1932, pp. 330–335.

15 Fries, *Chemical Warfare*, pp. 438–439.

16 Editorial, *BCW*, vol.1, no.9, 1919, p. 4.

17 William Mitchell, *Winged Defense*, Putnam, 1925, p. 163.

18 Between 1914 and 1918 between a third of a million and a million African-Americans moved north. J.H. Franklin, *From Slavery to Freedom*, Knopf, 1988, p. 306.

19 David Lewis, *W.E.B. Du Bois: Biography of a Race 1868–1919*, Macrae, 1993, pp. 537–542.

20 W.E.B. Du Bois, "Close Ranks", *The Crisis*, July 1918.

21 Lewis, *W.E.B. Du Bois*, pp. 556–557.

22 W.E.B. Du Bois, "The Pan-African Congress", *The Crisis*, April 1919, p. 274.

23 W.E.B. Du Bois, *The Crisis*, May 1919, p. 14.

10 The Gyroscope

1 Editorial, "The Control of Atomic Energy", *Scientific American*, November 1921, p. 21.

2 Dante, Alligeri, *The Divine Comedy*, book 1, Canto 3: "Abandon all hope, all you who enter here."

11 The Bomber/Poison Gas Combination

1 Frederic Brown, *Chemical Warfare: A Study in Restraints*, Greenwood, 1968, p. 22.

2 Fries, *Chemical Warfare*, McGraw-Hill, 1921, p. 411.

3 Bruno Latour, *Science in Action*, Open University, 1987, p. 129.

4 Thomas Hughes, "The Evolution of Large Technological Systems", in *The Social Construction Technological Systems*, ed. Thomas Hughes, MIT, 1987, p. 73; Thomas Hughes, *American Genesis*, Penguin, 1989, pp. 71–74.

5 US Department of State, *The Paris Peace Conference*, 4, p. 560; Quoted in Brown, *Chemical Warfare*, Greenwood Press, 1968, p. 53.

6 Michael Sherry, *The Rise of American Air Power: The Creation of Armageddon*, Yale, 1987, p. 14.

7 S.J.M. Auld, *Gas and Flame in Modern Warfare*, George H. Doran, 1918, pp. 22–23; quoted in Brown, *Chemical Warfare*, p. 43.

8 Sherry, *The Rise of American Air Power*, p. 14.

9 Ibid., p. 14.

10 "Chemical Warfare Inspires Peace", *CWB*, 6.5, 5 March 1921, p. 4.

11 Benedict Crowell, "Crowell Report", Reproduced in the *Aircraft Journal*, 23 August 1919.

12 Benedict Crowell, "Crowell on a United Air Service Before House Committee on Military Affairs", *Aircraft Journal*, 20 December 1919, p. 3.

13 Ibid., p. 6.

14 "Chemistry and War", Article in a pamphlet issued under the auspices of the National Research Council. Reproduced in *BCW*, vol.6, no.6, 20 March 1921, pp. 13–14.

15 Ibid.

16 Ibid.

17 A.M. Prentise, *Chemicals in War: A Treatise on Chemical Warfare*, McGraw-Hill, 1937, p. 519.

18 Amos Fries, "Chemical Warfare", *CWB*, 8.9 9 October 1919, p. 3.

19 "The First Decisive Air War", *Aircraft Journal*, 6.17, 24 April 1920, p. 3.

20 David Omissi, *Air Power and Colonial Control*, Manchester, 1990, p. 21.

21 "Civil Air Transport Committee Great Britain Report", *Air Service Journal* later *Aircraft Journal*, 4.3, 18 January 1919, p. 7.

22 G.O. Squier, "Squier's Victory Creed", *Air Service Journal*, 4.3, 18 January 1919, p. 12.

23 Editorial. *Aircraft Journal*, 12 July 1919, p. 8.

24 Francis Garvan, "Washington Letter", *JIEC*, 12.1 January, 1920, p. 91.

25 Garvan, "Washington Letter", p. 91.

26 P.D. Jones, "From Military to Civilian Technology: the Introduction of Tear Gas for Civil Riot Control", *Technology and Culture*, 19.2 April, 1978, p. 151–186.

27 US Congress, Senate, *Hearings on H.R. 5227, An Act Making Appropriations for the Support of the Army for the Fiscal Year Ending June 30, 1920*, 66th Cong. 1st sess., 18 June 1919, p 291; Quoted in Jones, "From Military to Civilian Technology", p. 155.

28 *New York Times* 20 July 1921; Quoted in P.D. Jones, "From Military to Civilian Technology", p. 160–161.

29 Jones, "From Military to Civilian Technology", p. 168.

30 E.P. Russell, "'Speaking of Annihilation': Mobilizing for War against Human and Insect Enemies", 1914–1945", *The Journal of American History*, March 1997, p. 1512.

31 "Chemical Warfare Making Swords into Plowshares", *BCW*, 8.2 1922.

32 L.O. Howard, "The War Against Insects", *Chemical Age*, vol.30, no.1, 1922, pp. 5–6.

33 R.C. Roark, "Household Insecticides", *Soap and Sanitary Chemicals*, 11 November 1935; Quoted in Russell, "Speaking of Annihilation", p. 1514.

34 R.C. Sawyer, "Monopolizing the Insect Trade: Biological Control in the USDA, 1888–1951", *Agricultural History*, vol.64, no.2 Spring, 1990, p. 276.

35 Russell, "Speaking of Annihilation", pp. 1515–1517.

36 H.W. Walker, "A Brief Resume of the Chemical Warfare Service Boll Weevil Investigation", *BCW*, 13.12 1927, pp. 231–233, especially 233; Quoted in Russell, "Speaking of Annihilation", p. 1517.

37 J.H. Perkins, "Insects, Food, and Hunder: The Paradox of Plenty for U.S. Entomology, 1920–1970", *Environmental Review*, 7.1 Spring, 1983; J.H. Perkins, *Insects, Experts and the Insecticide Crisis*, Plenium, 1982; T.R. Dunlap, "The Triumph of Chemical Pesticides in Insect Control, 1890–1920", *Environmental Review*, vol.1. no.5 1978; and Sawyer, "Monopolizing the Insect Trade: Biological Control in the USDA".

38 The argument here builds on Ian Hacking, "Weapons Research and the Form of Scientific Knowledge", *Canadian Journal of Philosophy*, Supplementary Volume 12, 1987, pp. 237–261; and Evelyn Fox Keller's *Secrets of Life: Secrets of Death*, Routledge, 1992, pp. 73–110.

39 Barry Barnes, David Bloor and John Henry, *Scientific Knowledge: A Sociological Analysis*, Athlone, 1996, pp. 129–139.

40 Hacking, "Weapons Research and the form of Scientific Knowledge", p. 254.

41 Fries, *Chemical Warfare*, pp. 292–294.

42 Charles Herty, "The Reserves of the Chemical Warfare Society", *Reprint and Circular Series of the National Research Council*, 16 February 1921, p. 17. See also Herty, "War Chemistry in the

Alleviation of Suffering", *JIEC*, vol.10, no.9 September 1918, p. 673, and "An Institute for Cooperative Research as an aid to the American Drug Industry: Addresses delivered before the New York Section of the American Chemical Society", *JIEC*, vol.10, no.12, December 1918, pp. 969–973.

43 Hacking, "Weapons Research and the form of Scientific Knowledge", p. 261.

44 R-D. Müller, "World Power Status through the Use of Poison Gas? German Preparations for Chemical Warfare, 1919–1945", *The German Military in the Age of Total War*, edited by Wilhelm Deist, Berg, 1985; and R.L. Metcalf, "The Impact of the Development of Organophosphorus Insecticide upon Basic and Applied Science"; and Peter Hayes, *Industry and Ideology: I G Farben in the Nazi Era*, Cambridge, 1987.

12 The Mind which is Destined to Govern the World

1 On the direction of science: Evelyn Fox Keller, "Critical Silences in Scientific Discourse: Problems of Form and Re-Form", and "Fractured Images of Science, Language and Power", *Secrets of Life, Secrets of Death*, Routledge, 1992; Ian Hacking, "Weapons Research and the Form of Scientific Knowledge", *Canadian Journal of Philosophy*, Supplementary volume 12, 1987; Bruno Latour, *Science in Action*, Open University, 1987; Barry Barnes, David Bloor and John Henry, *Scientific Knowledge: A Sociological Analysis*, Athlone, 1996.

2 The key secondary works used here are: (1) Books, Hunter Dupree, *Science and the Federal Government*, Belknap, 1957; Thomas Hughes, *American Genesis: A Century of Invention and Technological Enthusiasm*, Penguin, 1989; Daniel Kevles, *The Physicists: The History of a Scientific Community in Modern America*, Harvard, 1995; David Nobel, *America by Design: Science, Technology, and the Rise of Corporate Capitalism*, Knopf, 1977; Samuel Haber, *Efficiency and Uplift*, Chicago, 1964; Leonard Reich, *The Making of American Industrial Research*, Cambridge, 1985; and R.N. Proctor, *Value Free Science? Purity and Power in Modern Knowledge*, Harvard, 1991.

   (2) Articles, D.A. Hounshell, "Edison and the Pure Science Ideal in 19th Century America", *Science*, vol.207, 8 February 1980, pp. 612–617; George Daniels, "The Process of Professionalization in American Science", *Isis*, vol.58, 1967; Daniels, "The Pure Science Ideal and Democratic Culture", *Science*, vol.156, 30 June 1967, pp. 1699–1705; Daniels, "The Process of Professionalization in American Science: The Emergent Period, 1820–1860", *Isis*, 58 1967; J.W. Servos, "The Industrial Relations of Science: Chemical Engineering at MIT, 1900–1939", *Isis*, vol.71, 1980; J.J. Beer, "Coal Tar Dye Manufacture and the Origins of the Modern Industrial Research Laboratory", *Isis*, vol.49, 1958; G. Meyer-Thurow, "The Industrialization of Invention: A Case Study from the German Industry", *Isis*, vol.73, 1982; D.W. Eakins, "The Origins of Corporate Liberal Policy Research, 1916–1922: The Political-Economic Expert and the Decline of Public Debate", in Jerry Israel ed., *Building the Organizational Society*, The Free Press, 1972; Leonard Reich, "Research, Patents, and the Struggle to Control Radio: A Study of Big Business and the Use of Industrial Research", *Business History Review*, vol.51, no.2, Summer, 1977; Paul Forman, "Behind Quantum Electronics: National Security as a Basis for Physical Research in the United States, 1940–1960", *Historical Studies in the Physical and Biological Sciences*, vol.18.

3 The account given here is based on a survey of articles in the journals *Science* and *Nature* and on addresses to the American Association for the Advancement of Science. The most important of these are B.C. Brodie, "Science Research and University Endowments", *Nature*, vol.7, no.163, 12 December 1872, pp. 97–98; Roscoe. "Original Research As A Means of Education", *Nature*, 23 October 1873, pp. 538–539; "Lord Derby on the Endowment of Scientific Research", *Nature* vol.13, no.321, 23 December 1875, pp. 141–142; E.R. Lancaster, "The Endowment of Research", *Nature*, June 8, 1876, pp. 126–129; "Edison's Telephone", *Nature*, 20 March 1879, p. 471; W.R. Brown, "Science and Engineering", *Nature*, 15 November 1883, pp. 57–60; A. Brown, Endowment for Scientific Research and Publication", *Nature*, vol.51, no.1311 13 December 1894, pp. 164–166; Benjamin Gould, "Address", *American Association for the Advancement of Science Proceedings*, vol.18 1869, pp. 1–37; Henry Rowland, "A Plea for Pure Science", *Physical Papers*, John Hopkins, 1902, pp. 593–613; Rowland, "The Physics Laboratory in Modern Education",

Physical Papers: 614–618; "The Future of American Science", *Science*, vol.1, no.1, February 9, 1883, pp. 1–3; "The National Observatory", *Science*, vol.34, September 28, 1883, pp. 415–417; "Comment and Criticism", vol.6, no.144, 6 November 1885, pp. 397–398; "Comment and Criticism", *Science*, vol.6, no.101, 9 January 1885, p. 21; "The Government and its Scientific Bureaus", *Science*, vol.6, no.150 December 18, 1885, pp. 530–531; Alexander Agassiz, "The Coast Survey and "Political Scientists", *Science*, vol.6, no.137, 18 September 1885, pp. 253–255; "Official Science at Washington", *The Popular Science Monthly*, vol.27, 1885, pp. 844–847.

    See also D.A. Hounshell, "Edison and the Pure Science Ideal in 19th Century America", *Science*, vol.207, 8 February 1980, pp. 612–617; G. Daniels, "The Process of Professionalization in American Science", *Isis*, vol.58, 1967; and Daniels, "The Pure Science Ideal and Democratic Culture", *Science*, vol.156, 30 June 1967, pp. 1699–1705.

4 Gould, "Address", p. 8.

5 Ibid., p. 9.

6 Roscoe. "Original Research as a Means of Education", pp. 538–539; Rowland, "The Physics Laboratory in Modern Education", pp. 614–618.

7 Rowland, "The Physics Laboratory", p. 615.

8 Ibid., p. 614.

9 Ibid., p. 618.

10 Rowland, "A Plea for Pure Science", p. 596.

11 Roscoe. "Original Research as a Means of Education", p. 538.

12 Editorial. "The Future of American Science", *Science*, vol.1, no.1, 9 February 1883; Rowland, "A Plea for Pure Science", p. 594.

13 Rowland, "A Plea for Pure Science", p. 593–594.

14 Gould, "Address", p. 16–17.

15 Roscoe. "Original Research as a Means of Education", p. 539.

16 Gould, "Address", p. 17–18.

17 Ibid., p. 16.

18 Ibid., p. 4.

19 Ibid., p. 4.

20 Rowland, "A Plea for Pure Science", p. 38.

21 Ibid., p. 594.

22 Ibid., p. 594.

23 "The Future of American Science", p. 1. In the battle to claim that science is *the* creative force behind invention, Addison Brown went so far as to claim inventor's themselves admit they are absolutely dependent on science for everything they do by quoting an unnamed inventor. A. Brown, "Endowment for Scientific Research", *Nature*, vol.51, no.1311, 13 December 1894, p. 165.

24 Rowland, "A Plea for Pure Science", p. 613.

25 Ibid., p. 610.

26 Gould, "Address", p. 37; Rowland, "A Plea for Pure Science", p. 613.

27 Gould, "Address", p. 31.

28 Ibid., p. 32.

29 Ibid., p. 35.

30 "The National Observatory", *Science*, vol.34, 28 September 1883, p. 416.

31 "Comment and Criticism", *Science*, vol.101, 9 January 1885, p. 31.

32 Testimony 17 Dec. 1885 presented before the Allison Commission ["Joint Commission to Consider the Present Organization of the Signal Service, Geological Survey, Coast and Geodetic Survey, and the Hydrographic Office of the Navy Department, with a View to Secure Greater Efficiency and Economy of the Public Service in Said Bureau . . ." Quoted in George Daniels "The Pure Science Ideal and Democratic Culture", p. 1705.

33 "The Government and its Scientific Bureaus", *Science*, vol.6, no.150, 18 December 1885, p. 531.

34 Alexander Agazzis, "The Coast-Survey and "Political Scientists", *Science*, vol.6, no.137, 18 September 1885, p. 253.

35 "Official Science at Washington", *The Popular Science Monthly*, vol.27, 1885, p. 846.

36 Barnes, Bloor, and Henry, *Scientific Knowledge*, pp. 18–45.

37 Latour, *Science in Action*, pp. 80–81.
38 Ian Hacking, "Weapons Research", in his *The Social Construction of What?* Harvard, 2000.
39 Gould, "Address", p. 33.
40 For the early history of American science and the military see Hunter Dupree, *Science and the Federal Government*, Belknap, 1957.
41 Dupress, *Science and the Federal Government*, p. 30.
42 I owe this insight to Simon Schaffer.
43 Gould, "Address", p. 32.
44 Gould, "Address", p. 14.
45 J.L. Smith, *American Association for the Advancement of Science Proceedings*, vol.22, 1873, p. 18. Quoted in Daniels "The Pure Science Ideal and Democratic Culture", p. 1701.
46 Steven Shapin, *The Scientific Revolution*, Chicago, 1996, p. 164.

13 Permanent Mobilization

1 Simon Schaffer and Steven Shapin, *Leviathan and the Air Pump*, Princeton, 1985, pp. 283–331, Stevin Shapin *The Scientific Revolution*, Chicago, 1996, pp. 119–165, Stephen Toulmin, *Cosmopolis: The Hidden Agenda of Modernity*, Chicago, 1992, pp. 89–137, and Bruno Latour, *We Have Never Been Modern*, Harvard, 1993, pp. 15–32. On democracy and the Puritan revolution, see Sheldon Wolin, *Tocqueville Between Two Worlds*, Princeton, 2001, pp. 59–75.
2 Putney Debates (1647), in *Puritanism and Liberty*, ed. A.S.P. Woodhouse, London, Dent, 1958, p. 56.
3 Quoted in Shapin and Schaffer, *Leviathan and the Air Pump*, p. 290.
4 David Nobel, *The Religion of Technology*, Penguin, 1999, pp. 58–67.
5 On applied science see: T.C., Mendenhall, "The Relations of Men of Science to the General Public", *American Association for the Advancement of Science*, (hereafter *AAAS*), 1890; J. Johnson, "The Applied Scientist", *AAAS*, 1892; H.E. Armstrong, "The Appreciation of Science by the German Manufacturers", *Nature*, vol.48, no.1228, 11 May 1893; I. Remsen, "Scientific Investigation and Progress", *AAAS*, 1903–4; and V.C. Alderson, "Technical Education at Home and Abroad", *Nature*, vol.67, no.1737, 12 February 1903.
6 On organized research before America's entry into the First World War see: W.E. Ritter, "Organization in Scientific Research", *Popular Science Monthly*, vol.67, May 1905; W.E. Ritter, "Duties to the Public of Research Institutions in Pure Science", *Popular Science Monthly*, vol.80, January 1912; F.J. Crowell, "Science and Investment", *Science*, vol.29, no.745, 9 April 1909; A.D. Little, "The Chemist and the Community", *Science*, vol.25, no.643, 26 April 1907; W. Whitney, "Research as a Financial Asset", *JIEC*, vol.3, June 1911; W. Ferguson, "A Plan for Organized Research and Analytical Chemistry in Successful Chemical Manufacturing", *JIEC*, vol.4, December 1912; A.D. Little, "Industrial Research in America", *JIEC*, vol.5, October 1915; C.E. Lucke, "Research: What-Who-Where-Why", *JIEC*, vol.6, no.11, November 1914; C.E. Mees, "The Future of Scientific Research", *JIEC*, vol.6, no.8, August 1914; L.H. Baekeland, "Some Aspects of Industrial Chemistry", vol.6, no.9, September 1914; R. Bacon, "The Value of Research to Industry", *Science*, vol.50, no.1042, 18 December 1914; W. Walker, "Chemical Research and Industrial Progress", *JIEC*, vol.3, May 1911; W. Walker, "Education in Research", *JIEC*, vol.7, no.1 January, 1915; and R. Rossiter, "Knowledge and Research", *JIEC*, vol.7, no.4, April 1915.
7 T.C. Mendenhall, "The Relations of Men of Science to the General Public", *PAAAS*, 1890, pp. 10 and 14.
8 Johnson, "The Applied Scientist", p. 126.
9 Little, "Industrial Research in America", pp. 800–801.
10 J.R. Angell, "The Development of Research in the United States", *Reprint National Research Council*, vol.6, November, 1919, p. 8.
11 Johnson, "The Applied Scientist", p. 130.
12 Ritter, "Organization in Scientific Research", p. 49.
13 Ibid., p. 53.
14 Alderson, "Technical Education at Home and Abroad".

15 Arthur D. Little, "The Chemist's Place in Industry", *JIEC*, vol.2, no.2, February 1910, p. 64.

16 Editorial. "United States Forestry Service Investigations", *JIEC*, vol.5, no.8 August 1913, p. 626.

17 Baekeland, "Science and Industry", *Science*, vol.31, no.805, 3 June 1910, pp. 842–843.

18 Ibid., p. 845.

19 Leo Baekeland, "Introductory Address by the Chairman", *Science*, vol.28, no.725, 1908, and "Science and Industry".

20 Fernand Braudel, *Capitalism and Civilization*, Harper, 1979; Giovanni Arrighi, "The Three Hegemonies of Historical Capitalism", in Stephen Gill, ed., *Gramsci, Historical Materialism and International Relations*, Cambridge, 1993; Michael Hardt and Antonio Negri, *Empire*, Harvard, 2000; Immanuel Wallerstein, "The Rise and Future Demise of the Capitalist World System", *The Essential Wallerstein*, New Press, 2000.

21 Robin Blackburn, *The Overthrow of Colonial Slavery, 1776–1848*, Verso, 1988, pp. 3 and 11.

22 The American inventor, Robert Fulton, is a case in point.

23 David Nobel, *America by Design*, Oxford, 1977, pp. 86–87.

24 See Nobel "The Corporation as Inventor" and "Science for Industry" in his *America by Design*; Thomas Hughes, *American Genesis: A Century of Invention and Technological Enthusiasm 1870–1970*, Penguin, 1989; Leonard Reich, *The Making of American Industrial Research*, Cambridge, 1985, and his "Research, Patents, and the Struggle to Control Radio", *Business History Review*, vol.51, no.2, Summer 1977.

25 J. Beer, "Coal Tar Dye Manufacture and the Origins of the Modern Industrial Research Laboratory", *ISIS*, vol.49, 1958; and G. Meyer-Thurow, "The Industrialization of Invention", *ISIS*, vol.73, 1982.

26 Hughes, *American Genesis*, pp. 139–150.

27 Willis Whitney, "Research as a Financial Asset", *JIEC*, vol.3, no.6, June 1911, p. 429.

28 David Kevles, *The Physicists: The History of a Scientific Community in Modern America*, Harvard, 1995; Kevles, "The First World War and the Advancement of Science in America", *ISIS*, vol.59, Winter, 1968, pp. 427–437; Kevles, "'Into Hostile Political Camps': The Reorganization of International Science in World War 1", *ISIS*, vol.62, 1970, pp. 47–60; Nobel, *America By Design*; Hughes, *American Genesis*.

29 Ritter, W. "Organization of Scientific Research", p. 52.

30 Quoted in Kevles, *The Physicists*, p. 69.

31 Howard Zinn, *A People's History of the United States*, Harper, 1995, pp. 270–271.

32 G.E. Hale, *National Academies and the Progress of Research*, New Era Printing Co., 1915, pp. 53–54.

33 Quoted in Kevles, *The Physicists*, p. 112.

34 Quoted in Kevles, *The Physicists*, p. 114.

35 Elihu Root, "America on Trial", in Elihu Root, *The War, Russian and Political Addresses*, Harvard, 1918, pp. 27–38.

36 Quoted in Kevles, "The First World War and the Advancement of Science in America", *ISIS*, vol.59, Winter, 1968, p. 433.

37 Quoted in ibid., p. 433.

38 Quoted in ibid.

39 Quoted in ibid.

40 Quoted in ibid., pp. 434–435.

41 The members of the Industrial Division where J.J. Carty, chief engineer at AT&T; Raymond Bacon, director of the Mellon Institute; Frank Jewett, director of the Western Electric Laboratories; Arthur D. Little, president of America's largest engineering consulting firm; C.E. Skinner, director of research at Westinghouse; and Willis Whitney, director of research at General Electric. The Industrial Advisory Committee included Thodore Vale, chairman of the committee and president of AT&T, Cleveland Dodge; vice-president of Dodge mining interests; George Eastman, president of Eastman Kodak; Elbert Gary, president of US Steel; Andrew Mellon, head of Mellon bank interests; Pierre Du Pont; Elihu Root; Ambrose Swasey; E.W. Rice, president of General Electric; and Henry Pritchett, president of the Carnegie Foundation for the Advancement of Teaching.

42 Quoted in Kevles "The First World War and the Advancement of Science in America", p. 435.

43 Quoted in Kevles, *The Physicists*, p. 144.

44 George Hale, "National Academy of Sciences, Annual Report for 1918", pp. 41–50, quoted in Nobel, *America by Design*, p. 161.

45 Charles Rees, "Information Needs in Science and Technology, *Reprint and Circular Series of the National Research Council* (hereafter, *RNRC*), No.33, p. 1.

46 David Eakins, "The Origins of Corporate Liberal Policy Research, 1916–1922: The Political-Economic Expert and the Decline of Public Debate", in *The Organizational Society*, ed. Jerry Israel, Free Press, 1972, pp. 163–179.

47 Quoted in David Nobel, *America by Design*, p. 154.

48 Elihu Root, "The Need for Organization in Scientific Research", *Bulletin of the National Research Council* (hereafter, *BNRC*), vol.1, no.1, October 1919, pp. 7–10; George Elery Hale, "Cooperation in Research", *Science*, vol.51, no.1311, 13 February 1920, pp. 149–155.

49 J.J. Carty of AT&T in his presidential address to the Institute of Electrical Engineers, quoted by Hale in "The Purpose of the National Research Council", *BNRC*, vol.1, no.1 October 1919, p. 6.

50 Root, "The Need for Organization in Scientific Research", p. 8.; quoted in Hale, "Cooperation in Research", *Science*, vol.51, no.1311, 13 February 1920, p. 150.

51 J.R. Angell, "The Development of Research in the United States", *RNRC*, vol.1, no.6, November 1919, pp. 1–2.

14 Manifesto for a Global Deep Science Movement

1 The argument here draws on William Connolly, *Identity\Difference: Democratic Negotiations of Political Paradox*, Cornell, 1991, pp. 16–35, and Sheldon Wolin, *Tocqueville Between Two Worlds*, Princeton, 2001, pp. 20–45, and *The Presence of the Past: Essays on the State and the Constitution*, John Hopkins, 1989, pp. 100–119.

2 Connolly, *Identity\Difference*, pp. 16–35.

3 Theodore Adorno and Max Horkheimer, *Dialectic of Enlightenment*, Verso, 1989, p. 3.

4 The rise of a new imperial system located above national governments is explored by Michael Hardt and Antonio Negri in *Empire*, Harvard, 2000.

5 Sheldon Wolin, *Tocqueville Between Two Worlds*, pp. 20–45, and *The Presence of the Past*, pp. 100–119.

6 Judith Butler, "Restaging the Universal: Hegemony and the Limits of Formalism", in Judith Butler, Ernesto Laclau and Slavoj Žižek, *Contingency, Hegemony, Universality*, Verso, 2000.

7 Paul Rogers, *Losing Control: Global Security in the Twenty-First Century*, Pluto, 2000.

8 Michael Klare, "The Geopolitics of War", and Johnson Chalmers "Blowback", in Heuvel, ed., *A Just Response*, pp. 270–276.

9 Edward Herman and Gerry O'Sullivan, "'Terrorism' as Ideology and Cultural Industry", and Richard Falk "The Terrorist Foundations of Recent US Foreign Policy", in Alexander George, ed., *Western State Terrorism*, Routledge, 1991.

10 As Spinoza's discussion of Alexander the Great in the preface to his *Tractatus Theologico-Politicus* shows, this is nothing new.

11 Nichole Deller, Arjun Makhijani, & John Burroughs, *Rule of Power or Rule of Law*, Institute for Energy and Environmental Policy & Lawyers Committee on Nuclear Policy, May, 2002.

12 Richard Falk, "The New Bush Doctrine", *The Nation*, July 15, 2002, and Michael Byers, "Against Pre-Emption", *London Review of Books*, 25 July 2002. Byer's forthcoming *United States Hegemony and the Foundations of International Law*, Cambridge, is awaited with great expectation.

13 See Nancy Chang, *Silencing Political Dissent: How Post-September 11 Anti-terrorism Measures Threaten Our Civil Liberties*, Seven Stories Press, 2002, and also the Centre for Contitutional Right's website.

14 'Theses on the Philosophy of History", in *Illuminations*, Schocken, 1969.

15 On missile guidance technology see Donald McKenzie's pathbreaking work *Inventing Accuracy: A Historical Sociology of Nuclear Missile Guidance*, MIT, 1992.

16 World Health Organization, *Public health response to biological and chemical weapons*, section 2.4.

(Prepublication edition available at: http://www.who.int), and Brian Balmer, *Britain and Biological Warfare: Expert Advice and Science Policy 1930–1965*, Palgrave, 2001.

17 The classic reference here is Walter Benjamin's sixth, eighth, and eleventh theses. For a brilliant meditation on this work, see Rebecca Comay's "Redeeming Revenge: Nietzsche, Benjamin, Heidegger, and the Politics of Memory", in Clayton Koelb, ed. *Nietzsche as Postmodernist: Essays Pro and Contra*, Suny, 1990. See also Andrew Benjamin's *Present Hope: Philosophy, Architecture, Judaism*, Routledge, 1997.

18 Theodore Roosevelt, "Expansion and Peace", *The Strenuous Life*, Duckworth, 1911, p. 34, and see chapter six.

19 Eric Alterman, "'Blowback,' the Prequel", in Katrina Vanden Heuvel, ed., *A Just Response: On Terrorism, Democracy, and September 11, 2001*, Nation Books, 2002, pp.182–184; and Tariq Ali, *The Clash of Fundamentalisms: Crusades, Jihads and Modernity*, Verso, 2002, p. 207–208.

20 Giovanni Arrighi, "The African Crisis: World Systemic and Regional Aspects", *New Left Review*, May/June 2002. Here Zygmunt Bauman's *In Search of Politics*, Polity, 1999, provides key insights for an analysis that remains to be carried out.

21 Gar Alperovitz, *The Decision to Use the Atomic Bomb*, Vintage, 1995; J.S. Walker, "The Decision to Use the Bomb: A Historiographic Update", *Diplomatic History*, Winter, 1990.

22 Alperovitz, *Atomic Diplomacy: Hiroshima and Potsdam*, Pluto, 1985, p. 14.

23 Alperovitz, *The Decision to Use the Atomic Bomb*, pp. 321–365.

24 Michael Sherry, *The Rise of American Air Power: The Creation of Armageddon*, Yale, 1987.

25 Ibid., p. 239.

26 Ibid., p. 271.

27 Quoted in R.J. Lifton and G. Mitchell, *Hiroshima in America: Fifty Years of Denial*, Putnam, 1995, p. 4.

28 Alperovitz, *Atomic Diplomacy*, p. 8.

29 David Holloway, *Stalin and the Bomb*, Yale, 1994, p. 157.

30 Ibid., p. 132.

31 William Leahy, *I Was There*, Whittlesey House, 1950, p. 441. Quoted in Lifton and Mitchell, *Hiroshima in America*, p. 45.

32 Alperovitz, *The Decision to Use the Atomic Bomb*, p. 328.

33 Lifton and Mitchell, *Hiroshima in America*, p. 4.

34 Ibid.

35 Henry Rowlands, "The Physical Laboratory in Modern Education", *Physical Papers*, John Hopkins, 1902, p. 678.

36 For a discussion of what this might entail see Lyotard, *The Differend*, Minnesota, 1989, pp. 118–127.

37 Emmanuel Kant, "Perpetual Peace, A Philosophical Sketch", in *Kant's Political Writings*, ed. Hans Reiss, Cambridge, 1988, p. 95.

38 John Brewer, *The Sinews of Power*, HarperCollins, 1989.

39 Kant, *Critique of Judgement*, Hackett, 1987, p. 320; see also "Idea for a Universal History", *Kant's Political Writings*, p. 47.

40 Kant, "Perpetual Peace", p. 116.

41 William Connolly, *Identity/Difference: Democratic Negotiations of Political Paradox*, Cornell, 1991, pp. 28–31.

42 Two pathbreaking attempts to do just this are Jean-Luc Nancy, *The Inoperative Community*, Minnesota, 1991, and Giorgio Agamben, *The Coming Community*, Minnesota, 1993.

43 Evelyn Fox Keller, *Secrets of Life, Secrets of Death: Essays on Language, Gender and Science*, Routledge, 1992, p. 73–92.

44 Ibid., p. 82.

45 Stephen Toulmin, *Cosmopolis: The Hidden Agenda of Modernity*, Chicago, 1990, pp. 105–129.

46 Donald MacKenzie, "Tacit Knowledge and the Uninvention of Nuclear Weapons", *Knowing Machines*, MIT, 1998; and *Inventing Accuracy: a Historical Sociology of Nuclear Missile Guidance*, MIT, 1990.

47 Zygmunt Bauman, *Globalization: the Human Consequences*, Polity, 1998, pp. 106–118; Loic Wacquant, "From Slavery to Mass Incarceration", *New Left Review*, January, 2002.

Index